LORD SUMPTION AND THE

In *Lord Sumption and the Limits of the Law*, leading public law scholars reflect on the nature and limits of the judicial role, and its implications for human rights protection and democracy. The starting point for this reflection is Lord Sumption's lecture, 'The Limits of the Law', and, spurred on by this, the contributors discuss questions including the scope and legitimacy of judicial law-making, the interpretation of the European Convention on Human Rights, and the continuing significance and legitimacy, or otherwise, of the European Court of Human Rights. Lord Sumption ends the volume with a substantial chapter engaging with the responses to his lecture.

Lord Sumption and the Limits of the Law

Edited by
NW Barber
Richard Ekins
and
Paul Yowell

·HART·
OXFORD · LONDON · NEW YORK · NEW DELHI · SYDNEY

HART PUBLISHING
Bloomsbury Publishing Plc
Kemp House, Chawley Park, Cumnor Hill, Oxford, OX2 9PH, UK

HART PUBLISHING, the Hart/Stag logo, BLOOMSBURY and the Diana logo are
trademarks of Bloomsbury Publishing Plc
First published in Great Britain 2016

First published in hardback, 2016
Paperback edition, 2018

Copyright © The Editors 2016

The Editors have asserted their right under the Copyright, Designs and Patents Act 1988 to be
identified as the Authors of this work.

All rights reserved. No part of this publication may be reproduced or transmitted in any form or by
any means, electronic or mechanical, including photocopying, recording, or any information
storage or retrieval system, without prior permission in writing from the publishers.

While every care has been taken to ensure the accuracy of this work, no responsibility for loss or
damage occasioned to any person acting or refraining from action as a result of any statement in it
can be accepted by the authors, editors or publishers.

All UK Government legislation and other public sector information used in the work is Crown
Copyright ©. All House of Lords and House of Commons information used in the work is
Parliamentary Copyright ©. This information is reused under the terms of the Open Government
Licence v3.0 (http://www.nationalarchives.gov.uk/doc/open-government-licence/version/3) except
where otherwise stated.

All Eur-lex material used in the work is © European Union,
http://eur-lex.europa.eu/, 1998-2018.

A catalogue record for this book is available from the British Library.

Library of Congress Cataloging-in-Publication Data

Names: Barber, N. W. (Nicholas William), editor. | Ekins, Richard, editor. |
Yowell, Paul, 1969–, editor. | Sumption, Jonathan.

Title: Lord Sumption and the Limits of the law / edited by Nicholas Barber,
Richard Ekins and Paul Yowell.

Description: Oxford ; Portland, Oregon : Hart Publishing Ltd, 2016. | Series: Hart studies
in constitutional law ; volume 5 | "This volume arises out of a conference held in
the University of Oxford in October 2014." | Includes full text of lecture "The limits
of the law", originally presented as the 27th Sultan Azlan Shah Lecture, Kuala Lumpur,
Nov. 20, 2013. | Includes bibliographical references and index.

Identifiers: LCCN 2015049489 (print) | LCCN 2015049635 (ebook) | ISBN 9781849466943
(hardback : alk. paper) | ISBN 9781509902170 (Epub)

Subjects: LCSH: Sumption, Jonathan. Limits of the law—Congresses. | Judge-made
law—Congresses. | Judicial power—Congresses. | Political questions and judicial
power—Congresses. | European Court of Human Rights—Congresses.

Classification: LCC K574.A6 L67 2016 (print) | LCC K574.A6 (ebook) | DDC 341.4/8—dc23
LC record available at http://lccn.loc.gov/2015049489

ISBN: PB: 978-1-50992-205-5
HB: 978-1-84946-694-3

Typeset by Compuscript Ltd, Shannon
Printed and bound in Great Britain by
Lightning Source UK Ltd

To find out more about our authors and books visit www.hartpublishing.co.uk. Here you will find
extracts, author information, details of forthcoming events and the option to sign up for our
newsletters.

A Note on the Cover

'Fashion before ease; or, a good constitution sacrificed for a fantastic form'

By James Gillray, 1793.

The print shows an unhappy Britannia being laced into a corset by Thomas Paine. Paine was the author of, amongst other books, *The Rights of Man*—and the title of this volume can be seen on the measuring tap, which dangles from his pocket next to his tailor's shears. *The Rights of Man*, published a couple of years before Gillray's print, called for the introduction of a written constitution for the United Kingdom, the recognition that natural rights constrain the state, and a rejection of the aristocratic structuring of society. Paine's intellectual rival, Edmund Burke, would have sympathised with the manner in which Gillray has chosen to depict the scene. For Burke, the British state was an organic entity, one that had developed over time, intertwined with the community of which it was a part. The rationalist attempt to draw up a set of rights that limited the state was bound to create discomfort: the protection of liberties is a function of a well-formed state, and not something that can be imposed on it from outside.

Foreword: Beyond the Limits

TIMOTHY ENDICOTT

There is—as the last sentence of Lord Sumption's lecture[1] will remind you—no law of nature that things are going to get better in a political community. But things have undoubtedly got better in our constitutional order. In the youth of King Richard II, the Lords Appellant used the appearances of law to take over the government of the country, bringing proceedings in the High Court of Parliament against the King's councilors and against his judges. The charges were for treason in the policies that they had pursued and for treason in exercising undue influence over the King. There was no certainty as to what counted as a crime and no established authority for the process. The process included asking the Mayor and aldermen of London whether one of the defendants was guilty, and executing him when they prevaricated.[2]

Law has always captivated the English political imagination. Over many centuries, judicial process has offered an alluring alternative to other processes of governance. You can see that allure in legalistic abuses and also in the most intelligent steps toward the rule of law. Both involve rule by judges.

In the seventeenth century, Sir Edward Coke asserted three English constitutional fundamentals: the independence of judges, the peculiar preeminence of the judges in determining the content of the common law, and the jurisdiction of the judges to control the exercise of discretionary power by other servants of the King. 'Discretion', said Sir Edward, 'is a science of understanding, to discern between falsity and truth, between wrong and right, between shadows and substance, between equity and colourable glosses and pretences, and not to do according to their men's will and private affections.'[3] He imposed the rule of law on the will of other servants of the Crown; he subjected the country to the will of the judges.

Lord Sumption points out that people have expectations of the law today that they did not have in Coke's time, or some 60 years ago when British lawyers and politicians participated in the drafting of the European Convention on Human Rights. It is true, as he says, that: 'Popular expectations of law are by historical standards exceptionally high.'[4] Yet high and unrealistic expectations of law are an old English tradition. Already by the fourteenth century, in staging a coup d'etat,

---

[1] 'The Limits of Law', 27th Azlan Shah Lecture, Kuala Lumpur, 20 November 2013.
[2] *Oxford Dictionary of National Biography* (Oxford, Oxford University Press 2004–14), s.v. 'Lords appellant'.
[3] *Rooke v Withers* (1597) 77 ER 209, 210.
[4] See n 1 above.

the preferred way was under the guise of legal proceedings. And already by the seventeenth century, Sir Edward Coke was regulating the discretions of other public servants by claiming a massively important discretion for the judges. Coke's own maxim applies to that discretion: the judges are not to exercise it according to their men's and women's will and private affections, but they alone have jurisdiction to determine what would count as doing so.

The British lawyers and politicians who committed the UK to the Convention presumably thought that they were assuring, for the future of a continent, rights that had long been secure and uncontroversial in the UK. They presumably did *not* think that they were engineering the shift that Lord Sumption outlines towards governance of the UK by judges. Along with their responsibility for controlling other public authorities, the Strasbourg judges have incurred a correlative responsibility (which no one thought of at the time) to control themselves in their own use of public power. The rule of law imposes that same responsibility on UK judges exercising their authority under the Human Rights Act: not only to control the use of public power by other authorities, but also to control themselves and to use their power with humility.

The European Convention provides a salient and, now, politically contentious field for working out how a community is to be governed, and it forms a focus for much of the work in this volume. I think it is important to put that field of issues in the context of Lord Sumption's discussion of the *Witham* case.[5] On the proper effects of the European Convention, there is a wide and notorious diversity of opinions. But among English lawyers and judges, there is something very much like a consensus, or orthodoxy, that judges ought to use the common law 'principle of legality' to control governmental decisions over fees for access to the courts. So, in *Witham*, the Court of Appeal held that by increasing the cost of issuing a writ, the Lord Chancellor had unlawfully denied a constitutional right of access to the courts, which could only lawfully be denied by express legislation.[6]

The decision in *Witham* is part of a pattern of direct judicial control of the cost of litigation. The courts will not require claimants to give security for costs when they bring speculative claims for judicial review against public authorities.[7] In fact, the courts will make 'protective costs orders' to assure such claimants that they will not be faced with the ordinary order to pay the defendant's costs if they lose. The judges have done this even in cases that patently have no prospect of success.[8] These judicial innovations establish public subsidies for litigation. Lord Sumption says that 'the real question' in such cases concerns 'the relative importance of doing

---

[5] *R v Lord Chancellor ex p Witham* [1998] QB 575.

[6] ibid 586. The fee for issuing a writ where no monetary limit was specified became £500, and the new regulations repealed a provision that had allowed litigants in receipt of income support to issue a writ without a fee.

[7] See, eg, *R (Plantagenet Alliance) v Secretary of State for Justice* [2013] EWHC 3164.

[8] The first such reported case was *R v The Prime Minister ex p Campaign for Nuclear Disarmament* [2002] EWHC 2712. Perhaps the *Plantagenet Alliance* case is another example, although the judge who gave permission to seek judicial review thought that there was some prospect of success; the Divisional Court that heard the claim for judicial review disagreed.

so, relative, that is, to other possible uses of the money'.[9] He suggests that by treating access to the courts as a right at common law, the judges are imposing costs on a government that might legitimately have different spending priorities. In his challenge to the orthodoxy over judicial governance of access to the courts, Lord Sumption puts the debates over the European Convention on Human Rights in a new light: at every point, those debates concern not only the content of the Convention rights, but also the form of governance that can best respect the interests protected by the rights, and best reconcile them with other interests.

I am glad that the editors of this volume organised the discussion in the University of Oxford. During the Hundred Years' War, the University had not fully attained its potential, which is to put people in the predicament of defending views that they consider to be obviously true, in the face of the arguments of others who consider the contrary views to be obviously true. The University has still not fully attained that potential. But the colloquium on Lord Sumption's lecture was a step forward. I congratulate the editors on creating such an opportunity for the participants to experience the freedom of debate in the University and for publishing the conversation in this volume.

---

[9] See n 1 above.

Acknowledgements

This volume arises out of a conference held by the Programme for the Foundations of Law and Constitutional Government in Oxford in October 2014. The Faculty of Law, St John's College and Trinity College provided valuable help with the logistical arrangements. We thank the participants in the workshop for stimulating questions and comments, our colleagues who chaired the panels, and Timothy Endicott for his thoughtful remarks to open the proceedings. We are especially grateful to the contributors to this volume and to Lord Sumption for giving generously of their time and for their patience with the editorial process. Mikolaj Barczentewicz and Ewan Smith provided editorial assistance in the preparation of the text of the papers for publication, for which we are much obliged. Finally, we owe a special debt of gratitude to Mr Graham Child for providing the funding that made this project possible.

Nick Barber
Richard Ekins
Paul Yowell

Table of Contents

A Note on the Cover v
Foreword: Beyond the Limits by Timothy Endicott vii
Acknowledgements xi
List of Contributors xv

1. Introduction 1
   NW Barber, Richard Ekins and Paul Yowell

2. The Limits of Law 15
   Lord Sumption

3. Sumption's Assumptions 27
   Martin Loughlin

4. Living Trees or Deadwood: The Interpretive
   Challenge of the European Convention on Human Rights 45
   Sandra Fredman

5. Judges, Interpretation and Self-Government 67
   Lord Hoffmann

6. Judicial Law-Making and the 'Living' Instrumentalisation
   of the ECHR 73
   John Finnis

7. The Role of Courts in the Joint Enterprise of Governing 121
   Aileen Kavanagh

8. Three Wrong Turns in Lord Sumption's Conception
   of Law and Democracy 141
   Jeff King

9. The Human Rights Act and 'Coordinate Construction':
   Towards a 'Parliament Square' Axis for Human Rights? 153
   Carol Harlow

10. Limits of Law: Reflections from Private and Public Law 175
    Paul Craig

11.	The Limits of Lord Sumption: Limited Legal Constitutionalism and the Political Form of the ECHR..193 *Richard Bellamy*	
12.	A Response ....213 *Lord Sumption*	

Index 225

List of Contributors

Richard Bellamy is Professor of Political Science at University College London and Director of the Max Weber Programme at the European University Institute

Paul Craig is Professor of English Law in the University of Oxford

John Finnis is Professor Emeritus in Law and Legal Philosophy in the University of Oxford and Biolchini Family Professor of Law in Notre Dame University

Sandra Fredman is Rhodes Professor of the Laws of the British Commonwealth and the USA in the University of Oxford

Carol Harlow is Professor Emeritus at the London School of Economics

Lord Hoffmann was a Lord of Appeal in Ordinary (Law Lord) from 1995 to 2009

Aileen Kavanagh is Associate Professor of Law in the University of Oxford

Jeff King is Senior Lecturer in Law at University College London

Martin Loughlin is Professor of Public Law at the London School of Economics

Lord Sumption is a Justice of the Supreme Court of the United Kingdom

1

Introduction

NW BARBER, RICHARD EKINS AND PAUL YOWELL

THIS IS A book about the nature and limits of the judicial role. It examines the proper constitutional role of the judge by considering questions about relative institutional competence, the nature of law-making and legal reasoning in general, and rights adjudication in particular. These are questions that engage core constitutional principles, including the rule of law, parliamentary democracy and the separation of powers. All of these are matters of enduring scholarly and public interest. They are of particular importance in evaluating the exercise of judicial responsibilities under the Human Rights Act 1998 and the impact of the European Convention on Human Rights within the UK. Debates about the merits of that Act and the terms of the UK's continuing membership of the Convention are in large part debates about the powers that judges—British or European—ought to enjoy in our legal order.

The public conversation about the nature and limits of judicial power has long been enriched by the extra-judicial reflections of our leading judges. This book is framed around one such contribution, Lord Sumption's 2013 lecture, 'The Limits of Law'.[1] The lecture takes its place in a long tradition in which commitment to self-government by way of a sovereign Parliament has been shared by people who otherwise have a wide range of political views. Lord Sumption's lecture restates some central elements in this familiar understanding of fundamental principle, elucidating them from the distinctive perspective of a sitting judge and in relation to the latest developments in our constitutional law. With a view to exploring further the shape and implications of the argument, we invited nine leading scholars to reflect on Lord Sumption's lecture, in dialogue with him, at a conference held in Oxford in October 2014. This volume captures that conversation, opening with Lord Sumption's lecture, which is presented here in a format close to its original text, continuing through nine scholarly reflections and responses, and concluding with a reply from Lord Sumption.

---

[1] Lord Sumption, 'The Limits of Law', 27th Sultan Azlan Shah Lecture, Kuala Lumpur, 20 November 2013.

Following Lon Fuller,[2] the lecture takes as its framing question how best to separate responsibilities between judges and other officials, in particular, legislators. While noting that judicial law-making is widespread in the common law world, Lord Sumption discerns a growing tendency to characterise political questions as questions apt for judicial resolution, a tendency he sees in ordinary judicial review of executive action (the main focus of his FA Mann lecture in 2011,[3] a lecture to which a number of contributors refer), in American constitutional practice, and in the law and practice of the European Court of Human Rights. In particular, the Strasbourg Court's adoption of the 'living instrument' technique of interpretation has made possible the extension and modification of the content of the Convention beyond the text that was agreed by its signatories. The 'living instrument' doctrine, sometimes called the 'living tree' approach, provides that the judge may depart from the original meaning of the legal instrument, developing and extending the legal meaning over time. For its supporters, the 'living instrument' doctrine is a sensible way for courts to keep bills of rights up to date in line with changing needs and social mores. Lord Sumption takes a different view: he regrets the expansion of judicial power that this interpretive methodology has enabled. The problems with this mode of judicial action, he argues, are that it compromises the rule of law, departing from the disciplined legal technique that ought to govern a court's engagement with written legal instruments, and that it undermines democracy. These two claims, about proper legal technique and the rule of law, and about the relationship between judicial law-making and democracy, are in one way or another considered closely in every chapter in this book.

Judicial law-making may often involve a democratic deficit, Lord Sumption argues, but the deficit is at its most significant in relation to fundamental rights, which constrain the democratic process. The text of the Convention, he maintains, is wholly admirable: there was good sense in the decision to adopt the Convention and hence affirm some basic limits on state action, the breach of which clearly constituted oppression. However, when one sets these clear cases of real oppression aside, and when courts start to remake and extend the Convention, the democratic objection is, for Lord Sumption, compelling. He illustrates this point by way of the prisoner voting saga. In *Hirst v UK (No 2)*,[4] the European Court of Human Rights ruled that the UK's decision not to give prisoners the right to vote ran contrary to the Convention. The UK Parliament has yet to change the law in response to this ruling. The Strasbourg Court, Lord Sumption argues, ruled against the UK on the grounds of democratic legitimacy, grounding its decision in the obligation on the parties to hold free elections,[5] but in doing so demonstrated its lack of real

---

[2] L Fuller, 'The Forms and Limits of Adjudication' (1978) 92 *Harvard Law Review* 353.
[3] J Sumption, 'Judicial and Political Decision-Making: The Uncertain Boundary' (2011) 16 *Judicial Review* 301.
[4] *Hirst v UK (No 2)* [2005] ECHR 681.
[5] Protocol 1, art 3.

interest in democratic principle. Democracy, he says, has a straightforward meaning: it is 'a constitutional mechanism for arriving at decisions for which there is a popular mandate'. The Strasbourg Court, however, 'uses the word in a completely different sense, as a generalised term of approval for a set of legal values which may or may not correspond to those which a democracy would in fact choose for itself'. For Lord Sumption, Strasbourg's rejection of Parliament's decision to deny prisoners the vote was itself undemocratic: an unjustified restriction on the authority of Parliament. That the Convention's force in the domestic law of the UK is realised by way of Parliament's decision to enact the Human Rights Act does not remove the democratic deficit. Not every decision made by a democratic assembly is consistent with the maintenance of democracy: incorporating the case law of the Strasbourg Court, and the living instrument approach to interpretation, in effect transferred legislative power to a foreign court, which is remote from and uncontrolled by citizens of the UK.

Behind the expanding reach and significance of judicial law-making, of which European human rights law is just one example, Lord Sumption discerns a widespread disdain for democracy—for the political process—and a corresponding enthusiasm for the law—for the judicial process. He argues that neither the disdain nor the enthusiasm is warranted. There are very real advantages to according primacy to legislatures, to law-making by way of democratic means, both in terms of acting fairly in circumstances of disagreement *and* in terms of making substantively sound decisions. Arriving at a stable, peaceful decision about what is to be done in answer to the political questions that are the subject of so much rights adjudication is a task, he argues forcefully, for which the political process is much better suited than the judicial process. Echoing Fuller again, Lord Sumption argues that the problems in question are polycentric, with multiple consequences for parties not before the court. The institutional form of the court focuses the judge's attention on the parties before him or her, which entails the exclusion of much that is relevant to law-making in the context of polycentricity. The structure of the legislature, in contrast, permits a wider range of interests and arguments to be aired and considered before the decision is made. For this reason, the legislature is better placed than the court to decide what should be done, to make good law.

Lord Sumption is also concerned that shifting authority from the legislature to the courts imperils the capacity of the political process to facilitate compromise between groups of citizens. He argues that many public law questions which are presented to courts as issues between the state and an individual are really issues between different groups of citizens: these are questions on which people hold strong and divergent opinions, including matters of morality and social policy. 'The essential function of politics in a democracy', he argues, 'is to reconcile inconsistent interests and opinions, by producing a result which it may be that few people would have chosen as their preferred option, but which the majority can live with.' The political process, he acknowledges, might be characterised by opacity, fudge and even irrationality. But even though its results are 'intellectually impure', he defends them as in the public interest. Whilst the courts may appear to be 'animated by a combination of abstract reasoning and moral value-judgment, which at first sight appears to embody a higher model of decision-making than the messy compromises required to build a political consensus in a Parliamentary system', the price of these judicial virtues, he argues, is steep. Having courts attempt to resolve major policy issues deprives us of a mechanism through which compromises can be mediated. Lord Sumption concludes that without limitations on judicial law-making, without some minimally adequate separation of judicial from political authority, societies will be drained of what makes them democratic 'by a gradual process of internal decay and mounting indifference'.

The politics of the judicial role are at the core of Martin Loughlin's contribution to this volume. Loughlin seeks to locate Lord Sumption's theory of the judicial role within a wider account of the changing understanding of the place of the courts in the constitution. In company with Lord Sumption, Loughlin charts the emergence of the 'political court', as doctrinal barriers to review of political questions have fallen away, and more time and resources are expended promoting social reform through court decisions. As Loughlin notes, debates over the legitimacy of these developments—both whether it is appropriate for courts to engage in these tasks and the further question of how, if at all, this role should be undertaken—have been a staple of American constitutional scholarship for many years. Loughlin draws a link between Lord Sumption's preferred approach to interpretation and the American originalists: both call for a return to, and fidelity towards, the text of the law.

Reflection on the American experience also reveals some of the tensions that lie behind Lord Sumption's argument. Loughlin challenges the idea that democracy simply means majority rule. Potentially, democracy is a far richer idea that includes a commitment to the inclusion of groups within the decision-making processes of the state. Indeed, Lord Sumption acknowledges that not all decisions reached by an elected body are 'democratic' and that minorities may need protection from oppression. But if it is democracy that is at the core of Sumption's case for a more limited judicial role and if a richer account of democracy is embraced, this may warrant, Loughlin argues, a richer, not more limited, role for the judge. Whilst Loughlin agrees with Sumption that courts are now being asked to address issues that, 50 years ago, would have been regarded as 'political' and beyond their jurisdiction, he notes that the decision about the boundaries of the judicial role is itself a 'political' one. One's conception of the proper judicial role is grounded in evaluative judgments about what democracy—and other constitutional principles—requires and there is no 'neutral' position from which the limits of the law can be gauged. For Loughlin, then, Lord Sumption's apparent reluctance to detail the normative underpinnings of his argument or the ideological underpinnings of the British constitution limits his capacity to propose remedies for the ills he has identified.

The merits of fidelity to legal text are taken up directly by Sandra Fredman, who argues that theories of legal interpretation that purport to prevent judges from making decisions based on their personal values inevitably fail. More specifically,

Fredman argues that originalism and textualism do not deliver on their promise. Taking originalism to involve a search for original intentions, she contends that it fails to constrain judges because the intention of the founders is often impossible to ascertain. Sometimes this is a matter of evidence—there just is not a record of what the original authors intended, apart, that is, from the document they agreed. But sometimes the problem is deeper still: the authors of the document may not have had a collective view of how it should apply in a particular situation or even, perhaps, may have intended that the meaning of the document should develop over time. For example, she disputes Lord Sumption's originalist interpretation of Article 8 of the Convention, the right to a private and family life, which—she argues—is not supported by available evidence of what the states-parties intended when they agreed that text. Similar conceptual and practical problems mar textualism.

The alternative, Fredman says, is that judges should be open about all the values that are at play in adjudication: this is both more honest and more democratic. The 'living tree' or 'living instrument' approach, a theory of interpretation that contrasts sharply with originalism, is not only inevitable, once we realise that the constraints of originalism are illusory—it is also, she argues, to be welcomed and cherished. The advantage of the approach is that it allows the Strasbourg Court to respond to new challenges in a way that is open and persuasive, which in turn helps secure the legitimacy of the Court and the Convention.

Questions about interpretive theory, and the similarities and differences between the Convention and other legal documents, continue in Lord Hoffmann's chapter, which reinforces Lord Sumption's concerns about Strasbourg jurisprudence while developing its own parallel critique. Lord Hoffmann situates the 'living instrument' doctrine within a general theory of legal interpretation. He maintains that meaning turns not just on semantics or syntax, but crucially also on the *background* to the particular language used. In law, the document is usually drafted to make it possible for the reader to discern a clear meaning from the wording alone, but nonetheless recourse to the background is sometimes necessary. Lord Hoffmann takes the Vienna Convention to be a succinct statement of the usual approach to interpreting legal instruments, but cautions that there are no special rules for the interpretation of treaties in contrast to any other document. He states that he is an originalist because he considers the alternative to be unconstitutional amendment of the authoritative text under the guise of interpretation. But he contends that the authority of original meaning is consistent with the truth in the 'living instrument' idea and its domestic analogue of the 'always speaking' statute. Working through English and Privy Council authority, he distinguishes applying the concept in a statute to new facts—which is unremarkable—and replacing this concept with a new concept—which he rejects.

Noting the force of Lord Sumption's argument that the 'living instrument' doctrine wrongly transfers political questions to the courts, Lord Hoffmann considers the differences between rights adjudication under a domestic constitution and under an international human rights treaty. The challenge facing the international court is to apply generalities to the detail of so many different jurisdictions: such courts are often ignorant of the law and legal culture of any particular state, and the mediating idea of the margin of appreciation yields unpredictable results and often fails to constrain. Lord Hoffmann maintains that a foreign court's detachment from the national legal system undercuts its legitimacy because, unlike a domestic instrument, there is almost no chance of the Convention being amended. Rather than concluding that the difficulty of amending the Convention justifies a narrow construction of its demands, the Strasbourg Court has inverted this reasoning, arguing that because the Convention is hard to change the Court should amend it through interpretation. This, Lord Hoffmann claims, flouts the Vienna Convention and the analogous limits in domestic law. He concludes that the merits of the Strasbourg Court's rulings are not the issue: even if it rules well, the people should not be subject to the rule of a foreign court that answers to no one.

Like Lord Hoffmann, John Finnis takes Lord Sumption's lecture to have highlighted a serious problem in our constitutional arrangements. In his contribution to this volume, Finnis defends and extends Lord Sumption's argument about the constitutional role of the judge, exploring at length the nature of legal technique, the principle of the separation of powers and the risk of judicial usurpation. He begins by questioning Lord Sumption's assumption about judicial law-making in the common law. The declaratory theory of law, though it has now been largely discarded, contained a partial truth: that judges do not stand to the common law as the legislature stands to the statute book or to the law at large. Instead, judges are limited in their capacity to make changes in the law by their duty to adjudicate fairly and in accordance with the law settled by past legal decisions. The radical difference in object between judicial action and legislative action rules out simple accounts of judicial law-making and, Finnis continues, leading judges have recognised this truth in cases where the question about the relationship between judge and law has clearly arisen. Whilst judges may sometimes make or develop the law, within the common law structure, this creative capacity is limited by the pre-existing law: the judge and the legislator have profoundly differing tasks.

Whereas Lord Sumption confines his criticism to the European Court of Human Rights, stating that 'The text of the Convention is wholly admirable', Finnis is less impressed, calling it 'juridically … a mess'. The drafting of the Convention is problematic in a number of ways, which has encouraged the conflation of judicial and legislative power to which, Finnis says, Lord Sumption rightly objects. Finnis analyses the proportionality doctrine, which judges use to delimit the scope of the Convention, and the 'living instrument' doctrine, which judges call in aid to depart from the original meaning of the Convention. These doctrines invite and animate flawed and unwarranted exercises of supposedly judicial power on the part of the Strasbourg Court but also of British courts, most notably the Supreme Court. In line with Lord Sumption, Finnis argues that these departures from sound legal technique flout the original agreement amongst the Member States, compromise the rule of law and embody an inept, undemocratic mode of legislating. Finnis develops these arguments by way of two extended studies of judicial interference: first, with the ban on prisoner voting; and, second, with the capacity of states, especially in Southern Europe, to resist illegal migration. Finnis concludes his wide-ranging critique by arguing that Parliament ought to repeal the Human Rights Act and that Britain ought to exercise its right to exit the Convention.

In her contribution to the book, Aileen Kavanagh considers Lord Sumption's institutional analysis. It is true, Kavanagh maintains, that judges have neither the institutional legitimacy nor the competence to engage in radical law reform, and she endorses in large part Lord Sumption's identification of the institutional limitations of the courts and the corresponding strengths of the legislature. The legislature is well-placed to consider the broad public interest when setting the policies of the state and crafting legislation, whilst the courts, in contrast, are well-placed to assess the impact of general laws on individuals. It is the task of the judges to ensure that liberty and justice are respected in particular cases, ensuring that the broad policy decisions of the legislature do not imperil constitutional principle in the detail of their application. Thus, the courts should collaborate with the legislature, providing assistance but also being 'prepared to stand up for certain values and principles in the appropriate case'. Both of these functions are properly exercised by the courts even in complex—polycentric—cases that potentially have far-ranging consequences. The Human Rights Act, on Kavanagh's argument, makes it possible for the courts to complement the legislature, adjusting legislation to avoid breach of the Convention and authorising the courts to highlight other breaches.

Jeff King's contribution considers three themes in Lord Sumption's work: originalism, democracy and polycentricity. Placing Lord Sumption's theory in comparative perspective, he contrasts living tree interpretation with originalism. The distinction between these two modes of interpretation may be more problematic than it seems: King argues that the framers of constitutional documents generally intend the legal meaning of the document to develop over time. In particular, he argues that the European Convention on Human Rights was not intended by its drafters to be understood as limited to the conceptions of rights possessed by its framers; rather, the rights it lays down were intended to be subject to different interpretations at different times. Turning to the argument from democracy, King, like Loughlin, argues that only a very thin theory of democracy, one based on formal voting equality, demands the strict limits on judicial law-making called for by Lord Sumption. Democracy is compatible with institutions that have the effect of tempering voter equality, such as bicameralism or the consociational system found in Northern Ireland. Human rights law, King argues, can promote democratic equality by protecting marginalised groups within society. Giving individuals within these groups claims that they can make against the majority promotes rather than undermines the equality at the heart of democratic government.

Kavanagh and King thus each support human rights law as a tool for modifying legislation to avoid potentially unintended injustices by alerting the legislature to rights-related problems with its statutes or by protecting groups that would otherwise be marginalised within a formally equal democratic process. For King, this promotes democratic values; for Kavanagh, this limits democratic participation, but in a way that may be justified by the enhancement of good government.[6] Kavanagh and King also address an aspect of the broader question of the limited capacity of courts to acquire and process information: the argument from polycentricity. They argue that polycentricity is pervasive in adjudication, especially in the higher courts, and is not confined to the law on human rights.[7] The only alternative to allowing judicial decisions on polycentric matters would be to exclude adjudication across a large range of cases, including many in private law and international law. Thus, whilst polycentricity is a relevant factor for judges, even a reason for institutional restraint, it is not a reason for courts to withdraw altogether and treat polycentric issues as non-justiciable.

The complexity and stability, or otherwise, of the various modes of interaction between courts and legislatures are taken up further in Carol Harlow's chapter, which considers the prospects for fruitful dialogue or needless friction between institutions. Harlow makes clear the wide range of institutional interactions to which the Human Rights Act and the Convention give rise, a set of interactions sometimes described as forms of 'dialogue'. There is interaction between Parliament and the domestic courts, between Parliament and the European Court of Human Rights, and between the domestic courts and the European Court of Human Rights. When considering relative institutional competence, one should examine the difference not only between the courts and legislature, but also between the capacities of domestic courts and the capacities of transnational courts.

Harlow sketches four case studies of institutional interaction between the political authorities, the British courts and the Strasbourg Court. The studies—the regulation of political advertising, the ban on prisoner voting, the attempt to delimit the scope of Article 8 of the Convention in immigration cases, and the link of jobseekers' allowances to 'work-related activity'—are presented as a declining scale of cooperative dialogue between judicial and political bodies. She notes a split between two models of rights adjudication, in which the court either strives to respect Parliament's competence and distinctive capacities or purports to exercise an effectively legislative function to which other institutions must conform. The former may have been the promise of the Human Rights Act, Harlow suggests, and characterises the reasoning found in some cases, but the latter is a constant temptation, which overstates the judicial role and causes needless friction. Likewise, and relatedly, there are variations in the willingness of legislators to listen to judicial concerns and to respond to them on the merits, without calling (democratic) rank.

Having outlined the reasons why courts and political authorities may conflict in these ways, Harlow goes on to make the case for an alternative relationship,

---

[6] See further A Kavanagh, 'Participation and Judicial Review: A Reply to Jeremy Waldron' (2003) 22 *Law and Philosophy* 451.
[7] See further J King, 'The Pervasiveness of Polycentricity' [2008] *Public Law* 101.

in which the polycentric questions that are the subject of rights adjudication are addressed by way of a virtuous, rather than vicious, institutional dialogue. The required dialogue is both horizontal, between national institutions, and diagonal, between national and supranational institutions. Harlow highlights the role of mediating institutions already in place, such as the Joint Committee on Human Rights. For Harlow, this process of coordinate construction has the potential to constitute a 'Parliament Square Axis', in which contested questions of right are resolved intelligently, justly and democratically, and in which cooperation between the British courts and Parliament helps encourage restraint on the part of the Strasbourg Court.

The proper subject matter of judicial deliberation and action is a key theme of the lecture and this volume, to which the idea of polycentricity is closely related. This volume returns explicitly to the dilemmas of polycentricity in Paul Craig's response to Lord Sumption. Craig, noting that the focus of Lord Sumption's critique is excessive judicial law-making in public law cases, asks if the same conclusions apply to private law. If, as Lord Sumption suggests, it is inappropriate for judges to substitute normative judgment or to balance incommensurable values when considering politically controversial issues of public policy, how then should they approach a tort case? Everyday negligence cases are alive with implicit policy choices, whose consequences reach far beyond the claimants and respondents. These judicial choices reflect value judgments and have the effect of allocating resources within society.

Craig argues that the balancing exercises and the value judgments thought to mark out judicial activism in public law are common to judicial reasoning in public *and* private law. Moreover, to distinguish between these two systems on the grounds that matters of private right are binary whereas questions of public policy are polycentric is to ignore the extensive polycentric interests at stake in tort and other private law cases. If polycentricity is a problem for judicial reasoning, then it is a problem that is not limited to judicial review of administrative action.

In the volume's penultimate chapter, Richard Bellamy returns us to the question of how best to situate Lord Sumption's critique. At first (and maybe second) glance, Lord Sumption's critique of rights adjudication and defence of legislative primacy resonates with the tradition of political constitutionalism. This tradition, which has been dominant for so long in the Westminster constitution, provides that Parliament should not be subject to justiciable limits, but is nonetheless subject to the constitution, with the discipline of conventions, and the spur of political competition helping to avoid arbitrary legislative action. However, Bellamy, himself a leading scholar of political constitutionalism,[8] argues that Lord Sumption is in fact a limited legal constitutionalist. The grounds for his charge are twofold: first, Lord Sumption's concern for restrained legal technique overstates the

---

[8] See further R Bellamy, *Political Constitutionalism: A Republican Defence of the Constitutionality of Democracy* (Cambridge, Cambridge University Press, 2007).

determinacy of legal reasoning and undemocratically confines judges (and others) to original meaning rather than to present political will; and, second, Lord Sumption's account of politics is insufficiently *constitutional*, with his understanding of compromise failing to do justice to the difference between mere interest-group bargaining and fair settlement of contested questions about the equal terms of political association.

Bellamy argues that democratic principle does not limit courts—British or European—to the original meaning of the Convention, but rather requires them to update it in view of present concerns and priorities. Indeed, he maintains that political constitutionalism, properly understood, justifies (for the most part at least) the current shape of the Convention and the practices of the Strasbourg Court to which Lord Sumption objects. The courts are well-positioned to give voice to those who may lack it in the regular democratic process. On Bellamy's account, an important feature of courts that are structured to improve democratic deliberation is that they should not have a power to strike down laws—'strong form review'—but should instead engage in 'weak review' that leaves the last word to the legislature. Bellamy notes that the Strasbourg Court itself does not practise 'weak review'—any such analysis would be inconsistent with Britain's obligation as a matter of international law to conform to the decisions of that Court—and he advocates reform of that state of affairs. Such reform may be hard to realise, not least since it runs counter to the common refrain that the international rule of law demands Britain do as Strasbourg enjoins and, furthermore, the claim that the point of human rights adjudication is to limit the law-making freedom of legislatures, a limitation that would be weakened if compliance with Strasbourg's rulings was optional.

While the design and detail of the Convention and the Strasbourg Court may not be a perfect match for the role of courts in the political constitution, Bellamy defends them, and other international treaties and institutions of this kind, arguing that they are neither redundant nor democratically illegitimate. In view of the interconnected nature of the modern world, such treaties and institutions serve to bolster domestic democratic control. In more practical terms, they may be instruments for exporting democratic standards and for ensuring that other countries do not undermine our 'ability to operate in a democratic manner'. In this way, Bellamy maintains that courts, including an international court like the Strasbourg Court, that reject legalism may contribute to the project of democratic government.

The volume concludes with the text of Lord Sumption's rejoinder, delivered at the close of the Oxford conference. Ranging widely across the preceding chapters, Lord Sumption engages, inter alia, themes of private and public law (arguing against Craig that public law issues are distinctive both in the degree to which they engage popular interest and in their resilience to change by democratic law-making), democracy (defending his account of it as grounded in majority voting procedures against King's criticisms and against more substantive, value-laden accounts) and interpretation (rejecting Loughlin's criticisms of textualism and

Fredman's defence of the 'living instrument' approach, and arguing that some form of originalism is required for judges to respect democratic authority). Lord Sumption reiterates that the fundamental question to be decided is *who* should decide. He recalls the reasons why so many scholars and judges are sceptical about legislatures, but notes that they overlook the profound disadvantages of judicial settlement of political questions. The example of *Roe v Wade*[9] makes the problem clear, Lord Sumption contends: having abandoned legal technique, the American courts asserted an extreme rule (much more sweeping in its rejection of limits on abortion than is the norm in Europe), a rule that is effectively impossible to change and yet which has frustrated stable peaceful political settlement. This problematic mode of judicial law-making is what one increasingly sees, Lord Sumption argues, in the Strasbourg Court's Article 8 jurisprudence. The trend is also starkly visible in that Court's review of Britain's prisoner voting ban and in the reasoning of some members of the Supreme Court about assisted suicide. Legislation prohibiting assisted suicide or prisoner voting is not, Lord Sumption contends, majoritarian oppression. In a mature democracy, such questions should be decided openly by elected legislatures, not left to or taken over by courts, whether domestic or foreign.

What is to be done about this trend in our law and government? For some, it is a trend to welcome and to encourage: on this view, Lord Sumption's warnings, and other cautions about the expansion of judicial power, are overstated or misconceived and should be set aside. Perhaps the judicial power to protect rights should continue to expand. For others, the status quo has its appeal: the familiar case for the Human Rights Act is that it strikes the right balance between maintaining parliamentary authority and enabling judicial protection of human rights. On this account, 'weak form' judicial review captures the best of both legislative and judicial worlds. But critics might ask whether this is in fact the balance struck, whether we do have a system in which Parliament has the final say, or whether Britain's continuing membership of the Convention effectively commits us to a regime of strong form review, irrespective of the detail of the Human Rights Act. As Lord Sumption says in his rejoinder, it is by no means clear whether a half-way house of membership of the Convention is possible. And his concerns are not limited to the exercise of responsibilities under the Human Rights Act or the Convention. They extend to cases in administrative law, as his Mann lecture confirms, and would seem to also relate to recent decisions in which British judges have recognised rights in the common law. These cases might reflect a desire to secure Convention rights against possible legislative change or they may embody a re-discovery of common law values that, perhaps, themselves informed the drafting of the Convention.

The rise of common law rights, examined especially in Paul Craig's chapter, reminds us that the current system of rights protection in the UK may prove hard

---

[9] *Roe v Wade* 410 US 113 (1973).

to change. If the UK remains part of the Convention—a membership that bears on our relationship to the EU and to the Good Friday Agreement—the decisions of the European Court of Human Rights will continue to bind in international law, even if the Human Rights Act were modified to limit their domestic effect. And if the Human Rights Act is in the end repealed, there are other ways in which British courts might find themselves engaging in more or less the same reasoning in relation to similar, or identical, rights. First, common law rights could be extended to, in effect, recreate repealed provisions of the Human Rights Act, duplicating the interpretive force of section 3 and the declaratory power of section 4 through the common law. Second, European law is likely to play an increasing role in rights adjudication. The Charter of Fundamental Rights of the European Union echoes many of the Convention rights, and some Charter rights are regarded as general principles of European law. Furthermore, the EU may itself become a party to the Convention—such accession is provided for in the Lisbon Treaty, although the current accession agreement has been blocked by the Court of Justice of the European Union. As a result of these developments, when UK judges make decisions about the meaning and application of European law, they may be faced with many of the same issues as they now engage under the Human Rights Act, but the implications of the application of European law may be even more potent than under the Human Rights Act. The emerging rights jurisprudence of European law, combined with the doctrine of direct effect, may entail 'strong form' judicial review: statutes that are in conflict with these rights may be suspended or invalidated by UK courts.

Lord Sumption does not propose specific institutional remedies for the state of affairs he decries. Perhaps partly because of the institutional complications discussed in the last two paragraphs, Lord Sumption's lecture is first and foremost an appeal for judicial self-discipline. Ideally, the Strasbourg Court would limit itself, returning to restrained legal technique and adopting a much wider margin of appreciation, and domestic courts would also return to a more limited role in the area of rights. The prospects for any such change, especially in Strasbourg, Lord Sumption takes to be slim. Still, perhaps in view of the difficulties of unravelling the interlocking and overlapping bodies of positive law that invite an expansive judicial role, it may be that change in the legal culture is the most effective means to limit judicial power. The paramount importance of legal culture may be confirmed by the dynamic interaction between domestic political authorities, domestic courts and foreign courts. It is possible that British courts might resist overreach on the part of the Strasbourg Court or the Court of Justice of the European Union. But it also possible that fully domesticating the Convention, say by enacting a British Bill of Rights, will not limit the scope of judicial power, but rather will increase it; the interaction between the Supreme Court and the Strasbourg Court may prove to be a ratchet rather than a dampener for judicial intervention.

There are no easy options here. If the trend that Lord Sumption perceives is real, then the status quo may not long endure. Reform of Britain's constitutional arrangements by, for example, repealing and replacing the Human Rights Act may prove to be ineffective without exit from the Convention, which carries with it its own complications for maintaining the devolutionary settlements and for the conduct of British foreign policy. As this volume confirms, the separation of powers that ought to obtain between court and legislature, and between foreign courts and domestic authorities, is contested. In a self-governing political community, this separation is itself a matter for the community to decide and should therefore be the subject of informed public deliberation. In this deliberation, insight into the perspective of the judges, who, like Lord Sumption, have reflected on their capacities and on their responsibilities, will prove invaluable. However, as Lord Sumption would be the first to agree, the limits of law are too important to be left to the judges alone to draw. Self-government requires that we draw the limits; the rule of law and parliamentary democracy requires us to draw them well.

2

The Limits of Law

LORD SUMPTION

THE TITLE OF my lecture is not, I am afraid, calculated to tell you much about its contents. It is in part inspired by a well-known essay published in 1978 called 'The Forms and Limits of Adjudication' by Lon Fuller, the distinguished legal philosopher who held the chair of law at Harvard for many years. Professor Fuller took as his starting point the fact that the system of adjudication by courts of law was what he called 'a form of social ordering'. It was part of the complex mechanism by which the relations between people are governed and regulated. It operates side by side with other means of social control, such as legislation, administrative action, professional self-regulation and more or less powerful social or cultural conventions. The question which he asked himself was this: what kinds of social tasks can properly be assigned to judges and courts, as opposed to these other agencies of social control?

It is a much-debated question, and there are two features of our legal culture that make it a particularly important and difficult one. The first is that in the common law world, there are unquestionably some areas in which judges necessarily make law. In a precedent-based system, they lay down general statements of principle which then stand as authority in future cases. They do not merely discover legal principles concealed in the luxuriant undergrowth of ancient principle and scattered legal decisions, as the great eighteenth-century jurist Blackstone supposed and generations of common lawyers pretended. They make law within broad limits determined by statute and legal policy. In recent years, appellate courts in the UK have been increasingly open about this. In 2005, in *Re Spectrum Plus Ltd*,[1] Lord Nicholls of Birkenhead put the point in this way:

> Judges have a legitimate law-making function. It is a function they have long exercised. In common law countries much of the basic law is still the common law. The common law is judge-made law. For centuries, judges have been charged with the responsibility of keeping this law abreast of current social conditions and expectations.

Just as common law judges make law, so they also unmake it. They overrule past decisions, even those of the highest appellate courts. The declaratory theory of law

---

[1] *Re Spectrum Plus Ltd* [2005] 2 AC 680 [32].

holds that in that case, the earlier decisions must always have been wrong. It was just that the courts had taken a long time to realise it. As Lord Reid put it in *West Midland Baptist Association Inc v Birmingham Corporation*:

> We cannot say that the law was one thing yesterday but is to be something different tomorrow. If we decide that [the existing rule] is wrong, we must decide that it always has been wrong.[2]

But this is now overtly recognised as the fiction it always has been. The courts of the US, India, Ireland and the EU have all asserted the right in certain categories of case to overrule a decision only with prospective effect, a function previously regarded as the special domain of the legislature. In the *Spectrum Plus* case, the House of Lords held that in a suitable case, it would do so too. So judges can now not only say that the law was one thing yesterday and another tomorrow, they can actually admit that they are doing it. It is a very significant power.

It is not a power that would be recognised in all legal cultures. Article 5 of the French Civil Code, which has been part of the Code from its inception at the beginning of the nineteenth century, provides that 'judges are not permitted to adjudicate on cases before them by way of statement of general principle or statutory construction'. This means that judges may only formulate principles applicable to the particular facts before them. They may not purport to lay down general rules which would apply in any other case. That would be classified as an essentially legislative function. In keeping with that principle, there is with limited exception no doctrine of precedent in French law. This is one reason why the social and political implications of judicial decisions are usually more limited in civil law jurisdictions than they are in the world of the common law.

There is a second reason why we need to think seriously about the proper role of judges in the ordering of society. We live in an age of unbounded confidence in the value and efficacy of law as an engine of social and moral improvement. The spread of parliamentary democracy across most of the world has invariably been followed by rising public expectations of the state, of which the courts are a part. The state has become the provider of basic standards of public amenity, the guarantor of minimum levels of security and, increasingly, the regulator of economic activity and the protector against misfortune of every kind. The public expects nothing less. Yet protection at this level calls for a general scheme of rights and a more intrusive role for law. In Europe, we regulate almost every aspect of employment practice and commercial life, at any rate so far as it impinges upon consumers. We design codes of safety regulation designed to eliminate risk in all of the infinite variety of human activities. New criminal offences appear like mushrooms after every rainstorm. It has been estimated that in the decade from 1997 to 2007, more than 3,000 new criminal or regulatory offences were added to the statute book of the UK. Turning from statute to common law, a wide range of acts which a century

---

[2] *West Midland Baptist Association Inc v Birmingham Corporation* [1970] AC 874, 898–99.

ago would have been regarded as casual misfortunes or as governed only by principles of courtesy are now actionable torts.

This expansion of the empire of law has not been gratuitous. It is a response to a real problem. At its most fundamental level, the problem is that the technical and intellectual capacities of mankind have grown faster than its moral sensibilities or its cooperative instincts. At the same time, other restraints on the autonomy and self-interest of men, such as religion and social convention, have lost much of their former force, at any rate in the West. The role of social and religious sentiment, which was once so critical in the life of our societies, has been largely taken over by law. So when Lord Nicholls spoke, in *Spectrum Plus*, of the judiciary's duty to keep the law abreast of current social conditions and expectations, he was making a wider claim for the policy-making role of judges than he realised. Popular expectations of law are by historical standards exceptionally high.

These changes bring into sharper focus the question which I posed at the outset of this lecture: what sort of social reordering can properly be assigned to judges and courts, as opposed to other agencies of social control such as administrators or legislators? In theory, English law has a coherent answer to this question. It was given by Lord Diplock in his speech in the House of Lords in *R v Inland Revenue Commissioners ex p National Federation of Self-Employed and Small Businesses*.[3] Parliament is sovereign and has the sole prerogative of legislating. Ministers are answerable to the courts for the lawfulness of their acts. But they are accountable exclusively to Parliament for their policies and for the efficiency with which they carried them out, and of these things Parliament was the sole judge. This is neat. It is elegant. And it is perfectly useless, because it begs all the difficult questions. What is a question of law? What is a question of policy? The Diplock test will yield a different answer depending on how you define the issue.

Let me illustrate this point with an example, not particularly important in itself, but revealing nonetheless. In England, the administration and jurisdiction of the higher courts is governed the Senior Courts Act 1981. Section 130 of that Act, which remained in force until 2003, is not normally regarded as a great engine of social policy. It empowered the Lord Chancellor to fix the level of court fees. In 1997, the Lord Chancellor introduced new regulations. Their effect was to increase the court fees, while at the same time omitting provisions in the previous regulations which had exempted people on income support. They now had to pay the court fee just like anyone else. The object was to reduce the net cost to the state of funding the court system, but the effect was necessarily to make access to the courts more expensive for the poorest section of society. Mr Witham was a man on income support who wanted to bring an action for libel, but could not afford the court fee. So he applied for judicial review of the new regulations: *R v Lord Chancellor ex p Witham*.[4] Now there are at least three different approaches that

---

[3] *R v Inland Revenue Commissioners ex p National Federation of Self-Employed and Small Businesses* [1982] AC 617, 619
[4] *R v Lord Chancellor ex p Witham* [1998] QB 575.

one might take to a problem like this one. The first is to say that a service such as the administration of justice should be viewed in the same way as any other service provided by the state. It is simply one of a number of competing claims on a limited pot of money. All public services have an opportunity cost. The money that is spent on one service is not available to spend on another which might be equally beneficial. Who is to say whether it is more important that the poor should have affordable access to the courts or that they should have affordable access to hospitals, schools or any of the other publicly provided services of the state? This is precisely the kind of policy decision which on any orthodox view of English public law is not for judges. It is an inescapably political question. But there is a second approach. One could say that affordable access to justice was so fundamental a right that the state was under an absolute legal duty to provide it. From this it would follow that access to justice trumped all other calls on the state's budget. Put like that, the question ceases to be a political issue and becomes a legal one. A third approach is to recognise the absolute character of the duty to provide affordable access to the courts to the poor, while doing it in some other way. For example, one might make legal aid available on a more generous basis or increase income support payments so that the higher court fees became affordable. That approach raises yet further questions. The practical effect of providing legal aid is to increase the resources available to citizens provided that they spend it on litigation. Yet is litigation such a valuable part of our social culture that we should privilege it in this way? If Mr Witham's income support payments had been increased by enough to pay the court fee, he might have preferred to spend the money on a holiday than on suing his detractor. Is this a choice that should be denied to him? These are not straightforward questions. But more important than their inherent difficulty is that they are not legal questions. We are back in the realms of politics.

Mr Witham's case came before a Divisional Court of the Queen's Bench Division, which quashed the regulations. Laws J, one of the most thoughtful constitutional lawyers to have sat on the English bench in recent times, delivered the leading judgment. He considered that access to justice at an affordable price was not just another government service. It was a constitutional right, which could only be restricted with specific statutory authority. Since Britain does not have a written constitution, Laws J was exercising a purely judicial authority when he declared this constitutional right to exist. What he did not do was consider the implications of the question for the distribution of the government's resources or the appropriate method of helping the poor. Indeed, he seems to have thought that the question did not arise. This was because in his view, reduced court fees were not a state subsidy supported by taxpayers' money.[5] He thought that in this respect, they were different from legal aid, which the executive would be at liberty to regulate at its discretion. Now, I am not saying that the result of this case was necessarily wrong, and in any event it was subsequently given statutory force. But it cannot possibly be justified on these grounds. Since the cost of running the courts greatly exceeds

[5] ibid 586D–E.

the revenue derived from court fees, reducing court fees inevitably involves a large measure of public subsidy, just as legal aid does. The real question was not about the importance of keeping down court fees, but about the *relative* importance of doing so, relative, that is, to other possible uses of the money or other possible ways of helping the poor. What the Divisional Court did was reduce the question before it to a binary question. Was it fundamental to the legal order that the poor should be able to afford court fees? Yes or no? By classifying the question in that narrow way, the court turned it into a question of law. Had it confronted the real issue, it might have concluded that it wasn't a justiciable issue at all.

I cite this minor corner of English public law, because it perfectly illustrates the problems associated with the judicial resolution of questions with wider policy implications. But this is not a problem peculiar to English law. There has been a notable tendency in other common law jurisdictions to characterise as questions of law issues which do not really lend themselves to a legal solution. The tendency has been particularly marked in the US, where it was first noticed by the great French political scientist Alexis de Tocqueville as early as the 1830s. 'Scarcely any political question arises in the United States', de Tocqueville wrote, 'that is not resolved, sooner or later, into a judicial question.'

In Europe, much the most notable monument of this tendency to convert political questions into legal ones is the European Convention for the Protection of Human Rights and Fundamental Freedoms. This is such an important feature of the current British and European legal scene that it is worth dwelling on it for a while. The Convention is a treaty initially made between the non-communist countries of Europe in 1950, in the aftermath of the Second World War. It reflected the concern of European nations to ensure that the extremes and despotism and persecution characteristic of the German Third Reich were never repeated, as well as a growing fear of the new totalitarianism then coming into being in the Soviet-dominated communist bloc. In all countries of the Council of Europe, the Convention now has the force of law: that is to say, that it is not just an international obligation of the signatory states, but is part of their domestic legal order. In the UK, effect has been given to it since 2000 by the Human Rights Act 1998. Alone of the many national and international declarations of human rights, the European Convention provides for its enforcement by an international court, the European Court of Human Rights at Strasbourg, with the right to hear individual petitions and to make decisions which the contracting states bind themselves to put into effect. In the UK, this is achieved by conferring on all public authorities, including the courts, a statutory duty to give effect to the Convention so far as statute permits. Where statute does not permit, the courts may make a declaration of incompatibility. The understanding is that Parliament will then amend the law so as to remove the inconsistency. The Act provides that in applying the Convention, the courts are bound to have regard to the decisions of the Strasbourg Court.

The text of the Convention is wholly admirable. It secures rights which would almost universally be regarded as the foundation of any functioning civil society: a right to life and limb and liberty, access to justice administered by an independent judiciary, freedom of thought and expression, security of property, absence of arbitrary discrimination and so on. Nothing that I have to say this evening is intended to belittle any of these truly fundamental rights. But the European Court of Human Rights in Strasbourg stands for more than these. It has become the international flag-bearer for judge-made fundamental law extending well beyond the text which it is charged with applying. It has over many years declared itself entitled to treat the Convention as what it calls a 'living instrument'. The way that the Strasbourg Court expresses this is that it interprets the Convention in the light of the evolving social conceptions common to the democracies of Europe, so as to keep it up to date. Put like that, it sounds innocuous, indeed desirable. But what it means in practice is that the Strasbourg Court develops the Convention by a process of extrapolation or analogy, so as to reflect its own view of what rights are required in a modern democracy. This approach has transformed the Convention from the safeguard against despotism which was intended by its draftsmen into a template for many aspects of the domestic legal order. It has involved the recognition of a large number of new rights which are not expressly to be found in the language of the treaty. A good example is the steady expansion of the scope of Article 8. The text of Article 8 protects private and family life, the privacy of the home and of personal correspondence. This perfectly straightforward provision was originally devised as a protection against the surveillance state by totalitarian governments. But in the hands of the Strasbourg Court, it has been extended to cover the legal status of illegitimate children, immigration and deportation, extradition, aspects of criminal sentencing, abortion, homosexuality, assisted suicide, child abduction, the law of landlord and tenant, and a great deal else besides. None of these extensions is warranted by the express language of the Convention, nor in most cases are they necessary implications. They are commonly extensions of the text which rest on the sole authority of the judges of the court. The effect of this kind of judicial lawmaking is in constitutional terms rather remarkable. It is to take many contentious issues which would previously have been regarded as questions for political debate, administrative discretion or social convention, and transform them into questions of law to be resolved by an international judicial tribunal.

There appear to me to be a number of potential issues about this way of making law. In the first place, it is not consistent with the ordinary principles on which written law is traditionally elucidated by judges. A system of customary law like the common law may within broad limits be updated and reformulated by the courts which made it in the first place. But very different considerations apply to a written instrument like the Convention, which records not just an agreement between states but also the limits of that agreement. The function of a court dealing with such an instrument is essentially interpretative and not creative. The Vienna Convention of 1969 on the Law of Treaties requires every treaty to be interpreted in accordance with the ordinary meaning to be given to its terms, having regard to its object and purpose. While every one will have his own take on particular decisions, there are undoubtedly some cases in which the approach of the Strasbourg Court to the Human Rights Convention goes well beyond interpretation, and well beyond the language, object or purpose of the instrument. In practice, it seeks to give effect to the kind of Convention that the Court conceives that the parties might have agreed today. This process necessarily involves the recognition by the Court of some rights which the signatories do not appear to have granted, and some which we know from the negotiation documents that they positively intended not to grant.

Second, the power to extrapolate or extend by analogy the scope of a written instrument so as to enlarge its subject matter is not always easy to reconcile with the rule of law. It is a power which no national judge could claim to exercise in relation to a domestic statute, even in a common law system. It is potentially subjective, unpredictable and unclear. Beyond a very limited point, the reformulation of a written instrument so as to satisfy changed values since it was made is not necessarily an appropriate judicial function. Let me suggest an analogy drawn from recent English case law. In *Norris v United States of America*,[6] a bold attempt was made by a Divisional Court in England to rewrite the elements of the common law offence of conspiracy to defraud so as to cover economic cartels, which, although unlawful, had never hitherto been regarded as criminal. The Divisional Court's decision would have been perfectly acceptable by Strasbourg standards. It was a response to changing attitudes to economic manipulation. Cartels are less acceptable today than they were 100 years ago when the law in this area was made. But in the view of the House of Lords, which unanimously overturned the Divisional Court's decision, this was not an acceptable way for judges to change the law. Once a principle of law is established, Lord Bingham observed that 'the requirement of certainty is not met by asserting that at some undefined later time a different view would have been taken'.[7] There are of course particular reasons for insisting on the requirement of certainty in the criminal law. But, albeit within broader limits, the same principle must surely apply to all law.

Third, the Strasbourg Court's approach to judicial lawmaking gives rise, as it seems to me, to a significant democratic deficit in some important areas of social policy. This is a particular problem given the inherently political character of many of the issues which it decides. Most of the human rights recognised by the Convention are qualified by express exceptions for cases where the national law or action complained of was 'necessary in a democratic society' (or some equivalent phrase). The case law of the Strasbourg Court provides a good deal of guidance about how these qualifications are to be applied. The court must ask itself a number of questions. Is the measure being challenged necessary? Does it have a legitimate purpose? Does it conform to current practice among other signatories to the Convention? Does it pursue its purpose in a satisfactory way? What alternative and possibly less intrusive measures would have been enough? These questions have only to be stated for it to be obvious that they are questions of policy. Most people would regard them as inherently political questions. But their inclusion in

---

[6] *Norris v United States of America* [2008] 1 AC 920.
[7] ibid [21].

the Convention to a considerable extent removes them from the arena of legitimate political debate by transforming them into questions of law for judges.

Lack of democratic legitimacy is a potential problem about all judge-made law. In a common law system, it has to be accepted within limits. But it is potentially a rather serious problem in the case of judicial decisions about supposedly fundamental rights. It is important to bear in mind that in a parliamentary democracy, the legislature can selectively enact into law whatever parts of the Convention or the case law of the European Court of Human Rights it pleases. We do not need the Convention in order to introduce changes for which there is a democratic mandate.

The Convention and its judicial apparatus of enforcement are only necessary in order to impose changes for which there is no democratic mandate. It is a constraint on the democratic process. I think that most people would recognise that there must be some constraints on the democratic process in the interests of protecting politically vulnerable minorities from oppression and entrenching a limited number of rights that the consensus of our societies recognises as truly fundamental. Almost all written constitutions do this. But the moment that one moves beyond cases of real oppression and beyond the truly fundamental, one leaves the realm of consensus behind and enters that of legitimate political debate where issues ought to be resolved politically. An interesting illustration has recently been provided by a highly charged issue about the right of convicted prisoners in the UK to vote in elections. This rule has been part of the statute law of the UK since the inception of our democracy in the nineteenth century and has been regularly reviewed and re-enacted since. It has considerable public support. It may or may not be a good rule, but it has nothing to do with the oppression of vulnerable minorities. Yet in two cases, *Hirst v UK*[8] and *Scoppola v Italy*,[9] the European Court of Human Rights has held that the automatic disenfranchisement of convicted prisoners is contrary to the Convention. In both cases, the Court's reasoning revealed its limited interest in the democratic credentials of such policies. In the first, it declined to accept the argument based on democratic legitimacy on the ground that Parliament cannot have devoted enough thought to the penal policy involved. In the second, it disregarded it even more summarily on the ground that the issue was a matter of law for the court and implicitly, therefore, not a matter for democratic determination at all. But of course to say that it is a question of law is simply to point out the problem. The Strasbourg Court directed the UK to bring forward legislative proposals intended to amend the relevant statute. The government has brought forward legislative proposals, but the UK Parliament has declined to approve them. The resultant collision between an irresistible force and an immovable object was considered a month ago by the Supreme Court in *R (on the application of Chester) v Secretary of State for Justice*,[10] in which we held that we were bound to follow the

---

[8] *Hirst v UK* (2006) 42 EHRR 41.
[9] *Scoppola v Italy* (2013) 56 EHRR 19.
[10] *R (on the application of Chester) v Secretary of State for Justice* [2013] UKSC 63.

law repeatedly declared by the Strasbourg Court, although we declined to grant a remedy as a matter of discretion. The case law of the European Court of Human Rights, which is largely based on the Court's view of what is appropriate to a democratic society, is an interesting example of the ambiguity of political vocabulary. Properly speaking, democracy is a constitutional mechanism for arriving at decisions for which there is a popular mandate. But the Convention and the Strasbourg Court use the word in a completely different sense, as a generalised term of approval for a set of legal values which may or may not correspond to those which a democracy would in fact choose for itself. In his famous essay, 'Politics and the English Language', written in 1946, George Orwell observed that 'if thought corrupts language, language can also corrupt thought'. 'Democracy' was prominent in the catalogue of words that he singled out as having become largely meaningless in consequence. To give the force of law to values for which there is no popular mandate is democratic only in the sense that the old German Democratic Republic was democratic. Personally, if I may be allowed to speak as a citizen, I think that most of the values which underlie judicial decisions on human rights, both at Strasbourg and in the domestic courts of the UK, are wholly admirable. But it does not follow that I am at liberty to impose them on a majority of my fellow-citizens without any democratic process.

The answer which is normally put forward to defend of the democratic credentials of this kind of judge-made law is that Parliament has implicitly authorised it by not reversing the decisions which it disapproved or, in the case of decisions under the Human Rights Convention, by passing the Human Rights Act 1998. I would suggest that the reality, however, is somewhat more complicated. The treatment of the Convention by the European Court of Human Rights as a 'living instrument' allows it to make new law in respects which are not foreshadowed by the language of the Convention and which Parliament would not necessarily have anticipated when it passed the Act. It is in practice incapable of being reversed by legislation, short of withdrawing from the Convention altogether. In reality, therefore, the Human Rights Act involves the transfer of part of an essentially legislative power to another body. The suggestion that this is democratic simply confuses popular sovereignty with democracy. Of course, a sovereign Parliament may transfer part of its legislative power to other bodies which are not answerable even indirectly to the people of the UK. But it would be odd to deny that this undermines the democratic process simply because Parliament has done it. A democratic Parliament may abolish elections or exclude the opposition or appoint a dictator. But that would not make it democratic.

I have spoken mainly of these questions in a British context because that is where my own experience lies. But the frame of mind underlying the case law of the European Court of Human Rights is symptomatic of a much wider phenomenon, namely the resort to fundamental rights, declared by judges, as a prime instrument of social control and entitlement. The main casualty of that approach is the political process, which is no longer decisive over a wide spectrum of social policy. In many countries, including the UK, there is widespread disdain for the political process and some articulate support for an approach to lawmaking that takes the politics out of it. This reflects the contempt felt by many intelligent commentators for what they regard as the illogicality, intellectual dishonesty and the irrational prejudice characteristic of party politics. The American philosophers John Rawls and Ronald Dworkin have been perhaps the most articulate modern spokesmen for this point of view.

I think that their attitude, which is shared by some judges, overlooks some fundamental features of the political process. Democracy requires a minimum degree of social cohesion and tolerance of internal differences in order to function properly. But provided that these conditions exist, I would like to suggest to you that politics is quite simply a better way of resolving questions of social policy than judge-made law. The public law questions which come before the courts are commonly presented as issues between the state and the individual. But most of them are in reality issues between different groups of citizens. This applies particularly to major social or moral issues, and more generally to issues on which people hold strong and divergent positions. The essential function of politics in a democracy is to reconcile inconsistent interests and opinions by producing a result which it may be that few people would have chosen as their preferred option, but which the majority can live with. Political parties are rarely monolithic. Although generally sharing a common outlook, they are unruly coalitions between shifting factions, united only by a common desire to win elections. They therefore mutate in response to changes in public sentiment in the interest of winning or retaining power. In this way, they can often be a highly effective means of mediating between those in power and the public from which they derive their legitimacy. They are instruments of compromise between a sufficiently wide range of opinions to enable a programme to be laid before the electorate with some prospect of being accepted. The larger a democracy is and the more remote its political class from the population at large, the more vital this process of mediation is. It is true that the political process is often characterised by opacity, fudge or irrationality, and who is going to defend those? Well, at the risk of sounding paradoxical, I am going to defend them. They are tools of compromise, enabling divergent views and interests to be accommodated. The result may be intellectually impure, but it is frequently in the public interest. Unfortunately, few people recognise this. They expect their politicians to be not just useful but attractive. They demand principle, transparency and consistency from them. And when they do not get these things, they are inclined to turn to courts of law instead. The attraction of judge-made law is that it appears to have many of the virtues which the political process inevitably lacks. It is transparent. It is public. Above all, it is animated by a combination of abstract reasoning and moral value-judgment, which at first sight appears to embody a higher model of decision-making than the messy compromises required to build a political consensus in a parliamentary system. There is, however, a price to be paid for these virtues. The judicial resolution of major policy issues undermines our ability to live together in harmony by depriving us of a method of mediating compromises among ourselves. Politics is a method of mediating compromises in which we can all participate, albeit indirectly, and which we are therefore more likely to recognise as legitimate.

During the 1960s, the UK Parliament enacted a number of measures designed to liberalise long-standing features of our law. Two notable monuments of this period were the decriminalisation of homosexuality and the authorisation in certain circumstances of abortion. These measures were highly controversial and were strongly opposed by significant sections of the public. In both cases, the parliamentary debates squarely addressed the moral issues and represented the whole spectrum of contemporary opinion. The legislation which emerged contained carefully framed limitations and exceptions meeting some, although by no means all, of the objections. By and large, the results of these enactments have been accepted and the principles underlying them have become largely uncontroversial. This is the paradigm case of how the political process ought to work. It also suggests that it is perfectly capable of successfully addressing major moral issues which would today be characterised as engaging human rights. I venture to suggest that if similar reforms had been imposed judicially, they would not have been so readily accepted. The continuing controversy in the US about the decision of the US Supreme Court in *Roe v Wade*[11] to recognise judicially the almost unrestricted constitutional right of a woman to an abortion certainly suggests that that is so. Like other ancient nations, the UK has shown a remarkable ability to adapt peaceably to changing realities. Some of these changes have radically disturbed existing expectations and vested interests. Yet the law has adapted itself to them in a way which has generally been accepted by a broad consensus among its citizens. This process of compromise and adaptation in the face of disruptive social change owes almost everything to politics. Courts of law could not have done it. It is not their job.

I have already mentioned Professor Ronald Dworkin, whose death last year deprived us of one of the most formidable defenders of rights-based law defined by judges. He defended it against those who would leave this to the legislature by arguing that judges were more likely to get the answer right. 'I cannot imagine', he wrote, 'what argument might be thought to show that legislative decisions about rights are inherently more likely to be right than judicial decisions.' The problem is that this assumes a definition of 'rightness' which is hard to justify in a political community. How do we decide what is the 'right' answer to a question about which people strongly disagree without resorting to a political process to mediate that disagreement? Rights are claims against the claimant's own community. In a democracy, they depend for their legitimacy on a measure of recognition by that community. To be effective, they require a large measure of public acceptance through an active civil society. This is something which no purely judicial decision-making process can deliver.

But I would go further than this. Unlike Professor Dworkin, I *can* imagine why legislative decisions about rights are more likely to be correct than judicial ones, even if what one is looking for is the intellectually or morally ideal outcome.

---

[11] *Roe v Wade* 410 US 113 (1973).

The reason, as it seems to me, is that rights can never be wholly unqualified. Their existence and extent must be constrained to a greater or lesser extent by the rights of others, as well as by some legitimate collective interests. In deciding where the balance lies between individual rights and collective interests, the relevant considerations will often be far wider than anything that a court can comprehend simply on the basis of argument between the parties before it. Litigants are only concerned with their own position. Single-interest pressure groups, which stand behind a great deal of public law litigation in the UK and the US, have no interest in policy areas other than their own. The court, being dependent in the generality of cases on the material and arguments put before it by the parties, is likely to have no special understanding of other areas. Lon Fuller famously described these as 'polycentric' problems. What he meant was that any decision about them was likely to have multiple consequences, each with its own complex repercussions for many other people. 'We may visualise this kind of situation by thinking of a spider's web', he wrote; 'a pull on one strand will distribute tensions after a complicated pattern throughout the web as a whole'. In such a case, he suggested, it was simply impossible to afford a hearing to every interest affected. One of three consequences follows, and sometimes all three at once. First, the judge may produce a result which, because of its unexpected repercussions, is unworkable or ineffective or obstructive of other legitimate activities. Second, the judge may end up by acting unjudicially. He may consult third parties or make guesses about facts of which he has no sufficient knowledge and cannot properly take judicial notice. Third, he may reformulate the issue so as to make it a one-dimensional question of law in which the only relevant interests appear to be those of the parties before the court, which is what the Divisional Court did in Mr Witham's case. Decisions made in this way are necessarily made on an excessively simplified and highly inefficient basis.

Now, I would be the first to acknowledge that some degree of judicial lawmaking is unavoidable, especially in an uncodified common law system. It is a question of degree how far this can go consistently with the separation of powers. Even in a case where the limits have been exceeded, I am not going to suggest that the fabric of society will break down because judges, whether sitting in London, Strasbourg, Washington DC or anywhere else, make law for which there is no democratic mandate. The process by which democracies decline is more subtle than that. They are rarely destroyed by a sudden external shock or unpopular decisions. The process is usually more mundane and insidious. What happens is that they are slowly drained of what makes them democratic, by a gradual process of internal decay and mounting indifference, until one suddenly notices that they have become something different, like the republican constitutions of Athens or Rome or the Italian city-states of the Renaissance.

3
Sumption's Assumptions

MARTIN LOUGHLIN

I

THE APPOINTMENT OF Lord Sumption to the Supreme Court in January 2012 provoked a considerable amount of critical commentary. Initially, this was directed at the unusual circumstances of his appointment. But that controversy was soon overshadowed by his contention, expressed extra-curially in a series of public lectures, that the biggest challenge the judiciary presently faces is to ensure that, in developing the common law, care is taken not to stray into the political arena.

His call for judicial restraint, especially when reviewing matters of government policy, recollects the intense debates of the interwar period when the judiciary was criticised for allowing political prejudice to influence the manner in which they engaged in judicial review of administrative action.[1] But the circumstances now are different: whereas the interwar controversy focused on the ways in which a conservative judiciary was protecting property rights by striking down socially progressive administrative action, today Sumption expresses concern that an activist judiciary animated by liberal values is in danger of inappropriately interfering with (often conservative) governmental policy decisions. The interwar critics urging judicial restraint were on the side of progress. The question now to be asked is whether Sumption's call for restraint is progressive or reactionary.

This chapter suggests an answer to this question. It proceeds by first reflecting on the circumstances of Lord Sumption's appointment (his Assumption), then by examining the manner in which he has assumed responsibility to examine the appropriate boundary between law and politics, and finally by analysing the set of assumptions that would appear to underpin his analysis and remedy.

---

[1] See, eg, HJ Laski, 'Judicial Review of Social Policy in England' (1926) 39 *Harvard Law Review* 839; WI Jennings, 'The Courts and Administrative Law: The Experience of English Housing Legislation' (1936) 49 *Harvard Law Review* 42. *Per contra*, see Lord Hewart, *The New Despotism* (London, Benn, 1929); CK Allen, *Bureaucracy Triumphant* (Oxford, Oxford University Press, 1931).

II

In January 2012, Jonathan Sumption QC was appointed directly from the bar to the UK's highest court. This was a remarkable elevation, the first such in over 60 years. It is also an event that seems unlikely to recur any time soon. The last two occasions on which such elevations happened—James Reid in 1948 and Cyril Radcliffe in 1949—belong to an altogether different era. These two appointments were made at the tail-end of the period in which, given the informal and pragmatic character of the common law, close involvement in matters of politics and government and especially experience of high governmental office were regarded as significant qualifications for senior judicial appointment. This was especially important with respect to litigious questions of public law in which judges were expected, by virtue of a deep practical knowledge, to understand implicitly how and where to draw the line between matters within the court's jurisdiction and political questions. These appear to have been important factors in the appointments of Reid and Radcliffe.[2]

Political experience was evidently not a factor with respect to Sumption's candidature. Indeed, not only did he lack any significant political experience, he also happily conveyed the impression that, unless similarly elevated directly to a top political position, he would find politics 'uninteresting'.[3] Does this mean that intellect should now be regarded as a substitute for experience with respect to judicial appointment? This proposition is undoubtedly too broadly drawn. Most would accept that political experience is no longer a relevant factor, but what about judicial experience? Lord Sumption's appointment, it would seem, was controversial primarily because many, including significant numbers in the judicial ranks, opposed his appointment on the ground that promotion to the highest court should only go to someone with extensive judicial experience.[4] Their views evidently did not prevail.

---

[2] Reid had been a Scottish Unionist MP from 1931–35 and 1937–48, had served as Solicitor-General for Scotland (1936–41) and then as Lord Advocate (1941–45). Between 1945 and 1948, when he was appointed a Law Lord, he had acted as Dean of the Faculty of Advocates. During the Second World War, Radcliffe had served as Director-General of the Ministry of Information and after the war chaired several governmental inquiries, including the committee charged with drawing the boundaries between India and Pakistan following independence.

[3] In an interview with *The Independent*, it was reported of Mr Sumption that: 'Politics was discarded ... because of the "demands it makes on one's time. There is also a very narrow apex. There is not much of any interest below the top."' (*The Independent*, 15 October 2011). See also 'Interview with Jonathan Sumption' *The Lawyer* (18 December 2000): 'In the extremely unlikely event of somebody asking me whether I'd accept a peerage, I honestly don't know what I'd say. I can see the advantage of having some involvement in the political process without the awful grind of having to be elected.'

[4] Joshua Rozenberg, 'Likely Appointment of Jonathan Sumption to Supreme Court is Controversial' *Law Society Gazette* (14 April 2011).

III

It is not known whether Sumption's views on the law–politics boundary formed part of the judicial appointment process, but they are undoubtedly long-held. In an interview given to the BBC in 2010, he had already suggested that 'the biggest problem with the English legal system is drawing the boundary lines between politics and law'.[5] It is of particular significance given that the Supreme Court is likely to be exerting a greater influence on the development of public law in future and that presently relatively few Supreme Court judges possess extensive public law experience.[6]

On the occasion of his appointment, Sumption is reported to have said that: 'This is a challenging time for the development of the law, and I am honoured to have the opportunity of contributing to the work of one of the world's great common law courts.'[7] The challenge, it is suggested, is that of developing law while maintaining an appropriate boundary between legal and political questions. This concern was clearly signalled in the well-publicised Mann lecture he delivered after his appointment had been announced, but before he had taken office. Entitled 'Judicial and Political Decision-Making: The Uncertain Boundary', its main message was to warn the judiciary not to stray into the political arena.[8] Any doubt about his intention to assume responsibility as a Supreme Court judge for dealing with this matter was removed by subsequent public lectures: following his Mann lecture in 2011, he delivered lectures at the LSE in May 2012[9] and in Kuala Lumpur in November 2013,[10] both of which were devoted to aspects of the interface between law and politics.

What, then, is the basis of his concerns? Sumption began his Mann Lecture with the claim that 'one of the most significant constitutional changes to occur in Britain since the Second World War has been the rise in the political significance of the judiciary'.[11] This development has taken place because the expansion of judicial review has had the effect of blurring the line according to which the judiciary accepted that its function is 'to interpret and enforce law' and that it is concerned with neither policy questions nor with the determination of 'the public interest'.[12]

---

[5] '5 Minutes with Jonathan Sumption', *BBC News*, 2 August 2010: http://news.bbc.co.uk/1/hi/uk/8877049.stm.

[6] Interview, 'Jonathan Sumption: Donnish But Deadly', *The Independent* (15 October 2011): 'he [Jonathan Sumption] will bring a considerable and necessary boost of intellectual firepower to the roster of our senior judges, depleted by death and retirement over the past few years'.

[7] Clive Coleman, 'Jonathan Sumption QC Appointed Supreme Court Judge', *BBC News*, 4 May 2011, www.bbc.co.uk/news/uk-13287255.

[8] Jonathan Sumption, 'Judicial and Political Decision-Making: The Uncertain Boundary', FA Mann Lecture 2011.

[9] Lord Sumption, 'Foreign Affairs in the English Courts since 9/11', lecture at the LSE, 14 May 2012, available at: http://supremecourt.uk/news/speeches.html.

[10] Lord Sumption, 'The Limits of Law', 27th Sultan Azlan Shah Lecture, Kuala Lumpur, 20 November 2013, available at: http://supremecourt.uk/news/speeches.html.

[11] Sumption (n 8) 1.

[12] ibid 5, citing Lord Greene MR, 'Law and Progress' (1944) 94 *Law Journal* 349: discussed in Martin Loughlin, *Sword & Scales: An Examination of the Relationship between Law and Politics* (Oxford, Hart Publishing, 2000) 82–84.

Using illustrations from recent case law, he sought to show that judges are now engaged in an exercise that by its nature is political.

The main reason offered for this expansion is not the common one, that of the continuing growth of executive power; rather, it is the decline in the 'public reputation of Parliament and a diminishing respect for the political process generally'.[13] At the same time, Sumption recognised that an impetus for extending the scope of judicial review has been given by the incorporation into English law of the European Convention on Human Rights. This reform, enacted in the Human Rights Act 1998 (HRA), has 'shifted the boundaries between political and legal decision-making in areas some of which raise major political issues' and has 'extended the scope of judicial review from ministerial and administrative decisions to primary legislation'. It has generated a rights-based litigation that 'almost always turns ultimately on the question what inroads into them are justified in the public interest' and it therefore involves 'a difficult balance between competing public interests, which is an inherently political exercise'.[14]

The main danger, Sumption asserts, is that once this expansion in judicial power is fully recognised by the public, there will be pressure for some kind of democratic input into the selection of the judiciary, and this will lead to a politicisation of the bench. That development 'would undermine the reputation and perceived independence of the judiciary' and that 'would be a high price to pay'.[15] A better solution would be to 'sort out the law which judges administer'.[16] Crucially, this would require judges to pay greater respect to 'the constitutional separation of powers'.[17]

In his 2011 FA Mann lecture, Sumption acknowledged that the courts still recognise certain jurisdictional limits to their authority, including deference to the executive on questions of foreign affairs and national security.[18] But in his 2012 LSE lecture devoted to this subject, he suggests that these limits are being rapidly eroded and contends that 'the last decade has witnessed the progressive retreat of the non-justiciability theory and the advance of the qualified division of powers theory'.[19] A clear illustration is provided by the Court of Appeal's decision in *Al Rawi*, in which this shift is 'overtly acknowledged' and so 'rather strikingly', he adds, 'is the reason for it, namely the growing emphasis on the protection of human rights and the barely concealed revulsion of English judges against the [foreign policy] conduct of the United States'.[20] One prominent theme of his LSE lecture is that of the growing influence of the European Court of Human Rights, not least in extending the extra-territorial jurisdiction of the courts 'beyond those [populations] who were directly and effectively controlled by British troops to the

[13] Sumption (n 8) 16.
[14] ibid 11.
[15] ibid 19.
[16] ibid.
[17] ibid 20.
[18] ibid.
[19] Sumption (n 9) 8.
[20] ibid 13; *Al Rawi v Secretary of State for Foreign & Commonwealth Affairs* [2008] QB 289.

whole area for which Britain had responsibility as an occupying power'.[21] Sumption concludes that 'there is no doubt that they [the judges] will continue to scrutinise the impact of foreign policy decisions on individuals in a way that would not long ago have been unthinkable'.[22]

In the light of these earlier lectures, Sumption's 2013 'Limits of Law' lecture reads as a variation on the general theme, adding little in the way of legal analysis. He examines cases such as *Witham* 'because it perfectly illustrates the problems associated with the judicial resolution of questions with wider policy implications'[23] and he extends his critique to that of the Strasbourg Court's conversion of the Convention into a 'living instrument'.[24] But this extension of his thesis is informed less by legal analysis than political critique. The HRA 'involves the transfer of part of an essentially legislative power to another body'[25] and this, he contends, is corrosive of democracy. Democracy, he suggests, 'requires a minimum degree of social cohesion and tolerance of internal differences in order to function properly' and the maintenance of these qualities of tolerance and integration is the unique task of political practice.[26] Such practices may often be 'intellectually impure' and might even be 'characterised by opacity, fudge, or irrationality',[27] but they remain important features of civilised life. He alludes to the danger that the legalisation of political questions will lead to the politicisation of law, undermining cohesion and tolerance and ultimately leading to the corrosion of judicial legitimacy.

These are bold claims, but they are not original. They express general anxieties that have been the subject of widespread jurisprudential debate over the last 50 years. Such concerns have arisen mainly because of a transformation in understanding of the nature, purpose and method of constitutional law. In the Western world, this transformation has been promoted through the 'rights revolution', a movement that has shifted the focus from the role of constitutions in conferring powers on public institutions towards that of protecting the rights of citizens.[28] This rights revolution, which is expressive of deeper social trends, has resulted in the concept of 'the rule of law' being effectively converted from a political shibboleth into a juridical principle. Once this shift is transformed from thought into practice, the status of rights in constitutional ordering is enhanced, not least by providing a new platform of civil, political and social rights and considerably extending the range of anti-discrimination rights. This movement has led inexorably across the Western world to the emergence of 'political courts'.[29]

---

[21] Sumption (n 9) 18; *Al-Skeini v UK* (2011) 53 EHRR 23.
[22] Sumption (n 9) 20.
[23] Sumption (n 10) 6; *R v Lord Chancellor ex p Witham* [1998] QB 575.
[24] Sumption (n 10) 7.
[25] ibid 11.
[26] ibid 12.
[27] ibid 13.
[28] See, eg, Norberto Bobbio, *The Age of Rights* Allan Cameron(trans) (Cambridge, Polity Press, 1996).
[29] Ran Hirschl, 'The Judicialization of Mega-politics and the Rise of Political Courts' (2008) 11 *Annual Review of Political Science* 93.

Political courts exhibit certain standard features. Their jurisdictional ambit is expanded as the doctrinal barriers to the review of political questions are removed. The discretionary powers of supreme court judges grow as they assume control over their own dockets and are more easily able to determine which cases they are prepared to hear, and this generally results in an increased proportion of public rather than private law cases being given leave to be heard. There is innovation in the fashioning of public law remedies which often require continued judicial involvement in the management of governmental change. Finally, their emergence leads to huge legal, political and financial resources being mobilised in the cause of promoting social reform through judicial action.[30]

The dramatic nature and scale of these changes has generated an extensive debate over legitimate methods of constitutional interpretation. From a great variety of approaches, three basic positions might be identified. The first is that the constitution is to be treated as law and interpreted as such through the normal canons of legal interpretation. Second, rather than being regarded as ordinary law, the constitution must be viewed as a special 'fundamental law' of governmental ordering that has been drafted at a specific moment in time and through an extraordinary process of constitutional convention and ratification. Third, the constitution may indeed be a unique document, but its special character flows from the fact that it is an attempt to express and safeguard the distinctive ethos of a nation, and it must therefore be interpreted in a singular manner, one which requires creative re-interpretation as the values and practices of the nation continue to evolve.

The first approach suggests that the normal canons of positivist legal interpretation should be deployed and constitutional adjudication should be subject to such standard judicial disciplines as *res judicata* and *stare decisis*. The second approach gives rise to what American constitutional scholars call 'originalism', a method of constitutional interpretation that requires careful attention to be paid to the intention of those who drafted the document. The third treats the constitutional text as a 'living instrument', whose meaning can be re-interpreted as the mores of the nation change over time.

These developments have rendered constitutional analysis a treacherous undertaking. One problem is that considerable variation exists amongst the judiciary over the correct method of interpretation. But even when it is possible to identify a particular judge's favoured method, the relative weight given to precedent, to the framer's intent, and to evolving ethos often alters from case to case.[31] This creates considerable uncertainty in the field of constitutional litigation. Given the nature of that activity, it also feeds the sense that constitutional adjudication has become a highly politicised engagement.

---

[30] See, eg, Charles R Epp, *The Rights Revolution: Lawyers, Activists, and Supreme Courts in Comparative Perspective* (Chicago, University of Chicago Press, 1998). On the change in judicial role, see Abram Chayes, 'The Role of the Judge in Public Law Litigation' (1976) 89 *Harvard Law Review* 1281.

[31] See, eg, Robert Post, 'Theories of Constitutional Interpretation' (1990) 30 *Representations* 13.

Because of the peculiarities of Britain's unwritten and evolutionary constitutional arrangements together with the subordinate role of judges within the frame of parliamentary sovereignty, such debates have been slow to reach the UK. But recent developments—including the increased volume of judicial business, the rise of interest group litigation, the dramatic growth in judicial review, the impact of European law, the emergence of a rights-based public law and the enactment of the HRA—have now combined to bring comparable questions to the forefront of public attention. Sumption is evidently tapping into these concerns. It had to come. Perhaps the only surprising element is that his various interventions make no reference to the extensive literature on this subject and deploy little comparative analysis.[32] His argument is presented as a parochial phenomenon that has arisen mainly because of recent changes in juristic fashion.

In raising this issue for debate, Sumption is performing an important service. But it should be noted that he also holds out the promise of a prescription. What is his solution? His repeated interventions suggest an ambition to take the lead in reining in the judiciary, but thereafter the message is ambiguous. Yet without an accurate diagnosis, which might require consideration of the deeper-seated structural aspects of these developments, it is unlikely that any proposed remedy will prove effective. It is on these issues that I will now focus. The critical question is: what assumptions is Sumption making when he expresses a desire to maintain and reinforce a clear 'boundary line' between law and politics? In particular, what juristic presupposition does he utilise when proposing to 'sort out the law which judges administer'?[33] Although significant differences exist between the constitutional traditions of the US and the UK, some help with an answer can be found by first undertaking a brief review of the recent American experience.

IV

The expansion of constitutional review in the US over the last 50 years has arisen primarily because of the implicit recognition among many judges in the higher judiciary that the Constitution is to be understood as an artefact that expresses the nation's public ethos. This is the key factor that has driven the search for innovative interpretative methods. There have been variations in technique or presentation, but one of the earliest coherent statements of this innovation remains one of the most influential. This is Alexander Bickel's *The Least Dangerous Branch*.[34]

Taking his cue from Hamilton's account in the *Federalist Papers*, which highlighted the point that the judiciary department lacks both the power of the

---

[32] See, though, Sumption (n 8) 13–16 (mainly on the experience of the European Court of Human Rights).
[33] ibid 19.
[34] Alexander Bickel, *The Least Dangerous Branch: The Supreme Court at the Bar of Politics*, 2nd edn (New Haven, Yale University Press, 1986), 1.

purse and the sword,[35] Bickel contends that the 'least dangerous branch of the American government' is becoming 'the most extraordinarily powerful court of law the world has ever known'.[36] The source of this transformation is the fact that Americans have come to regard the Constitution as 'the symbol of nationhood, of continuity, of unity and common purpose'.[37] Consequently, when exercising its constitutional jurisdiction, the US Supreme Court no longer conceives its role merely as an institution that (to use Lord Sumption's term) 'administers' the law, but also regards itself as 'a legitimating force in society'.[38] The Supreme Court has become 'an institution charged with the evolution and application of society's fundamental principles'.[39]

With this transformation, the traditional materials of legal analysis—formal text and judicial precedents—no longer set the parameters of the judicial task. These materials become merely one type of source from which the judiciary may draw inspiration. When engaging in constitutional interpretation, judges must also 'immerse themselves in the tradition of our society ... in history and in the sediment of history which is law, and ... in the thought and the vision of the philosophers and the poets'.[40] The overriding objective when engaging in constitutional adjudication is to extract the 'fundamental presuppositions' of the evolving political morality of the American tradition.

This shift, one of revolutionary proportions, comes about because the US Constitution can no longer be read primarily as a legal text or as a document drafted in the late eighteenth century; it should instead be regarded as a cultural artefact bound up with the life of the nation. Many theories of constitutional interpretation have been crafted to explain and justify the judicial role in the light of this transformation. But the critical point for our purposes is that it has exposed a major gulf between judges and scholars who treat the Constitution as an expression of a nation's ethos and those who continue to treat it as a legal text. The most prominent of those in the latter camp are legal positivists and originalists.

The gulf between these two camps was vividly exposed in 1987, when President Reagan nominated Robert Bork, a US Court of Appeals judge and leading originalist scholar, to a Supreme Court vacancy. Bork's nomination provoked a national debate over his judicial philosophy, or at least over the political consequences of that philosophy, culminating in his candidature being rejected by the Senate. Bork's argument was that the transformative shift signalled by Bickel had had the effect of conferring arbitrary power on the judicial branch of the state. Once the Constitution is no longer treated as a type of positive law, then its interpretation becomes subject to the morality and politics of what he called

---

[35] James Madison, Alexander Hamilton and John Jay, *The Federalist Papers*, I Kramnick (ed) (London, Penguin, 1987) no 87; *Federalist Papers*, no 78.
[36] Bickel (n 34) 1.
[37] ibid 31.
[38] ibid.
[39] ibid 109.
[40] ibid 236.

the 'intellectual or knowledge class'.[41] Bork's thesis was that the effect of this transformation had been to convert the Constitution into 'a weapon in a class struggle about social and political values' and that political struggle had resulted in 'the transportation into the Constitution of the principles of a liberal culture that cannot achieve those results democratically'.[42] Judges, in short, have been seduced into substituting politics for law.

Bork's stance is today most forcefully expressed by the Supreme Court Justice Antonin Scalia. Scalia adopts an interpretative methodology with respect to the Constitution based on three primary factors: textualism, originalism and democracy.[43] Textualism means that judges should pay close attention to the precise formulation of the rules as enacted in the constitutional text, in statutes or in the ratio of precedent cases. Rather than adopting creative techniques suggested by purposive or so-called teleological interpretation, judges should strive to give effect to the plain meaning of legal rules. Originalism conveys the belief that when seeking to understand and give effect to a document like the Constitution, the judiciary must begin by seeking to ascertain the drafter's intent and thereafter should try to discern the meaning of the words as they would have been understood at the time they were written. Scalia's third factor expresses a commitment to democracy. Judges should never seek to breathe their own value preferences into the meaning of general claims exhibited in constitutional texts. Instead, they must be mindful of their subordinate position in the political system and should leave policy matters and value choices to those branches of government that are accountable to their electorates.

V

This sketch of the parameters of US constitutional debates helps us identify the basic assumption that underpins Sumption's argument: judges must stick to the task of applying the law. Specifically, UK judges should not be seduced into seeing themselves as guardians of their constitution, viewing their task as interpreters and enforcers of the nation's political morality. Judges should keep to received methods of legal interpretation and the traditional techniques of the common law, and retain faith in the rule of ordinary law. Of particular significance is the political conviction that Sumption and the American originalists have in common. This is the claim that a positivist adherence to the strict canons of legal interpretation has the inestimable value of bolstering the democratic foundation of the polity.

---

[41] Robert H Bork, *The Tempting of America: The Political Seduction of the Law* (London, Sinclair-Stevenson, 1990) 8.
[42] ibid 9.
[43] Antonin Scalia, *A Matter of Interpretation: Federal Courts and the Law* (Princeton, Princeton University Press, 1998); Antonin Scalia and Bryan A Garner, *Reading Law: The Interpretation of Legal Texts* (St Paul, West Publishing, 2012).

Sumption alluded to this conviction in his 'Limits of Law' lecture when referring to the dangers inherent in the enactment of the HRA. A similar point has also been vigorously asserted by Justice Scalia. In his widely cited dissenting opinion in *Lawrence v Texas*, for example, Scalia criticised the majority ruling in the US Supreme Court for failing to respect the principle of *stare decisis*, for taking sides in 'the culture war' and, most significantly, for departing 'from its role of assuring, as a neutral observer, that the democratic rules of engagement are observed'.[44] What force does this type of argument possess?

Bickel had been conscious of its power. His response was that the most important restraint guarding against an arbitrary and unjustified judicial usurpation of political power is that 'judicial review brings principle to bear on the operation of government'.[45] The main limitation on the accretion of judicial power is, in short, 'society's striving for the rule of principle'.[46] Bickel's argument throws into relief the political significance of recent debates between positivists and rights-theorists on whether it is rules or principles that form the fundamental building blocks of legal and constitutional ordering. Its significance for our purposes is to illuminate the point that Sumption's assumption that a line is capable of being drawn between the legal and the political is founded on a legal positivist philosophy.

There is clearly something to be said in favour of the positivist position. With a constitutional text of such longevity as that of the US, originalism might seem a highly restrictive device, but textualism, underpinned by a conception of law as the attempt to subject human conduct to the governance of rules, is surely an important means both of limiting governmental power and of ensuring that judges charged with determining the limits of governmental authority do not abuse their power through the imposition of their own values. Originalism and textualism are devices that aim to bolster democracy by reinforcing a belief that the business of policy-making should be left to those agencies of government that are politically and administratively accountable. There is also general consensus that judicial review should not be used as a vehicle to enable those who lose out in the democratic process to petition the judiciary to support their policies. Judicial review can be justified only if it establishes a set of procedures and principles that strengthen democratic government. But is this necessarily an argument that bolsters the legal positivist position?

When defending their position, positivists have a tendency to promote a one-dimensional view: democracy is equated to majority rule. But democracy is a complex and contested concept. Majority rule is certainly a democratic principle of primary importance, but democrats deploy this technique for a reason. Majority rule gives effect to a basic principle of equality, and especially of equal liberty. In a world of value conflict, the rule that the majority prevails is adopted as one that best expresses the principle that we should accord equal respect to each citizen's

---

[44] *Lawrence v Texas* 539 US 558 (2003).
[45] Bickel (n 34) 199.
[46] ibid 204.

view. But democrats recognise that there are occasions in which majorities might use that technique not only to institute prevailing value preferences but also to oppress minority views. In certain circumstances, majority rule can operate to deny certain groups their right to equality and thereby to corrode the underlying value of democracy.

This problem has been referred to as the paradox of democracy: 'each generation wants to be free to bind its successors, while not being bound by its predecessors'.[47] The way democrats resolve this paradox continues to be the subject of intense debate.[48] But since this aspect of democratic culture does not much engage the interests of positivists,[49] it is uncertain how serious they are about protecting democracy rather than simply bolstering the principle of legislative supremacy. What remains controversial about the so-called originalist position in the US, for example, is that contrary to Scalia's claims to be performing a neutral role in ensuring that the rules of democratic engagement are observed, their rulings tend not to result in even-handed treatment, but to politically conservative outcomes.[50]

This discussion throws up a more basic question: is it ever possible for judges operating in a public law context to avoid getting entangled in political questions? When they are drawn actively into the ambit of constitutional interpretation, it would appear that they have no alternative but to pay respect to the basic political values on which a state seeks to found itself. These must include the values of social cohesion and toleration of difference that Sumption has identified as being basic to democracy. But this does not exhaust the value catalogue. Judges will be obliged to pay attention to history, to have respect for the structural integrity of institutional arrangements, to maintain fidelity to the basic texts that found or shape a regime, and to adhere to such underlying values as democracy, liberty and equality that give meaning to that institutional configuration. Consequently, constitutional interpretation is demonstrably not the type of exercise with respect to which objectively correct answers are likely to be found within the authoritative sources of positive law. But if this lack of certainty and predictability is the problem that Sumption foresees, what is the remedy? Can the limits of law be specified?

---

[47] Jon Elster, *Ulysses and the Sirens* (Cambridge, Cambridge University Press, 1979) 94.

[48] From a voluminous literature, see only Stephen Holmes, *Passions and Constraint: On the Theory of Liberal Democracy* (Chicago, University of Chicago Press, 1995), especially ch 5; Jürgen Habermas, 'Constitutional Democracy: A Paradoxical Union of Contradictory Principles' (2001) 29 *Political Theory* 766.

[49] But see Jeremy Waldron, 'The Core of the Case against Judicial Review' (2006) 115 *Yale LJ* 1346–1406.

[50] Critics deploy this argument with particular effect with respect to the First (free speech), Fifth (due process of law), Eighth (cruel and unusual punishment) and Fourteenth (equal protection) Amendments. Consider, eg, the equal protection clause. Adopted after the Civil War, it was designed to bring African Americans into the civil nation by according them equal rights. But in the hands of Scalia and his followers, it is said, the equal protection clause has been altered from a provision that protects minorities into one that prohibits particular types of classification irrespective of who benefits and who is burdened. And this is not a very cogent interpretation of the text of the Fourteenth Amendment, the original intent of its drafters or the conception of democracy it seeks to enforce.

VI

Lord Sumption believes that judges should confine themselves to the task of interpreting and enforcing the law and avoid interfering in policy questions or determining what 'the public interest' might entail. What in practice might this mean? What precisely is the appropriate role of the judiciary in the British system? Since the evidence provided in his lectures is sparse, various answers could be offered depending on what is perceived to form the core of his argument. I will outline these possibilities under the headings of constitutionality, democracy, competence and admonition.

The *constitutional* aspect has the most far-reaching consequences. If Sumption's analysis about the dire consequences of being drawn into constitutional interpretation is sound, it follows that judges should refrain altogether from engaging in such constitutional speculation. Sumption might therefore be read as hankering after a return to the high Victorian era when judges sat 'as servants of the Queen and the legislature'[51] and when it could be said that the duty of the scholar was 'neither to attack nor to defend the constitution, but simply to explain its laws'.[52] In this milieu, a leading work on the constitution could be written with no mention at all of any constitutional responsibilities of the judiciary,[53] for the simple reason that answers to constitutional questions were felt to lie entirely within the remit of Parliament. As 'the mirror of the nation', Parliament acted as the guardian of constitutional values; the judiciary's role was merely to act as the precision instrument of parliamentary intention.

From this constitutional perspective, Sumption presents himself as an arch-exponent of so-called 'political constitutionalism'.[54] This might indeed be the British inheritance, but the problem with it is that many now question whether it is still capable of offering an adequate account of Britain's constitutional arrangements. Sumption himself concedes in his Mann lecture that the rise of judicial review is attributable to the decline in the reputation of Parliament. As the business of government changes and as Parliament is no longer believed to have a monopoly of wisdom on the expression of British constitutional values, it is perhaps not surprising to find the judiciary beginning to play some role in both the explication and the institutional protection of those values.

---

[51] *Lee v Bude & Torrington Junction Rly Co* (1871) LR 6 CP 582, per Willis J, who elaborates: 'The proceedings here are judicial, not autocratic, which they would be if we could make laws instead of administering them.'

[52] AV Dicey, *Introduction to the Study of the Law of the Constitution*, 8th edn (London, Macmillan, 1915) 3.

[53] Walter Bagehot, *The English Constitution*, Miles Taylor (ed) (Oxford, Oxford University Press, 2001). But interestingly Bagehot does suggest that 'the supreme court of the English people ought to be a great conspicuous tribunal, ought to rule all other courts, ought to have no competitor, ought to bring our law into unity, ought not to be hidden beneath the robes of a legislative assembly' (at 96).

[54] Richard Bellamy, *Political Constitutionalism: A Republican Defence of the Constitutionality of Democracy* (Cambridge, Cambridge University Press, 2007)

The argument from *democracy* is related, but it comes from a different source. The recent extension of judicial review is not simply a response to the perceived relinquishment of Parliament's historic constitutional role; it has also been expressly legislated for by Parliament in the provisions of the HRA and implicitly also in the European Communities Act 1972. Sumption recognises that 'the Human Rights Act involves the transfer of part of an essentially legislative power to another body'.[55] But he argues that the fact that this is done by Act of Parliament does not make it democratic. If the decision of a democratically elected Parliament to 'abolish elections or exclude the opposition or appoint a dictator' cannot, as he contends, be a democratic decision,[56] then neither can this transfer of what is in effect legislative authority to the judiciary.

It is difficult to derive conclusions from this argument. Sumption here accepts that democracy cannot be equated with majority will; in that sense, the transfer by majority will of a power to legislate to the judiciary is not a democratic decision. But what are the implications for the judiciary? Is the appropriate judicial response a refusal to comply with that parliamentary intention on the ground that judges cannot interpret the ECHR without legislating, something that would undermine the constitutional value of Parliament's legislative monopoly? If so, the judiciary are only able to do so: (i) by challenging Parliament's monopoly of constitutional wisdom; and (ii) by undermining the constitutional principle that the judiciary should give full and faithful effect to Parliament's will. Alternatively, we could draw the conclusion that the concept of democracy underpinning the British system is both fundamental and more nuanced than that of simple majority will. If so, then, contrary to the positivist position, the idea of democracy expresses not only tolerance of difference but also a respect for the values of liberty and equality on which the democratic will is founded. If that is indeed the case, then Parliament has charged the judiciary with the task of protecting these foundational principles of democracy. With respect to the argument from democracy, Sumption's lectures offer little guidance.

The third critique is founded on *institutional competence* rather than constitutional or political legitimacy. Sumption's critical assessment of the recent development of judicial review may be that British judges, being constitutional neophytes, are simply not up to the task of extending their jurisdictional authority into this sphere and undertaking rigorous constitutional analysis. If there is a concern that Parliament can no longer monopolise the role of guardian of constitutional values and the judiciary lacks competence to assume the role while maintaining fidelity to common law values, then what might now be needed is a new type of institution charged with the task of reconciling law and right, that is, of balancing legal rules and constitutional principles. The implication is that Britain needs to establish a special constitutional court comprising judges appointed as much for their political nous (once again) as for their forensic legal skills.

---

[55] Sumption (n 10) 11.
[56] ibid 11–12.

That, I suspect, is not what Sumption expects or wishes us to draw from an argument founded on institutional competence; rather, it is that judges should stick to the task of administering the law, maintaining a clear distinction between legal and policy questions. But is this a conceivable undertaking? This argument returns judicial review to the mindset prevailing in the post-war period up to the 1960s, a frame of thought that even Sir William Wade, a leading positivist disciple of Dicey, characterised as one that entailed 'a dreary catalogue of abdication and error'.[57]

Some might find this point far-fetched, but the leading cases of the 1960s that brought about the 'weather change'[58] all contain the seeds of the errors in contemporary practice that Sumption criticises. Whether considering the shift from natural justice to procedural fairness,[59] from jurisdiction to illegality,[60] from Crown privilege to public interest immunity challenge,[61] or of activism in review of government policy decision-making,[62] it is impossible to draw a clear line between law and politics in judicial review without reverting to the 'sporadic and peripheral' culture of mid-twentieth-century review practices.[63]

The old practices were hardly without their ambiguities and discretionary aspects, and they therefore provided opportunities for judges to impose their political views. But they did at least operate as a discrete set of doctrines, rules and practices that had evolved through the 'artificial reason' of the common law and they did seek to enforce a strict conception of legality. If Sumption really wants to ensure that courts maintain a clear distinction between law and policy, avoid involving themselves in questions of what constitutes the public interest and adhering to a 'constitutional separation of powers', then he must surely be advocating a return to the basics of jurisdictional review that dominated

---

[57] As cited by Sumption (n 8) 16.
[58] ibid.
[59] *Ridge v Baldwin* [1964] AC 40 might not itself have made a radical breakthrough in procedural protection (since, holding an office, it could be argued that the Chief Constable should never have been deprived of his 'property' without due process), but it did lead to the erosion of clear rules of natural justice applied to administrative bodies exercising quasi-judicial tasks. It also led to a highly flexible standard of procedural fairness, reinforced by the novel concept of legitimate expectations, which operated only if the judiciary immersed themselves in policy questions. See, eg, Martin Loughlin, 'Procedural Fairness: A Study of the Crisis in Administrative Law Theory' (1978) 28 *University of Toronto Law Journal* 215.
[60] *Anisminic v FCC* [1969] 2 AC 147 might not explicitly have held that all errors of law go to jurisdiction, but, as the judiciary soon recognised, that was its logical consequence. This led to legality replacing jurisdiction as the basis of review, which consequently meant that Parliament could no longer determine that, notwithstanding pressing policy reasons for a privative clause, the allocation of a task to an administrative tribunal could never be insulated from review.
[61] *Conway v Rimmer* [1968] AC 910 might not have jettisoned the notion of 'Crown privilege', but, following its logic, it was soon replaced by public interest immunity claims that were subject to judicial policy assessment of the strength of the executive's claim to maintain the secrecy of its material.
[62] *Padfield v Minister of Agriculture* [1968] AC 997 might not constitute a case of the court second-guessing the Minister's policy decision, but in holding that the Minister's refusal to establish an investigation frustrated the policy of the statute, the ruling opened up a line of review of ministerial discretionary policy-making in which issues of law and policy remain forever entangled.
[63] SA de Smith, *Judicial Review of Administrative Action*, 3rd edn (London, Stevens, 1973) 1.

mid-twentieth-century practice.[64] The difficulty with this argument, though, is that it requires the judiciary to set aside a body of precedents that have been built up over the last 30 or more years. It is therefore an argument as radical as the US originalist stance.

Since the arguments from constitutionality, democracy and institutional competence all seem to raise major problems for which no solution is offered, it might be the case, finally, that Sumption's public engagement should be understood purely as *admonition*. He might simply be intending to issue a warning that if judges continue down this road there will soon be calls for a greater political involvement in their appointment and that could jeopardise the independence of the institution. The experience of Judge Bork provides an obvious case in point, though in Britain presently the main threat might be over the ratification of judges with rights-protecting instincts. Nevertheless, I have some difficulty in accepting this account. Sumption has after all made the case that maintenance of the law—policy boundary is the 'biggest problem' facing English law today and has developed his argument in several public forums over the last few years. If this is not a purely rhetorical, or even political, intervention—and it might be noted that it is an intervention entirely in tune with the policies of today's Conservative Party[65]— then it might be expected that he would offer an account of what a scheme of judicial review founded on these positivist assumptions would look like. Without this constructive dimension, his public lectures, despite his protestations to the contrary,[66] look very much like the exercise of a value choice.

VII

Sumption's elevation directly from the bar to the Supreme Court remains an enigma. It marks a break with the traditions of common law practice, traditions he apparently strives to uphold. His sustained advocacy of the need to maintain a clear boundary between law and politics sits uneasily with the trajectory of contemporary practice in judicial review and consequently raises the question of whether his was a politicised appointment. And although expressing a bold stance, his lectures offer a diagnosis without any clear remedy. We can discern a particular juristic assumption—a strict legal positivism and distaste for abstract

---

[64] This was a problem of which Sir William Wade was acutely aware and who struggled, arguably with limited success, to resolve: see Martin Loughlin, *Public Law and Political Theory* (Oxford, Clarendon Press, 1992) 184–90.

[65] See, eg, *Judicial Review—Proposals for Further Reform: The Government Response* (Cm 8811, February 2014); Conservative Party, *Protecting Human Rights in the UK: The Conservatives' Proposals for Changing Britain's Human Rights Laws* (October 2014), expressed as a 2015 election manifesto commitment in https://www.conservatives.com/manifesto.aspx at 58.

[66] See Sumption (n 10) 11: 'Personally, if I may be allowed to speak as a citizen, I think that most of the values which underlie judicial decisions on human rights, both at Strasbourg and in the domestic courts of the United Kingdom, are wholly admirable. But it does not follow that I am at liberty to impose them on the majority of my fellow-citizens without any democratic process.'

principles masquerading as objective law—but beyond that, there are considerable ambiguities. This may, as some have suggested, be a consequence of his relative lack of knowledge or experience in public law matters,[67] but if so, this only increases speculation on why he has determined on this course of action. After all, it is likely to lead only to that which he apparently dreads: the politicisation of the process of Supreme Court appointments. And if he is so far out of step with the contemporary practice of judicial review, we might also wonder why he sought judicial appointment in the first place.

I am left with one final speculation. Some might argue that Lord Sumption's argument expresses a deep respect for Parliament and, by requiring observance of the limits of law, he is striving to uphold the values of democracy. Perhaps. But we should at least bring into consideration the point that this stance can also be explained as an expression of what Albert Hirschman labelled 'the rhetoric of reaction'.[68] Lord Sumption's arguments in fact read as a classic illustration of what Hirschman calls 'the jeopardy thesis': that certain reforms and social developments, though ostensibly desirable in principle, are capable of being realised only by incurring unacceptable social costs.

This type of argument has been made at many stages of modern British constitutional development. It was a feature of debates surrounding the Reform Act of 1832 and it came to prominence during the mid-nineteenth century in a series of shrill interventions complaining that the coming of democracy would imperil liberty.[69] There have since been various refrains at critical junctures. One such is exhibited by commentaries to the effect that the enactment of the Parliament Act 1911 has 'destroyed our last effective constitutional safeguard'.[70] Another followed the passing of social legislation and consequent extension of administrative government during the interwar period, leading to a chorus of common lawyers protesting the emergence of a 'new despotism' of organised 'administrative lawlessness'.[71] Sumption's contemporary variant, on its face, strikes a rather different tone: whereas the earlier calls sought to uphold constitutional values against

---

[67] This is the thrust of the critical analysis of Sumption's Mann Lecture (n 8) offered by Sir Stephen Sedley, a retired Court of Appeal judge: Stephen Sedley, 'Judicial Politics' (2012) 34 *London Review of Books* 15–16 (23 February).

[68] Albert O Hirschman, *The Rhetoric of Reaction: Perversity, Futility, Jeopardy* (Cambridge, MA, Belknap Press, 1991).

[69] See only HS Maine, *Popular Government* (London, John Murray, 1885) 97–98: 'The delusion that democracy ... is a progressive form of government, lies deep within the convictions of a particular political school; but there can be no delusion grosser ... [W]e may say generally that the gradual establishment of the masses in power is the blackest omen for all legislation founded on scientific opinion, which requires tension of mind to understand it, and self-denial to submit to it.'

[70] See, eg, AV Dicey, 'The Parliament Act, 1911, and the Destruction of all Constitutional Safeguards' in Sir William R Anson et al, *Rights of Citizenship: A Survey of Safeguards for the People* (London, Frederick Warne & Co, 1912) 81–82: 'The first truth is that the Parliament Act has destroyed our last effective constitutional safeguard. The second truth is that the whole experience of every country, which enjoys popular government, proves that the absence of constitutional safeguards imperils the prosperity of the State. The last truth is that the absence of constitutional safeguards is full of danger to England; for it enables a party, or a coalition of parties, to usurp the sovereignty of the nation.'

[71] Hewart (n 1) 14.

the threat posed by the democratisation of Parliament, he now warns that the judicial enforcement of civil and political rights corrodes democracy. The problem here is that his argument seems to be much less concerned with democracy than with authority. His claims are best understood as advocating the need to bolster parliamentary authority. While there is a serious issue here to be addressed, I doubt whether the analysis Lord Sumption has offered is able to provide a sound basis for advancing that claim. The question he raises cannot properly be addressed without undertaking a much broader investigation into the workings of the institutional arrangements of contemporary British government. And while that is so, his intervention reads most cogently as the recurrence of a distinctive English voice. This is the voice of a privileged elite who find intellectual stimulation in dwelling on the evident deficiencies in the functioning of modern constitutional democracies without offering any serious analysis or any practical remedy. This is the authentic voice of reaction, one that accompanies strident critique with vague allusions to some earlier mythical age, in which law was the 'golden metwand' and legislation remained the province of 'the upper ten thousand'.

4

Living Trees or Deadwood: The Interpretive Challenge of the European Convention on Human Rights

SANDRA FREDMAN

> 'But at the moment the hobbits noted little but the eyes. One felt as if there was an enormous well behind them, filled up with ages of memory and long, slow, steady thinking; but their surface were sparkling with the present' (*Lord of the Rings*)

> '… my name is growing all the time, and I've lived a very long, long time; so my name is like a story.' (Treebeard: *Lord of the Rings*)

ONE OF THE chief sources of criticism of the European Court of Human Rights (ECtHR) is its approach to interpretation. In an oft-repeated dictum, the Court in the case of *Tyrer* stated: 'The Convention is a living instrument which … must be interpreted in the light of present-day conditions.'[1] Lord Sumption, among others, argues that this doctrine is an illegitimate extension of judicial power, particularly in the hands of a supranational court. Such a critique assumes that there is an objective or non-contentious meaning of such terms as 'inhuman and degrading treatment', 'equality', 'freedom of speech' or 'fair trial'. It is argued here that even if judges claim to be providing the true meaning of such terms, they are in fact adopting an interpretive theory which demands background value choices. Adjudicating human rights inevitably involves value judgments. Even the choice as to whether to defer to other decision-makers, be they the current legislature or the original drafters, is value-laden. It is crucial that judges acknowledge this. Judicial accountability does not arise from their relationship to elected representatives, whether directly or indirectly, or from resort to apparently mechanical formulae about the intention behind the provision or its natural meaning. This merely disguises judges' real values. Instead, judges should be able to explain and defend their choice of values and show that they are drawn from a recognised store of possibilities. Some of these are institutional, including principles of separation of powers, legitimacy and competence. Others are based

---

[1] *Tyrer v UK* (1979–80) 2 EHRR 1 (ECHR) [31].

on adjudicative issues such as stare decisis and interpretive theories of how texts should be construed. Others are philosophical, historical or social. The danger lies, it is argued, in disguising value judgments rather than acknowledging them. It is more honest, and in the end more democratic, to require courts to give an interpretation of open-textured terms which can be defended in a deliberative manner. The question then becomes not so much whether the decision is based on judges' personal values, but whether the reasons given are persuasive, both in terms of their substantive reasons and of their consistency with specific constraints of legal reasoning, such as their relationship with the constitutional text, previous decisions and institutional factors.[2]

One need only look more closely at *Tyrer* itself to demonstrate this. In *Tyrer*, the question was whether sentences of 'birching' (judicially imposed corporal punishment) constituted a breach of the right in Article 3 not to be subjected to 'inhuman and degrading treatment or punishment'. The Court held that 'his punishment—whereby he was treated as an object in the power of the authorities—constituted an assault on precisely that which it is one of the main purposes of Article 3 to protect, namely a person's dignity and physical integrity'.[3] In his dissenting opinion, Sir Maurice Fitzgerald, the British judge in the case, argued that birching, while possibly undesirable, could not be considered degrading. But while the majority drew on 'the developments and commonly accepted standards in the penal policy of the member States of the Council of Europe in this field',[4] Sir Maurice drew on his own, arguably idiosyncratic experience. He admitted that:

> [M]y own view may be coloured by the fact that I was brought up and educated under a system according to which the corporal punishment of schoolboys ... was regarded as the normal sanction for serious misbehaviour, and even sometimes for what was much less serious ... They also not infrequently took place under conditions of far greater intrinsic humiliation than in this case. Yet I cannot remember that any boy felt degraded or debased.[5]

These points are defended below by looking at theories of human rights interpretation in a comparative context, drawing on case law from the US, Canada, South Africa and the ECtHR. On closer inspection, the dichotomy between original intent and 'living tree' or evolutionary approaches often proves to be more one of polemic than practical reality. The open-textured nature of many human rights concepts makes it impossible in some contexts to rely on the intent of drafters who could not have envisaged the issue in the current context. Text and history are factors which need to be considered. But so do current understandings and

---

[2] For an elaboration of the deliberative approach to adjudication, see S Fredman, *Human Rights Transformed: Positive Rights and Positive Duties* (Oxford, Oxford University Press, 2008); S Fredman, 'From Dialogue to Deliberation: Human Rights Adjudication and Prisoners' Right to Vote' [2013] *Public Law* 292.

[3] *Tyrer v UK* (n 1) [33].

[4] ibid [31].

[5] ibid [23]–[24].

values. Judgments on human rights issues in practice end up considering a variety of factors before coming to a conclusion, whether they claim to be referring to original intent, text or 'living tree' doctrines. The major difference lies in the extent to which this is acknowledged.

I. ORIGINALISM OR THE INTENTION OF THE DRAFTERS

Given that the task of judges is not to answer fundamental moral questions, but to apply the law, one way of resolving contested questions about the meaning of human rights instruments is to ask what the drafters intended them to mean. This is a well-known approach to statutory construction: since judges are said to be responsible for interpreting rather than drafting laws, they will frequently justify their interpretation of an enactment by reference to parliamentary intention. Thus, it seems to make sense to do the same for the interpretation of constitutional human rights. Rather than rely on judges' own values or predilections, so the argument goes, the intentions of the framers of the document should be determinative. An analogous argument might be made in relation to international or regional human rights arguments and the role of preparatory documents or *travaux préparatoires*. On one view, since international treaties are potentially an incursion on the sovereignty of states, signatory states cannot be bound beyond the extent to which they actually agreed, and these original intentions should be sought in the *travaux préparatoires*.

Several advantages are claimed for this approach. The first and most important is concerned with legitimacy. Dworkin frames the originalist position thus:

> Suppose judges can discover how the Framers intended uncertain provisions of the Constitution to be understood. If judges follow that original intention, they would not be making substantive choices themselves but only enforcing choices made long ago by others, choices that have been given authority by the people's ratification and acceptance of the Constitution.[6]

For the US Supreme Court Justice Antonin Scalia, one of its main modern proponents, originalism is more compatible with the nature and purpose of a constitution in a democratic system than its alternatives. He argues that it is not the function of constitutional guarantees of human rights to ensure that they reflect current values. This is the function of elections. On the contrary:

> The purpose of constitutional guarantees—and in particular those constitutional guarantees of individual rights that are at the centre of this controversy—is precisely to prevent the law from reflecting certain *changes* in original values that the society adopting the Constitution thinks fundamentally undesirable. Or, more precisely, to require the society to devote to the subject the long and hard consideration required for a constitutional amendment before those particular values can be cast aside.[7]

---

[6] R Dworkin, *A Matter of Principle* (Oxford, Oxford University Press, 1985) 34.
[7] A Scalia, 'Originalism: The Lesser Evil' (1988–89) 57 *University of Cincinnati Law Review* 849, 862.

48 *Sandra Fredman*

Lord Sumption takes an even stronger position in relation to the ECHR. He argues that the only legitimate approach to interpretation is to look to the original intentions of the drafters. States should be bound to their original promises and not to far-reaching interpretations that they could never have envisaged. Any other interpretation, he argues, gives rise to a significant democratic deficit. He acknowledges that there should be some constraints on majoritarianism 'in the interests of protecting politically vulnerable minorities from oppression and entrenching a limited number of rights that the consensus of our societies recognises as truly fundamental'. Beyond this, issues should remain in the political sphere.

The second advantage of originalism, as Scalia puts it, is to insulate judges from the temptation to:

> [M]istake their own predilections for the law. Avoiding this error is the hardest part of being a conscientious judge; perhaps no conscientious judge ever succeeds entirely. Non-originalism, which, under one or another formulation invokes 'fundamental values' as the touchstone of constitutionality, plays precisely to this weakness. It is very difficult for a person to discern a difference between those political values that he personally thinks most important, and those political values that are 'fundamental to our society'. Thus, by the adoption of such a criterion, judicial personalization of the law is enormously facilitated.[8]

Similarly, Sumption vehemently criticises the ECtHR for extending the provisions of the Convention well beyond the original intention and instead basing its decisions on its view of what is appropriate for a democratic society. For example, he argues that Article 8 of the Convention, the right to respect for home, family, private life and correspondence, was 'originally devised as a protection against the surveillance state by totalitarian governments'.[9] However, in his view, it has been extended well beyond the express language of the Convention, so that its scope rests on the 'sole authority of the judges of the Court'.[10] The third advantage is, in Scalia's view, a negative one: the absence of any constructive alternatives or rather 'the impossibility of achieving any consensus on what, precisely, is to replace original meaning once that has been abandoned'.[11]

Although Scalia regards this last defect as 'fundamental and irreparable', he himself admits to being only a 'faint-hearted originalist'.[12] He acknowledges that he would not, as a judge of the US Supreme Court, uphold a statute which imposes public flogging, even though the Framers of the US Constitution might not have considered that public flogging was a 'cruel and unusual' punishment.[13] However, it is hard to see how he can sustain his originalist stance in the face of this concession. For if he rejects both the values of the Framers and the values of those who

---

[8] ibid 863.
[9] Lord Sumption, 'The Limits of Law', p 20 in this volume.
[10] ibid 8.
[11] Scalia (n 7) 862–63.
[12] ibid 863.
[13] ibid 864.

passed the statute imposing public flogging, where does he get his 'values' from? It is not enough to say, as he does, that he cannot imagine being faced with such a statute or that the practical defects of originalism are less corrosive than those of non-originalism. This is because as soon as he allows other values to enter into the discussion, he needs to be able to find a plausible way of defending them. If not, he falls foul of his own criticism of those who disguise their value judgments behind apparently objective legal techniques.

There are several other difficulties with an originalist position. First, parliamentary intention is notoriously difficult to gauge. How much more so is the intention of the original founders? The 'cruel and unusual punishment' clause in the Eighth Amendment of the US Constitution is particularly challenging. In the death penalty case of *Furman v Georgia*, several of the Supreme Court Justices looked to the debates in the First Congress in 1789 in an attempt to ascertain the meaning of 'cruel and unusual punishment clause' in the Eighth Amendment. However, they found that this clause received very little attention, evidence of consideration being confined to comments by two opponents of the Clause in the House of Representatives, one of whom regarded its meaning as simply too indefinite.[14] The conclusion, as Brennan J acknowledged, was that 'we have very little evidence of the Framers' intent in including the Cruel and Unusual Punishments clause ... in the Bill of Rights'.[15] Dworkin takes this one step further: 'There is no such thing as the intention of the framers waiting to be discovered, even in principle. There is only some such thing waiting to be invented.'[16]

A similar approach can be seen in relation to international human rights law. Preparatory documents are considered 'notoriously unreliable'[17] in relation to treaty interpretation generally and therefore were given only a supplementary role by the Vienna Convention on the Law of Treaties.[18] This approach was accepted by the ECtHR in the seminal case of *Golder*[19] when the Court was asked to decide whether the right to a fair trial in Article 6 of the Convention included a right of access to court. Even the strongly worded dissent in that case acknowledged that 'It is hardly possible to establish what really were the intentions of the Contracting States under this head'[20] and that 'to go into the drafting history of Article 6(1) ... would be both tedious and unrewarding because, like so many drafting histories, the essential points are often obscure and inconclusive'.[21]

---

[14] See *Furman v Georgia* 408 US 238 (1972) (US Supreme Court) per Brennan J at 261–62; Douglas J at 244. Nevertheless, the Eighth Amendment was passed by a considerable majority: see Brennan J at 262, citing 1 Annals of Congress 754 (1789).

[15] ibid 258.

[16] Dworkin (n 6) 39.

[17] C Ovey and R White, *Jacobs, White & Ovey: The European Convention on Human Rights*, 5th edn (Oxford, Oxford University Press, 2010) 66.

[18] Article 32.

[19] *Golder v UK* (1979–80) 1 EHRR 524 (ECtHR).

[20] ibid [40].

[21] ibid [41].

Lord Sumption confidently asserts that the ECHR was intended by its draftsmen as a 'safeguard against despotism', and that Article 8 was 'originally devised as a protection against the surveillance state by totalitarian governments'.[22] However, a glance at the *travaux préparatoires* on Article 8 reveals that no mention is made of these objectives.[23] What we do know from the documentation is that at the Conference of Senior Officials, which met in June 1950, the UK delegation proposed that the Article should be worded as a 'right to freedom from governmental interference with his privacy, family, house or correspondence'. However, the version adopted by the Conference and eventually accepted by the Committee of Ministers framed this instead as a positive right to respect for private and family life, home and correspondence. If anything, this suggests that the right was intended to mean more than freedom from government surveillance. We also know that in the earlier Committee on Legal and Administrative Questions, objections had been raised to the proposed inclusion of all the 'family' rights, which grouped the proposed Article 8 with the right to marry and found a family, and the right of parents to choose the kind of education to be given to their children. The objectors had argued that none of these rights was essential for the functioning of democratic institutions, so that it was preferable to exclude them. These objections did not, however, prevail. The majority of the Committee regarded it as crucial that these rights be retained, for example, to ensure that racial restrictions on the right to marriage should be absolutely prohibited. This decision did not give rise to any further discussion in the Consultative Assembly. To the extent that anything can be gleaned from the *travaux préparatoires*, it seems that Article 8 was regarded as a positive right rather than merely a freedom from surveillance and that objections to the effect that only rights essential to the functioning of democratic institutions could be included were emphatically rejected. What is certainly clear is that there is no support in the preparatory documents for the view that Article 8 was intended only as a protection from surveillance.

This problem of discerning the intention of the drafters might seem easier to confront when a bill of rights has been drafted within living memory of adjudicators, as has been the case with the Canadian Charter and the South African Constitution. Yet the Supreme Court of Canada has emphatically rejected the originalist approach, partly because the records left by the drafters were intrinsically unreliable. Thus, in one of its earliest Charter cases, the Court stated that although it was prepared to admit in evidence the Minutes of Procedure of the Special Joint Committee tasked with drafting the Charter, these should be given minimal weight. This is because they were inherently unreliable.[24] 'Were this Court to accord any significant weight to this testimony, it would in effect be assuming a fact which is nearly impossible of proof, i.e. the intention of the legislative bodies which adopted the Charter.'[25]

---

[22] Sumption (n 9) 7.
[23] www.echr.coe.int/LibraryDocs/Travaux/ECHRTravaux-ART8-DH(56)12-EN1674980.pdf.
[24] *Re BC Motor Vehicle Act* [1985] 2 SCR 486 (Supreme Court of Canada), 508.
[25] ibid 508.

The same dilemma was thrust before the South African Constitutional Court almost immediately after its inception. In *Makwanyane*,[26] the second case that came before the newly constituted Court, the Court was faced with the explosive question of whether the death penalty remained lawful under the Interim Constitution. In its argument, the government wished to refer to the records of the Multi-Party Negotiating Process responsible for drafting the Constitution. The relevance of the drafters' intentions immediately arose. Chaskalson J agreed that the reports of the technical committees which advised the Multi-Party Negotiating Process could provide a context for the interpretation of the Constitution.[27] However, taking his cue from the Canadian Court, he emphasised that the Constitution was a product of a multiplicity of persons, and therefore the comments of individual actors should be regarded with great caution, no matter how prominent a role they might have played.[28] For the case in hand, he held, they could only be relied on to show why a provision was or was not included, provided the record on this point was clear, not in dispute and relevant.

In the case of *Makwanyane* itself, however, resort to the drafting materials did not assist the Court in deciding the substance of the case. All they did was indicate clearly that no agreement had been reached on the lawfulness of the death penalty and that the baton had been passed to the Constitutional Court. As Chaskalson J put it:

> Capital punishment was the subject of debate before and during the constitution-making process, and it is clear that the failure to deal specifically in the Constitution with this issue was not accidental. In the constitutional negotiations which followed, the issue was not resolved. Instead, the 'Solomonic solution' was adopted. The death sentence was, in terms, neither sanctioned nor excluded, and it was left to the Constitutional Court to decide whether the provisions of the pre-constitutional law making the death penalty a competent sentence for murder and other crimes are consistent with … the Constitution.[29]

Of course, it is possible to widen the original intent by arguing that the Framers deliberately chose to use standards which could reflect changing mores. The US Supreme Court Justice Brennan J, although generally eschewing original intent, still felt moved to support his conclusion in *Furman* by stating that 'the Framers … [did not] intend simply to forbid punishments considered "cruel and unusual" at the time. The "import" of the Clause is, indeed, "indefinite", and for good reason'.[30] Scalia, however, argues that there is little evidence that the Framers did intend to leave the interpretation to later generations. Indeed, he points out that the death penalty was specifically permitted by the Framers of the US Constitution:[31] the

---

[26] *S v Makwanyane* 1995 (3) SA 391 (CC); 1995 (6) BCLR 665 (CC) (South African Constitutional Court).
[27] ibid [17].
[28] ibid [18].
[29] ibid [20], per Chaskalson CJ.
[30] *Furman v Georgia* (n 14) per Brennan J at 263.
[31] Scalia (n 7) 863.

52 *Sandra Fredman*

Fourteenth Amendment provides expressly that the state shall not 'deprive any person of life, liberty, or property, without due process of law'.[32]

A similar resort to original intention to justify evolving norms can be seen in the jurisprudence of the ECtHR. In the recent case of *Markin v Russia*,[33] the concurring opinion stated: 'The petrification of the Convention would not only depart from the common rules of treaty interpretation … it would also ultimately disregard the true intention of the founding fathers, namely to create an instrument for the guarantee of rights that are practical and effective, not theoretical and illusory'.[34] However, here too, the resort to original intention to justify evolving norms is risky; it could quite easily be argued that the Framers meant to limit the right to its original meaning. The dissenting opinion in the earlier case of *Golder* made this kind of point in order to show that the absence of a right of access to court in the right to a fair trial should be seen as intentional. According to Judge Sir Gerald Fitzmaurice: 'It is hardly possible to establish what really were the intentions of the Contracting States under this head; but that of course is all the more reason for not subjecting them to obligations which do not result clearly from the Convention.' Indeed, it was 'quite inconceivable that governments intending to assume an international obligation to afford access to their courts, should have set about doing so in this roundabout way—that is to say should, without stating the right explicitly'.[35] For Dworkin, this resort to what he calls the Framers' interpretive intent is fundamentally misplaced. The problem is not the difficulty in determining the Framers' own interpretive theory; it is 'to think the interpretive intention of the Framers matters one way or the other'.[36]

The second and more far-reaching objection to original intent questions its very foundations in legitimacy. Indeed, this objection turns Lord Sumption's reference to a democratic deficit on its head. Why should the intentions of the drafters be given such significance? One way of responding would be to argue that democracy requires that those who have been selected by the people to draft a constitution should determine its meaning. However, as Dworkin points out, the framers of the US Constitution were 'remarkably unrepresentative of the people as a whole'.[37] The majority of the population, including women, slaves and the poor, were excluded from the selection and ratification process. Even if the drafters were representative of the people at the time of drafting, it is difficult to explain 'why people now should be governed by the detailed political convictions of officials elected long ago'.[38] The result is that even if the intention of the drafters is clear

---

[32] Article XIV of the US Constitution: see http://memory.loc.gov/cgi-bin/ampage?collId=llsl&fileName=014/llsl014.db&recNum=389.
[33] *Markin v Russia* (2013) 56 EHRR 8 (ECtHR).
[34] ibid 53.
[35] *Golder v UK* (n 19) 40–41.
[36] Dworkin (n 6) 53.
[37] R Dworkin, *Law's Empire* (London, Fontana, 1986) 364; see also J Waldron, *Partly Laws Common to Mankind: Foreign Law in American Courts* (New Haven, Yale University Press, 2012) 151.
[38] Dworkin (n 37) 364.

from the legislative history, this may not be a relevant issue for later generations. Thus, in the famous US case of *Brown v Board of Education*,[39] the US Supreme Court was required to decide whether state-imposed racial segregation in schools was a breach of the Fourteenth Amendment's command that no state shall 'deny to any person within its jurisdiction the equal protection of the laws'. It was clear from the legislative history that the congressmen who proposed the Fourteenth Amendment did not regard state-imposed racial segregation as unconstitutional.[40] As Vicki Jackson points out: 'Not only did the 1789 US Constitution contemplate the continued existence of slavery and a voting structure favouring slave states, but there is evidence that the Framers and ratifiers of the Fourteenth Amendment did not necessarily understand the Equal Protection Clause to prohibit state imposed segregation of the races.'[41] However, this fact was no longer relevant, opening the way for the Court in *Brown* to strike down official segregation in schools.

The ECtHR faced a more complex situation when faced with the question of whether the right to freedom of association in Article 11 ECHR also included the right not to join an association. This had been a highly controversial issue when the Convention was drafted, due to the prevalence in the UK of the 'closed shop' or a system of compulsory trade union membership. In *Young, James and Webster v UK*,[42] three workers who had been dismissed because they did not belong to a union claimed that this breached their right of freedom of association. The Court's attention was drawn to the following paragraph in the *travaux préparatoires*:

> On account of the difficulties raised by the 'closed-shop system' in certain countries, the Conference in this connection considered that it was undesirable to introduce into the Convention a rule under which 'no one may be compelled to belong to an association' which features in the United Nations Universal Declaration.[43]

The Court nevertheless held that the applicants' rights had been breached by the requirement to join the union. Even if such a general rule had been deliberately omitted from the Convention, it held, this did not mean that every compulsion to join a union was compatible with the intention of Article 11.[44]

The Canadian courts have been even more emphatic. For them, the opinion of senior public servants, however well respected, cannot be determinative:

> The simple fact remains that the Charter is not the product of a few individual public servants, however distinguished, but of a multiplicity of individuals who played major roles in the negotiating, drafting and adoption of the Charter. How can one say with any confidence that within this enormous multiplicity of actors ... the comments of a few federal civil servants can in any way be determinative?[45]

---

[39] *Brown v Board of Education* 347 US 483 (1954) (US Supreme Court).
[40] Dworkin (n 37) 389.
[41] V Jackson, 'Constitutions as "Living Trees"? Comparative Constitutional Law and Interpretive Metaphors' (2006) 75 *Fordham Law Review* 921, 955.
[42] *Young, James and Webster v UK* (1982) 4 EHRR 38 (ECtHR).
[43] Report of 19 June 1950 of the Conference of Senior Officials, Collected Edition of the 'Travaux Préparatoires', vol IV, p 262.
[44] *Young, James and Webster v UK* (n 42) [52].
[45] *Re BC Motor Vehicle Act* (n 24) 508.

Dworkin concludes that searching for intention is a 'mischievous' idea because it covers up the substantive decisions which judges inevitably make and pretends that this has not occurred.[46] The content of the Framers' intention cannot be regarded as 'just a matter of historical, psychological or other fact'; it can only be resolved through political theory. That 'judges can make apolitical constitutional decisions by discovering and enforcing the intention of the Framers' is a promise that cannot be redeemed. Judges can only discover that intention by 'making the decisions of political morality they were meant to avoid'.[47]

II. TEXTUALISM

Closely related to theories of original intent are those that focus on the language of the constitutional provision or the bill or rights as the primary source of meaning. Textualism comes close to originalism in that its rationale is often stated to be in originalist terms; that is, that the text is the surest guide to the intentions of those who framed it.[48] However, it resolves the difficulty of ascertaining the Framers' intentions by resort to the 'plain meaning rule'. This assumes that the Framers must have intended words to have the plain meaning that words bear. This in turn permits textualism to go beyond some of the strictures of originalism. Textualists are not concerned with the subjective intentions of the Framers or with idiosyncratic use of language, but rather with the way in which such language is understood.

However, this introduces a crucial ambiguity which could undermine the raison d'etre of textualism. If 'plain meaning of words' is impossible to gauge without the linguistic and social contexts in which they are used,[49] should this meaning be sought by reference to that of the society in which the Framers found themselves or the current social context? Brest argues that the interpreter of a constitutional text 'cannot assume that a provision adopted one or two hundred years ago has the same meaning as it had for the adopters' society today. She must immerse herself in their society to understand the text as they understood it'.[50] For example, she needs to ask what words like the 'equal protection of the laws' meant to those who adopted the Fourteenth Amendment in 1868.[51]

The difficulty with this is that, like originalism, such an approach turns judges into historians and, even then, might not yield sufficiently determinate results. As Easterbrook points out, the interpretive community of 1791 or 1868 might not have thought about the issues that arise in the application of constitutional terms

---

[46] Dworkin (n 6) 34.
[47] ibid 55–56.
[48] P Brest, 'The Misconceived Quest for the Original Understanding' (1980) 60 *Boston University Law Review* 204, 205.
[49] ibid 206.
[50] ibid 208.
[51] ibid 209.

in later eras. For example, 'because official action favouring racial minorities was unheard of in 1871, we do not know (and cannot reconstruct) how the interpretive community of that era would have understood the Fourteenth Amendment'.[52] In particular, we cannot know whether the phrase 'equal protection of the laws' means 'no official use of race', therefore precluding affirmative action in favour of minorities, or only 'no use of race to harm minorities', which would permit affirmative action.[53] In any event, as Brest argues, we may be too hopelessly imprisoned in our current perspectives even to appreciate that our view of previous social understandings is tempered by our own conceptual framework.[54]

This problem is not, however, solved by turning to current interpretations. Given that there may be well-founded disagreements amongst current communities as to the meaning of key terms such as 'reasonable' and 'cruel', the question inevitably gravitates towards why the arbiter of such meaning should be the judge, rather than the political sphere, which resolves disagreements through democratic elections and accountability to the public. This leads Easterbrook to argue that the interpretive task should track closely to institutional legitimacy and capability. Only if there is a strong textual claim should judges interfere with legislative majorities:

> If the age or generality of the text frustrates the statement of a rule, then it also defeats the claim of judicial power. If the living must indeed chart their own course, then the question is political, outside the domain of judicial review ... Judicial review depends on the belief that decisions taken long ago are authoritative.[55]

The conclusion he draws is that judges should enforce 'against the contrary views of other governmental actors, only the portion of the text or rule sufficiently complete and general to count as law'.[56]

Easterbrook's approach in the human rights context leads to a highly restrictive judicial approach, potentially leaving human rights exposed to executive or legislative override. Waldron takes a very different view. He regards himself as a textualist, particularly in relation to statute, but also on constitutional matters.[57] However, he is concerned that constitutional textualism sometimes veers into originalism in an indefensible way.[58] Indeed, he regards Scalia as a textualist who lapses into an appeal to the historic intent of the framers whenever politically convenient.[59] Waldron's defence of textualism is based on the authority given to the text by the laborious processes of enactment rather than on fidelity to original intention.[60] He argues that 'textualism requires a judge to focus his (sic) interpretive energies

---

[52] F Easterbrook, 'Abstraction and Authority' (1992) 59 *University of Chicago Law Review* 349, 361.
[53] ibid 361.
[54] Brest (n 48) 221–22.
[55] Easterbrook (n 52) 375.
[56] ibid 376.
[57] Waldron (n 37) 155.
[58] ibid.
[59] ibid 167.
[60] ibid 155.

on a particular piece of constitutional text, binding on him and his society on account of the circumstances of its framing and ratification in that country'.[61] Moreover, the main reason for textualists' emphasis on natural language is the constancy of language, which can be used to coordinate understanding among diverse communities in a given culture.

This leads Waldron to take a very different view of how to discern the plain meaning of words from that portrayed by Brest and Easterbook. While Waldron acknowledges that language can change over time, he argues that most of the words in current bills of rights mean what they used to mean. The words 'cruel and unusual', for example, mean the same now as they did when they were first used in the English Bill of Rights 1689. 'Cruel' means 'causing or characterized by great suffering' and unusual still means 'uncommon'.[62] The application of the term may have changed—people today apply the term 'cruel' to practices which previously were not considered to cause considerable pain and suffering—without changing the meaning of the word.[63] This avoids many of the problems above and certainly leads to a less restrictive approach than that of Easterbrook. However, in accepting that the word 'cruel', while maintaining its meaning, can refer to practices which change over time, Waldron's approach begins to converge with a 'living tree' or evolutionary approach, as the discussion below demonstrates.

III. THE 'LIVING TREE' OR EVOLUTIONARY APPROACH

Rather than search for meaning in the original intention of the Framers, several jurisdictions, such as Canada and the ECtHR, prefer to regard the bill of rights as an evolving document, a 'living tree', capable of growing and changing to reflect current values. Canada has been at the forefront of the development of the organic metaphor of the living tree, while other jurisdictions use the less graphic terms of 'living instrument' or living constitution. This approach is highly challenging: once the veneer of legitimacy achieved by referring to text or original intent is finally abandoned, the need to justify the source of human rights values is laid bare. As Sharpe and Roach point out: 'The judges are called upon to delve deeply into the very foundations of our legal system and political culture to answer questions of the most fundamental nature, and many of these questions cannot be answered adequately by reference only to traditional legal sources.'[64]

The 'living tree' metaphor was first used in the oft-cited Privy Council case of *Edwards v Attorney-General for Canada*.[65] The context was auspicious, concerning

---

[61] ibid 156.
[62] ibid 165.
[63] ibid 165.
[64] R Sharpe and K Roach, *The Charter of Rights and Freedoms*, 5th edn (Toronto, Irwin Law Inc, 2013) 55.
[65] *Edwards v Attorney-General for Canada* [1930] AC 124 (Privy Council).

as it did the question whether the word 'persons' in the British North America Act 1867[66] referred only to men, thereby perpetuating the long-standing prohibition on women's right to vote and stand for public office. Rather than seeking out the original meaning or intent of the relevant provision, the Court made it clear that 'the British North America Act planted in Canada a living tree capable of growth and expansion within its natural limits ... Their Lordships do not conceive it to be the duty of this Board—it is certainly not their desire—to cut down the provisions of the Act by a narrow and technical construction, but rather to give it a large and liberal interpretation so that the Dominion to a great extent, but within certain fixed limits, may be mistress in her own house'.[67] The Court rejected an originalist approach, regarding it as impossible to speculate whether the drafters of the British North America Act purposely followed one or other of the existing models of legislative composition. Even more importantly, the Court recognised that 'customs are apt to develop into traditions which are stronger than law and remain unchallenged long after the reason for them has disappeared'.[68] Whatever 'persons' meant at the time that the Act was passed, in the present there was no reason to hold that it excluded women. This principle has been consistently followed by the Supreme Court of Canada in interpreting the *Charter of Rights and Freedoms*.[69] In a recent emphatic re-endorsement, in the *Same-Sex Marriage* case, the Court referred to it as 'one of the most fundamental principles of Canadian constitutional interpretation: that our Constitution is a living tree which, by way of progressive interpretation, accommodates and addresses the realities of modern life'.[70]

The Supreme Court of Canada has robustly defended this evolutionary approach. Most importantly, whereas originalists and textualists regard the legitimacy of constitutional interpretation as deriving from the document's history, the Canadian Court views the document as intrinsically future-oriented. Unlike a statute, which is 'easily enacted and easily repealed', a constitution 'is drafted with an eye to the future. Its function is to provide a continuing framework for the legitimate exercise of Governmental power, and when joined by a Bill or a Charter of Rights, for the unremitting protection of individual rights and liberties. Once enacted, its provisions cannot easily be repealed or amended. It must, therefore, be capable of growth and development over time to meet new social, political and historical realities, often unimagined by its framers'.[71] Nor is its evolving

---

[66] The only constitutional text prior to the enactment of the Canadian Charter.
[67] *Edwards v Attorney-General for Canada* (n 65).
[68] ibid.
[69] *Hunter v Southam* [1984] 2 SCR 145 (Supreme Court of Canada); *Law Society of Upper Canada v Skapinker* [1984] 1 SCR 357 (Supreme Court of Canada); *R v Big M Drug Mart Ltd* [1985] 1 SCR 295 (Supreme Court of Canada); *Blais v Her Majesty the Queen* (2003) SCC 44 (Supreme Court of Canada); *United States v Burns* (2001) SCC 7 (Supreme Court of Canada); *Reference re Same-Sex Marriage* (2004) SCC 79 (Supreme Court of Canada); *Reference Re Provincial Electoral Boundaries (SASK)* (1991) 2 SCR 158 (Supreme Court of Canada).
[70] *Reference re Same-Sex Marriage* (n 69) [22]–[23].
[71] *Hunter v Southam* (n 69).

interpretation therefore left to the political process, as Easterbrook would have it. The Canadian Court has been unabashed in its readiness to assume responsibility for such interpretation. Thus, in another of the early cases, Estey J stated: 'The fine and constant adjustment process of these constitutional provisions is left by a tradition of necessity to the judicial branch.'[72]

However, abandoning original intention is not sufficient to create a coherent theory of interpretation. Scalia's challenge of finding a plausible alternative source of values, short of judges' personal preferences, must still be faced. The Canadian Court has sought these values through a purposive approach. By determining the purpose of a provision, guidance as to its meaning may be found. This is an avowedly complex and value-laden approach. An early example of its application is in *Hunter v Southam*,[73] where the Court was required to determine the meaning of the right to 'be secure against unreasonable search or seizure' in section 8 of the Charter, a guarantee which the Court acknowledged was 'vague and open'.[74] Dickson J noted that the meaning of 'unreasonable' could not be determined by recourse to a dictionary, nor was there any particular historical, political or philosophical context capable of guiding the court as to the meaning of the section.[75] Instead, he re-affirmed what he regarded as obvious: 'The *Canadian Charter of Rights and Freedoms* is a purposive document. Its purpose is to guarantee and to protect, within the limits of reason, the enjoyment of the rights and freedoms it enshrines.'[76] But how is purpose to be assessed? The first step is to delineate the nature of the interests that the right is meant to protect. These, the Court held, were wider than had been the case at common law,[77] where only property interests were protected. Instead, it was held, the underlying purpose was to protect individuals from unjustified state intrusions on their privacy. Equally important, the assessment of reasonableness must focus on the 'impact on the subject of the search or the seizure, and not simply on its rationality in furthering some valid government objective'.[78]

The search for purpose of the provision means that history plays a very different role from that under the doctrine of original intent. As McLachlan CJ put it: 'The doctrine of the constitution as a living tree mandates that narrow technical approaches are to be eschewed. It also suggests that the past plays a critical but non-exclusive role in determining the content of the rights and freedoms granted by the *Charter*. The tree is rooted in past and present institutions, but must be capable of growth to meet the future.'[79] In relation to the right to vote as much as to the right to freedom of religion, the right, 'while rooted in and hence to some

---

[72] *Law Society of Upper Canada v Skapinker* (n 69) 366.
[73] *Hunter v Southam* (n 69).
[74] ibid 154.
[75] ibid 155.
[76] ibid 156.
[77] *Entick v Carrington* (1765) 19 St Tr 1029; 1 Wils KB 275 (House of Lords) at 1066.
[78] *Hunter v Southam* (n 69) 157–59.
[79] *Reference Re Provincial Electoral Boundaries (SASK)* (n 69).

extent defined by historical and existing practices, cannot be viewed as frozen by particular historical anomalies. What must be sought is the broader philosophy underlying the historical development of the right to vote—a philosophy which is capable of explaining the past and animating the future'.[80]

Thus, the purposive approach signified by the metaphor of the living tree is a complex one, drawing together multiple factors: from 'the character and the larger objects of the *Charter* itself, to the language chosen to articulate the specific right or freedom, to the historical origins of the concepts enshrined, and where applicable, to the meaning and purpose of the other specific rights and freedoms with which it is associated within the text of the *Charter*'. The interpretation should be 'a generous rather than a legalistic one, aimed at fulfilling the purpose of the guarantee and securing for individuals the full benefit of the *Charter*'s protection. At the same time it is important not to overshoot the actual purpose of the right or freedom in question, but to recall that the *Charter* was not enacted in a vacuum, and must therefore … be placed in its proper linguistic, philosophic and historical contexts'.[81]

A similar set of issues has been played out before the ECtHR early on in its jurisprudence. The Court, like its counterparts in other jurisdictions, found itself confronted with the application of open-textured terms in contexts possibly not envisaged by the original drafters. Thus, in *Golder*, the Court was asked to decide whether the right to a fair trial in Article 6 of the Convention included a right of access to court. In the face of a strongly worded dissent, which argued that the absence of express mention of such a right should be regarded as strong evidence against its implication, the Court decided to be guided by the Vienna Convention on the Law of Treaties[82] and, in particular, its focus on interpretation of terms in the context of the treaty's object and purpose. Thus, Article 31(1) of the Vienna Convention states: 'A treaty shall be interpreted in good faith in accordance with the ordinary meaning to be given to the terms of the treaty in their context and in the light of its object and purpose.'

This paved the way for the development of a contextual approach, which regards the Convention as a 'living instrument'. As we have seen, the earliest mention of this approach arose in *Tyrer*,[83] where the Court decided that judicially imposed corporal punishment for crimes committed by juveniles constituted a breach of Article 3.[84]

The living instrument approach has allowed the Court to develop the Convention both to respond to important new challenges not envisaged at the time of its adoption and to change its mind when it appeared that society had evolved. Possibly the clearest manifestation of this evolutionary approach has been in relation

---

[80] ibid 180–81.
[81] *R v Big M Drug Mart Ltd* (n 69) 344.
[82] Although it was not yet in force
[83] *Tyrer v UK* (n 1).
[84] ibid [33].

60 *Sandra Fredman*

to discrimination on grounds of sexual orientation. The case of *Dudgeon*[85] was the Court's first robust intervention in this area, holding that the criminalisation of sodomy in Northern Ireland was a breach of the right to respect for privacy and family life in Article 8 of the Convention. Since then, there has been a series of cases challenging many aspects of inequality for same-sex couples, which Contracting States have regularly attempted to justify by arguing that the aim was to protect the traditional family. In responding to these cases, the Court has consistently re-affirmed the evolutionary nature of the Convention. Thus, it has repeatedly stated, most recently in *X v Austria* in 2013:

> Given that the Convention is a living instrument, to be interpreted in the light of present-day conditions, the state, in its choice of means designed to protect the family and secure, as required by art.8, respect for family life must necessarily take into account developments in society and changes in the perception of social, civil-status and relational issues, including the fact that there is not just one way or one choice in the sphere of leading and living one's family or private life.[86]

This raises the same dilemma encountered in Canada and the US: how does the Court determine relevant social developments from which it can draw its conclusions as to the changing meaning of the Convention? One important source is the common traditions and values of the Member States that make up the Council of Europe. The Court will regularly require a comparative survey of the laws of the Member States in order to discover a common tradition, and consensus has frequently been invoked to justify a dynamic interpretation of the Convention.[87] Thus, in *Dudgeon*, the Court stated:

> As compared with the era when that legislation [criminalising sodomy] was enacted, there is now a better understanding, and in consequence an increased tolerance, of homosexual behaviour to the extent that in the great majority of the member States of the Council of Europe it is no longer considered to be necessary or appropriate to treat homosexual practices of the kind now in question as in themselves a matter to which the sanctions of the criminal law should be applied; the Court cannot overlook the marked changes which have occurred in this regard in the domestic law of the member States.[88]

But consensus is a problematic criterion. Is the Court a norm-setter or a norm-reflector, doing no more than making sure that outliers are keeping pace with the dominant position within Europe? Certainly, in *X v Austria*, the dissenting judges thought the majority were moving too fast. They protested that 'the point of the evolutive interpretation, as conceived by the Court, is to accompany and even

---

[85] *Dudgeon v UK* [1982] 4 EHRR 149 (ECtHR).
[86] *Kozak v Poland* (2010) 51 EHRR 16 (ECtHR) [98]; *X v Austria* (2013) 57 EHRR 14 (ECtHR) [139].
[87] *A, B and C v Ireland* (2011) 53 EHRR 13 (ECtHR) [234]: *Marckx v Belgium*, judgment of 13 June 1979, Series A no 31, § 41; *Dudgeon v UK*, judgment of 22 October 1981, Series A no 45, § 60; *Soering v UK*, judgment of 7 July 1989, Series A no 161, § 102; *L and V v Austria*, nos 39392/98 and 39829/98, § 50, ECHR 2003-I; and *Christine Goodwin v UK* [GC] 35 EHRR 18 (ECHR), § 85.
[88] *Dudgeon v UK* para 60; see also *Smith and Grady v UK* (2000)29 EHRR 493 (ECHR) para 104.

channel change; it is not to anticipate change, still less to try to impose it'.[89] Simply reflecting existing norms might assist the Court in its relationships of comity with Member States. However, the mere fact that a majority of countries do not agree that their practices are a breach of fundamental human rights should not itself be a reason for holding that no breach has occurred. Conversely, is the existence of a consensus sufficient to require outliers to change their practices?

The Court has attempted to address this tension by delineating principles which it regards as impervious to a lack of European consensus. In particular, 'where a particularly important facet of an individual's existence or identity is at stake', such as in relation to discrimination on grounds of gender or sexual orientation, the Court will give little latitude to Member States to make their own decisions.[90] However, it will be reluctant to intervene where 'there is no consensus within the member States of the Council of Europe, either as to the relative importance of the interest at stake or as to the best means of protecting it, particularly where the case raises sensitive moral or ethical issues'.[91] This is because 'by reason of their direct and continuous contact with the vital forces of their countries, the State authorities are, in principle, in a better position than the international judge to give an opinion, not only on the "exact content of the requirements of morals" in their country, but also on the necessity of a restriction intended to meet them'.[92]

The Court uses the concept of a 'margin of appreciation' to calibrate the extent to which it will insist on a common standard on the one hand or permit Member States to determine their own standards on the other. However, a closer look at the formulae used by the Court reveals their malleability. The category of 'sensitive moral or ethical issues' is not self-defining: it is not clear why issues of individual identity, such as gender and sexual orientation discrimination, have been held to fall outside of this category, warranting a robust human rights standard, while others, such as abortion, have been held to be issues solely for the Member State. Even the concept of consensus can be malleable. In *X v Austria*, the Court found only 10 relevant comparators within the Council of Europe, of which six treated heterosexual couples and same-sex couples alike, while four adopted the same position as Austria. It held that the narrowness of this sample meant that no conclusions could be drawn as to the existence of a possible consensus.[93] Nevertheless, the Court held that the right to equality for same-sex couples should be upheld. On the other hand, in *A, B and C v Ireland*,[94] the existence of a strong European consensus in favour of abortion was not sufficient for the Court to reject

---

[89] *X v Austria* OII-23 (Joint Partly Dissenting Opinion of Judges Casadevall, Ziemele, Kovler, Jočienė, Šikuta, De Gaetano and Sicilianos).
[90] ibid [149].
[91] ibid.
[92] *A, B and C v Ireland* (n 87) [232].
[93] *X v Austria* (n 86) 149.
[94] *A, B and C v Ireland* (n 87).

Ireland's justification for prohibiting abortion.[95] It did this by shifting the focus from whether Member States afforded a right to abortion to the question of when the right to life begins. Because it found no consensus on this issue, it held that it was up to Ireland to balance the rights of the mother against the rights of the unborn.[96]

Even more complex is when the Court considers that values have changed enough for it to reverse its previous position. This dilemma has been faced in relation to the right of lesbian and gay people to adopt and in relation to paternity leave, both issues which have seen rapid change in recent years. Thus, in *Fretté v France*,[97] the Court found that the French authorities' decision not to allow a gay man to adopt a child was not discriminatory within the meaning of Article 14 of the Convention. It noted that the law appeared to be going through a transitional phase and that there was little common ground between Member States of the Council of Europe. Moreover, the scientific community was divided over the possible consequences of children being brought up by one or more homosexual parents. However, the Grand Chamber reversed its position only four years later in *EB v France*.[98] It concluded that in refusing the applicant (who was living with another woman in a stable same-sex relation) authorisation to adopt a child, the French authorities had made a distinction on the basis of her sexual orientation, which was not acceptable under the Convention and constituted a breach of Article 14 in conjunction with Article 8, the right to respect for family life.

A similar shift occurred in relation to the right to paternity and family leave and allowances. In *Petrovic v Austria*[99] in 2001, the Court was faced with a claim that it was discriminatory to make parental leave allowances available only to mothers and not fathers. The Court rejected the claim, holding that as the majority of Contracting States did not provide for parental leave or related allowances for fathers, there was no European consensus on this issue. However, in 2012, it was able to discern a sufficient evolution in social attitudes in Europe to uphold a similar claim.[100] By that time, an absolute majority of European countries provided for parental leave for both mothers and fathers, indicating that 'contemporary European societies have moved towards a more equal sharing between men and women of responsibility for the upbringing of their children and that men's caring role has gained recognition'. According to the judgment, 'the Court cannot overlook the widespread and consistently developing views and associated legal changes to the

---

[95] The first applicant could have obtained an abortion justified on health and well-being grounds in approximately 40 Contracting States and the second applicant could have obtained an abortion justified on well-being grounds in some 35 Contracting States. Only three states have more restrictive access to abortion services than in Ireland, namely, a prohibition on abortion regardless of the risk to the woman's life: *A, B and C v Ireland* (n 87) [235].

[96] ibid [237].

[97] *Fretté v France* (2004) 38 EHRR 21 (ECtHR).

[98] *EB v France* (2008) 47 EHRR 21 (ECtHR); see also *X v Austria* (n 86) [102].

[99] *Petrovic v Austria* (2001) 33 EHRR 14 (ECtHR).

[100] *Markin v Russia* (n 33).

domestic laws of Contracting States concerning this issue'.[101] On the other hand, it refused to shift ground in relation to abortion. The fact that this was a highly contentious issue in Ireland and that the people of Ireland had recently voted in a referendum in favour of a continuation of the prohibition meant that the Court should not intervene.

The above discussion has shown that judges in fact use an eclectic mix of approaches to interpretation. An unadulterated adherence to original intent, text or other historical sources will often be inconclusive or implausible. Instead, history and text are often dealt with as part of the context, which also includes prevailing understandings and objective values. There are thus significant convergences between the different approaches. Balkin, for example, presents this convergence as part of an understanding of a constitution not as a finished product, but as a framework for governments: 'We look to original meaning to preserve this framework over time, but it does not preclude us from a wide range of future constitutional constructions that implement the original meaning ... In this model of originalism, the Constitution is never finished, and politics and judicial construction are always building up and building out new features.'[102] He therefore sees the goal as 'creating a set of key values and commitments that set the terms of political discourse, and that future generations must attempt to keep faith with'.[103] This is comes very close to an evolutionary or living tree approach, which also seeks to retain its roots in the history and text, while growing with the society and adapting to social change.

IV. CONCLUSION

Lord Sumption takes issue with the way in which the ECtHR has interpreted the European Convention. He argues that the ECtHR has interpreted the Convention in ways which were never intended by the signatories. This he regards as illegitimate and undemocratic. Instead of sticking to the understanding of the original signatories to the Convention, he argues, the ECtHR has simply and illegitimately imposed their view of what values a democracy should subscribe to.

The arguments from democracy are of course familiar, their best-known proponent being Jeremy Waldron.[104] This chapter has not addressed this set of arguments directly; I have done so elsewhere.[105] Here I argue that the theory of original

---

[101] ibid [140].

[102] J Balkin, 'Framework Originalism and the Living Constitution' (2009) 103 *Northwestern University Law Review* 549, 557.

[103] ibid 554–55.

[104] Lord Sumption's argument, although not citing Jeremy Waldron, is remarkably similar, including his examples, comparing *Roe v Wade* and the UK Abortion Act: J Waldron, *Law and Disagreement* (Oxford, Oxford University Press, 1999).

[105] S Fredman, 'Judging Democracy: the Judiciary and the Human Rights Act 1998' (2000) 53 *Current Legal Problems* 99; S Fredman, 'From Deference to Democracy: the Role of Equality under the Human Rights Act 1998' (2006) 122 *Law Quarterly Review* 53–81; S Fredman, 'From Dialogue to Deliberation: Human Rights Adjudication and Prisoners' Right to Vote' (2013) *Public Law* 292.

intent does not solve these problems. Nor does the similar theory which urges judges not to stray beyond the 'natural meaning' of words. Many proponents of these theories eschew the notion that they are using an interpretive theory at all. They argue that they are simply requiring courts to stick to the intended meaning of the words. Yet the arguments of uncertainty and democratic deficit apply equally to them. This is because human rights principles are necessarily couched in open-textured terms. There is no objectively 'true' interpretation. It does not help to resort to the intention of the drafters. As a start, the latter may well have had several different, even conflicting intentions. The argument from democracy is even less compelling. Even if the intention of the original drafters can be discerned, it is not clear that they have any continuing democratic mandate.

There can of course be very good institutional reasons why judges, and particularly the ECtHR, should defer to domestic decision-making and, in practice, it does do so on many occasions, the most recent decision in *SAS v France* being an example. I have attempted elsewhere to argue for a democratic role for judges in the human rights context, particularly through the concept of deliberative democracy.[106] It is beyond the scope of this chapter to tackle these institutional issues, except to reiterate, as argued above, that resort to the original intention of the signatories or drafters of the Convention does not resolve these problems.

Much of the difficulty in the above discussion stems from an attempt to find an interpretive theory which does not require judges to make substantive decisions on the basis of their own personal or political values. It has been argued here that there is no objective or value-free method to interpret human rights documents. This is true too of the choice of interpretive theory itself. As Karl Klare puts it: 'Judges' personal/political values and sensibilities *cannot be* excluded from interpretive processes or adjudication. Not because judges are weak and give in to political temptation, but because the exclusion called for by the traditional rule-of-law ideal is quite simply impossible.'[107] But these values need to be convincingly defended as furthering the human rights standards committed to judicial oversight. Klare argues that since 'we have no solely legal criteria of correctness for resolving contested cases ... then there is nothing legal practitioners can do but acknowledge their political and moral responsibility in adjudication and share the secret with their publics in the interests of transparency'.[108] The question then becomes not so much whether the decision is based on judges' personal values, but whether the reasons given are persuasive, both in terms of their substantive reasons, and for their consistency with specific constraints of legal reasoning, such as their relationship with the constitutional text, previous decisions and institutional factors. This suggests that it is not merely the outcome that matters, but

---

[106] ibid.
[107] K Klare, 'Legal Culture and Transformative Constitutionalism' (1998) 14 *South African Journal on Human Rights* 146, 163 (italics in original).
[108] ibid 163.

also the process of reasoning leading to the outcome. The reasoning leading to the outcome needs to be clear and transparent: it is the temptation to manipulate ostensibly mechanical legal doctrines that constitutes the most serious risk for the development of human rights jurisprudence.

How these key values are shaped and determined remains a source of both the challenge and the dynamism of human rights law. By remaining responsive to evolving social values, at the same time as insisting on continuity with the values and the aspirations of the past, and by subjecting both to a rigorous process of deliberative scrutiny, human rights law can continue to play an essential role in modern democracies.

5

Judges, Interpretation and Self-Government

LORD HOFFMANN

IN THIS CHAPTER I propose to take up Lord Sumption's discussion of the 'living instrument' doctrine and discuss it in the context of a general theory of the interpretation of legal documents.

Utterances having legal effect, such as wills, contracts, statutes, treaties or constitutions, have to be interpreted in order to be applied to the facts of a particular case. In order to say that the written instrument or other utterance applies to some state of affairs in the real world, one has to ascertain what meaning the use of those words and syntax was intended to convey.

This interpretation will almost invariably be objective, that is to say, it will not be concerned with the meaning which the author of the utterance subjectively intended to convey, but with the meaning that a reasonable member of the intended audience would have understood from the use of those words in that particular context. Usually this objectivity is unavoidable because the author is not an individual who can have a subjective consciousness, but a construct of social reality such as 'the university', 'the company', 'the state', 'Parliament', or 'the parties to the contract'. Thus, when one speaks of the 'intention of Parliament', Parliament is obviously not something which can have an individual subjective consciousness, but a reference to the rules by which an instrument which has been approved at the various stages of the parliamentary process has the force of law. One uses the language of authorship as if Parliament were an individual author, but the absence of individual consciousness means that the utterances of the notional author can only be given an objective interpretation. There are of course sometimes rules of attribution by which the consciousness of a particular individual is attributed to a social construct such as a company, but these need not concern us now. There are no such rules for legislative bodies or parties to international treaties.

The ability to convey meaning by the use of language rests primarily upon a general consensus among users of any particular language as to the meanings which will be given to the use of given words or syntax. The effect of this consensus will be found set out in dictionaries and grammars. But language is so rich and subtle that anyone who has tried to learn a foreign language with a dictionary and grammar will know that they need to be supplemented with knowledge of the context in which the words are being used and the assumptions which the author is making about the knowledge of his intended audience—knowledge of, for example, the Bible or Shakespeare or recent political events or popular music or television. All this is conventionally called the background to the language of the utterance. The extent to which knowledge of background is essential to understanding meaning will vary with the nature of the utterance. On the whole, legal instruments are drafted in order so far as possible to avoid ambiguities of language which can be resolved only by knowledge of background. Judges or other interpreters will therefore give primacy to the words and will assume that the draftsman was using conventional meanings and syntax. But resort to background is often unavoidable. The usual approach to legal instruments is succinctly conveyed by Article 31.1 of the Vienna Convention on the Law of Treaties:

> A treaty shall be interpreted in good faith in accordance with the ordinary meaning to be given to the terms of the treaty in their context and in the light of its object and purpose.

This provision gives primacy to the conventional meanings, but allows for the use of context and in particular the background which shows the object and purpose of the treaty. The requirement of good faith is to discourage literalism: the use of ambiguities to attribute to the parties meanings which they could not reasonably have intended.

I should at this stage emphasise, because it is an important point for the purposes of later discussion, that the fact that there is a special provision in a treaty dealing with the interpretation of treaties does not mean that treaties are subject to a special interpretative regime which does not apply to other utterances. Nor is there a special regime for contracts or wills because books are written on the interpretation of contracts and used to be written on the interpretation of wills. Fundamentally, treaties, constitutions, contracts, statutes, political speeches and chat shows are all speech acts which are subject to the same form of interpretation, namely by considering the language against the background to its use. The point about treaties, statutes and other such formal instruments is that part of the background is the prima facie assumption—which, simply as a matter of common sense, the interpreter should take into account—that the language of such documents is likely to have been carefully considered and often heavily negotiated. Primacy is therefore given to the conventional meaning of the language. But the general principle of interpretation is the same and one cannot draw lines between the methods of interpreting one category of instruments and another.

The question is therefore whether the 'living instrument' doctrine in relation to human rights instruments, as practiced by the European Court of Human Rights, is a legitimate form of interpretation of the language of the treaty or whether, as its opponents claim, it is an illegitimate form of judicial legislation. The same controversy exists in the US between originalists such as Justice Scalia and the liberal proponents of the living instrument doctrine.

I shall say at once that, like Justice Scalia, I am an originalist. I do not see how one can interpret a Constitution framed in 1787 except by considering what its language would have been understood to mean by its audience, the American people, in 1787. Otherwise one is committed to the proposition that the meaning of an utterance can be changed by events of which the actual or deemed author of that utterance would completely unaware because they lay in the future. That is updating and amendment, not interpretation. Having said that, I think that a perfectly respectable case can be made, as a matter of originalist construction, for treating some provisions of constitutions or statutes or even contracts as 'living instruments' or, as another popular phrase goes, 'always speaking'. In the domestic context, this form of construction was discussed by Lord Wilberforce in *Royal College of Nursing of the UK v Department of Health and Social Security*:

> In interpreting an Act of Parliament it is proper, and indeed necessary, to have regard to the state of affairs existing, and known by Parliament to be existing, at the time. It is a fair presumption that Parliament's policy or intention is directed to that state of affairs ... When a new state of affairs, or a fresh set of facts bearing on policy, comes into existence, the courts have to consider whether they fall within the Parliamentary intention. They may be held to do so, if they fall within the same genus of facts as those to which the expressed policy has been formulated. They may also be held to do so if there can be detected a clear purpose in the legislation which can only be fulfilled if the extension is made. How liberally these principles may be applied must depend upon the nature of the enactment, and the strictness or otherwise of the words in which it has been expressed. The courts should be less willing to extend expressed meanings if it is clear that the Act in question was designed to be restrictive or circumscribed in its operation rather than liberal or permissive. They will be much less willing to do so where the subject matter is different in kind or dimension from that for which the legislation was passed. In any event there is one course which the courts cannot take, under the law of this country; they cannot fill gaps; they cannot by asking the question 'What would Parliament have done in this current case—not being one in contemplation—if the facts had been before it?' attempt themselves to supply the answer, if the answer is not to be found in the terms of the Act itself.[1]

Thus, a provision in a statute may be applied in circumstances which were not contemplated at the time of its enactment because the statute, on its true originalist construction, invites its application to new or changed circumstances. This is how I once described the way this form of interpretation applied to the human rights provisions in a constitution:

> Parts of the Constitution ... are expressed in general and abstract terms which invite the participation of the judiciary in giving them sufficient flesh to answer concrete questions. The framers of the Constitution would have been aware that they were invoking concepts of liberty such as free speech, fair trials and freedom from cruel punishments which went back to the Enlightenment and beyond. And they would have been aware that sometimes the practical expression of these concepts—what limits on free speech are acceptable, what counts as a fair trial, what is a cruel punishment—had been different in the past and might again be different in the future. But whether they entertained these thoughts or not, the terms in which these provisions of the Constitution are expressed

---

[1] *Royal College of Nursing of the UK v Department of Health and Social Security* [1981] AC 800.

necessarily co-opts future generations of judges to the enterprise of giving life to the abstract statements of fundamental rights. The judges are the mediators between the high generalities of the constitutional text and the messy detail of their application to concrete problems. And the judges, in giving body and substance to fundamental rights, will naturally be guided by what are thought to be the requirements of a just society in their own time. In so doing, they are not performing a legislative function. They are not doing work of repair by bringing an obsolete text up to date. On the contrary, they are applying the language of these provisions of the Constitution according to their true meaning. The text is a 'living instrument' when the terms in which it is expressed, in their constitutional context, invite and require periodic re-examination of its application to contemporary life. Section 15(1) is a provision which asks to be construed in this way. The best interpretation of the section is that the framers would not have intended the judges to sanction punishments which were widely regarded as cruel and inhuman in their own time merely because they had not been so regarded in the past.[2]

It is thus a caricature of the originalist position to say that it requires the constitution to be interpreted as it would have been by a court sitting on the day after it was enacted. In cases of the kind I have been describing, that would have been contrary to the intention of the framers of the constitution. But, as Lord Wilberforce pointed out in the *Royal College of Nursing* case, the adoption of a living instrument approach must be justified as a proper interpretation of the statutory or constitutional provision as it would have been understood at the time of its enactment. It is the framers of the instrument who must have given life to that provision, and it must demonstrate their intention that it should be always speaking. And the extent to which it is able to accommodate later events, inventions and changes in attitude will depend upon the interpretation of the language itself. New embodiments of the same concept may readily be admitted. On the other hand, if contemporaries would have understood a provision as dealing with one concept, its extension to an altogether different concept could not be described as interpretation. If I may quote again from the judgment in which I discussed the living instrument doctrine:

> The 'living instrument' principle has its reasons, its logic and its limitations. It is not a magic ingredient which can be stirred into a jurisprudential pot together with 'international obligations', 'generous construction' and other such phrases, sprinkled with a cherished aphorism or two and brewed up into a potion which will make the Constitution mean something which it obviously does not.[3]

Lord Sumption has dealt with some of the dangers of extending the scope of rights conferred by a statute or treaty by analogy rather than interpretation of the language of the instrument. In particular, it carries the risk of judicialising political questions which ought properly to be decided by democratic institutions. But I want to draw a distinction between domestic statutes or constitutions on the one hand and international human rights treaties, in particular the European

---

[2] *Boyce v R (Barbados)* [2005] 1 AC 400.
[3] ibid [59].

Convention on Human Rights, on the other. A court which deals with the human rights provisions of a domestic constitution or constitutional statute is in a number of respects in a very different position from the European Court of Human Rights.

First, there is the conceptual problem of a court trying to apply the generalities of the rights enumerated in the Convention to specific situations in 47 countries with widely different legal systems, histories, cultures and religions. This is something I have discussed on other occasions and I will not dwell on it here.[4] It is partly mitigated by the doctrine of the margin of appreciation, but that doctrine is unpredictable in its application. The Strasbourg Court seems, for example, more sensitive to the religious prejudices of some of its Member States than to differences in legal culture. Occasionally the Court displays straightforward ignorance of a legal system with which its members are unfamiliar. These are obviously not problems which would concern a national court like the Supreme Court of the United States in its interpretation of the constitution.

Second, there is the question of democratic control. Most constitutions can be amended. Sometimes there is a special procedure which makes it more difficult to amend a constitution than to pass ordinary legislation, but in the end, if a sufficient majority are in favour, the constitution can be amended. Even the US Constitution has been amended 27 times. Furthermore, the democratically elected organs of government can usually exercise some indirect influence on the activities of a constitutional court through the selection of judges. In countries in which many questions which would usually be a matter for political debate are regarded as fit for judicial decision, such as the US, it is not surprising that politicians take a lively interest in the politics of prospective appointees to the Supreme Court. In Germany, appointment to the constitutional court is alternately in the gift of one or other of the main political parties. An amendment to the European Convention, however, is in practice virtually impossible. It would require the consent of the 47 Members of the Council of Europe. The people and politicians of each individual Member State therefore have virtually no control over the law binding upon their country and can influence the appointment of only one of the 47 judges of the court.

Third, there is the question of legitimacy. A national court, even though it does and should consist of unelected judges, has a legitimacy simply from being part of the national legal system. Even if the judges are not known to the public, as they are in the US, the people know the institution and understand its function. A court comprising 47 foreign judges is in a very different position. It lacks the same legitimacy and has to tread more warily so as not to antagonise the people of a Member State. Even if the effect of their decision is not of any great importance, such as whether prisoners can vote or not, the intervention of a foreign court may arouse nationalist sentiments and hostility to the court and the whole concept of international human rights.

---

[4] See L Hoffmann, 'The Universality of Human Rights' (2009) 125 *LQR* 416.

These differences between the situation of a national court interpreting a constitution and the European Court interpreting the Treaty are not only pragmatic considerations which the Court should take into account; they are also relevant to the question of interpretation itself, as forming part of the background against which the treaty must be construed. All the distinctive features which I have described—the disparity in the laws and cultures of the Member States, the inability of the people of the Member States to have any control of the terms of the treaty or the choice of its interpreters and the exogenous character of the decision-maker—were clear at the time of when the Treaty was concluded. They form part of the background which should influence its meaning. And they seem to me quite antithetical to the way in which the jurisprudence of the Court has developed: the search for what is alleged to be a European consensus which is then imposed upon Member States who have no wish to subscribe to it; the use of living instrument doctrine to apply provisions of the Treaty which could not possibly have been regarded as within the concepts originally intended to be covered; the development of the law by analogy without regard to the language of the instrument.

The Strasbourg Court seems to have regarded the fact that the Treaty would be very difficult to amend as a reason why it should assume a legislative function and, by looking for a European consensus, to undertake the task of amending the Treaty to bring it into line with what it considers the Member States, or at any rate a majority of them, would have been willing to agree to today. But this is the very exercise which Lord Wilberforce, in the *Royal College of Nursing* case, said was not the function of a judicial body. Interpretation means ascertaining the meaning of the utterance in question, in this case, an instrument made in 1950. As I have explained, there is no reason why such an instrument should not use language that indicates that it expects future courts to interpret its concepts according to the standards of their own day. But that is interpretation of the original treaty, not the repair or updating of its terms. Nor is the practice of the Strasbourg Court in accordance with the provisions of the Vienna Convention on the interpretation of Treaties, which gives primacy to the language of the instrument and requires the context and background surrounding its creation to be taken into account.

Supporters of the Strasbourg Court point out that some of its decisions have improved the jurisprudence of this country. That may well be true. There are cases in which I have myself thought they produced a better answer than the House of Lords. But that is an argument for a benevolent dictatorship, a rule of wise guardians. It is not a function which should be assumed by a foreign judicial body which is responsible to no one.

6

Judicial Law-Making and the 'Living' Instrumentalisation of the ECHR

JOHN FINNIS

'THE LIMITS OF Law' reflected and anticipated two notable judgments delivered in the Supreme Court by its author: *Chester* (October 2013) and *Nicklinson* (July 2014). The first had gently exposed the absurd ('very curious') position maintained by the Strasbourg Court[1]—in tacit reliance on its 'living instrument' doctrine[2]—against the UK's long-standing statutory exclusion of voting by convicted prisoners.[3] The second would indicate much of what was wrong with the seeming willingness[4] of five Supreme Court justices to rule, against both Parliament and the Strasbourg Court, that the historic statutory prohibition of assisting suicide is incompatible with Convention rights. Lord Sumption's *Nicklinson* judgment amplifies his lecture's theses about 'political questions' by giving 'political' its most specific, paradigmatic focus—the processes and act of legislating—and by then comparing these with processes and acts appropriate to adjudication.[5]

Taking up the elements of the Shah Lecture that are thus linked with some of its legal-political circumstances, this chapter's first section considers the Lecture's brief general remarks, conceding that (at least in the domain of common law rules) judges properly make law. This concession, I will suggest, would better have been more hedged, even for that domain. Section II questions whether it is right to describe the European Convention on Human Rights (ECHR)—albeit in diplomatic courtesies—as wholly admirable. Section III supplements the Lecture's remarks about the 'living instrument' doctrine or mantra, which has enticed both Strasbourg and the Supreme Court into profoundly flawed and unwarranted exercises of purportedly judicial power. To make good this critical claim in a way

---

[1] *Hirst v UK (No 2)* (74025/01) 6 October 2005 (GC); *Scoppola v Italy (No 3)* (126/05) 22 May 2012 (GC). See at n 81 below.
[2] See n 70 below.
[3] *R (on the application of Chester) v Secretary of State for Justice* [2013] UKSC 63 [135].
[4] On the uncertainties in this assessment of the relevant judgments, see John Finnis, 'A British "Convention Right" to Assistance in Suicide?' (2015) 131 *LQR* 1.
[5] *R (on the application of Nicklinson) v Ministry of Justice* [2014] UKSC 38 [224]–[235].

74 John Finnis

that is accessible to readers unfamiliar with the ECHR system and its Court's jurisprudence, section IV takes up *Hirst (No 2)* and *Scoppola* and their antecedents at sufficient length to make clear their errors and peculiar recklessness. Section V does likewise with *Hirsi Jamaa* and its antecedents in the construction of a rigidly absolutist asylum regime antithetical to the original intentions of the founding states and, in its completion (so far) in *Hirsi Jamaa*, prejudicial to their territorial integrity and dominion. The brief final section gives another iteration of the Lecture's investigation of the limits of law, understood as interdefined with the limits of appropriate adjudication—of adjudicative integrity. These are limits grounded in and illuminated by the profound difference, in terms of aim, responsibility and method, between adjudicating and legislating.

As just indicated, neglect of that difference is of more than academic interest: there are good reasons to conclude that among the usurpations of legislative power by the Strasbourg Court (and by courts that loyally follow it) are some that unconscionably prejudice the European domain's rights of self-determination and, without logically sound or juridically valid warrant, block its peoples' escape from possible catastrophe. That needs to be said, from time to time, occasionally even in a context like the Lecture's and this chapter's, where the question is neither existential—about what 'threatens the life of the nation'[6]—nor in other ways essentially predictive, but is essentially about the *norms* or directive principles of constitutional *propriety*. The chapter's ventures in prediction supplement rather than replace: (a) the historical and juridical case it sketches for concluding that the UK would be justified in exercising its Convention right to withdraw from the Convention (and in exercising any other treaty rights to withdraw from any treaties that make membership of the ECHR system a precondition of participation); and (b) the parallel constitutional case it suggests, not develops, for repealing (without replacing) the Human Rights Act 1998.

I. DON'T JUDGES MAKE LAW ANYWAY?

The Lecture holds that 'in the common law world there are unquestionably some areas in which the judges necessarily make law' and 'do not merely discover legal principles concealed in the luxuriant undergrowth of ancient principle and scattered legal decisions'. For generations, it says, common lawyers 'pretended' that judges do not make law and were committed to the 'declaratory theory of law', which held that decisions overruled by judges 'must always have been wrong'— a 'theory' articulated, as the Lecture recalls, by Lord Reid in 1970 in *West Midland Baptist Association v Birmingham Corp*.[7] But this, the Lecture affirms, 'is now overtly recognised as the *fiction* it always has been'.[8] We can add that, within a year

---

[6] See n 89 below.
[7] *West Midland Baptist Association v Birmingham Corp* [1970] AC 874, 879.
[8] Lord Sumption, 'The Limits of Law', Ch 2 in this volume, p 16 (emphasis added).

or two of articulating it, Lord Reid himself declared the declaratory theory to be a mere 'fairy tale'.[9]

This vivid expression of scepticism was recalled with approval by the dissenting Law Lords (Browne-Wilkinson and Lloyd) in a case that wrestled with this theoretical issue in a very practical, serious way: *Kleinwort Benson v Lincoln City Council* (1998).[10] But, as was recognised by the majority (especially by Lord Goff),[11] the declaratory theory, though too simply stated by Lord Reid in 1970, is when properly understood quite sound: not fiction, but an important truth about the proper responsibility and authority of judges. We can add, again, that Lord Reid's 1972 denunciation of the theory was accompanied and tempered by a fair statement of that proper responsibility, and by constitutional observations[12] highly concordant with the critique of ECtHR doctrine offered below in sections IV–VI. And even his 1970 statement itself, read in context,[13] intended little or no more than the sound thesis about *judicial* responsibility.

The majority in *Kleinwort Benson* recognised, of course, that the common law changes as a result of judicial decisions. After all, the judgments of this same majority (like those of the minority) were 'abrogating', with 'retrospective effect',

---

[9] Lord Reid, 'The Judge as Law Maker' (1972) 12 *Journal of the Society of Public Teachers of Law* (NS) 22.

[10] *Kleinwort Benson v Lincoln City Council* [1998] UKHL 38, [1999] 2 AC 349.

[11] I was inclined to write 'especially by Lords Goff and Hoffmann', but the latter said to me at the Oxford conference about the Shah Lecture that his judgment in *Kleinwort Benson* had no relevant theoretical concerns or content. (And certainly its first three pages, 39–400, are resolutely and ingeniously focused on dealing with the issues in a rigorously legal practice-oriented context and perspective. As to its final page, see n 18 below.) In any event, I simplify in speaking of majority and minority: Lord Hope, while not affirming the declaratory theory of adjudication expressed by Lord Goff and implied (at 401, I would say) by Lord Hoffmann, did join them in holding it inappropriate for judges, as distinct from legislatures, to introduce a rule, of the kind proposed by the minority, denying restitutionary recovery for mistake where the payments were made in accordance with 'a settled view of the law'.

[12] See n 62 below.

[13] I am indebted to Paul Yowell's contextualisation of Lord Reid's pair of quoted dicta. In *West Midland Baptist Association*, the rule being abrogated by the House of Lords was adopted in the mid- to late nineteenth century at a time of great price stability, as a general rule for identifying the date at which compulsorily acquired property should be valued for the purposes of giving effect to the stable principle that such taking should be compensated at full value. The abrogation was justified because in the conditions of the mid- to late *twentieth* century, application of that rule (value as at the date of the initiating notice to treat) would defeat rather than apply the overriding (and statutory) principle, and abrogation, even when done on the basis assumed by Lord Reid that the rule 'had always been wrong', entailed no upset to existing contracts or property rights. The 1972 Lecture reiterates rather than repudiates this: 'And there is another sphere where we have got to be very careful. People rely on the certainty of the law in settling their affairs, in particular in making contracts or settlements. It would be very wrong if judges were to disregard or innovate on what can fairly be regarded as settled law in matters of this kind. When Parliament passes an Act there is always objection to any proposal to make it retrospective. But judge-made law is always retrospective. We cannot say that the law until yesterday was one thing, from tomorrow it will be something different. That would indeed be legislating' (Lord Reid (n 9) 23). A weakness in both of Lord Reid's iterations of his position is that, as the facts of and recounted in *West Midland Baptist Association* disclose, the rule which that case abrogated could well have been regarded as sound for the era in which it was adopted and as *not wrong* in that era (save insofar as it might have been understood as a free-standing rule rather than as the overriding principle's best application in that era's conditions).

a common law rule (no restitutionary recovery for money paid under mistake of law) applied in England since 1802! The dispute between majority and minority was, directly, about what counts as a 'mistake *of law*'. Suppose the courts in case A in 1990 have overruled a settled view of the legal profession, and/or earlier (say 1983) judicial decisions (whether at common law or in application of statute), about the validity of a certain kind of transaction. Was money paid in say 1986, in reliance on the rule or view of the law overruled in 1990, paid 'under mistake of law'? Or was the payment—as John Austin (judges are subordinate law-*makers*) and Oliver Wendell Holmes (a rule is just a prediction of judicial action) and Lord Reid vintage-1972 (declaratory theory is mere fairy tale) would say—made under a *true view* of the law as it was in 1986 (the only mistake, if any, being one of *prediction* of what the courts would in fact decide in, say, 1990)?

The latter was the minority view, and it has the sheen of academic sophistication and gritty professional realism. But, right at its surface, it has a profound practical awkwardness. The transactions adjudicated on in case A in 1990 will have been treated by the court in that case as void *ab initio*, and all transactions like them will have been and are treated likewise. And this standard (in practice virtually universal) common law approach the *Kleinwort Benson* minority peacefully accepted. That minority's position focused on a lesser, collateral class of transactions—payments of moneys in reliance on the rule or view overruled in case A—and in relation to *these* reasoned on the basis that, or as if, the transactions held void-in-1986 in 1990 were in law (the 'true, not mistaken, view' of the 1986-era law!) valid-in-1986. This makes little or no sense in law or justice, even on the 'practical man's' no-fictions-please view of law from which the minority were seeking to reason.

The problem with saying 'no-fairy-tales please, judges are law-makers' goes deeper, however. The declaratory theory of law is not and never was put forward as a description of the history of our law—a history that includes many changes in the common law and in interpretations of statute law, changes which may go beyond development to abrogation. Rather, it is a statement of the judge's vocation and responsibility. So I called my case-note on *Kleinwort Benson* 'The Fairy Tale's Moral'[14] and argued that the view mocked as mere fairy tale is not a fictional assertion about facts—a fairy tale—but a normative moral/juridical doctrine about judicial responsibility. Since the issues in *Kleinwort Benson*, and in its essential resolution, manifest the elements of the problem of adjudication and law-making so well, and show that hereabouts subtlety cannot be abandoned without high cost, I shall venture to quote the case-commentary at some length. Calling the judicial responsibility a duty, I tried to articulate it like this:

> [A]djudication is not the telling of some story which if accurate might be called history—or prescient prediction—and if inaccurate a myth or fairy tale. Adjudication is the effort

---

[14] John Finnis, 'The Fairy Tale's Moral' (1999) 115 *LQR* 170–75; also in 'Adjudication and Legal Change', essay 20 in John Finnis, *Philosophy of Law: Collected Essays Volume IV* (Oxford, Oxford University Press, 2011) 397–403.

to identify the rights of the contending parties *now* by identifying what were, in law, the rights and wrongs, or validity or invalidity, of their actions and transactions *when entered upon and done*. If those [actions and transactions] rested on a view of the law then widely settled, the judge may nonetheless have the duty now to take and act upon a contrary view of the law if (a) adhering to that former view would conflict with other elements of our law—notably with principles of law and other judicially cognizable policies and standards—applicable then and now to the parties, (b) departing from that former view would not collide with duties specific to the judge (for example the duty to follow a recent decision of the court immediately superior in the hierarchy), and (c) departing from the formerly settled view would not be an injustice to the parties before the court. The facts about precedent and about currently or predictably prevalent opinion enter into judicial reasoning, but even when decisive (as is usual) they have their directiveness only by virtue of legally normative standards—a set of legal standards which, just as they are the source of the authoritativeness of opinion and precedent, can on occasion give reason to reject and depart from even a well-settled and judicially approved understanding of the law.[15]

And again:

> Mistakes of law, because identifiable only by using a legal rule to assess the correctness of beliefs, need not and should not be understood as simply another kind of mistake of fact. Correctly identifying a belief as having been mistaken in law need involve no denial or neglect of any historical fact. The law, in our metaphor,[16] has a double life. One can switch between the descriptive (historical or predictive) and the normative ways of thinking and talking about it, and everyone regularly does. Shifting between these warranted, complementary perspectives, one can without contradiction make statements which, if made from one and the same perspective, would be contradictory. One can say both that a settled rule of common law existed [for many years], *and* that all those years the settled view that the supposed rule is part of our law was an error awaiting correction by better legal reasoning and sound adjudication.

That is what the 'declaratory', no-real-change view holds, and it can be explained and made more precise by making explicit how the adjudicative contexts to which the theory speaks differ from each other. For although, on the one hand:

> The institutional duty of the Court of Appeal and lower courts to apply the supposed rule until the House of Lords declared the newly clarified law does provide good reason— even within a strictly normative perspective—to speak of the declaration as a 'change', an

---

[15] ibid, 'The Fairy Tale's Moral', 172 ('Adjudication and Legal Change', 399–400).

[16] 'Law has a double life. It is in force as a matter of fact; historians and contemporary observers can describe—and make predictions about—its content and effect by attending to the opinions and practices prevalent among certain persons and groups, especially courts and their officers. But it has its force by directing the practical reasoning of those persons and groups. And since one engages in practical reasoning to reach nonnormative conclusions (such-and-such ought to be done, or ought not, or is desirable, or permissible, etc.), facts count in practical reasoning only by virtue of some further, normative premise(s), the source of the reasoning's directiveness for decision and action. Law stated *in* such reasoning, not least in judicial reasoning, is stated as a norm, and exists *as* directing one towards or away from decisions and actions, validating or invalidating one's transactions, and so forth, precisely by being itself justified as part of a set of such standards. Law's existence, force, and effect—its life—can always thus be understood as sheer fact (historical or predictable) or alternatively as directive standard.' ibid 170 (397).

'abrogation', and a 'development', with retrospective effect', and to treat the superseded rule as having thus been more than merely 'supposed' …

nevertheless, on the other hand:

> A higher tribunal, looking beyond prevalent opinions and the purely institutional duties of, say, lower courts, and considering our law as a principled and lasting whole, could with equally good reason declare a contrary rule, and apply it to the parties, their transactions, and their supporting beliefs, as having been at all relevant times legally correct and an authentic legal rule. From this highest-level view of our law as a justifying because justified whole, the newly declared rule would not, in the last analysis, be retroactive—would, in the last analysis, abrogate no part of our law's substantive content. The judicial reasoning towards, and act of declaring, the rule would be fundamentally different from the enactment of new statutory provisions; only in result would it coincide even with that rare form of legislative action which, sometimes reasonably, makes new statutory provisions retroactive.

For indeed (and this is really the point), in relation to common law rules and taking 'legally appropriate' to mean appropriate given the content of *our* law (as it stands at the time of the adjudication):

> [A]djudication involves the duty not to declare and apply a rule unless it can fairly be said to have been all along a legally appropriate standard, more appropriate than alternatives, for assessing the validity and propriety of the parties' transactions. When that can fairly be said, the same rule, having been declared and applied, is clearly the only legally appropriate standard for assessing the *correctness* of the parties' belief in the legal validity and propriety of their transactions. And it will equally be the appropriate standard for judging correct or mistaken the similar belief of parties to legally similar transactions during the period stretching *at least* as far back as it would be reasonable to allow the results of completed but invalid or improper transactions to be disturbed.[17]

So, Lords Goff and Hoffmann need not have been *pretending* to 'discover legal principles concealed in the luxuriant undergrowth of ancient principle and scattered legal decisions' when they, with the rest of the Appellate Committee, set aside the old 1802 rule about recovery for mistake of law. Lord Goff, reflecting on the very issue addressed in the Lecture passages quoted at the beginning of this section—and doing so in closest proximity to a striking exercise in developing the common law of restitution—articulated what one might call a reformulated declaratory theory, in resistance to the fiction/fairy tale jibe:

> When a judge decides a case which comes before him, he does so on the basis of what he understands the law to be … In the course of deciding the case before him he may, on occasion, develop the common law in the perceived interests of justice … This means not only that he must act within the confines of the doctrine of precedent, but that the change must be seen as a development … of existing principle and so can take its place as a congruent part of the common law as a whole.

---

[17] ibid 173–5 (401–03).

And Lord Hoffmann said:

> The [no recovery for mistake of law] rule is ... not founded upon any defensible logic or principle. It is the proper business of your Lordships in a judicial capacity to clarify and develop the common law by restating rules in accordance with principle, even when this may require the *correction of ancient heresies*.[18]

In short, I think the view expressed on common law 'law-making' in the Lecture is an over-simplification. Neither 'pretence' nor 'fiction' is apt to describe the long-settled resolve of conscientious judges to do justice *according to law* with full and self-disciplined awareness that—whatever may be said about prospective overruling, a possibility very significantly more talked about than put into practice—their determinations of the law will in reality be applied to *past* dealings and inter-relations of the parties before the court, and can only be just and properly judicial if they state law that can reasonably be said to *have been* the law that, *all things now considered*, was properly applicable at the time (even if not then generally recognised as such).

It would be facile and unwise to write off this judicial awareness and corresponding responsible self-discipline as double-think. For doing justice *according to law*—the peculiarly judicial responsibility—is a matter neither of mediating nor of legislating, but of finding the law that is applicable to the *lis* because it was the law governing the parties as they interacted (at the relevant past time(s)) in a way allegedly giving rise to a cause in action, and then by applying that law so as to give to each their legal entitlement. To ignore or belittle the internal, normative point of view from which judges can discern their adjudicative, interpretative responsibility is to adopt the strategy—whether predictive/descriptive or also bootstrapping, liberated normative/justificatory—which in the early to middle of the last century was called 'Realism'. Such not fully realistic realism is a seed-bed or hothouse, softening up judges and their communities for the 'living instrument' doctrine. That doctrine claims that anxiously drafted, debated and agreed-in-detail documents, establishing propositions of law with high authority, on matters perhaps remote from the domains traditionally left to common law development, are legitimately interpreted so as to introduce, later, propositions contrary to or at odds with those earlier established propositions—that is, departing, often widely,

---

[18] *Kleinwort Benson v Lincoln City Council* [1999] 2 AC 401 (emphasis added). My case-note paraphrased Lord Hoffmann's further reflections, with some context: 'In this way, he adds (reinforcing the echoes of Dworkin), a properly judicial change in the "settled view of the law" is to be distinguished from a new rule's adoption "founded purely upon policy; upon a utilitarian assessment" that the new rule "would, on balance, do less harm than good"—an adoption which would be improper even for the House of Lords because it "would be a legislative act in a sense in which the abrogation of the mistake of law rule would not". (Of course, in saying that the Lords can properly reaffirm principles against even ancient heresies, Lord Hoffmann was not saying that every "heresy" can properly be corrected by the supreme judicial tribunal. In a case decided six weeks after *Kleinwort Benson*, he said [*White* [or *Frost*] *v Chief Constable of South Yorkshire Police* [1999] 2 AC 455, 500] that recent Lords' decisions restricting recoverability in tort for psychiatric injury are a departure from principle, a wrong turning, but one that "it is too late to go back on"; "until there is legislative change, the courts must live with them").' Finnis (n 14) 173 (401).

from what those who settled them provided by deliberate inclusion and exclusion. Section III below discusses that doctrine, in sympathy with the Lecture's critique of it. But first there is something to be said about the European 'instrument' that judges in 1978 started to call 'living': the ECHR.

II. HOW ADMIRABLE?

'The text of the Convention is wholly admirable.' Is it? To be sure, it identifies a number of true and important rights. It is a helpful *aide-memoire* for legislators, and in this way could be useful in a country where courts had no power to review primary legislation for non-compliance with the Convention. But juridically, that is, as a helpfully precise guide to adjudication, it is a mess. Some of these defects are mentioned in my Maccabean Lecture, 'A Bill of Rights for Britain?' (1985).[19] I mention now only three salient points, one of which my lecture failed to anticipate.

1. *The wording of certain key articles* postulates, presupposes or implies that there are justifiable and justified interferences with rights and/or justified restrictions on the 'exercise' of those rights.[20] Notably, Article 8 postulates first the 'enjoyment' by A of a 'right to respect' from/by B for A's private life, and then a perhaps wholly justified 'interference'—so-called—by the state with that enjoyment (and thus with that 'right to respect' or 'right to private life').[21]

    Sometimes the Strasbourg Court circumvents the main conceptual source of such confusion by departing from the article's terms, and speaking instead of the right's being (not 'interfered with', but merely) 'engaged'.[22] But the problem is not fully surmounted until what is called a right (say, in Article 8(1)) is understood to be no more (and no less) than an important human *interest* or aspect of human wellbeing. State conduct impinging negatively on this human good requires justification, and this duty not *unjustifiably* to harm the interest/good entails—has as its jural correlative—a human right that the

---

[19] 'Human Rights and their Enforcement', essay 1 in John Finnis, *Human Rights and Common Good: Collected Essays Volume III* (Oxford, Oxford University Press, 2011) 19–46 at 27–31, 39–42; also in 'A Bill of Rights for Britain? The Moral of Contemporary Jurisprudence' (1985) 71 *Proceedings of the British Academy* 303–31.

[20] On all this, see Grégoire Webber, *The Negotiable Constitution: On Limitation of Rights* (Cambridge, Cambridge University Press, 2009): ch 2 describes the received approach, ch 3 critiques it as 'constraining and unbecoming of our commitment to rights' (115); ch 4 offers an alternative conception of rights as specified or constituted by their limits (118) and then not subject to balancing or 'optimization'; ch 5 locates the legislature as the paradigmatic specifier of rights by construction rather than interpretation *stricto sensu*; ch 6 reflects upon the justifying of rights by public reason in a free society, with the role of the judiciary (in reviewing the legislature's specification) appropriately restricted to very clear mistakes (210).

[21] '8. *Right to respect for private and family life* 1. Everyone has the right to respect for his private and family life, his home and his correspondence. 2. There shall be no interference by a public authority with the exercise of this right except such as is in accordance with the law and is necessary in a democratic society in the interests of...'.

[22] *Pretty v UK* (2346/02) 29 April 2002 (4th Section) [86].

state not interfere unjustifiably with one's private life. So the subject matter and content of the Article 8 right are not even definable, or juridically identifiable, until one has taken into account, at least in outline, all those kinds of state action that are justifiable under Article 8(2), including all those countless kinds of law that do justifiably[23] restrict what one can legitimately do in private—and the outlines of all those many kinds that *might*.[24]

2. *The standard for justifying* so-called 'restrictions on' or 'interferences with' the freedoms or immunities in Articles 7, 8, 9, 10 and 11 is: 'necessary in a democratic society'. This 'necessary' sets the bar at the highest level, called by US constitutional doctrine *strict scrutiny* and reserved in that doctrine to provisions involving a very few 'suspect classifications' (notably race and national origin or lawful alienage within the country). That this level of scrutiny is for most (other) purposes and contexts intolerably high helps explain why the ECtHR has cobbled together the proportionality doctrine: to *water down the necessity* denoted by 'necessary'. The ECtHR and national courts alike apply this doctrine (or test, or mantra) in a highly variable and results-oriented manner, capable of landing anywhere along a spectrum stretching from 'rational-basis', highly deferential review to, at the other end, the real practical necessity demanded by strict scrutiny or 'most intensive' review.[25] But juridically unsound slackness in application and explanation was inevitable, in view both of the Convention's excessively demanding term 'necessary' and of the more or less legislative assessments called for by the incommensurables and imponderables that, in many if not all kinds of case, are inherent[26] in the 'proportionality' test(s).

Perhaps 'appropriate' would have made better sense in the text of these articles than 'necessary'. That this is so confirms that subjecting general laws to assessment of the kind called for when 'rights' are 'engaged' is often more legislative than judicial in the deliberative and decision-making intellectual processes, and the radically under-determined choices, that it demands. After

---

[23] One necessary though not sufficient condition of justifiability is that the restriction be not purely paternalist (in relation to the purely private acts of consenting adults), but be motivated by concern for the public good: see Finnis (n 14) essay 11 ('Hart as a Political philosopher') 268.

[24] Lord Hughes in *Nicklinson* (n 5) clarifies art 8 considerably at [263]: 'There are times when, as a sphere of personal activity is identified as falling within the reach of article 8, it is tempting to say that there is therefore a fundamental right to that particular form of activity. The better view is that the fundamental right is to what article 8.1 actually speaks of—namely *respect for private and family life. Whether there is a right to do the particular thing under consideration depends on whether the State is or is not justified in prohibiting it, or placing conditions upon it,* and that in turn depends on whether the State's rules meet the requirements of article 8.2' (emphasis added; see also [264]). Lord Sumption's remarks in [216] move in this direction.

[25] See my examination of the reasoning in *R (Begum) v Denbigh High School* [2006] UKHL 15; [2007] 1 AC 100: John Finnis, 'Endorsing Discrimination between Faiths: A Case of Extreme Speech?' in Ivan Hare and James Weinstein (eds), *Extreme Speech and Democracy* (Oxford, Oxford University Press, 2009) 431ff.

[26] See Francisco Urbina, 'A Critique of Proportionality' (2012) 57 *American Journal of Jurisprudence* 49; *Momcilovic v R* [2011] HCA 34, Heydon J (dissenting) at [428]–[432]; John Finnis, 'Response to Harel, Hope and Schwartz' (2013) 8 *Jerusalem Review of Legal Studies* 147, 150–52, especially fns 7, 12.

showing this in action in section IV, I will revisit proportionality briefly in section VI.

3. *The true absolute rights* which in 1980 I celebrated as correlative to the true absolute duties—notably, not to choose to torture someone (or to arrange for, counsel or facilitate his torture) and not to subject someone to inhuman or degrading treatment—have turned out to have a wording wide open to misinterpretation and have been subjected to unwarrantable 'interpretative' extension (as components of a 'living instrument'). For the Strasbourg Court, as section V will show, has adopted the ultimately self-contradictory proposition that a state has an exceptionless duty not to do anything which, despite genuine precautions against this result, *risks* having as a *result* someone's being tortured or subjected to such treatment by someone else's choices, choices which, moreover, the state is not complicit in and has taken bona fide steps to avert. The bad consequences of that shift in public meaning include some real risk that the ECHR itself, and European states themselves, will be wrecked. Whether that existential risk will materialise, nobody knows. What is clear is that the Strasbourg Court's extension of these provisions has become philosophically and juridically indefensible.

III. LIVING INSTRUMENTS

The Shah Lecture points to the Strasbourg Court as 'the international flag-bearer for judge-made fundamental law extending well beyond the text which it is charged with applying' and as thus converting essentially political into purportedly legal questions. The ECtHR's claim to treat the Convention as a 'living instrument' grounds (the Lecture says) the Court's 'development' of the Convention, by 'extrapolation or analogy',[27] so as to reflect not so much the Convention's language, object or purpose as agreed between its signatories, but rather the judges' 'view of what rights are required in a modern democracy'—a view controlled only by the evolution of 'conceptions common' (more or less) 'to the democracies of Europe', that is, of 'changed values' (changed since the text was agreed). Thus, the Court comes to 'recognize' rights which 'we know from the negotiation documents that [the signatory states] positively intended not to grant'.

Quite so. And one can add a footnote: besides the 'negotiation documents', there are further resources available to all lawyerly and bona fide interpretations of an agreed instrument—contract, constitution, treaty or convention—resources for discerning with objectivity and (often) reliability what its expressed and intended meaning included. Often, too, these resources enable us to discern reliably what that public meaning, the agreement embodied in the instrument, was intended *not* to include. Correspondingly, judges and advocates being reasonably competent

---

[27] The reflections deployed in this chapter suggest that 'extrapolation' and 'analogy' may not adequately describe the range of adventurous Strasbourg decisions. See n 100 on 'spirit and intendment' going beyond 'analogy with' and extending to 'or within the spirit of…'.

and honest, their claim that proposition X is warranted by the instrument *because it is a 'living instrument'* is excellent backhanded evidence: evidence that proposition X is not within the instrument's agreed, expressed or intended public meaning; or even good evidence that X is a proposition which the instrument's makers considered and agreed (or accepted) was *no part of* the undertakings they were entering into by settling, agreeing and subscribing to the instrument.

Such backhanded or negative evidence, though by no means necessary, is often helpful. For, beyond certain easy cases, it is hard to articulate abstractly how competent lawyers reasonably judge that certain propositions are 'contrary to' (or 'outside') an agreement and the instrument that embodies it. The difficulty arises, in part, from the fact that expressed and public meaning does reasonably include, or at least warrant, some implications that are not themselves directly expressed.[28] Such implications may extend the range of propositions beyond those fully and directly articulated. Or, depending on the context, they may narrow the range that might otherwise have been taken to be agreed: 'If we had meant to include proposition X we obviously would have spelled it out (or in some other way adjusted the wording), but we thought about it and meant *not* to include it—indeed, at least some of those among us whose agreement was necessary meant to exclude it—so we chose the wording you now find.'

It follows that, in many cases, the appeal by judges or advocates to notions of the 'living instrument' (or 'living tree', or 'evolutionary' or 'developmental' interpretation) is, presumptively, warrant for *rejecting* the interpretation (proposition of law) they advocate. In other words, such appeals are evidence that agreements and understandings, in reasonable reliance upon which at least some of the parties (the others being aware of this reliance) entered into or ratified the agreement, are being set aside. But for their reliance on this meaning, they might well not have become party to the whole. Such parties, in such circumstances, are presumptively being *pro tanto* betrayed. Often these parties knew that they and their successors would be vulnerable to serious harm or loss as a result of entering the agreement and making the compromises they did. In such cases, the judges' imposition of the living instrument interpretation will be an injustice, which in some cases will smack of ambush or cynicism: 'You or your naïve forebears acting for you should have tried harder to exclude the meaning we have minted and are now imposing.'

***

Meaning and origins of 'living instrument'. Besides its own utility (just indicated) as a guide to its own inappropriateness, the phrase as used about, say, the ECHR[29]

---

[28] See n 36 below.

[29] As used about the whole body of the law (constitutional, statutory and common)—the whole set of true propositions of our law—'living instrument' signifies no more and no less than the *means* of doing justice *according to law*. Thus, Dixon CJ, addressing Bench and Bar on first presiding in Melbourne as Chief Justice on 7 May 1952, said: 'In this Court ... the use of academical writings has been very great indeed; and yet I believe that the Court has always administered the law as a

seems on its face an affront to reason, a category mistake. An instrument cannot be living. What would it be for a valid and controlling instrument to be dead or lifeless? Why don't we talk about living contracts?

Societies and states, of course, can reasonably be called 'living', by an acceptable *analogy* with living human persons and (different analogy) with families. Judicial appeal to the 'life/living' metaphor in the context of constitutional interpretation perhaps began with Holmes J's argument for an expansive interpretation of the effect of treaties under the US Constitution in *Missouri v Holland* (1920).[30] But precisely here, life or living is predicated *not* of the Constitution or any of its terms (nor of any treaty), but of the nation whose constitution it is.[31] Similarly, talk of living *trees* began in Canada as a reference *not* to any instrument, or even to any set of propositions (such as the Constitution, including conventions, of Canada),[32] but to the political community itself—in that case to the political community, the confederation of Canada, established by the British North America Act 1867.[33]

---

living instrument and not as an abstract study. Indeed, I think the Court has shown an ever-growing tendency to decide cases upon the minor premises and not to concern itself with general propositions but to go to the precise facts and circumstances.' Owen Dixon, *Jesting Pilate and Other Papers and Addresses* (Melbourne, Law Book Co, 1965) 251.

[30] *Missouri v Holland* 252 US 416 (1920), 434.

[31] '[W]hen we are dealing with words that also are a constituent act, like the Constitution of the United States, we must realize that they have *called into life a being* the development of which could not have been foreseen completely by the most gifted of its begetters. It was enough for them to realize or to hope that they had created *an organism*; it has taken a century and has cost their successors much sweat and blood to prove that they created *a nation*. The case before us must be considered in the light of our whole experience, and not merely in that of what was said a hundred years ago. The treaty in question does not contravene any prohibitory words to be found in the Constitution. The only question is whether it is forbidden by some invisible radiation from the general terms of the Tenth Amendment ['powers not delegated to the United States by the Constitution, nor prohibited by it to the States, are reserved to the States respectively, or to the people']. *We must consider what this country has become in deciding what that Amendment has reserved.*' *Missouri v Holland* (ibid) 434 (emphases added). So far as it concerned a treaty with a genuinely international subject matter (migratory birds), the decision in *Missouri v Holland* in relation to the internal enforcement of treaties was more defensible than the decisions of the High Court of Australia in and since 1982 to treat the Commonwealth Parliament's paramount power over 'external affairs' as including the internal enforcement of human rights (qua the matter of treaties to which Australia is party): see John Finnis, 'Power to Enforce Treaties in Australia—The High Court Goes Centralist?' (1983) 3 *Oxford Journal of Legal Studies* 126–30.

[32] *Pace* Bradley W Miller, 'Origin Myth: The Persons Case, the Living Tree, and the New Originalism' in Grant Huscroft and Bradley W Miller (eds), *The Challenge of Originalism: Theories of Constitutional Interpretation* (Cambridge, Cambridge University Press, 2011) 136–37. With this illuminating essay I disagree only on the point made in n 33 below about the referent of 'living tree'. Miller's interpretation gets its plausibility from Lord Sankey's glissade at [1930] AC 136 from community to Constitution/constitution: 'The British North America Act [1867] planted in Canada a living tree capable of growth and expansion within its natural limits. The object of the Act was to grant a Constitution to Canada. Like all written constitutions it has been subject to development through usage and convention.'

[33] Read in context, it seems likely that the primary or sole referent of Sankey LC's phrase 'living tree', in the *Persons* case (*Edwards v Attorney-General of Canada* [1930] AC 124)—a tree said by him to be 'planted' in North America by the British North America Act and 'capable of growth and expansion within its natural limits'—was not what Justice Miller ((n 32) 132) calls 'the Canadian Constitution in its entirety—written and unwritten, convention and law'. Rather, the living tree intended and spoken of was (at least primarily) *the Dominion itself*, as (what Lord Sankey in the preceding paragraph called) one of the 'communities included within the Britannic system ... and undergoing a continuous process of evolution', and referred to again on the judgment's last page (143) as 'a responsible and developing

But in later decades the phrase 'living tree' was co-opted and converted into talk of something equivalent or close to 'living instrument/document'.[34]

The Strasbourg Court's first use of the latter metaphor to articulate and justify its approach was in *Tyrer* in 1978: the Convention is a 'living instrument which … must be interpreted *in the light of present-day conditions*'.[35] The formula I have italicised remains in use. It conceals the statement's real thrust. For no one is likely to object to the statement's literal sense.[36] But its real and intended meaning is different and far more extensive: that the instrument can and should be deployed by courts 'in the light' not merely of 'present-day conditions' but also *of present-day attitudes and/or opinions* (so far as these are shared by a majority of some court, commission or tribunal) *about better political or social arrangements*,[37] or about (as the Lecture reports) 'what rights are required in a modern democracy'[38]—such deployments being not included in, or being even contrary to, its original public meaning (intent). The instrument's actual meaning, as it was envisaged, agreed and adopted, is thus *pro tanto* replaced by a meaning in line with those present-day and judicially shared value judgments.

State'. If so, Canadian 'living tree constitutionalism', so far as it has appealed to Lord Sankey's dictum, is a touch more myth-ridden than Miller contends. As Miller in substance agrees, the decision in the *Persons* case did not involve 'living tree' doctrine understood as treating the British North America Act as a 'living instrument'; the Judicial Committee summarises its position on that final page of Lord Sankey's judgment: 'having regard—(1) to the object of the Act, viz., to provide a constitution for Canada, a responsible and developing state; (2) that the word "person" is ambiguous and may include members of either sex; (3) that there are sections in the Act above referred to which show that in some cases the word "person" must include females; (4) that in some sections the words "male persons" is expressly used when it is desired to confine the matter in issue to males, and (5) to the provisions of the *Interpretation Act*; their Lordships have come to the conclusion that the word "persons" in sec. 24 includes members both of the male and female sex'.

[34] In Canada, see *Hunter et al v Southam Inc* [1984] 2 SCR 145; *Re BC Motor Vehicle Act* [1985] 2 SCR 486; and commentary in the essays by Miller cited in nn 32 above and 37 below. This arguably mistaken reading is adopted by Lord Bingham in *Brown v Stott* [2003] 1 AC 681, 703, albeit in the context of counselling attention to the 'natural limits' which (on this misreading) the text to be interpreted imposes on its 'living' interpretation. Likewise, Lady Hale takes it to be 'the Constitution of Canada' ('Beanstalk or Living Instrument: How Tall Can the European Convention on Human Rights Grow?' (2011), www.gresham.ac.uk/print/2666 at fn 3).

[35] *Tyrer v UK* [1978] ECHR 2 (5856/72), 25 April 1978 [31].

[36] As Bradley Miller says, in relation to 'changing circumstances, such as unanticipated technological changes like the telephone and atomic energy, as well as social changes such as the full participation of women in the workforce', the sort of 'progressive interpretation' that is 'a matter of specification, or gap-filling, of the *eiusdem generis* variety' is 'equally supported by originalist and non-originalist interpreters': Miller (n 32) 136–37.

[37] On the fundamental equivocation here between conventional morality and morality taken by the speaker (say, the Court) to be true, see Miller's critique (of Aileen Kavanagh, 'The Idea of a Living Constitution' (2003) 16 *Canadian Journal of Law and Jurisprudence* 55, 69–86) in his 'Beguiled by Metaphors: The "Living Tree" and Originalist Interpretation in Canada' (2009) 22 *Canadian Journal of Law and Jurisprudence* 331, 338–39, 350–52. The present chapter does not explore this defect in the Strasbourg Court's approach; cf Finnis (n 14) essay 1, s III; Finnis (n 19) essay 11 ('Hart as a Political Philosopher') 269–72.

[38] And see n 56 below.

The court in *Tyrer* may well[39] have picked up the term 'living instrument' from the 'first conclusion' of a 'report',[40] to a colloquium on the ECHR held in Rome in November 1975, by the Danish international lawyer Max Sørensen: 'The [Convention] is a living legal instrument ... Its provisions are capable of being interpreted in such a way as to keep pace with social change.'[41] The conclusion about what Sørensen also called 'evolutive interpretation methods' rested largely on a number of reports of, and friendly settlements sponsored by, the Commission. He gave only slight attention to the decision of the Court itself, in February 1975, in *Golder*[42] (and none at all to Judge Fitzmaurice's elaborate and far-seeing partial dissent).[43] The uncritical slackness in Sørensen's general approach in this report is exemplified by his astonishing remark that the judicial organs of the Convention should avoid 'a narrow interpretation that would make the provisions [of Article 3] utterly meaningless in the normal conditions prevailing in Western Europe'[44]—as if a provision is meaningless because it is fully complied with (yet would doubtless be violated if 'normal conditions' were to be replaced in some states by the totalitarian takeover—or excessive counter-measures—against which the founders intended the Convention to be a bulwark)! As we will see, five years later Sørensen had come to a sounder view. But the decisions of the Court itself, by and large, have gone on exemplifying his fallacy, deploying it as the almost articulated major premise for imposing an unending flow of reforms of law and culture.[45]

Now when the ECtHR took up the phrase 'living instrument' in *Tyrer* in April 1978, the words were pointing not only forward but also backward, to what the Court itself had already done in half a dozen major cases. These went back to *Golder*. There Fitzmaurice[46] demonstrated that the Contracting States *certainly* intended that Article 6's elaborate guarantee of a right to a fair trial (in the determination of

---

[39] As is observed by Eirik Bjorge, *The Evolutionary Interpretation of Treaties* (Oxford, Oxford University Press, 2014) 12.

[40] The question addressed by Sørensen was: 'Do the rights set forth in the European Convention on Human Rights in 1950 have the same significance in 1975?'

[41] 'Report Presented by Max Sørensen to the Fourth International Colloquy about the European Convention on Human Rights, Rome 5–8 November 1975': reprinted in *Professor, dr. jur. Max Sørensen: A Bibliography* (Aarhus, Aarhus University Press, 1988) 23, 54–55.

[42] *Golder v UK* (4451/70), 21 February 1975 (Plenary).

[43] The report seems to have been completed before the judgment (again with extensively argued partial dissent by Fitzmaurice), delivered 10 days before the colloquium, in *National Union of Belgian Police v Belgium* (4464/70), 27 October 1975 (Plenary). Fitzmaurice, while accepting perhaps too easily ([10]) that the ECHR should 'be given a reasonably liberal construction that would also take into consideration manifest changes or developments in the climate of opinion which have occurred since the Convention was concluded', persuasively excoriated (a) the free-wheeling approach to interpretation adopted by the Commission in this and other cases, and (b) the interpretation of Article 14 adopted by the majority of the Court, which in effect: 'set up that Article (art. 14) as an independent autonomous provision under which all discrimination in the general field of human rights would be prohibited. Such a process may have its attractions, and it may be tempting to follow it. Yet a natural and creditable distaste for discrimination in any form cannot justify a conclusion for which no sufficient legal warrant exists, or can exist. The Court is not a court of ethics but a court of law'.

[44] 'Report' (n 41) 40.

[45] See this chapter's final paragraph.

[46] Judges Verdross and Zekia wrote partially dissenting judgments to like effect as Judge Fitzmaurice's.

civil rights or criminal charges) would *not* guarantee a Convention *right of access* to a court in the 'determination of civil rights' (in relation to criminal charges the position is less clear, because of sub-arts (2) and (3)). The founding states carefully and purposefully omitted everything that in the Universal Declaration of Human Rights 1948 (UDHR) connoted such a right. And it is scarcely conceivable that states intending or contemplating that Article 6 should secure or declare a right of access to a court or judicial tribunal would have drafted Article 6 as they did, limiting its provisions about the countervailing interests of morals, public order, security, other rights etc *only* to the minor issue of *public* pronouncement of judgment, and with the defining term 'civil rights' shrouded in an ambiguity that innumerable decisions over 35 years have done little to resolve in a principled way.

Of course, if *Golder* was the Court's original sin of 'living' (mis)interpretation, the occasion for committing it was peculiarly seductive. For, as Fitzmaurice's dissent accepts, a Convention without any guarantee of access to a judicial tribunal is somewhat defective, and Article 6's wording, when read apart from its historical context, easily seems to take such a guarantee for granted. But the defect was one the Contracting States were knowingly content to accept; they intended to live with it.

The *Golder* decision was a *coup de main*, an *overriding* of original public meaning, *including* the Convention's original object and purpose as precisely conceived by its makers and stated in Article 1(1): 'to secure to everyone within their jurisdiction the rights and freedoms defined … in the Convention'. All this was cheerfully accepted at the Court's seminar, 'Dialogue between Judges' in January 2011, by Jan Erik Helgesen, the first President of the Venice Commission (the Council of Europe's European Commission for Democracy through Law). He recounted with satisfaction how, as a law student in Oslo in 1974, he wrote a dissertation predicting and proleptically defending the majority decision in *Golder*:

> [T]he evaluation committee at the Law School looked with great scepticism at my dissertation. Never during my time at Law School did I receive such a poor grade … *One of the members of the evaluation committee was among the founding fathers of the Convention in 1950. He told the young law student that Article 6 was never meant to be interpreted like that!*[47]

Indeed. And what the founding father doubtless meant, more precisely put, was that Article 6 was *meant never to be interpreted* like that.[48] The ECtHR's living instrument jurisprudence is founded on the grasping of legislative power, a power of constructing new law,[49] by judges whose jurisdiction extended, in truth, only to 'interpretation and application' (Article 32(1)), not to legislative improvement. As

---

[47] European Court of Human Rights, *Dialogue between Judges 2011: What are the Limits to the Evolutive Interpretation of the Convention?* (Strasbourg, 2011) at 19 (emphasis added).

[48] As Lord Sumption's Lecture puts it, there are rights 'which we know from the negotiation documents that they [the signatories] positively intended not to grant'.

[49] On construction, in this sense, as opposed both to interpretation and to textual amendment, see Webber (n 20) 165–68; on the necessity of such construction and the ordinary appropriateness of reserving it to the legislature, see 167–73.

Baroness Hale said in the same seminar, the ECtHR holds itself ready to override even a definite intention of the drafters and signatories to exclude a right from the ambit of (as Article 1 puts it) 'the rights and freedoms defined in [Articles 2–18] of this Convention'.[50]

Baroness Hale points here to *Young, James and Webster*,[51] in which the plenary ECtHR of 21 judges in 1981 outlawed key 'closed shop' provisions of UK trade union law on the ground that *even though*[52] (i) the Convention's makers deliberately excluded any equivalent of the UDHR's 'negative right' of free association (the right in Article 20(2) UDHR not to 'be compelled to belong to an association', complementing the positive Article 20(1) UDHR 'right to freedom of association'), and even though (ii) it also was clear that the makers formed this exclusory intention precisely so as to protect provisions such as then existed in UK and some other national laws for permitting, setting up and maintaining union 'closed shops', still such provisions contravened the 'substance' of the positive Article 20(1) right to 'freedom of association'. Just to the extent that points (i) and (ii) are clear (whether by concession or sound historical judgment), *Young, James and Webster* is a stark instance of *giving a new answer to an old question*, a question *that had been answered* in the decisions made in drafting Article 11(1) ECHR to secure a Convention right going no further than (positively) 'to freedom of association with others, including the right *to form and to join* trade unions for the protection of [one's] interests' and thus, by the *decision to omit* any phrase such as 'or not to join' or 'not to be compelled', to leave closed shop laws undisturbed. So, however desirable we may think the result, this was not genuine or bona fide evolution, giving a new answer (or adapting an old answer) to a *new* question arising out of *changed circumstances*.[53] It is simply judicial law-making—or rather, since law-making is non-judicial, it is law-making by judges and was a usurpation.

---

[50] Baroness Hale of Richmond, 'What are the Limits of the Evolutive Interpretation of the Convention?', http://echr.coe.int/Documents/Dialogue_2011_ENG.pdf, 18: 'What are the natural limits to the growth of the living tree? They are not set by the literal meaning of the words used. They are not set by the intentions of the drafters, whether actual or presumed. *They are not even set by what the drafters definitely did not intend* [n 49]. But there must be some limits … Perhaps there are no real limits. Perhaps the Convention is a magic beanstalk rather than a living tree.'

[51] *Young, James and Webster v UK* (7601/76, 7806/77), 13 August 1981 (Plenary).

[52] Strictly, 'even if', for the Court granted this (assumed it *arguendo*) without conceding or finding it to be so, though the point, as Lady Hale rightly presupposes, is historically clear.

[53] Professor Helgesen's contribution to the seminar distinguished (but without explanation or illustration) between 'evolutive' and 'dynamic' interpretation: 'I would rather use the word "evolutive" as covering the situation where the Court gives answers to new facts, issues resulting from societal changes, and issues that have never been considered before by the Court; whereas "dynamic" interpretation, to my mind, refers primarily to the situation of when the Court gives new answers to old facts.' The most obvious reference of the phrase 'new answers to old facts' is to the giving of new answers to issues that are old in the sense that they *were* issues *addressed* by the Convention's makers and *at that constitutive time were given* an explicit or implicit but publicly clear response ('answer')—whether it be to include or to exclude a then specifiable right from the Convention's protection—a response now set aside and overridden and replaced by a contrary ('dynamic') answer declared and imposed by a majority of the Court. Whichever way Helgesen intended his useful distinction to apply, cases such as *Golder* or *Young, James and Webster* exemplify not evolutive, but dynamic, illegitimately creative 'interpretation'.

Strikingly, Judge Max Sørensen (with two others) dissented. The concluding words of his convincing judgment are of wide relevance as a repudiation of the general approach for which he had provided the prevailing name:

> Objectionable as the treatment suffered by the applicants may be on grounds of reason and equity, the adequate solution lies, not in any extensive interpretation of that Article (art. 11) but in safeguards against dismissal because of refusal to join a union, that is in safeguarding the right to security of employment in such circumstances. But this right is not among those recognised by the Convention *which—as stated in the Preamble—is only a first step for the collective enforcement of human rights*. At present, it is therefore a matter for regulation by the national law of each State.[54]

But within two months, Sørensen was dead, and lawyerlike views such as this have not prevailed. In the Court's 2011 seminar, Baroness Hale took up the appointed question: are there limits to living, evolutive interpretation? Immediately after saying that 'there must be some limits', she floats the conclusion called for by her seminar paper's analysis (and her own role in interpreting the Convention over the years): 'Perhaps there are no real limits. Perhaps the Convention is a magic beanstalk rather than a living tree.' The metaphor is one she leaves unpacked, but its meaning is obvious enough: the will of judicial majorities can and does prevail, and

---

[54] Dissenting opinion of Judge Sørensen in *Young, James and Webster* at [7] (see also [5]) (emphasis added). Fitzmaurice had retired from the Court not long before the hearing. His successor, Sir Vincent Evans, was of a different stamp and was of the majority opinion in the case. The *Oxford Dictionary of National Biography* says of Evans: 'Evans's style in the [Strasbourg] court was, however, noticeably different from his predecessor's: less pugnacious, less prone to dissent, persuasive not by the brilliance of his reasoning but out of respect for his character and principles and his straightforward good sense, as well as his sheer hard work in mastering every detail of the cases with which he dealt ... In the court's judgments he was mostly with the majority, nudging the court from within towards a realistically liberal view of the development of European convention rights. The great respect in which he was held throughout government in Britain contributed materially to the acceptance of adverse decisions out of Strasbourg when they came, and he was wholeheartedly in favour of the incorporation of the convention into UK law when in due course that occurred.' In short, Evans was a consolidator of the living instrument approach and of its supercharging by the architects of the Human Rights Act 1998. For they hoped that whenever Strasbourg happened to lag behind liberal progressive opinion but recognised a margin of appreciation, its conservatism would be ignored by the British courts in favour of a British 'Convention right' embodying that opinion: see Lady Hale's quotation from the White Paper of 1997 in the first case to accept this invitation to apply the one-way ratchet (when Strasbourg is liberal, it must be followed; when it is conservative, it need not be) in *Re G (A Child) (Adoption: Unmarried Couple)* [2008] UKHL 38; [2009] 1 AC 173 [119]:

> The Government's white paper, *Rights brought home: the Human Rights Bill*, 1997, Cm 3782, said this at para 2.5:
>
>> 'The convention is often described as a 'living instrument' because it is interpreted by the European Court in the light of present day conditions and therefore reflects changing social attitudes and the changes in the circumstances of society. In future our judges will be able to contribute to this dynamic and evolving interpretation of the Convention.'
>
> For what it is worth, there were also clear statements by the Home Secretary in the House of Commons (*Hansard (HC Debates)*, 16 February 1998, Vol 306, col 768) and by the Lord Chancellor in the House of Lords (*Hansard (HL Debates)*, 18 November 1997, Vol 583, cols 514-515) that the courts must be free to develop human rights jurisprudence and to move out in new directions.

Re G was approved by at least a majority in *Nicklinson* and was not challenged there by Lord Sumption; see Finnis (n 4) 2.

knows no limits other than their predictive sense of what changes in the law they can or cannot accomplish without provoking a backlash strong enough to imperil the Convention (people axing the beanstalk) or at least to imperil the continued appointment of judges committed to such a methodology of political progress.

***

A warranted deployment of specifically judicial authority and technique? Perhaps the best defence that can be offered for the setting aside of original public meaning in favour of 'interpreting' a 'living instrument' is that framed by George Letsas. Letsas stresses frankly the extent to which the use of this judicial liberty entails law-making by the court and argues that that is legitimate:

> [S]tates gave the Court the legal mandate to provide institutional remedies for the violation of people's human rights, **whatever these moral rights happen to be. The Convention is meant to protect whatever human rights people *in fact* have,** and not what human rights domestic authorities or public opinion *think* people have[55] … As a result, a better understanding of the nature of human rights and the principles that justify [sic] will require an evolving interpretation of the Convention.[56]

Now there are indeed truths about human rights (identifying the 'rights people *in fact* have'), and those truths can be better or worse understood. But: (i) understanding of them can regress as well as progress; (ii) the judges do not occupy an Archimedean position outside the possibility of error which afflicts 'domestic authorities or public opinion'; and (iii) the Strasbourg Court's legal mandate is to uphold *those* human rights that the States Parties *agreed would be protected by the Convention* and the compulsory jurisdiction it eventually established. As we have seen, the obligation assumed by the parties to the ECHR, and their 'object and purpose' in stating and assuming it, was to secure 'the rights and freedoms *defined … in the Convention*' (Article 1(1)).

So *those* rights should be understood by the Court in their morally true sense, so far as that is compatible with the original public meaning of the Convention, and taking into account the laws that had then been judged morally appropriate (or might reasonably be so judged) by a given state in pursuit of one of the countervailing interests (eg, of children, in having a mother and father) for the sake of

---

[55] George Letsas, 'The ECHR as a Living Instrument: Its Meaning and Its Legitimacy' (March 2012) http://ssrn.com/abstract=2021836, 23. Note the discordance between this and the Strasbourg Court's constant appeal to emerging *trends* of (elite) opinion. For example (among countless instances), *Christine Goodwin v UK* (28957/95), 11 July 2002 (GC) [85]: 'The Court accordingly attaches less importance to the lack of evidence of a common European approach to the resolution of the legal and practical problems posed, than to the clear and uncontested evidence of a continuing international trend in favour not only of increased social acceptance of transsexuals but of legal recognition of the new sexual identity of post-operative transsexuals.' And [90]: 'In the twenty first century the right of transsexuals to personal development and to physical and moral security in the full sense enjoyed by others in society *cannot be regarded as a matter of controversy* requiring the lapse of time to cast clearer light on the issues involved' (bold emphasis added).

On 'emerging consensus', see eg, *Stafford* (n 142) at [68].

[56] Letsas, ibid, 23.

which the *interest* (say, in private and family life) which is foundational to the right properly and strictly so called may be impinged upon (justifiably and thus without violating the right).[57] Transposing the conclusion into the domestic realm, courts considering the implications of the Human Rights Act 1998 should recognise that *all public authorities*—indeed, all citizens and others—have the duty to accord to others the rights they 'in fact have' (including those the 1998 Act calls human) and that the particular mandate of the courts is to uphold *our law* about what human rights people in fact have. That law, today, includes prior judgments of the superior courts (including Strasbourg) and Acts of Parliament, all presumptively made on the basis of (or at least presupposing) an understanding of (ie, an opinion about) what human rights people in fact (ie, in truth) have. Each or any of these judgments, understandings or opinions may be in error. But so too may the countervailing judgments, understandings or opinions being pressed upon the court by advocates of a 'living instrument' interpretation (that is, in the last analysis, amendment or abrogation) of the existing law. To the extent that the judicial precedents themselves are founded upon a living instrument (mis)interpretation of the Convention, they may rightly be set aside by the appropriate institution constitutionally authorised to rectify our law—the 'correction of ancient [or a fortiori modern] heresies'.[58]

The Lecture's remarks about justiciability begin to open up this issue of judicial overreach and fallibility. But what the issue involves is less explained than labelled by the Lecture's contrast between the legal and the 'political'; it is illuminated more by Lord Sumption's searching and extended discussion of the importance, and variety of kinds, of *evidence* (and in his allusions to the relevance of *moral* judgment) in *Nicklinson*.[59] To that might be added a reference to that experience

---

[57] See text at n 24 above.
[58] See text at n 18 above.
[59] *Nicklinson* (n 5) [224]–[229] ('the role of evidence') and [230]–[235] ('Parliament or the Courts). At [229] Lord Sumption says: 'The question whether the protection of the health of the vulnerable requires a general prohibition on assistance for suicide cannot be a pure question of fact susceptible to decision on evidence alone. Like many issues in the area of human rights, it turns at least partly on a judgment about the relative importance of the different and competing interests at stake.' At [230], he concludes: 'the issue involves a choice between two fundamental but mutually inconsistent moral values, upon which there is at present no consensus in our society. Such choices are inherently legislative in nature. The decision cannot fail to be strongly influenced by the decision-makers' personal opinions about the moral case for assisted suicide. This is entirely appropriate if the decision-makers are those who represent the community at large. It is not appropriate for professional judges. The imposition of their personal opinions on matters of this kind would lack all constitutional legitimacy'. At [232], he says: 'the Parliamentary process is a better way of resolving issues involving controversial and complex questions of fact arising out of moral and social dilemmas. The legislature has access to a fuller range of expert judgment and experience than forensic litigation can possibly provide. It is better able to take account of the interests of groups not represented or not sufficiently represented before the court in resolving what is surely a classic "polycentric problem". But, perhaps critically in a case like this where firm factual conclusions are elusive, Parliament can legitimately act on an instinctive judgment about what the facts are likely to be in a case where the evidence is inconclusive or slight … Indeed, it can do so in a case where the truth is inherently unknowable'. At [235], he adds some words about a moral dimension over and above that involved in the protection of the vulnerable, and concludes: 'The criminal law is not a purely utilitarian construct. Offences against the person engage moral considerations which may at least arguably be a sufficient justification for a general statutory prohibition supported by criminal sanctions. The fact that the parties to these proceedings chose not to argue a point which might nevertheless legitimately influence Parliament illustrates one of the difficulties of deciding an issue of this kind judicially in the course of contested forensic litigation.'

92 *John Finnis*

and good judgment in human affairs[60] which would reasonably lead responsible *legislators* to judge that the scheme of court-supervised permissions (in a very narrow range of types of case) of assisting suicide, imagined by the two Justices who in *Nicklinson* were willing to declare the general prohibition of assisting suicide a violation of human (Convention) rights (in that very narrow range of cases), would be bad legislation, neither rationally nor (in all probability) actually sustainable as the sole exception or range of exceptions to the prohibition of suicide and mercy-killing. Freed from the accidental constraints of litigation and forensic tactics, legislators can be at least as well placed as judges to decide 'what human rights in fact require':

> For that is a matter of bearing in mind the ends and the means *and the side-effects* of actual or proposed provisions, in their relation not just to art. 8 [the right to private life] and the justifications it happens to list, but equally to art. 2 [the right not to be intentionally killed] and the rest of the Convention and of our constitution and law, and to the whole future of their community with all its members, in their private lives and their morally significant (and therefore wellbeing-affecting and wellbeing-constituting) relations with each other—all envisaged by legislators, each drawing upon their whole experience of, and reasonable belief about, life and death in their community.[61]

There is no need to stress the deficiencies of legislatures' deliberations, the fallibility of their judgments and the damage they thus can do, have often done and will do to the natural rights of persons and other elements of the common good. Given that each of these constitutional organs (legislature and judiciary) is fallible, the question which of them should have the decisive determination of those human rights the Convention's references to which cannot be applied in individual cases without further specification/determination—ie, which need to be made more specific by deliberation, judgment and decision about likely circumstances and

---

[60] But this is a slippery term, to be understood here by what follows in the paragraph as a whole and in light of, for example, Dixon's observations in his address to the Royal Australasian College of Surgeons, 'Jesting Pilate' (1957) in Owen Dixon, *Jesting Pilate and Other Papers and Addresses* (Melbourne, Law Book Co, 1965) 3: 'The courts are not, as is a man who is called upon to decide upon action in general affairs, concerned with a general situation defined neither in its ambit nor its consequences. The courts in their way seek truth only upon some narrow or restricted question defined in advance by the law, a question which is submitted to them because it supplies the standard of decision between the parties. A much wider field must be covered in great affairs of state for there can be no limit to the considerations that may be relevant or the consequences that may ensue.' The immediate context concerns executive and military decisions (and some of the decisions of the surgeon), but was undoubtedly also framed with an eye to exercises of legislative and constituent authority, calling for experience, knowledge and above all *judgment*. For Dixon's view of the issue discussed in section I, a view similar to Lord Goff's, see, eg, *Jesting Pilate*, 157–59 ('Concerning Judicial Method' (1955)). Dixon's often-quoted remarks (on being sworn in as Chief Justice in 1952) in favour of 'strict and complete legalism' by judges and his less quoted accompanying remark that 'it is not [lawyers'] business to contribute to the constructive activities of the community, but to keep the foundations and framework steady' (*Jesting Pilate*, 249) must not be understood to favour the Benthamite condemnation of all judicial *development* of the common law, or principled reconsideration of constitutional or statutory interpretations, a condemnation he rejected (ibid 157: 'Concerning Judicial Method', Yale, 1935).

[61] Finnis (n 4) 7.

probable consequences—is a question that, speaking generally, should be left to general constitutional distribution of responsibilities.[62]

The scheme of the Human Rights Act 1998 does presuppose and instantiate one such distribution. But it will work acceptably well only if members of the legislature (and citizens generally) become much more aware that many of the judicial determinations of incompatibility (or of compatibility by strenuous 'so far as possible' interpretation under section 3 of the Act) *were not really applications of law*, but rather were more legislative in character—were instances of legislating, quite often of poor quality, and were always arrived at in the somewhat inauspicious circumstances of litigious proceedings. The reasons for this state of affairs will become clearer in sections IV and V, and are given a brief summary in section VI.

And in relation to the 1998 scheme, there remains always available a perhaps superior alternative way of effecting the appropriate distribution: the way followed in the UK until the end of the last millennium and in Australia[63] to this day.

---

[62] About which Lord Reid's 1972 address on judging and law-making said: 'Parliament is the right place to settle issues which the ordinary man regards as controversial. On many questions he will say: "That is the lawyers' job, let them get on with it." But on others he will say: "I ought to have my say in this. I am not going to accept dictation from the lawyers." Family law is a good example. It is not for judges to say what changes should be made on big issues. Now that we have Law Commissions they can and do prepare the material and opportunities are being found for Parliament to take action. On such issues the ordinary man can form just as good an opinion as the lawyer or at least he thinks he can, and that is what matters' (Lord Reid (n 9) 23). A more sophisticated statement of this thesis is offered at [7] of the dissenting judgment of Judge Wojtyczek in *Firth v UK* (47784/09), 12 August 2014 (Fourth Section):

> 7. The rights enshrined in Article 3 of Protocol No. 1 have a very special dimension closely connected with a broader problem, often referred to by the scholarship as the 'counter-majoritarian difficulty' (see in particular A. M. Bickel, *The Least Dangerous Branch*, 2nd edition, New Haven and London 1986, p. 16 et seq.). The issue is one of the most vividly discussed in constitutional law and political theory. For the purpose of the present opinion, it suffices to note briefly that the provision under consideration guarantees the right to vote in elections to the legislative bodies and to determine—through elections—legislative policies. The elected bodies should have broad legislative powers. Depriving the legislature of its legislative powers infringes the citizens' right protected by the provision in question. In this context, Article 3 of Protocol No. 1 is the explicit legal basis for the preservation of the margin of appreciation of the States in the implementation of the Convention. This doctrine protects first and foremost the freedom of choice of the people in the democratic decision-making processes and ensures a proper balance between the citizens' rights to political participation and other rights protected by the Convention and the Protocols thereto. It is one of the fundamental guarantees of an effective democracy at national level in the High Contracting Parties.
>
> Human rights are by definition counter-majoritarian claims. They are restrictions imposed on the freedom of choice of the people and especially on the scope of legislative powers protected under Article 3 of Protocol No. 1. There is no effective human rights protection without real protection against the democratic legislator. History teaches us that the parliamentary majority may be tempted to infringe the rights of different vulnerable groups. The right to elect a legislature with effective powers necessarily conflicts with other rights. At the same time, one has to bear in mind that unduly extended rights may erode the substance of the right protected under Article 3 of Protocol No. 1. In disputes concerning the scope of Convention rights there should be a—rebuttable—presumption that questions on which two or more reasonable persons strongly disagree should be decided by democratic national legislatures rather than by courts, let alone international courts, unless there are serious reasons for a particularly thorough judicial review of the disputed measures.

[63] See Finnis (n 26) 152.

94 John Finnis

IV. OVERREACH AND IRRATIONALITY: *HIRST (NO 2)* AND *SCOPPOLA*

Like the Lecture, both this section and section V take their exemplary materials from the decisions of the Strasbourg Court. But that court's decisions have no monopoly on unsoundness explicable only by desire that certain propositions be made part of our law, a desire imperiously neglecting both the judicial duty to decide according to law and the significant inaptness of court proceedings as a forum for legislative deliberation. Earlier essays of mine have pointed to decisions of the highest English[64] court exhibiting comparable defects[65] in the human rights domain, defects that cannot be said to have been forced or directed by Strasbourg jurisprudence.

The cases to be considered in section V concern Article 3 of the Convention itself. Those considered in the present section concern Article 3 of the ECHR's First Protocol, adopted in 1951, which reads:

> 3. Right to Free Elections. The High Contracting Parties undertake to hold free elections at reasonable intervals by secret ballot, under conditions which will ensure the free expression of the opinion of the people in the choice of the legislature.

Not until *Mathieu-Mohin v Belgium* (1987) did the Strasbourg Court hold that Article 3, Protocol 1 creates or recognises rights and freedoms that, like other Convention rights, are 'directly secured to' individuals within the States Party to the Convention. The Court here referred, appropriately, to some aspects of the wording of the Convention's preamble and made use of the Protocol's *travaux préparatoires* and drafting history; indeed, some sound use. It further held—again with reference to the *travaux préparatoires*—that the implied rights to vote and to stand for election are subject to implied limitations and conditions: each state has 'a wide margin of appreciation' in determining these conditions for its own elections, provided 'that the conditions do not curtail the rights in question to such an extent as to impair their very essence and deprive them [the rights] of their effectiveness; that they [the conditions] are imposed in pursuit of a legitimate aim; and that the means employed are not disproportionate ... In particular,

---

[64] And other essays point to comparable lawlessness in the uppermost judicial reaches of other jurisdictions, such as Canada and Australia; see John Finnis, 'Prisoners' Votes and Judges' Power', Oxford Legal Studies Research Paper No 58/2015; SSRN: http://ssrn.com/abstract=2687247.

[65] On the indefensibility of the House of Lords' decision in *A v Secretary of State for the Home Department* [2004] UKHL 56; [2005] 2 AC 68 (foreign terrorist suspects imprisoned in Belmarsh pending deportation), see John Finnis, 'Nationality, Alienage, and Constitutional Principle' (2007) 123 LQR 127; on the errors in *R (Purdy) v Director of Public Prosecutions* [2009] UKHL 45; [2010] 1 AC 345 (persons contemplating the crime of assisting suicide entitled to guidance about the likelihood of their prosecution), see John Finnis, 'Invoking the Principle of Legality against the Rule of Law' [2010] *New Zealand Law Review* 601 (and in Richard Ekins (ed), *Modern Challenges to the Rule of Law* (Wellington, LexisNexis, 2010) 129–42), or in part in 'The Lords' Eerie Swansong: A Note on *R (Purdy) v Director of Public Prosecutions*' (2009), http://ssrn.com/abstract=1477281. On the rational weakness albeit right result of *R (Begum) v Denbigh High School Governors* [2006] UKHL 15, [2007] 1 AC 200 (school ban on jilbab lawful to protect rights of other Muslim girls), see Finnis (n 25) 430–41; (2008), http://ssrn.com/abstract=1101522. On the deeply flawed majority judgments in *Nicklinson*, see n 4 above.

such conditions must not thwart "the free expression of the opinion of the people in the choice of the legislature".[66] So far, so good.

But the judgment in *Mathieu-Mohin* has a flaw at its centre. At a crucial stage in its own argumentation towards the conclusion that Article 3, Protocol 1 creates legal rights in individuals, the judgment recounts without criticism the Commission's practice, initiated in the 1960s, of basing that conclusion on the premise that Article 3, Protocol 1 requires universal suffrage.[67] And that premise is quite contrary to the Protocol's *travaux préparatoires* and drafting history—to which, in *this* connection, neither the Commission nor the Court made any reference whatever. Early drafts of Article 3-P1 contained a clause *substantially* identical to the final form of Article 3-P1 with this sole significant difference: the final version speaks of 'free elections at reasonable intervals by secret ballot', whereas the versions prior to August 1950 said 'free elections at reasonable intervals with universal suffrage and secret ballot.' So, all reference to universal suffrage was deliberately omitted from Article 3-P1. For the UK raised objections to including 'universal suffrage'.[68]

---

[66] *Mathieu-Mohin and Clerfayt v Belgium* (1987) (9267/81), 2 March 1987 (GC) [52].

[67] ibid [51]: 'As to the nature of the rights thus enshrined in Article 3 (P1-3), the view taken by the Commission has evolved. From the idea of an "institutional" right to the holding of free elections … the Commission has moved to the concept of "universal suffrage" (see particularly the decision of 6 October 1967 on the admissibility of application no. 2728/66, *X v. the Federal Republic of Germany, Yearbook of the Convention*, vol. 10, p. 338) and then, as a consequence, to the concept of subjective rights of participation—the "right to vote" and the "right to stand for election to the legislature" (see in particular the decision of 30 May 1975 on the admissibility of applications nos. 6745-6746/76, *W, X, Y and Z v. Belgium*, op. cit., vol. 18, p. 244). The Court approves this latter concept.' But the Commission decision of 6 October 1967 simply asserts (without the slightest argument or apparent consideration of relevant materials on the drafting of art 3) by way of preamble, not of substantive decision (and subject to a restriction substantially rejected in *Hirst (No 2)*): 'whereas this undertaking of the Contracting Parties to hold free elections implies the recognition of universal suffrage; whereas, consequently, the complaint by an individual under Article 25 (Art. 25) of the Convention that he was prevented from voting gives rise to an examination by the Commission of the implementation of this obligation; whereas, however, it does not follow that Article 3 (P1-3) accords the right unreservedly to every single individual to take part in elections; whereas, indeed, it is generally recognised that certain limited groups of individuals may be disqualified from voting' (*X v Federal Republic of Germany* (2728/66), 6 October 1967). X was a convicted prisoner denied voting papers while serving his sentence, and the Commission's dismissal of his application as manifestly unfounded is in substance overruled by *Hirst (No 2)*. But the Commission's acceptance of a principle of universal suffrage, as if it were self-evidently implied rather than intentionally omitted after objection, is used to boot-strap that principle into the evolutionary/evolutive doctrine of the Court. Under the cloak of the juridical reason—in this instance diaphanously threadbare—the Court in substance legislates against the states signatory to art 3, Protocol 1.

[68] At the Experts' Committee meeting in Strasbourg on 2 February 1950, the UK representative objected to draft art 3, Protocol 1, especially the reference it then made to 'universal suffrage': 'It is probable that the suffrage is as wide in the United Kingdom as in any other country; yet even in the United Kingdom as in any other country it is inaccurate to speak of the suffrage as "universal". In no State is the right to vote enjoyed even by citizens without qualifications. The qualifications required differ from State to State … And it is our view that the variety of circumstances to be considered may justify the imposition of a variety of qualifications, as a condition of the exercise of suffrage' (www.echr.coe.int/LibraryDocs/Travaux/ECHRTravaux-P1-3-Cour(86)36-BIL1221606.pdf, 8). The response of the other experts is given in the Committee's report on 9 or 10 March 1950: 'The other Committee members, however, were of the opinion that the term "universal suffrage" had a sufficiently clear and precise meaning for the European countries and did not exclude the usual restriction[s] on the right to

The omission of these facts allowed the Grand Chamber in *Hirst* to say (with a spice of equivocation between reporting and endorsing and adopting as a premise): 'Universal suffrage has become the basic principle (see *Mathieu-Mohin* ... para 51 citing *X v Federal Republic of Germany* [1967]).'[69] When *Hirst* was reaffirmed (against the UK) in *Scoppola v Italy* in 2012, the equivocation fell away, the ratcheting was completed, and the past and its promises and reliances were openly left behind:[70] 'In the twenty-first century, the presumption in a democratic

vote' (www.echr.coe.int/LibraryDocs/Travaux/ECHRTravaux-P1-3-Cour(86)36-BIL1221606.pdf, 11. The singular 'restriction' in the English typescript is a typographical error: the French is '*les restrictions de droit de vote qui y sont d'usage*'). And by late August, the article had taken (via other organs of the drafting and negotiating process) the form it now has, essentially identical to that objected to by UK representatives in February and March, but now omitting reference to universal suffrage and warmly welcomed by the UK. Thus, both the omission of the phrase and concept, and the assurances given (and reasonably given) when it was still in the draft combine to show that making universal suffrage the very principle of the article is an act of legislation by the Commission and the Court. But what was agreed by those who drafted art 3-P1 is true of the rest of the Convention too: 'No one expected that the minority would modify their legal systems in order to bring them into line with a Protocol acceptable to the majority. It was thus the task of the experts to find texts ... which represented the minimum standards obtaining in Western Europe as a whole' (AW Brian Simpson, *Human Rights and the End of Empire: Britain and the Genesis of the European Convention* (Oxford, Oxford University Press, 2004) 791 (ch 15, text at fn 121), quoting a formal and, it seems, universally well-received British statement to the meeting of Ministers and Advisers, 30 April to 1 May 1951). Simpson comments that this corresponds to the position taken more generally by the Juridical Section (committee) that launched the drafting of the Convention itself in 1949 and that said of its proposals: 'It is applicable to States possessing different constitutional systems, and which do not have precisely the same criteria in the matter of rights and liberties. In addition, this provisional solution appears as readily acceptable to governments, since *it does not require any modification of the constitutional laws of their countries*' (ibid 661, commentary by the Juridical Section on its draft Convention, 12 July 1949, emphasis added). Again, the motion proposed by the chairman of that Section and 44 others and acted upon if not adopted in August 1949 by the Consultative Assembly was for a Convention: 'to maintain intact the human rights and fundamental freedoms assured by the constitutions, laws, and administrative practices *actually existing in the respective countries at the date of the signature of the convention*' (ibid 671, emphasis added).

[69] *Hirst v United Kingdom (No 2)* (2005) (74025/01), 6 October 2005 (GC) [59]: 'As pointed out by the applicant, the right to vote is not a privilege. In the twenty-first century, the presumption in a democratic State must be in favour of inclusion, as may be illustrated, for example, by the parliamentary history of the United Kingdom and other countries where the franchise was gradually extended over the centuries from select individuals, elite groupings or sections of the population approved of by those in power. Universal suffrage has become the basic principle' (see *Mathieu-Mohin and Clerfayt* (n 66) § 51, citing *X v Germany* (2728/66), Commission decision of 6 October 1967, Collection 25, 38–41).

[70] As the principal dissenting judgment of five judges in *Hirst* says:

> 6. It has been part of the Court's reasoning in some cases in recent years to emphasise its role in developing human rights and the necessity to maintain a dynamic and evolutive approach in its interpretation of the Convention and its Protocols in order to make reforms or improvements possible.... The majority have not made reference to this case-law, but that does not in our opinion change the reality of the situation that their conclusion is in fact based on a 'dynamic and evolutive' interpretation of Article 3 of Protocol No 1.
>
> We do not dispute that it is an important task for the Court to ensure that the rights guaranteed by the Convention system comply with 'present-day conditions', and that accordingly a 'dynamic and evolutive' approach may in certain situations be justified. However, it is essential to bear in mind that the Court is not a legislator and should be careful not to assume legislative functions. An 'evolutive' or 'dynamic' interpretation should have a sufficient basis in changing conditions in the societies of the Contracting States, including an emerging consensus as to the standards to be achieved. We fail to see that this is so in the present case.

State must be in favour of inclusion and universal suffrage has become the basic principle (see *Mathieu-Mohin*, § 51, and *Hirst (No 2)* [GC], § 59).'[71]

A word about the proceedings that culminated in this decision. Shortly before the fiftieth anniversary of the Protocol's adoption and his own birth, John Hirst had applied to the English courts for a declaration that the 1983 statute disqualifying him from voting violated Article 3-P1. He had been imprisoned since 1980 after conviction on indictment for murder; he had pleaded guilty to manslaughter on the grounds of diminished responsibility, a plea accepted 'on the basis of medical evidence that he was a man with a severe personality disorder to such a degree that he was amoral'.[72] So, since mid-1994, he was in detention (under the original sentence of discretionary life imprisonment) on the grounds of risk and dangerousness. The High Court in April 2001, having reviewed the case law in the US, Canada, South Africa and under the ECHR, found that the 1983 Act, disenfranchising everyone in prison pursuant to sentence, is fully compatible with Article 3-P1; its aims are legitimate aims and its criteria fall within the range of 'proportionate means' of pursuing them. After his applications for leave to appeal were refused as hopeless, Hirst applied to the Strasbourg Court, a seven-judge Section Chamber of which in March 2004 unanimously held that the 1983 statute violates Article 3. The 17-judge Grand Chamber upheld this ruling 12:5. The long but weak majority judgment has at least three substantial flaws.

First, its review of proportionality lacks competence and care. The judgment *said*[73] that it accepted the UK's case that disenfranchisement has two legitimate *aims*: (i) to promote civic responsibility by giving expression to the *link* between the exercise of social rights (such as voting) and the acceptance of social duties such as respect for the lawful rights of other citizens—acceptance and respect plainly violated by the commission of an offence serious enough and/or an offender cumulatively culpable enough to be met by imprisonment; and (ii) to enhance the essential retributive rationale of punishment by accompanying the punitive deprivation of liberty of movement with pro rata punitive deprivation of the right to have a say (as elector) in the making of rules of the kind breached

---

Apart from the idea that an 'emerging consensus in the societies' somehow renders an 'interpretation' non-legislative, this is a sound statement.

[71] *Scoppola v Italy (No 3)* (2012) (126/05), 22 May 2012 (GC) [82]; see also [84]: 'However, it is for the Court to determine in the last resort whether the requirements of Article 3 of Protocol No. 1 have been complied with; it has to satisfy itself that the conditions do not curtail the rights in question to such an extent as to impair their very essence and deprive them of their effectiveness; that they are imposed in pursuit of a legitimate aim; and that the means employed are not disproportionate (see *Mathieu-Mohin and Clerfayt*, cited above, § 52). In particular, any conditions imposed must not thwart the free expression of the people in the choice of the legislature—in other words, they must reflect, or not run counter to, the concern to maintain the integrity and effectiveness of an electoral procedure aimed at identifying the will of the people through universal suffrage. Any departure from the principle of universal suffrage risks undermining the democratic validity of the legislature thus elected and the laws it promulgates. Exclusion of any groups or categories of the general population must accordingly be reconcilable with the underlying purposes of Article 3 of Protocol No. 1 (see *Hirst (No. 2)* [GC]...).'

[72] *Hirst (No 2)* (n 69) [12].

[73] ibid [75].

by the convicted prisoner.[74] But when purporting to assess the proportionality of disenfranchisement as a means, the Court paid the ends (these aims) no attention whatever. It silently substituted its own end or aim, which was stated a little earlier in the judgment: the protection of democratic society against 'activities intended to destroy the rights or freedoms set forth in the Convention ... [protections by] restrictions on electoral rights ... imposed on an individual who has, for example, seriously *abused a public position* or whose conduct threatened to *undermine the rule of law or democratic foundations*' (paragraph 71, emphasis added). Having made this tacit substitution, the judgment can effortlessly hold that disenfranchising imprisoned burglars, muggers, rapists and non-terrorist murderers is quite disproportionate to the end dreamed up in place of the statutory ends that the judgment had pretended to accept.

Second, the judgment is viciously circular, helping itself to the conclusion by treating it as a premise. For it takes as an axiom that a sentence of imprisonment involves the forfeiture of no other right save the right to liberty (plus such other exercises of rights as would prejudice prison security).[75] But English law, like the laws of most states, has long defined the consequences of *such* a sentence as including the forfeiture of both personal liberty *and* legal capacity to vote.

Third, the Court's ruling that disenfranchisement of all convicted prisoners during their imprisonment is arbitrary and disproportionate was itself arbitrary. It did nothing more than restate the content of the British disenfranchisement rule in opprobrious terms: 'general, automatic and indiscriminate'. But sentences to prison in the UK are simply not indiscriminate. Indeed, in England, only eight per cent of convictions for crime result in such a sentence.[76] The British disenfranchisement was no more a 'blanket ban' than a rule disenfranchising all persons serving a sentence of (say) 10 years or more. The *link* between the exercise of social rights (such as voting) and the acceptance of social duties (such as respect

---

[74] For example: '37. The minority opinion given by Gonthier J [in *Sauvé (No 2)* [2002] 3 SCR 519; 2002 SCC 68] found that the objectives of the measure were pressing and substantial and based upon a reasonable and rational social or political philosophy. The first objective, that of enhancing civic responsibility and respect for the rule of law, related to the promotion of good citizenship. The social rejection of serious crime reflected a moral line which safeguarded the social contract and the rule of law and bolstered the importance of the nexus between individuals and the community. The "promotion of civic responsibility" might be abstract or symbolic, but symbolic or abstract purposes could be valid of their own accord and should not be downplayed simply for being symbolic. As regards the second objective, that of enhancing the general purposes of the criminal sanction, the measure clearly had a punitive aspect with a retributive function. It was a valid objective for Parliament to develop appropriate sanctions and punishments for serious crime. The disenfranchisement was a civil disability arising from the criminal conviction. It was also proportionate, as the measure was rationally connected to the objectives and carefully tailored to apply to perpetrators of serious crimes. The disenfranchisement of serious criminal offenders served to deliver a message to both the community and the offenders themselves that serious criminal activity would not be tolerated by the community. Society, on this view, could choose to curtail temporarily the availability of the vote to serious criminals to insist that civic responsibility and respect for the rule of law, as goals worthy of pursuit, were prerequisites to democratic participation.'
[75] *Hirst (No 2)* (n 69) [69]–[70].
[76] See *Chester* (n 3) [29] (Lord Sumption).

for the lawful rights of other citizens) is properly *expressed* by the straightforward and very moderate rule that, of convicted violators of the rights of others, those eight per cent or so whose violations are so serious that they are in prison for it cannot exercise the right to vote. The 'link' expresses the reciprocity that leading liberal thinkers such as HLA Hart[77] and John Rawls[78] made the foundation of their account of the obligation to obey the law: those who have benefited from others' compliance with the law should accept the same burden of compliance when the law bears on their own choices: reciprocity of benefits and burdens. The great liberal philosophers Kant and Mill assented to this disqualification of serious criminals, as an implication of the social contract and 'as aid to the great object of giving a moral character to the exercise of the suffrage' (Mill).[79]

So the Grand Chamber's judgment was much inferior in quality to the sort of reasoning on display in some legislative discussions of such matters. The arbitrariness and indefensibility of its ruling that the disenfranchisement was disproportionate because 'blanket'-like in its ban on eight per cent of all convicted offenders was surely noticed and understood, albeit tacitly, by the ECtHR section that in *Frodl* (2010) ruled against Austria's disenfranchisement of prisoners serving sentences of one year or more for an offence involving criminal *intent*. This seven-judge court pulled together some stray elements in the disorderly *Hirst* judgment to find a coherent basis for a finding of disproportionality: all disenfranchisement is disproportionate *unless* it is imposed on a case-by-case basis by a judge and for an offence linked to 'issues relating to elections and democratic institutions'.[80]

This was a gain in integrity of doctrine (though scarcely of juridical adherence to the Convention's text and intent), but it did not last. Confronted with Italy's law (and with the UK's seven-year-long defiance), the Grand Chamber in *Scoppola* in 2012 abandoned the two requirements extracted from *Hirst* in *Frodl*. Italy's main disenfranchising provisions were *legislative* 'blanket bans' on voting by any prisoner serving a sentence of three years or more and a (revocable) lifetime ban on those sentenced to five years or more. Despite the much greater severity of the latter ban, *Scoppola* upheld all of Italy's voting bans. Unlike the UK's, which the Court again explicitly condemned, Italy's were declared to be not 'general, automatic and indiscriminate'.

In *Chester*, with great moderation, Lord Sumption described the ECtHR's position as 'very curious':

[T]he Strasbourg Court has arrived at a very curious position. It has held that it is open to a Convention state to fix a minimum threshold of gravity which warrants the disenfranchisement of a convicted person. It has held that the threshold beyond which he

---

[77] HLA Hart, 'Are There Any Natural Rights?' (1955) 64 *Philosophical Review* 175, 185.
[78] John Rawls, *A Theory of Justice* (Cambridge, MA, Harvard University Press, 1971) 112; and see Finnis (n 14) s 18 at 49–51.
[79] See JS Mill, *Thoughts on Parliamentary Reform* (London, 1859) 20. See the review of Mill's opinion (and of the mishandling of Mill by the majority of the Supreme Court of Canada) in David M Brown, '*Sauvé* and Prisoners' Voting Rights: the Death of the Good Citizen?' (2012) 20 *Supreme Court Law Review* (2d) 297, 319–27.
[80] *Frodl v Austria* (20201/04), 8 April 2010 (First Section).

will be disenfranchised may be fixed by law by reference to the nature of the sentence. It has held that disenfranchisement may be automatic, once a sentence above that threshold has been imposed. But it has also held that even with the wide margin of appreciation allowed to Convention states in this area, it is not permissible for the threshold for disenfranchisement to correspond with the threshold for imprisonment. Wherever the threshold for imprisonment is placed, it seems to have been their view that there must always be some offences which are serious enough to warrant imprisonment but not serious enough to warrant disenfranchisement. Yet the basis of this view is nowhere articulated.[81]

The criticism is illuminating and fully merited. There is no need here to ask whether the Supreme Court erred in judging that Strasbourg's error was not sufficiently egregious[82] to warrant departing from its ruling against the UK in *Scoppola*, or to delve into the *arcana* of the relationship between 'Convention rights' as declared authoritatively by Strasbourg and 'Convention rights' as declared by British courts in some sort of opposition to Strasbourg and perhaps other Convention countries' courts.[83]

For this chapter's concern is not with the place of the Human Rights Act 1998 in the vast engine of contemporary human rights law bearing upon the UK, but with the judicial transformation of the ECHR by a series of juridically unsound decisions. The chapter seeks also to contribute to deliberations about two distinct questions. Is it constitutionally desirable either to remain party to a Convention now so untethered by genuine juridical fidelity to law? And is it desirable to retain any of the novel judicial powers brought into being by the 1998 Act, given that any retention of them is highly likely to perpetuate our own judges' recent practice of exercising legislative power, in the guise of interpretation. So the point for the present purposes is that *Scoppola* is rationally indefensible—inexplicable save as a political compromise foreign to the proper exercise of *judicial* power.[84] A legislature could rationally adopt the UK disenfranchisement *or* the Italian *or* (say) the *via media* Canadian law struck down in *Sauvé (No 2)*. But there is no juridical basis whatever for a court to declare one of these schemes compliant with Article 3-P1 and another non-compliant. Such a declaration, by a court, is irrational (it fails the *Wednesbury* test); the reasons offered[85] are empty.

---

[81] *Chester* (n 3) [135] Lord Sumption (with Lord Hughes, concurring). The paragraph adds that a basis for the view could perhaps have been found by demonstrating that the principles on which UK courts sentence to imprisonment are unsound, but no such demonstration was attempted.

[82] *Chester* (n 3) [27] Lord Mance.

[83] See Finnis (n 4) and the 'timeline' assembled by Lord Wilson (dissenting) in *Moohan v Lord Advocate* [2014] UKSC 67 at [104].

[84] The decision of the majority of the High Court of Australia in *Roach v Commonwealth* [2007] HCA 43—that a UK-type disqualification of all convicted prisoners is unconstitutional, but a disqualification of prisoners serving sentences of three years and above is constitutional—is equally unreasonable *as an exercise of judicial power* (even before one considers the objections made to it by the dissenting Justices on Australian constitutional-historical grounds), but lacks the appearance of merely political compromise.

[85] Most recently by Lord Clarke JSC in *Chester* (n 3) [109].

Judicial 'Living' Instrumentalising of ECHR 101

The Divisional Court in *Hirst*—in the course of an examination that the Strasbourg Grand Chamber would later, unreasonably, say omitted to make a proportionality assessment—quoted the following from the Canadian Court of Appeal judgment in *Sauvé (No 2)* (reversed on appeal):

> Where someone, by committing a serious crime, evinces contempt for our basic societal values, their right to vote may be properly suspended. Indeed, *not* to do so undermines our democratic values.[86]

One could also put it like this. *Allowing* criminals to vote during incarceration under sentence says to each of the law-abiding that *your* vote (nullifiable by the contrary vote of some such prisoner) does not count very much and says to the criminal that his own vivid defiance *of the communal project of self-government* (so far as that project called upon him to respect his victim) leaves his right to continued participation *in that project* unimpaired, *entirely* unimpaired. It says to him that he can defy the rules, even grossly or repeatedly, and treat his victim(s) and his fellow citizens as unequals, but *go on* claiming equality with them in terms of rights of participation in communal self-government, without even temporary interruption. Correspondingly, disqualification of such criminals points out to them their contempt for reciprocity and, in doing so, gives effect to a reciprocity entirely fundamental to respect for law, and particularly to adjudication and judicial awards of compensation, restitution and punishment. True, a legislature responsible for the entire common good in all its complexity might nonetheless properly find reason, in some circumstances, to temper these demands of reciprocity and limit the disqualification by some 'via media'. But the Grand Chamber's unwillingness even to envisage and acknowledge the relevance of the fundamental conception of reciprocity *across time*—one could also call it proportionality—is rationally inexplicable. (However, it fits with the Court's displacement of judicial method by its own legislative activities.) The unwillingness seems to me to manifest both a deep-going political complacency that could reasonably be called decadent, and a judicial indifference to the separation of powers inherent in entrusting self-government primarily to an elected legislature. It gives the political philosophy and preferences of unelected, unaccountable and philosophically maladroit[87]

---

[86] *Sauvé v Canada (No 2)* [2000] 2CF 117 [139]; *Hirst v Attorney-General* [2001] EWHC Admin 239 [37] (emphasis added).

[87] The majority judgment of the Supreme Court of Canada in *Sauvé (No 2)*, treated with respect in *Hirst (No 2)*, exemplifies this strikingly: '[31] In a democracy such as ours ... delegation from voters to legislators gives the law its legitimacy or force. Correlatively, the obligation to obey the law flows from the fact that the law is made by and on behalf of the citizens. In sum, *the legitimacy of the law and the obligation to obey the law flow directly from the right of every citizen to vote*. As a practical matter, we require all within our country's boundaries to obey its laws, whether or not they vote. But this does not negate *the vital symbolic, theoretical and practical connection between having a voice in making the law and being obliged to obey it. This connection, inherited from social contract theory and enshrined in the Charter*, stands at the heart of our system of constitutional democracy ... [32] ... The "educative message" that the government purports to send by disenfranchising inmates is both anti-democratic and internally self-contradictory. *Denying a citizen the right to vote denies the basis of democratic legitimacy. It says that delegates elected by the citizens can then bar those very citizens, or a portion of them, from*

judges a reach and sway that have no adequate support in the justice, law and constitutional arrangements entrusted to their administration.

In sum, the judicial disarray in Strasbourg, the unprincipled to-ing and fro-ing between the pre-*Hirst* ECHR (Commission) jurisprudence, then *Hirst*, then *Frodl* and then *Scoppola* shows adjudication collapsing into legislation by judges. Such paradigmatically legislative action as drawing—for the whole nation—a line between disenfranchising eight per cent of convicted criminals—unlawful!—and disenfranchising (say) five per cent of them—lawful!—or between the whole class of one-year sentences and the whole class of three-year sentences is the kind of exercise that ought to be repudiated in principle by our judges when the warrant for the line-drawing is no more than the Convention obligation to hold 'free elections'.[88]

V. UNREASONABLY EXTENDING ARTICLE 3 AS AN ABSOLUTE: *SOERING, SAADI* AND *HIRSI JAMAA*

Article 3 ECHR says simply 'No one shall be subjected to torture or to inhuman or degrading treatment', and there can be no doubt that its original public meaning

---

participating in future elections ... [33] ... the history of democracy is the history of progressive enfranchisement. The universal franchise has become, at this point in time, an essential part of democracy. From the notion that only a few meritorious people could vote (expressed in terms like class, property and gender), there gradually evolved the modern precept that all citizens are entitled to vote as members of a self-governing citizenry. ... *The disenfranchisement of inmates takes us backwards in time and retrenches our democratic entitlements.*' Thus, a proportionality analysis purporting to measure a rational connection between legislative aims purportedly accepted as legitimate and enacted means (disqualification of imprisoned convicts with sentences of two years or more) not only entails the impossibility of legitimately disenfranchising any imprisoned criminal, however gross or treasonable or subversive of elections. The majority's analysis also employed premises from a home-made grand political-philosophical theory of singular ineptness. For their theory that your obligation to obey the law depends on your having the right to vote is absurd. It entails that convicted prisoners lawfully disenfranchised in mature democracies such as the UK or Italy have no obligation to comply with the law. (The absurdity is half-recognized by the inconclusive sentence half-conceding that 'as a practical matter', non-citizens have the obligation to obey the law.) The only relevant proposition that could be defended is this: your obligation to comply with the law is impaired (though still not by any means dissolved) if your participation in government is *unjustly* denied—a proposition of no use to the majority, since what they are here trying to *show* is that *this* denial is unjust (is contrary to acknowledged rights). The reliance, finally, on 'social contract theory', implausibly asserted to have been adopted into the Canadian constitutional order, ignores the oft-demonstrated disqualifying weaknesses of every such theory, save those versions that limit themselves to observing the justice of reciprocity, of relating benefits to burdens, and of regulating many present rights by reference inter alia to past performance of related obligations—those versions, in other words, that lend support to the disenfranchisement of criminals.

[88] There is hereabouts no constitutional problem of the kind that has sometimes made plausible certain line-drawing judicial interventions, such as the problem of apportioning electoral boundaries by a legislature presumptively motivated by self-interest to leave them malapportioned—the 'democracy and distrust' or democratic process theory elaborated by John Hart Ely. Nor is there in Britain or Europe or South Africa or Canada any suggestion that either the electoral or the criminal justice system is biased or manipulated against racial or other discrete and insular minorities in need of protection from legislative or popular majorities.

was and is that it absolutely, ie, exceptionlessly, indefeasibly, prohibits every choice to subject someone to torture or to inhuman or degrading treatment—every choice to do or omit something *in order that* someone be subjected to some such treatment. That meaning, with that exceptionless force, is confirmed by Article 15(2)'s stipulation that Article 3 (like Articles 2, 4(1) and 7) cannot be derogated from on the ground that the exigencies of war or public emergency, even emergency threatening the life of the nation, call for it to be set aside.[89]

The Strasbourg Court has used Article 3 ECHR to erect a vast system of compulsory political and non-political asylum.[90] In doing so, it has: (i) defied (or been unconscious of) the logic of absolute norms; and (ii) defied the intentions of the signatories of the Convention, intentions very deliberately formed (as we shall see) and plainly indicated in the nearly contemporaneous adoption of Article 33 of the UN Convention on the Status of Refugees.

A. *The logic of norms* that absolutely exclude from deliberation and choice any and every act (or deliberate omission) of a certain type has been explored by philosophers. Both scholars who hold and scholars who deny that there are some absolute moral norms (picking out and excluding from deliberation such types of act) can agree that—if there are any such norms—such a norm's specification of the type of act it purports to exceptionlessly exclude must be *by reference to the intentions* (object(s), purpose(s)) of, with and/or for the sake of which the conduct or behaviour involved in the act is chosen (and carried out).[91] In other words, the purposes of the conduct or behaviour, however benevolent and beneficial their further ends are, must not include *a purpose (intention, object) of engaging in or bringing about, whether as a means or an end*, an excluded state of affairs or activity.[92]

---

[89] 1. In time of war or other public emergency threatening the life of the nation any High Contracting Party may take measures derogating from its obligations under this Convention to the extent strictly required by the exigencies of the situation…
2. No derogation from Article …3… shall be made under this provision.

[90] This regime is not the only vast doctrinal structure erected by the Court on the back of art 3 and 'living instrument' methodology. A concertina-like range of state duties to investigate serious crimes or even civil wrongs (whether committed by public officials or not) and to compensate persons for failures to carry out these duties sufficiently is now growing alongside and (despite judicial protestations) in competition with classic principles of tort: see the discussion of authorities and doctrine in *Commissioner of Police of the Metropolis v DSD* [2015] EWCA Civ 646, especially [44]–[46], [50] (Dyson MR for the Court). But the ECtHR accepts that these affirmative (positive) art 3 duties (even if non-derogable under art 15) are *not* absolute (but rather are circumstance-relative in strength), whereas its asylum regime, discussed below, is constructed largely on the basis of art 3's negative and therefore exceptionless ('absolute') obligations.

[91] Some philosophers argue that the specification could be by reference to *actions* as opposed to omissions. But this goes against the entire movement of modern criminal law, and the sense of ethical responsibility extending to deliberate omissions intended to result in effects which the chooser has some responsibility and capacity to avert (parent deliberately starving child; co-pilot deliberately omitting to open cockpit door to allow captain to return and save aircraft etc).

[92] Torture, as defined in the UN Convention against Torture or Other Cruel, Degrading or Inhuman Treatment (1984), exemplifies such an act-specification in terms of object, ie, of what is *intended/purposed as a means*: 'For the purposes of this Convention, the term "torture" means any act by which severe pain or suffering, whether physical or mental, is *intentionally inflicted on a person for such*

In the case of the moral and legal absolute against torture, it is obvious why reference to intention/purpose is essential to the definition of the type(s) of act exceptionlessly excluded by the norm: no one doubts that it is legitimate for anyone, including public officials, to resort to means of legitimate defence of self or others against actual ongoing attack, even though those means are in many cases certain to cause agonisingly severe pain and suffering. Normally, means of legitimate defence are selected *without* purpose of inflicting such pain, which remains entirely in the domain of side-effects.[93]

The basis of the rational necessity is this. If the types of states of affairs *exceptionlessly* excluded by the norm from choice (that is, absolutely prohibited as options) extended beyond what is chosen-as-intended (that is, chosen as a means) and included *unintended* effects of the chosen behaviour—call them side-effects—the norm would necessarily entail contradictory directives. For, even when restricted to the foreseeable or even the foreseeably probable, the side-effects caused by choosing *not* to make and carry out an option because it is of an exceptionlessly excluded/prohibited type—and therefore choosing some alternative option—may well include states of affairs of the very kind that (on this extended, cause-not-intention understanding of the exceptionless norm) *it is exceptionlessly prohibited to cause (even as only a side-effect)*. So it would inevitably sometimes be impossible to comply with such a directive, a directive *both* to abstain from a certain type of act *and* to make no choice which results (as a side-effect) either in a real risk that an act of that type *will* be performed by others, and/or in a real risk that persons will by some other causality suffer bad consequences of the kind that the norm seeks to exclude. An ethics including *such* absolutes would be self-contradictory and thus irrational. The Strasbourg Court's doctrine that Article 3 is absolute, and

---

purposes as obtaining from him or a third person information or a confession, punishing him for an act he or a third person has committed or is suspected of having committed, or intimidating or coercing him or a third person, or for any reason based on discrimination of any kind, when such pain or suffering is inflicted by or at the instigation of or with the consent or acquiescence of a public official or other person acting in an official capacity.' Note that 'intentionally', by itself, without the 'for such purposes as', would not necessarily connote *intent* or *purpose*, since in idiomatic English, it is contrasted with 'unintentionally', which connotes accident or mistake or lack of foresight. See John Finnis, *Intention and Identity: Collected Essays Volume II* (Oxford, Oxford University Press, 2011) at 142, 184, 190.

[93] But, as even so stern an upholder of the absolute norm against torture as Jeremy Waldron has told me he accepts, it is legitimate to cause an unjust aggressor pain *as a means* of getting him to drop his weapon or relax his strangling grip on the innocent; his wrongful attack entails a kind of *pro tanto* forfeiture of his right to be immune from such a purpose. The forfeiture does not, I think, go wider, or qualify the absoluteness of the norm as stated (though it calls for a tight definition of 'for a purpose of coercing'). But this underlines the essentiality of the intention/purpose element in the definition of the exceptionlessly excluded act-type and invalidates Waldron's general proposition that any attempt to seek a precise practical definition of torture is corrupt, a proposition he makes plausible partly by oscillating between 'torture' and 'deliberate infliction of severe pain *for purposes of interrogation*'. See Jeremy Waldron, 'Torture, Suicide and *Determinatio*'(2010) 55 *American Journal of Jurisprudence* 1, 19–29; for some counter-commentary, see Finnis, 'Invoking the Principle of Legality '(n 65) fns 5 and 15 (and 20 and 29).

absolutely prohibits *causing* a real risk of conduct[94] or effects[95] of a kind referred to in the article, entails precisely this sort of self-contradiction.[96]

A rational ethics does include some moral absolutes, exceptionlessly excluding some types of action defined by their precise intention (object, purpose etc), and treats the causing of the foreseeable side-effects of choices (to act or omit/forbear) as a matter of moral responsibility governed by *non-absolute* moral norms (of fairness, fidelity to commitments etc): in the zone of side-effects, the justice of the acting person's *reasons for* doing what foreseeably causes these side-effects (eg, in order to protect the rights of others) will be of great justificatory significance, even though it is incapable of justifying *intending* to cause such effects.

The rationality deficit of absolute norms defined by causation rather than intention can be restated without reference to issues of contradiction. Once the scope of a norm is conceived as prohibiting me not only from causing *intended* effects of kind X, but also from causing (or 'direct' or 'foreseeable' causing) *side-effects* (*un*-intended effects) of kind X *even in cases where I in no way intend any such effects*, it is irrational (especially in the latter kind of case) to refuse to compare the side-effects of kind X with (i) the intended effects caused by the same option, and/or with (ii) the side-effects (whether of kind X or of other bad kinds) caused by not choosing that option but some alternative (including inaction). For example, if the scope of Article 2 ECHR is conceived as prohibiting exceptionlessly not only my intentionally depriving P of his life but also my doing anything that *foreseeably causes* a real risk that someone will be deprived of his life, it would be irrational (especially in any case where I have no intent to kill) to treat an option's *causing that risk* to person P as settling the norm's application *without first comparing* that risk to P with both (i) the intended effect of (say) saving Q and R from death and/or torture, and/or (ii) the side-effects of choosing (for the sake of P) not to save Q and R, namely the real risk (or fact) of Q and R suffering death.

To be more concrete: even if preventing P from entering a country or domain causes by side-effect a real risk that he will be killed outside by his enemies, it is nonetheless irrational not to compare with that risk the real risk that if he *is* allowed to enter, *he* will kill *his* enemies Q, R and S. Or again, judges choosing to impose a sentence of imprisonment are well aware that doing so imposes on the convict a real risk of abusive, degrading treatment (eg, homosexual rape), but letting the convict go free is to create a real risk that he will commit offences which his fellow-citizen victims would otherwise have been spared; thus, sentencing to imprisonment is not ruled out by an absolute norm against subjecting anyone to

---

[94] eg, *Chahal v UK* (22414/93), 15 November 1996 (GC), text at nn 106–07 below.
[95] eg, *D v UK* (30240/96) 2 May 1997 (Chamber), and n 98 below.
[96] Robert D Anderson, 'The Moral Permissibility of Accepting Bad Side Effects' (2009) 83 *American Catholic Philosophical Quarterly* 255, 262–63 shows this, with some reference to the attempt by early Jainist philosophy or religion to abstain from any and every causing of harm. On the points made in this paragraph, see generally John Finnis, *Fundamentals of Ethics* (Oxford, Oxford University Press, 1983) 112–20; John Finnis, *Moral Absolutes* (Washington DC, CUA Press, 1991) 67–73; GEM Anscombe, *Ethics, Religion, and Politics* (Oxford, Blackwell, 1981) 58.

106   *John Finnis*

degrading treatment (Article 3 ECHR), although it would be unjust not to make some effort to reduce the risk of abuse.

The unilateral prioritising of one sort of side-effect is indeed doubly or triply unreasonable. For the Court, compounding its inattention to the logic of moral absolutes, has committed the positive fallacy of treating Article 3's *force* (as exceptionless) as grounds for measuring its *scope*. And it has made the fallacy doubly fallacious[97] by inferring that this scope must, precisely by reason of the article's force, be expansive.[98]

B. *The Court's descent*: at first, when the Court was launching its 'living instrument' extension of Article 3 in *Soering* (1989),[99] its decision (in substance if not in all its articulations) remained at least mainly or in large part within, and respectful of, the rational requirements of an exceptionless norm. For that decision prohibited the UK from *extraditing* Soering—surrendering him to a foreign state[100] *so*

---

[97] The fallacious inference is made and rhetorically enforced, but not vindicated, in Waldron (n 93); the article never confronts the serious reasons of justice that can make it reasonable to cause and accept side-effects of the kind that it is impermissible to intend to cause—reasonable, that is to say, to treat the *absolute* prohibition as no wider than it rationally must be.

[98] Thus, *D v UK* (n 95) [49]: 'To limit the application of Article 3 (art. 3) [to cases where the source of the risk of proscribed treatment in the receiving country stems from factors which [can] engage either directly or indirectly the responsibility of the public authorities of that country, or which, taken alone, [...] in themselves infringe the standards of that Article (art. 3)] would be to *undermine the absolute character* of its protection' (emphasis added). The criminal deportee in that case (having been earlier deported for crime had promptly returned solely to commit serious crimes) was dying of AIDS, despite the extensive and expensive treatment he was receiving (without charge to him) from UK government medical agencies, and if returned to his home country St Kitts would die in distressing circumstances simply because of that country's lack of advanced medical facilities and his own lack of family there. The judgment is further confused in that its eventual holding is not that there would be 'proscribed treatment in the receiving country', but instead that the UK's act of deportation itself would be the (only) proscribed treatment. The subsequent course of decisions essentially confines *D v UK* to persons about to die: see *N v Home Secretary* [2005] 2 AC 296; [2005] UKHL 31 and the 14:3 decision in the same case, *N v UK* (26565/05), 27 May 2008 (GC), upholding *D v UK*, but limiting it lest its application of art 3 'place too great a burden on the Contracting States' ([44]), given that 'inherent in the whole of the Convention is a search for a fair balance between the demands of the general interest of the community and the requirements of the protection of the individual's fundamental rights' ([44]). The dissenting minority in *N v UK* correctly observed ([7]) that these dicta are incompatible with the absolutist interpretation of art 3 adopted in *Soering, Chahal* and *Saadi*, and were willing to impose limitless burdens on states of providing expensive medical care to anyone indigent from an indigent country who can set foot in a Convention state—a burden that (in light of *Hirsi Jamaa*) would extend to a right to be permitted to set foot and enter to obtain such treatment. The minority's tacit acknowledgment of the rational vulnerability of their own position—and thus of art 3 jurisprudence (of liability for side-effects) as a whole—is to be found in their implausible intimations (see [8]) that there is no likelihood that any more than a few (or 'rather few') will ever claim these rights and that the burden on states is only 'budgetary'. Note that in *N v UK*, the majority (unlike the minority) seem to take some care not to adopt the *D v UK*, reasoning that art 3's scope can be inferred from—and must be wide because of—its absolute character, preferring instead to infer its width (as extending to *D*-like situations) from 'the Article's fundamental importance in the Convention system'. (Whether or not that is in the last analysis a distinction without a difference, this 'importance' premise is a *petitio principii*; the question is whether the side-effects it forbids states to cause are more important than the side-effects of states respecting this prohibition.)

[99] *Soering v UK* (14038/88), 7 July 1989 (Plenary) [102].

[100] Thus, the key interpretative sentences in *Soering*, ibid [88]: 'were a Contracting State *knowingly to surrender a fugitive to another State where there were substantial grounds for believing that he would be*

that he *would* be subjected to the legal processes and process-based treatment of the requesting state (treatment which in this case the Court declared to be inhuman insofar as it conditionally included the purpose of sentencing Soering to death, thus subjecting Soering to conditions—death-row delays—that the Court judged inhuman treatment). Thus, whatever the hopes and desires of UK officials involved in the extradition, the purposes/intentions of the UK tracked those of the US and included the conditional intent that he be punished in any manner authorised in the US—which includes a manner that the Court judged (and ordered the UK to regard as) inhuman. This conjunction or overlapping of intentions/purposes we can describe as *complicity* of the UK in the inhuman US treatment, a kind of complicity that involves mens rea and no element of 'strict' liability.

But the next relevant extension of Article 3, in *Cruz Varas* (1991),[101] concerned expulsion, not extradition. Ignoring the consequent difference in the intentionality of the removing state, the plenary Strasbourg Court held that Article 3 applied equally to expulsion, since this too was 'action which has as a direct consequence the exposure of an individual to proscribed ill-treatment'.[102] The Court in *Soering* had put in place this broad formulation, in which causality ('direct consequence') silently replaces complicity in the proper sense, and the Court in *Cruz Varas* takes it up and runs with it, leaving all trace of complicity behind. As is usual if not universal in ECtHR jurisprudence, profound shifts of doctrine are made without acknowledgement of their significance,[103] whether in logic or in consequences for the future of states, their governments or their peoples.

---

in danger of being subjected to torture, however heinous the crime allegedly committed. Extradition in such circumstances, while not explicitly referred to in the brief and general wording of Article 3 (art. 3), would plainly be contrary to the *spirit and intendment* of the Article, and in the Court's view this inherent obligation not to extradite also extends to cases in which the fugitive would be faced in the receiving State by a real risk of exposure to inhuman or degrading treatment or punishment proscribed by that Article (art. 3)' (emphases added). By appealing to the 'spirit and intendment' of art 3 rather than to 'ordinary meaning' as required by the Vienna Convention on the Law of Treaties, the Court implicitly concedes that it is departing from the Convention as intended and meant by its signatories. The eccentric phrase 'spirit and intendment' is taken from English charity law; before the Charities Act 2006 codified what counts as a 'charitable purpose', the test was whether a purpose was within 'the spirit and intendment' of the preamble to a statute of 1601, and the flexibility with which the courts deployed the phrase over the centuries is captured by the codifying provision (s 2(2) with 2(4)), which lists 12 classes of purpose and then a thirteenth: 'any purpose that may reasonably be regarded as analogous to, or within the spirit of,' a purpose falling within' those 12 classes; and a fourteenth: 'any purpose that may reasonably be regarded as *analogous to, or within the spirit of*, a purpose that has been recognized under charity law as falling within' any of the classes referred to.

[101] *Cruz Varas v Sweden* (15576/89), 20 March 1991 (Plenary).

[102] ibid [69], citing *Soering* (n 99) [91]. On the facts, the 18:1 majority held that this expulsion did not expose Cruz Varas to a real risk of torture etc in Chile and so did not violate art 3. The nine judges who dissented on a more procedural aspect of the case alleged that *Soering* itself extended to 'extradition and expulsion' and that: 'It cannot be otherwise, since the Convention provides for a real and effective protection of human rights for all persons present in the member State; their governments cannot be permitted to expose such persons to serious violations of human rights in other countries.' Here 'expose' equivocates between intention and effect, to the extent that it refers to side-effects, the passage is a *petitio principii*.

[103] '70. Although the present case concerns expulsion as opposed to a decision to extradite, the Court considers that the above principle also applies to expulsion decisions and a fortiori to cases of actual expulsion.'

But deprived of the savour of complicity, the extension of Article 3 initiated in *Soering* is rationally defenceless against the UK's principal argument in that case (an argument the Court buries in its fleeting report of six UK arguments and then evades): 'it would be straining the language of Article 3 (art. 3) intolerably to hold that by surrendering a fugitive criminal the extraditing State has "subjected" him to any treatment or punishment that he will receive following conviction and sentence in the receiving State'.[104] The linguistic strain is tolerable when there is *complicity*—intent to assist, say, torture, or intention's functional equivalent, recklessness: knowledge of probability along with an unwarrantable ('reckless') inattention to the reasons for trying to avert the evil or to avoid making it possible. But when complicity is replaced by efforts to *avert* an evil considered to be possible (really possible) rather than probable and the action that happens to have the side-effect of making (as one necessary causal condition among others) that evil possible is motivated only by urgent concern to protect the rights of citizens, the now-ignored UK point shows its truth. It is impossible to say that 'the ordinary meaning to be given to the words ['to subject to torture...'] in their context'[105] extends to a case where the expelling state has no complicity, but, rather, urgent rights-based reasons for expulsion. For instance, it would be unreasonable to say that (to adapt the facts in *Chahal*)[106] the *UK subjected Chahal to torture or ill-treatment contrary to Article 3* if, in the event and in line with the assurances extracted by the UK from India, he was left unmolested by India after his expulsion from the UK and return to India, and ridiculous to say so if, in the event, he was unexpectedly welcomed by a new government with garlands and honour; however, in cases where there is no complicity, the Court's doctrine entails these absurdities.

For *Chahal* (1996) definitively advanced beyond grounding the sending state's Aricle 3 liability on its *complicity* in the torturous or inhuman intentions of the receiving state. The UK actively and (it seems) bona fide sought (and received) assurances and re-assurances that Chahal 'would have no reason to expect to suffer mistreatment of any kind at the hands of the Indian authorities';[107] for the UK wished to deport him not in order to advance any purpose of India, but exclusively to protect the UK's own citizens (and others in the UK) from bad consequences (including human rights violations) really possible at the hands of Chahal were he not deported. The extreme implications of the *Chahal* decision became explicit in *Saadi v Italy* (2008).

In *Saadi*, the UK intervened to argue (in effect)[108] that where a removing state: (1) had no intentions of the kind prohibited by Article 3; and (2) had no complicity in any intentions of that kind on the part of the receiving or any other state, and (3) had sought and obtained assurances from the receiving state that it too had

---

[104] *Soering* (n 99) [83].
[105] Vienna Convention on the Law of Treaties, art 31(1).
[106] *Chahal* (n 94).
[107] ibid [35].
[108] See *Saadi v United Kingdom* (2008) (13229/03), 29 January 2008 (GC) [119]–[122].

no such intentions and forbad them, and (4) was proposing to remove the alien national of the receiving state exclusively to protect the rights of persons in the removing state, rights—especially the right to life under Article 2—that were at real risk from the presence of the deportee, then (5) its removal of him need be no violation of Article 3. The UK argument was, in substance, that once intention and complicity (intention or recklessness) are excluded, there rationally remains only a comparison of risks of bad consequences of the kind which Article 3 seeks to avert; outside the zone of intention (complicity), the reach and force of Article 3 cannot be absolute, but rationally must be relative to comparative risks in the various possible circumstances. This sound argument was brushed aside or overlooked by the Strasbourg Court in a judgment notable for its viciously circular refusal to engage with the UK argument that Article 3 cannot rationally be absolute across its full reach, the Court instead referring repetitiously[109] to the 'absolute nature of Article 3'.[110]

But *that* absoluteness is part of the problem, not of the solution. Call the following the problem or the objection:

> [T]he interpretation summed up in the mantra 'art. 3 is absolute' entails contradiction in *at least* any circumstances where choosing non-removal imposes on citizens of the would-be removing state real risks of inhuman treatment or death broadly equivalent to or greater than the risks of inhuman treatment imposed on the persons removed because of the bad dispositions of official or other[111] persons in the receiving state (or some eventual receiving state).

The force of the objection and the self-imposed incapacity of the Court to respond to it are illustrated in exemplary fashion in *Hirsi Jamaa v Italy* (2012).[112]

On 6 May 2009, pursuant to an agreement with the then effective government of Libya, Italy intercepted three vessels on the Mediterranean high seas 35 miles south of the Italian island of Lampedusa. On board were some 230[113] Somalis and Eritreans seeking to reach the Italian coast; all were taken by Italian ships back to Libya. Subsequently, some of the 24 applicants (from among the 230 shipped back to Libya) were granted refugee status either by the UN or the Italian authorities.

---

[109] *Chahal* (n 94) [127], [137], [138], [140].

[110] ibid [138]: 'Accordingly, the Court cannot accept the argument of the United Kingdom Government, supported by the [Italian] Government, that a distinction must be drawn under Article 3 between treatment inflicted directly by a signatory State and treatment that might be inflicted by the authorities of another State, and that protection against this latter form of ill-treatment should be weighed against the interests of the community as a whole ... Since protection against the treatment prohibited by Article 3 is absolute, that provision imposes an obligation not to extradite or expel any person who, in the receiving country, would run the real risk of being subjected to such treatment.'

[111] 'Owing to the absolute character of the right guaranteed, the Court does not rule out the possibility that Article 3 of the Convention may also apply where the danger emanates from persons or groups of persons who are not public officials' (*Hirsi Jamaa v Italy* (27765/09), 23 February 2012 (GC) [120]). The phrase 'does not rule out the possibility' is deceptive; provided the danger (risk) is real and the government unable to obviate it, the Court clearly regards art 3 as applicable: ibid [120]. And its case law illustrates this abundantly: start the list with *D v UK* (n 95).

[112] *Hirsi Jamaa* (ibid) (GC).

[113] See ibid [33].

The Strasbourg Grand Chamber in February 2012 unanimously held that Italy's actions violated not only Protocol 4 (prohibiting 'collective expulsion of aliens'), but also, and primarily, Article 3 as interpreted in *Soering, Chahal* and *Saadi*, because of the real risk that Libya would arbitrarily (and against the terms of its agreement with Italy) repatriate the applicants to countries where they faced a real risk of inhuman treatment. The judgment held—but as inconspicuously as could be contrived—and the concurring judgment of Judge Pinto de Albuqueque extensively emphasised that Article 3 is violated by *any exercise of state A's jurisdiction* that prevents a would-be immigrant *from gaining entry to state A* and has the effect—however contrary to state A's intentions and despite its bona fide precautionary measures—that he is exposed to some real risk of inhuman treatment, if not by state B (the receiving state, or the state from which he set out to gain entry to A), then by a subsequent receiving state C or D ... or by persons within state C or D ...

In reflecting on this seminal judgment for the purposes of this chapter, it is right to start with the law posited by, and in, the Convention as established by the signatory states in November 1950.

C. *The intention of the signatory states* was, unquestionably, that their Convention should contain *no* right to asylum,[114] not even a right as restricted as had appeared in the Universal Declaration of Human Rights 1948.[115] When the ECHR was finalised, the UN's Geneva Convention relating to the Status of Refugees had begun, 11 months earlier, to take concrete shape. And even *that* convention does not recognise or establish a right to asylum, or regulate the granting of asylum;[116] it deals with the status of those refugees granted asylum (and to some extent with other refugee non-nationals who have been permitted to be present in the territory of a state).[117] The states that created the ECHR and the Refugee Convention fully recognised the humanitarian case for asylum and indeed the reasonable *moral* claims in justice of many who might seek asylum. But they judged it reasonable and right to neither recognise nor create such a *right*, but instead to leave states legally free to decide how far to live up to humanitarian and moral ideals or responsibilities by granting asylum in specific cases (individual or group). They

---

[114] See, eg, Simpson (n 68) 672, 688, 690, 811.

[115] 'Article 14(1) Everyone has the right to seek and to enjoy in other countries asylum from persecution. (2) This right may not be invoked in the case of prosecutions genuinely arising from non-political crimes or from acts contrary to the purposes and principles of the United Nations.' Simpson (n 68) 451–52 shows that art 14(1) was, at the urging of the UK, watered down so as to eliminate the statement of a right to be *granted* asylum and/or of right of *admission* to a country.

[116] Paul Weis, *The Refugee Convention 1951: The Travaux Préparatoires Analyzed with a Commentary by Dr Paul Weis* (Refugee Studies Programme, University of Oxford, and Cambridge Research Centre for International Law, International Documents Series, nd, c 1994: www.unhcr.org/4ca34be29.pdf), text after fn 59: 'the Convention itself does not regulate asylum'.

[117] As drafted and adopted in 1951, it applied only to persons fleeing events prior to 1951, a temporal restriction removed by Protocol in 1967.

completely rejected the absolutist view strongly urged upon them by the Drafting Committee.[118]

As the preceding pages have displayed in outline, the Strasbourg Court, pursuant to its 'living instrument' doctrine, has set about *creating* wide rights of asylum, utilising Article 3, but crabwise, step by step, rarely if ever revealing or foreshadowing its next step, and never articulating the implications and probable consequences of the step it is taking at each stage. Its law-making has been, as usual, far removed from rational legislative debate. As far as one can tell from the Court's judgments, even the parties to cases have not explored the matters of history and likely consequence that would reasonably be prominent in a legislative debate.[119]

The decisive step over the threshold, taken in *Hirsi Jamaa*, is in plain though unadmitted defiance of the *travaux préparatoires* relating to the meaning of *refouler/refoulement* in the Refugee Convention 1951. In immediate and direct response to the UK representative's observation—in line with prior Swiss, French, German, Italian and Swedish observations—that he assumed 'refoulement' had no wider meaning than 'return', the President of the meeting of Plenipotentiaries (11 July 1951) proposed, and all states agreed, that the French word be inserted in parentheses wherever the English word appeared. Certainly a more perspicuous means of making the firmly requested clarification would have been, instead, to insert 'return' in parentheses wherever the French word appeared. But in the context of the discussion,[120] the intention—and therefore the meaning—of the insertion actually made was then entirely clear to any reasonable observer, and

---

[118] Weis (n 116) text at fns 647–50:

> *The Drafting Committee* proposed the following text: 'No Contracting State shall expel or return, in any manner whatsoever, a refugee to the frontiers of territories where his life or freedom would be threatened on account of his race, religion, nationality or political opinion.' Article 28 was adopted. It read:
>
> 'No Contracting State shall expel or return a refugee in any manner whatsoever to the frontiers of territories where his life or freedom would be threatened on account of his race, religion, nationality or political opinion.'
>
> The Committee made the following comment: While some question was raised as to the possibility of exceptions to Article 28, the Committee felt strongly that the principle here expressed was fundamental and that it should not be impaired.

That is, it should be exceptionless, ie, absolute; see likewise Guy S Goodwin-Gill, *Convention relating to the Status of Refugees* (Audiovisual Library of International Law, 2008), Introductory Note, 'Non-refoulement', http://legal.un.org/avl/ha/prsr/prsr.html, accessed 14 October 2015. Article 28 was renumbered 33(1) and its exceptionlessness was deliberately impaired by art 33(2).

[119] But the UK submissions in *Saadi* observed that the doctrine adopted in *Chahal* 'was in contradiction with the intentions of the original signatories of the Convention' ([122]). The judgment does not contest this and tacitly concedes it in its brief remark ([138]) on art 33 of the Refugee Convention.

[120] On 11 July 1951 (Weis (n 116) 239–40):

> The Netherlands representative recalled that at the first reading the Swiss representative had expressed the opinion that the word 'expulsion' related to a refugee already admitted into a country, whereas *the word 'return' ('refoulement') related to a refugee already within the territory but not yet resident there. According to that interpretation, Article 28* [which had subsequently become art 33] *would not have involved any obligation in the possible case of mass migration across frontiers or of*

112 John Finnis

so is entirely clear to an informed observer now:[121] to limit the term *refouler/refoulement* so that it extended only to removing from within, and not to refusal

> *attempted mass migration.* He wished to revert to that point, because the Netherlands Government attached very great importance to the scope of the provision now contained in Article 33. The Netherlands could *not accept any legal obligation in respect of large groups of refugees seeking access to its territory.*
>
> At the first reading, the representatives of Belgium, the Federal Republic of Germany, Italy, Netherlands, and Sweden had supported the Swiss interpretation. From conversations he had had since with other representatives, he had gathered that the *general consensus of opinion was in favour of the Swiss interpretation.* In order to dispel any possible ambiguity and to reassure his Government, he wished to have it placed on record that the Conference was in agreement with the interpretation, that *the possibility of mass migration across frontiers or of attempted mass migrations was not covered by Article 33.*
>
> There being no objection, the President ruled that the interpretation given by the Netherlands representative should be placed on record.
>
> *The UK representative remarked that the Style Committee had considered that the word 'return' was the nearest equivalent in English to the French term 'refoulement'. He assumed that the word 'return' as used in the English text had no wider meaning.*
>
> The President suggested that in accordance with the practice followed in previous Conventions, the French word 'refoulement' ('refouler' in verbal use) should be included in brackets and between inverted commas after the English word 'return' wherever the latter occurred in the text.
>
> He further suggested that the French text of paragraph 1 should refer to refugees in the singular. .....
>
> The two suggestions made by the President were adopted unanimously.

The record (at 235) of the Swiss intervention, earlier that day, wholly confirms the accuracy of the Dutch observations and the meaning of the UK's final intervention:

> The Swiss representative said the Swiss Federal Government saw no reason why Article 28 should not be adopted as it stood, for the Article was a necessary one. He thought, however, that its wording left room for various interpretations, particularly as to the meaning to be attached to the words 'expel and return'. In the Swiss Government's view, the term 'expel' applied to a refugee who had already been admitted to the territory of a country. *The term 'refouler' on the other hand, had a vague meaning; it could not, however, be applied to a refugee who had not yet entered the territory of a country. The word 'return' used in the English text, gave that idea exactly.* Yet, Article 28 implied the existence of two categories of refugees: refugees who were liable to be expelled, and those who were liable to be returned. In any case, *the States represented at the Conference should take a definite position regarding the meaning to be attached to the word 'return'. The Swiss Government considered that in the present instance the word applied solely to refugees who had already entered a country, but were not yet resident there. According to that interpretation, States would not be compelled to allow large groups of persons seeking refugee status to cross its frontiers.* He would be glad to know whether the States represented at the Conference accepted his interpretations of the terms in question. If they did, Switzerland would be willing to accept Article 28, which was one of the Articles in respect of which States could not, under Article 36 of the Draft Convention, enter a reservation.

Nothing in the extensive discussions on 11 July, the day that the text of art 33 was settled, leaves any room for Judge Pinto de Albuquerque's argument in n 123 below or for his open (or the Court's wrapped-up) conclusion on the meaning here of *refouler/refoulement*.

[121] On intent, meaning and the reasonable observer (aware of context), see, eg, *Mannai Investment* [1997] AC 749, per Lord Hoffmann; Finnis, *Intention and Identity* (n 92) at 31–33.

of initial entry into, the state.[122] The Court in *Hirsi Jamaa*, in indicating (and the concurring judgment in arguing for)[123] the opposite, is producing not so much a 'living' interpretation as a sheer misinterpretation.

The effect of this error is precisely what was feared in 1951 by the Dutch, the Swiss, the British, the Italian, the German and the Swedish governments (to mention only those that articulated their fears): irrevocable, exceptionless exposure of signatory countries to massive influxes—mass migration of persons coming directly or indirectly from failed or vicious states (or indeed from impoverished or relatively poor states)—without recourse to resistance by *denial of entry*.[124] If there is a real risk that even one among 1,000 sturdy young men seeking entry (say, by being landed openly or clandestinely[125] from a boat or flotilla) is fleeing some real risk of death or inhuman conditions and if that one person would be at some real risk of that risk materialising unless granted entry (and not subsequently expelled

---

[122] Lord Bingham's excellent discussion of the drafting of art 33(1) in *R v Immigration Officer Prague Airport ex p Roma Rights* [2004] UKHL 55 recalls (at [13]) that each party to the 1933 Convention relating to the International Status of Refugees undertook 'not to remove or keep from its territory by application of police measures, such as expulsions *or non-admittance at the frontier (refoulement)*, refugees who have been authorized to reside there regularly, unless the said measures are dictated by reasons of national security or public order' and 'undertakes in any case not to refuse entry to refugees at the frontiers of their countries of origin', and comments: 'This language might be understood to oblige contracting states to admit refugees coming to seek asylum, but in the opinion of a respected commentator the word *refouler* in the authoritative French text was not used to mean "refuse entry" but "return", "reconduct" or "send back", and the provision did not refer to the admission of refugees but only to the treatment of refugees who were already in a contracting state.'

[123] *Hirsi Jamaa* (n 111) concurring judgment of Judge Pinto de Albuquerque at 67: 'the French term of *refoulement* includes the removal, transfer, rejection or refusal of admission of a person. The deliberate insertion of the French word in the English version has no other possible meaning than to stress the linguistic equivalence between the verb return and the verb *refouler*'. This is the opposite of the truth. The actually intended meaning of the deliberate insertion was to limit the reference of *refouler* to the reference of 'return', as demanded by the many states above-mentioned (which all assented then and there to the insertion because they, like doubtless everyone there, knew its intent). The nature of this elaborately documented concurring judgment may be gauged from its final words: 'Refugees attempting to escape Africa do not claim a right of admission to Europe. They demand only that Europe, the cradle of human rights idealism and the birthplace of the rule of law, cease closing its doors to people in despair who have fled from arbitrariness and brutality. That is a very modest plea, vindicated by the European Convention on Human Rights. "We should not close our ears to it".' The first and second sentences state a distinction without difference, and the first is false: the Court was upholding precisely such a claim of right made by 24 such persons. And in unascertainably many cases, the 'demand' reported in the second is made from motives other than any that are connoted by 'in despair'. Above all, a plea that is modest when stated by a few dozen could be deafening and unprocessable when stated or stateable—and devastating when acted upon—by millions or, as it might well be, tens or scores or hundreds of millions. The exhortation not to close our ears comes well from a legislator or citizen, but ill from a judge professing to honour the rule of law.

[124] As is obvious, the nullification of littoral states' pushback operations is tantamount to permission to set foot ashore, with all that that footfall connotes in high practical probability of acquiring a new and 'better life', a new country. The incentivising effect is vast, and an immediate side-effect is that thousands perish at sea.

[125] The EU border agency Frontex reports that one modus operandi is to land immigrants at unpoliced beaches where they can come ashore by mingling with the swimmers (and from there making their way to wherever they will in the Schengen Area). Frontex, *FRAN Quarterly Q3 2014* (Warsaw, 2014) 22–23, http://frontex.europa.eu/assets/Publications/Risk_Analysis/FRAN_Q3_2014.pdf.

or returned), *all 1,000* must be allowed entry. Indeed, so as to make possible an investigation, individual by individual, of their personal circumstances (however slight the chance that those circumstances could be discovered accurately by enquiry directed to persons overwhelmingly motivated to fabricate accounts of their circumstances and destroy all evidence of their true origin or status), all 1,000 must be admitted and, once admitted, can never be returned if at risk that they would find themselves in—or be sent on by some ECHR or non-ECHR state to—a country racked by violence, oppression or other dire conditions. Since in 2014 alone scenarios, or rather events, like this were played out hundreds of times—Italy alone received by sea some 200,000 unauthorised persons,[126] almost all in such circumstances as to be de facto unreturnable, and as the writing of this chapter was being finished in March 2015 the responsible EU official predicted up to five times as many for 2015[127]—receiving states are subjected to rapid *and effectively irreversible* change in their demography and conditions of existence.

It is neither difficult nor extravagant to envisage circumstances in which such changes, forced on receiving states by mass immigration the reception of which is mandated by the Strasbourg Court under the living instrument interpretation of Article 3, would reasonably be regarded as threatening the life of the nation. If the 1,000 persons in a flotilla or the 200,000 (or some day a million) in a succession of ships were to include many persons suffering from contagious and lethal disease, these might exceed by scores or hundreds of times the capacity of the receiving state's hospitals to handle them. The response of the Strasbourg Court has in principle already been given, again and again: Article 3 is an absolute. And Article 3 cannot be derogated from merely because the life of the nation is threatened.[128]

---

[126] And found the corpses of 3,000 who had drowned, in the absence of the pushback operations prohibited by *Hirsi Jamaa* (n 111).

[127] www.ibtimes.co.uk/libya-one-million-migrants-ready-reach-europe-says-eu-border-chief-1490831 (6 March 2015).

[128] See n 89 above. The Court in *Hirsi Jamaa* (n 111) states all this with its usual reticent delicacy:

> 134 ... the rules for the rescue of persons at sea and those governing the fight against people trafficking impose on States the obligation to fulfil the obligations arising out of international refugee law, including the *non-refoulement* principle (see paragraph 23 above).

Paragraph 23 consists in substance of a UNHCR Note, which para 134 will then endorse:

> 23. In its Note on International Protection of 13 September 2001 (A/AC.96/951, § 16), UNHCR, which has the task of monitoring the manner in which the States Parties apply the Geneva Convention, indicated that the principle of *non-refoulement* laid down in Article 33, was:

>> '... a cardinal protection principle... In addition, **international human rights law has established** *non-refoulement* **as a fundamental component of the absolute prohibition of torture and cruel, inhuman or degrading treatment or punishment.** The duty not to *refoule* is also recognized as applying to refugees irrespective of their formal recognition... It encompasses any measure attributable to a State which could have the effect of returning an asylum-seeker or refugee to the frontiers of territories where his or her life or freedom would be threatened, or where he or she would risk persecution. **This includes rejection at the frontier, interception, and indirect** *refoulement*, **whether of an individual seeking asylum or in situations of mass influx.**' (emphasis added).

The immigrant thousands might include—or there is a real risk that they include—hundreds or thousands or tens of thousands of members of more or less disciplined forces intent on overthrowing the government and social order of the receiving state and of abrogating the sway of the ECHR itself. The wider mass, too, while lacking such intent, might be (if not already are) in large numbers and proportion adherents of a religion which the Strasbourg Court itself has declared without ambiguity to be, in 'its changeless dogmas', incompatible with the principles of the ECHR,[129] and which anyone who studies it can confirm can tend, by the recorded dicta, circumstances and *personalia* of its founding, to imbue intensely loyal and informed or enthusiastic adherents with a motivating vision of domination and submission, most relevantly by migration (*hijra*) and conquest.[130] Or again, the immigrants may simply be so numerous, and so culturally different from the community they enter, that the state, though rich, powerful and mature, could be colonised or simply overwhelmed.[131]

To any or all of these kinds of possible scenario, the Strasbourg Court has its response ready, grounded in its living-instrument position on Article 3 as stated in *Hirsi Jamaa* (as in *Saadi*). Article 3 prohibits torture and inhuman treatment absolutely; this prohibition holds regardless of its bearing on any threat to the life of the nation; the signatories to the ECHR intended Article 3 to exclude the dishonourable practice of inflicting torture and inhuman treatment exceptionlessly, '*ruat caelum*, though the heavens fall' and though the life of the nation fail; under a living instrument like our Convention and instrumentality like this Court, refusal of entry of many refugees, even to protect the life of the nation, is by interpretation to be treated as simply a way of being guilty, then and there, as party to their torture (and guilty of strict-liability complicity in it, even if never takes place)—and/or guilty of their deliberate subjection (whether or not it materialises or was ever more probable than not) to inhuman or degrading conditions. The fact that the same state signatories fully intended to retain all their powers of refusing initial

---

[129] The 18 judges of the ECtHR held unanimously, in *Refah Partisi (No 2) v Turkey* (2003) 37 EHRR 1 [123] (quoting *Refah Partisi (No 1)* [72]) that: 'the Court considers that *sharia, which faithfully reflects the dogmas and divine rules laid down by religion, is stable and invariable. Principles such as pluralism in the political sphere or the constant evolution of public freedoms have no place in it ... [A] regime based on sharia ... clearly diverges from Convention values*, particularly with regard to its criminal law and criminal procedure, its rules on the legal status of women and the way it intervenes in all spheres of private and public life in accordance with religious precepts ... [A] political party whose actions seem to be aimed at introducing sharia ... can hardly be regarded as an association complying with the democratic ideal that underlies the whole of the Convention'. See Finnis (n 25) ss II and III.

[130] See Finnis (n 19) essay 9 at 149 and essay II.7 (2008a); Finnis (n 14) essay 11, s IV; John Finnis, *Religion and Public Reason: Collection of Essays Volume V* (Oxford, Oxford University Press, 2011) essay 1, s VII and essay 4, s VII; and John Finnis, 'Does Free Exercise of Religion Deserve Constitutional Mention?' (2009) 54 *American Journal of Jurisprudence* 44, s VII.

[131] The possibilities are evident, but (as in other imaginative fictitious enactments of real possibilities such as Huxley's *Brave New World* and Orwell's *Animal Farm*) have been acutely and vividly imagined (not without some moral coarseness and rebarbative editorialising) in Jean Raspail, *The Camp of the Saints*, Norman Shapiro(trans) (New York, Charles Scribner, 1975), on which see Samuel Huntington, *The Clash of Civilizations and the Remaking of World Order* (New York, Free Press, 2002) 203–04.

entry, especially under conditions of mass migration threatening the life of the nation, is now (the Court holds) quite irrelevant. It need not be explicitly mentioned or frankly admitted. For *this instrument is alive* and its prohibitions must be made *effective* to their fullest extent, so as to protect human rights as they are *now* conceived in elite circles in these states, or at any rate in the 'human rights community' in which we judges are leading, creative participants; that is, the human right of *some* to be free from consequences of actions taken to protect the human rights of *others*.

That line of judicially sponsored argument has only one sound element, the thesis that *the signatory states intended to condemn and renounce unconditionally all intentional infliction by them of torture or inhuman or degrading treatment, and to make a commitment to run the risk that such renunciation might materially, even fatally, hamper their efforts to defend themselves* against war, terror or other subversion.[132] They (or the main signatories among them) had run that risk in their war against the Nazis, who freely engaged in such practices. What is unacceptable is the notion that the signatories thereby committed themselves to accepting mass influx of purported refugees who might almost all be purely economic migrants, or might include countless terrorists, or fleeing perpetrators of genocide, or bearers of contagious and lethal disease, or some combination of these classes mixed unascertainably in with a small (or even a large) proportion of bona fide refugees from persecution or torture or the deliberate imposition of inhuman or degrading treatment. Every self-respecting and self-determining nation would, instead, wish to respond to such circumstances by legislative (or legislature-ratified) decisions taken after debates unhampered by the artificialities of judicial/juridical methods with their narrow premises, and their systematic neglect of various probable but unprovable consequences. And a fortiori would wish to respond unhampered by the relentlessly superficial and generally erroneous juridical/judicial handling both of Article 3 ECHR and of the conditions under which it makes sense to think in terms of morally (and therefore ECHR-legally) absolute, exceptionless norms of humanly fitting choice.

Though all this will instantly incur imputations of hard- and cold-heartedness, not to mention inequity or iniquity (and any number of more severely opprobrious epithets), it is permissible to point out how unconstitutional is the Court's *method* of responding to this kind of situation by making, in the exercise of judicial power, a purely legislative extension of Article 3 so as to *wedge open* the doors of Convention states (and flatten the walls, and tie down the sentries, of many of them) and denounce as complicity in inhuman treatment the attempt to respond to a humanitarian challenge in the manner provided for by the architects alike of the Convention to which Article 3 belongs and the Refugee Convention—that is, in the manner of a free people. Such a people should and would decide for itself[133] with full advertence to the likely consequences for its members' freedom

---

[132] Art 15(2) ECHR (see n 89 above) is the primary expression of this commitment.

[133] International Covenant on Civil and Political Rights 1966, art 1(1): 'All peoples have the right of self-determination. By virtue of that right they freely determine their political status.'

(in every sense of that protean political word) *and* for the future wellbeing of desperate and deprived peoples everywhere—a wellbeing significantly dependent on the maintenance of well-functioning states of generous cultural heritage—*and* for the survival of the constitutional system in which the Convention was meant to have its place.[134]

VI. SUMMING UP

It will be objected that the latter parts of the preceding section are an argument *in terrorem* or *ex horribilibus*, appealing to extremes of possible bad consequences. The objection would come ill from the Strasbourg Court, which launched its 'living instrument' doctrine in *Golder* with a resounding appeal to the spectre that, were the text of Article 6 not to be given a 'living' interpretation, a signatory state 'could, without acting in breach of that text, do away with its courts, or take away their jurisdiction to determine certain classes of civil actions and entrust it to organs dependent on the Government'.[135] That spectre, moreover, was and remains hypothetical, while several of the consequences that I have mentioned as possibilities are already vivid actualities, as effects and causes, with only their scale and the insuperability of the further effects yet to be settled by the course of future events. And the reference to consequences only reinforces, but does not substitute for, the prior, independent demonstrations of the logical and juridical unsoundness of the judicial legislation that, as now in place, would render states and peoples spectators in their own ruin.

In *Golder*, Judge Fitzmaurice's dissent drew attention to the distinction between the issues discussed above in section I and those discussed in sections III–V. Though common law judges sometimes 'make new law', 'legislate', it is quite another thing, said Fitzmaurice, 'for this method to be imposed ab extra on States parties to an international convention supposed to be based on agreement'.[136] The point has some force, but that force decays as states subjected to Strasbourg's judicial legislation acquiesce in it, and actively confirm the Court's jurisdiction and

---

[134] On the considerations of justice that are important in any such deliberation about such existential acts of self-determination, see Finnis (n 92) essay 6 ('Law, Universality and Social Identity') especially 119, and essay 7 ('Cosmopolis, Nation States, and Families') especially 125–26; Finnis (n 19) essay 9 ('Nationality and Alienage') especially 146–48.

[135] *Golder* (n 42) [35].

[136] *Golder* (n 42), dissenting opinion of Judge Fitzmaurice [37] fn 21. He went on: 'It so happens however, that even in England, a country in which "case law", and hence—though to a diminishing extent—a certain element of judicial legislation has always been part of the legal system, a recent case led to severe criticism of this element, and another decision given by the highest appellate tribunal went far to endorse this criticism in the course of which it had been pointed out that the role of the judge is jus dicere not jus dare, and that the correct course for the judge faced with defective law was to draw the attention of the legislature to that fact, and not deal with it by judicial action. It was also pointed out that no good answer lay in saying that a big step in the right direction had been taken—for when judges took big steps that meant that they were making new law. Such remarks as these are peculiarly applicable to the present case in my opinion.' His use of the phrase 'judicial legislation' is looser than in this chapter; the difference of positions is verbal, not substantial.

even extend its reach. A more important reason for countries like ours to reject systems like the Strasbourg Court's is the consideration with which I concluded the Maccabean Lecture 1985: adopting a system of judicially enforced rights of the programmatic character of the ECHR, and all the more so a system in which the decisive word rests with a Court that decides in the post-1975 Strasbourg manner, 'means accepting into our country's institutional play of practical reasoning and choice a new, or greatly expanded, element of make-believe, and new or ampler grounds for alienation from the rule of law'.[137]

The make-believe is in fact the modern form of the 'fairy tale'; Lord Reid is widely taken to have used the metaphor to ridicule[138] as fantasy the common law's self-understanding, and section I has argued that the ridicule was undeserved and perhaps only half-meant; more worthy of the ridicule, as sections III–V suggest, is the claim which every Strasbourg judgment *must* make: that its purpose and effect is 'to ensure the observance of the engagements undertaken by the High Contracting Parties' (Article 19), and that it does so by 'interpretation and application of the Convention' (Article 32). The 'living instrument' method ensures that much of the time, the Court is instead interpreting not text or agreement, but 'attitudes', that is, opinions (not least prejudices and ideologies, 'memes' and 'tropes') that have emerged since the Convention was adopted and won favour among transnational elites and a majority of the Court. These the Court 'applies' in order to promote the future observance of norms that were rejected or not adopted (or *at best* neither implied nor envisaged) by the High Contracting Parties—norms which, as Convention obligations, are thus created by the Court.

Highly visible from sections IV and V are the two most important reasons for rejecting the ECHR system as it has been administered and remoulded, indeed transformed, since 1975. The first is that courts are a poor forum for creating norms—legislating—when the issues at stake engage the self-understanding and future destiny of all or very many of the members of a political community faced with competitions of interest and judgment (*prudentia*) as profound as are involved in such *frontiers* as—for example—those between a wide franchise and voting by prisoners; or between maternal health, maternal autonomy and unborn children; or between the marital and the non-marital; or between palliative care (or living disabled or depressed), autonomy and homicide (voluntary or would-be voluntary); or between the members of the nation, the hundreds of millions who wish or may soon wish to join or perhaps supplant them in their homeland, the fact or ideal of multiculturalism, and what can be judged to be its normal eventual

---

[137] Finnis (n 19) 44. The preceding sentence had made clear that doing without a justiciable bill of rights 'means accepting some real risks of injustices.' That Lecture was 15 years before the Human Rights Act 1998 came into effect, and now, after 15 years under that Act, it seems clear that its operation has been more damaging to the rule of law and more transgressive of the limits of adjudication than even the Maccabean Lecture had anticipated. The cases mentioned in n 65 above are some of the evidence.

[138] Michael Kirby's Hamlyn Lectures in 2003, *Judicial Activism* (London, Sweet & Maxwell, 2004) 1, 88, take Reid to have been using laughter and humour to explode the myth (etc).

consequence (racial and/or religious civil wars and/or partitions; and before that a surveillance state overseeing eruptions of disorder, networked criminality and terrorism; and meanwhile escalating inter-group grievances, resentments and mistrust, insecurity and so forth). Litigation, with its focus on the posited sources of existing law, proves itself again and again to be an inept means of making the acts of political-communal self-determination demanded by such issues and the uncertainties that surround them. Even when the acts of legislatures are profoundly misguided and/or unjust to present or future generations, as they not rarely are, the deliberative processes involved (in mature political communities of our broad tradition)—and above all the transparent orientation of those processes towards taking responsibility for the impact of the *changes* in our law that the legislature openly intended to make—render the legislative acts of legislatures *appropriate* in their constitutional and procedural form.

The second reason for rejecting justiciable bills of rights specifies the first by pointing to the *juridical* unsoundness of the Strasbourg Court's two principal juridical premise- or framework-concepts: (1) proportionality; and (2) effectiveness for object.

Proportionality provides the framework for countless judgments of the Court, but its appearance of juridical craftsmanship barely conceals the unbounded, essentially legislative character of the assessments it involves, which frequently include both: (a) unbound moral reasoning and moral judgment; and (b) speculation about the range of possible future consequences of the measure impugned, alternative measures and/or some regulatory status quo ante free from 'any measures'. For (i) the legitimacy of the measure's aim, and (ii) the efficacy or 'suitability' of the means adopted, each involve both (a) and (b) even before we reach (iii) the measure's 'necessity' in the sense that *no* alternative can be envisaged that would be *both* as effective as a means *and* less harmful to or restrictive of the right being relied upon to impugn the measure, while all this leaves open (iv) 'proportionality' in the narrow sense that *all things considered*, the measure is a proportionate (reasonable) response to a social need (considering especially the degree of legitimacy and desirability of the aim; the degree of importance of the right asserted; the likelihood of the means' efficacy for aim and impact on that right; the side-effects of the measure on *other* rights and interests; *and* the side-effects for those rights and interests of *forgoing* the measure).[139] Almost all of these elements may involve matters of fact and evaluative opinion in which legal learning is of little assistance and forensically ascertainable evidence is unavailable. Though judicial competence can be deployed in applying a proportionality test to some classes of executive decision within the context of a dense web of legal rules (whether legislative or common law in origin) and culturally and conventionally established expectations, there is

---

[139] This fourth element, 'proportionality' *stricto sensu*, tends to swallow up the other criteria concerning means ((ii) and (iii)) and itself depends on views concerning the aim (element (i)): see, eg, the ECtHR cases cited in the leading judgment of Lord Mance in *Recovery of Medical Costs for Asbestos Disease* [2015] UKSC 3 [48].

little or nothing judicial about judgments about (assessments of) proportionality in relation to rights such as those in the ECHR, as brought to bear upon general legislative or legislatively approved arrangements for social life. The judicial opinions reporting or expressing such assessments/judgments can muster only the appearance of juridical character by reciting the facts about the measure's enactment, the disputed contentions of the parties and previous opinions of judges. Debacles of assessment such as *Hirst (No 2)* and *Scoppola*, or the majority judgment of the Supreme Court of Canada in *Sauvé (No 2)*,[140] illustrate the problem, which is less one of competence than one of intrinsically legislative, non-judicial character.

Effectiveness for object is the criterion deployed by the Court particularly when dealing with absolutes such as Article 3 ECHR,[141] where proportionality is on its face inappropriate: 'it is essential that the Convention is interpreted and applied in a manner which renders the guarantees practical and effective and not theoretical and illusory'.[142] When a guarantee is taken by the Court to be absolute not only in the defensible moral sense which relates to and governs a state's *intentions* but also in the sense which extends it to unwanted side-effects of a state's action (even effects, like illness, remote from anybody's behaviour anywhere), the criterion embodies a morally optional preference for one kind of social life over other reasonable kinds. The adoption of such a preference is an act of communal self-determination that ought to be taken transparently, and not clad in garments of judicial rhetoric deployed by judges who are in a position to disclaim personal political responsibility for their decisions as decisions 'required by law' and made in its 'application'. Judges disqualify themselves from making that disclaimer when they constitute themselves—like the ECtHR since 1975—a permanent instrumentality for reforming the culture by changing the law.[143]

---

[140] See n 87 above.

[141] Thus, *Soering* (n 99) [87]: 'the object and purpose of the Convention as an instrument for the protection of individual human beings require that its provisions be interpreted and applied so as to make its safeguards practical and effective'. This has a benign and legitimate meaning, and a wrongheaded extremist meaning such as is plain in the Sørensen Report remark discussed at n 41 above. The Court tends to use it in the latter sense when rebutting arguments that its 'interpretation' of an article is a misinterpretation in terms of original public meaning and/or of constitutional principle.

[142] *Hirsi Jamaa* (n 111) [175]. Behind this is *Stafford v UK* (46295/99), 28 May 2002 (GC)—not an art 3 or other absolute rights case, but applying or extending art 5(4)'s guarantee of court decision on lawfulness of detention—[68]: 'Since the Convention is first and foremost a system for the protection of human rights, the Court must however have regard to the changing conditions in Contracting States and respond, for example, to any emerging consensus as to the standards to be achieved (see, among other authorities, *Cossey v. the United Kingdom*, judgment of 27 September 1990, Series A no. 184, p. 14, § 35, and *Chapman v. the United Kingdom* [GC], no. 27238/95, § 70, ECHR 2001-I). *It is of crucial importance that the Convention is interpreted and applied in a manner which renders its rights practical and effective, not theoretical and illusory*. A failure by the Court to maintain a dynamic and evolutive approach would risk rendering it a bar to reform or improvement.'

[143] The justification offered by the Court in *Stafford* (n 142) is, as so often, confused and self-deceptive: 'failure by the Court to maintain a dynamic and evolutive approach would risk rendering it a bar to reform or improvement'. How could the Court's refusal to *order* 'reform or improvement' constitute a bar to such (supposed) reforms or improvements at the hands of those whose responsibility it is to reform and improve?

7

The Role of Courts in the Joint Enterprise of Governing

AILEEN KAVANAGH[*]

IN HIS LECTURE 'The Limits of Law', Lord Sumption poses a fundamental question of institutional design, namely: what kinds of social tasks can properly be assigned to judges and courts, as opposed to other institutions such as administrators or legislators? This is a vexed question which has preoccupied judges, politicians and legal philosophers for decades. How does Lord Sumption answer it? He starts by considering a common way of expressing the appropriate division of labour between the courts and Parliament.[1] This is the seductively simple idea that the courts deal with questions of law, whereas Parliament deals with issues of social policy. Lord Sumption is not so easily seduced. Whilst he acknowledges its superficial attractions, he dismisses the law/policy distinction as 'perfectly useless, since it begs all the difficult questions'.[2] What is a question of law? What is a question of policy?' Lord Sumption worries that these questions will yield different answers depending on how one defines the issue.[3] The terms 'law' and 'politics' are so flexible that they are subject to manipulation to achieve the desired result. If judges want to intervene, they will characterise an issue as one of 'law', whereas if they do not, they will characterise it as one of policy. Lord Sumption seems most exercised by the danger of judicial manipulation on the interventionist side. Thus, he gives examples where, in his view, the courts were wrong to 'characterise as questions of law issues which do not lend themselves to a legal solution'.[4] If the judges had opened their eyes to 'the real issue'[5] before them, they would have concluded that it was a political question and therefore non-justiciable.[6]

---

[*] I wish to thank the British Academy for funding my research in 2014–15 on a project called 'Rights in the Collaborative Constitution'. I am also grateful to all the participants at the Lord Sumption workshop in Oxford for helpful feedback on this chapter, and to Paul Yowell for insightful written comments.

[1] Lord Sumption, 'The Limits of Law', 27th Sultan Azlan Shah Lecture, Kuala Lumpur, 20 November 2013, www.supremecourt.uk/docs/speech-131120.pdf, 4.

[2] ibid.

[3] ibid.

[4] ibid 6.

[5] ibid 6.

[6] ibid.

And yet, though he knows it is misleading, these remarks show that Lord Sumption is not completely immune to the charms of the law/policy distinction. In fact, it is a leitmotiv of his lecture and is embedded in its central thesis, namely, that 'politics is quite simply a better way of resolving questions of social policy than judge-made law'.[7] The critical question then becomes: how does he define 'questions of social policy' and how does he distinguish them from 'questions of law'? This is of the utmost importance, because it is difficult to evaluate the claim that judges should not decide questions of social policy unless we know exactly what 'policy' means.

Lord Sumption pursues two lines of thought on this question. The first is an endorsement of Lon Fuller's classic and still-influential view that 'polycentric' problems are unsuitable for adjudication by the courts. Any decisions about polycentric problems are 'likely to have multiple consequences, each with its own complex repercussions for many other people'—consequences which judges are ill-placed to judge.[8] The inappropriateness of judges attempting to resolve polycentric problems underpins much of Lord Sumption's discussion. Thus, when discussing the *Witham* case, he bemoans the fact that the Divisional Court 'reduce[d] the question before it to a binary question' of whether Mr Witham had a fundamental right to access to the courts. But the 'real question' was about the importance of funding litigation relative to 'other possible uses of the money or other possible ways of helping the poor'.[9] If access to the courts had been viewed instead as 'one of a number of competing claims on a limited pot of money', then we can see that a judicial decision on Mr Witham's claim has broader consequences and repercussions. It is a polycentric issue and therefore non-justiciable.[10]

The second line of thought is to explore the institutional credentials of the courts and the legislature in order to evaluate which institution is suited to questions of policy. In doing so, Lord Sumption highlights the institutional limitations of the courts and the institutional advantages of the legislature. It may be that he is drawn to this rather one-sided institutional picture because he wants to show that the legislature is best placed to decide 'questions of social policy' or 'polycentric issues'. Be that as it may, the institutional limitations of the courts he identifies are undoubtedly true. Courts have access to a narrow range of information, ie, the information presented to them by legal counsel for the litigants. Legal disputes before the courts are presented in a 'bivalent form'[11] where the broader implications for society as a whole are not, and cannot be, fully canvassed. Judges have expertise and training in the law and how to apply legal techniques, but nothing equips them to engage with radical law reform. They have neither the institutional legitimacy nor the competence to do so.

---

[7] ibid 12.
[8] ibid 15.
[9] ibid 6.
[10] ibid.
[11] Timothy Endicott, 'The Impossibility of the Rule of Law' (1999) 19 *OJLS* 1, 15.

Lord Sumption's presentation of the institutional strengths of the legislature is similarly unassailable. Elected politicians have an institutional incentive to heed the views and interests of their constituents, to strike compromises between them and to integrate them into their policy agenda. Only they can actively garner popular support for proposed changes and evaluate how to strike the correct balance between the need for change and extent of popular resistance to that change.[12] Only they can 'reconcile inconsistent interests and opinions' in the required way and work out 'what the majority can live with'.[13] Members of Parliament are elected and this gives people a sense of identification with, and participation in, political decisions.[14] In short, elected politicians have the advantages of being democratically legitimate, accountable to the people, able to consult interest groups when forming policy, able to gauge the levels of popular support for a measure and able to deliberate on legislative proposals by canvassing a broad range of expertise which is then subjected to scrutiny.

I agree with all of these points, and I join Lord Sumption in warning against the temptation to assume a posture of disdain for the political process, messy though it may sometimes appear.[15] It is precisely because of the institutional strengths Lord Sumption outlines that we give elected politicians the prominent role as primary decision-makers about what the law will be in our society. As in all democratic systems, elected politicians (acting through the institutional structures of the executive and the legislature) have the primary role in devising and setting the policy agenda. Elected politicians are the primary decision-makers in a democratic society, and rightly so. They have 'the general initiative in the project of governing'.[16]

However, despite agreeing with Lord Sumption on these and other points, I part company with him in various ways. First, I believe that Fuller's idea of polycentricity cannot bear the weight Lord Sumption places on it. It does not provide us with a discerning or meaningful criterion for demarcating the job of the courts from the job of the legislature. Second, whilst the points Lord Sumption makes about the institutional limits of the courts and the strengths of the legislature are incontrovertible, I believe they suffer from being incomplete and one-sided. To answer the fundamental question of institutional design posed at the outset of Lord Sumption's lecture, we need to appreciate the strengths and weaknesses of *both* institutions. Third, I have to disagree with Lord Sumption's conclusion, namely, that if judges are faced with claims which have 'multiple consequences' and 'complex repercussions', they should declare them to be non-justiciable. I believe that

---

[12] See Dimitrios Kyritsis, 'Constitutional Review in Representative Democracy' (2012) 22 *OJLS* 297, 303.
[13] Lord Sumption (n 1) 12; see also Jonathan Sumption, 'Judicial and Political Decision-Making: The Uncertain Boundary' (2011) 16 *Judicial Review* 301, 312.
[14] Lord Sumption (n 1) 13.
[15] ibid 12.
[16] Kyritsis (n 12) 312.

this conclusion is too sweeping. I will argue that judicial awareness of their epistemic and other institutional limitations has an important role to play in judicial reasoning. It *may* lead judges to conclude that the issue is non-justiciable and not amenable to judicial evaluation at all, but it should not automatically have that absolute or preclusive effect. It should lead judges to exercise an appropriate degree of judicial restraint, depending on the extent of the limitations and their importance in the individual case before them. Judges should adjudicate the claim, but should do so with caution. They should recognise their limits, whilst not abdicating their proper constitutional role. In making these points, I will sketch out a role-conception for the courts—one where judges are partners with the legislature in the joint enterprise of governing.

I. POLYCENTRICITY AND OTHER FALSE STARTS

The enduring attraction of the idea of polycentricity is due to the obvious and commonsensical point which lies at its core. By virtue of their legal training and the nature of court processes, judges are good at resolving disputes about the application of the law to concrete facts, as well as resolving questions arising from the application of existing legal doctrines and the interaction between them. They are generally not good at evaluating the broader knock-on effects of changes in the law for society as a whole. They make their decisions on the basis of a narrow range of information (legal arguments presented by necessarily partisan litigants who are focused on a single issue) and do not generally have the requisite institutional tools to acquire a broader range of information. On the basis of these well-known facts, Fuller proposed the idea of polycentricity as a way of demarcating the appropriate domain of judicial (as opposed to legislative) decision-making. Judges should be confined to the adjudication of non-polycentric issues.

But the problems of trying to confine the judicial role using the idea of polycentricity become apparent the moment we turn to examine what courts typically do. When we look at judicial practice and the issues which judges are asked to resolve on a daily basis (particularly in the higher courts), polycentricity is everywhere. As Jeff King has pointed out, from private law to public law, from tax law to tort law, from contract law to competition law, polycentricity is pervasive in judicial decisions.[17] In fact, when we get to the Supreme Court level, polycentricity seems to be an explicit requirement for leave to appeal to the Court. As it says on its website, the UK Supreme Court hears appeals on 'arguable points of law of general public importance'. It concentrates on 'cases of the greatest public and constitutional importance', the impact of which 'extend far beyond the parties involved in any given case, shaping our society and directly affecting our everyday lives'.[18] So, in

---

[17] Jeff King, 'The Pervasiveness of Polycentricity' [2008] *PL* 101.
[18] The Supreme Court, 'Role of the Supreme Court', www.supremecourt.uk/about/role-of-the-supreme-court.html.

order to be heard by the Supreme Court, the case must necessarily have importance and consequences for the general public over and above its significance to the individual parties before the court. In short, the case must have polycentric features.

The pervasiveness of polycentricity (and its ubiquity at the Supreme Court level) should lead us to be wary of concluding that non-justiciability should follow automatically from polycentricity. After all, such a conclusion would put the Supreme Court (and probably all courts) out of a job. We should either reject the idea as unhelpful, or draw more nuanced conclusions about the implications of polycentricity for judicial reasoning. Perhaps we could refine the idea by emphasising that polycentricity is a matter of degree (as Fuller occasionally seemed to concede).[19] It is only when it reaches a certain level that courts should conclude that the issue is non-justiciable, or at least warrants significant judicial restraint. Either way, it is clear that the idea of polycentricity cannot do the main work it purported to do in Fuller's analysis, namely, to provide us with a single criterion to mark out the kinds of issues suitable for legal adjudication, as opposed to other institutional actors such as administrators and legislators.

Another well-known distinction which attempts the same daunting feat of distinguishing the roles of the courts and legislatures using a single criterion is Ronald Dworkin's distinction between principles and policy. Dworkin defined principle as a 'requirement of justice or fairness or some other dimension of morality'[20] and policy as 'a kind of standard that sets out a goal to be reached, generally an improvement in some economic, political or social feature of the community'.[21] Arguments of principle identify rights, whereas arguments of policy assert that some decision or law will promote the general welfare, the public interest or the collective good. Famously, or perhaps notoriously, Ronald Dworkin thought that judicial reasoning was characterised by arguments of principle, whereas legislators justified their decisions by reference to arguments of policy.

Like Fuller's idea of polycentricity, this distinction has an intuitively plausible idea at its core. This is that we know that there is something different about the reasoning of the courts and the legislature. Judicial decisions are directly responsive to the arguments presented on both sides. Judges present their conclusions in a publicly reasoned form, justified in accordance with the relevant laws and the legal principles which underpin them. We know that legislative decision-making is open to forms of compromise and negotiation which we would think inappropriate in the judicial sphere. Despite this grain of good sense at its core, Dworkin's distinction suffers from the same problems as Fuller's idea of polycentricity, whilst having the further negative side-effect of popularising an idealistic

---

[19] See King (n 17) 101.
[20] Ronald Dworkin, *Taking Rights Seriously* (Cambridge, MA, Harvard University Press, 1977) 22.
[21] ibid.

image of courts and judicial reasoning on the one hand, together with an irredeemably negative view of legislative reasoning on the other.[22]

The reality is that both policy and principle feature in the reasoning of the courts and the legislature.[23] Courts often consider arguments based on the public interest and the common good. Indeed, they are sometimes legally required to do so. Judicial evaluation of the consequences of their decisions is part of 'the traditional judicial toolkit'.[24] We would be appalled if judges were not alert to the consequences of deciding in one way or the other.[25] Similarly, it must be wrong to say that principles do not figure in legislative proposals. Principles are not the exclusive preserve of the courts and policy arguments are not the exclusive preserve of the legislature. Both institutions rely on both types of reasoning. This means that the principle/policy distinction does not provide us with a meaningful criterion for marking out the exclusive province of the courts vis-a-vis the other branches of government. Like Fuller, Dworkin strives to demarcate the domains of the courts and the legislature by separating out the kinds of issues each institution addresses or the kind of reasoning each is said to employ. But this cannot work because of the overlap in subject matter each institution has to address, and the commonality in the types of reasons on which each relies.

What about the idea of function, ie, that each branch of government is distinguished by the function it performs? This seems to follow from a traditional understanding of the separation of powers, whereby each branch has a function which gives it its name: the legislature legislates or makes law, the executive executes it and the courts adjudicate disputes and apply the law.[26] But problems beset any attempt to account for the distinctness of the three branches of government in terms of one single function which it exercises to the exclusion of the other branches.[27] Overcoming these problems has been a notoriously difficult challenge for writers on the separation of powers for centuries. Lord Sumption points out one reason why it obviously does not work in common law systems. This is that,

---

[22] Paul Yowell, 'A Critical Examination of Dworkin's Theory of Rights' (2007) 52 *American Journal of Jurisprudence* 93, 137; Dimitrios Kyritsis, 'Principles, Policies and the Power of Courts' (2007) XX *Canadian Journal of Law and Jurisprudence* 1, 9.

[23] For critical discussion of the principle/policy distinction, see Kyritsis (n 22); Aileen Kavanagh, *Constitutional Review under the UK Human Rights Act 1998* (Cambridge, Cambridge University Press, 2009) 186ff; Jeff King, 'Institutional Approaches to Judicial Restraint' (2008) 28 *OJLS* 409, 416–19.

[24] Antonin Scalia, 'Judicial Deference to Administrative Interpretations of the Law' [1989] *Duke Law Journal* 511.

[25] One common example of judicial attentiveness to consequences is the floodgates argument. For discussion, see Kavanagh (n 23) 185.

[26] MJC Vile calls this the 'pure' view of the separation of powers: see *Constitutionalism and the Separation of Powers* (Oxford, Oxford University Press, 1967), 12; Nick Barber, 'Prelude to the Separation of Powers' (2001) 60 *CLJ* 59.

[27] Aileen Kavanagh, 'The Constitutional Separation of Powers' in David Dyzenhaus and Malcolm Thorburn (eds), *Philosophical Foundations of Constitutional Law* (Oxford, Oxford University Press, 2016, forthcoming); M Elizabeth Magill, 'The Real Separation in the Separation of Powers' (2000) 86 *Vanderbilt Law Review* 1127; Victoria Nourse, 'The Vertical Separation of Powers' (1999) 49 *Duke Law Journal* 749.

in such systems, the courts have a significant law-making role. But the problem strikes wider than this in any system. This is because all branches of government perform all three functions. Therefore, the distinctive features of the branches of government cannot lie in the functions they perform. A rigid 'one branch—one function' view is descriptively inaccurate. Indeed, many would argue that it also practically unfeasible and normatively undesirable.[28]

What, then, is the solution? I think the answer lies in the idea of institutional *roles* and the way in which each branch carries out its respective tasks as part of what I will call 'the joint enterprise of good government'. Institutional roles have a normative character. They are constituted by the standards that define what the people who perform them can legitimately do in their institutional capacity.[29] In order to work out which tasks to assign to which institutions, we need to relate those tasks to appropriate decision-making processes and the values which they various institutional roles are meant to serve.

Note that the distinction between the institutional roles of the courts and the legislature does not map directly onto a distinction between two different functions (such as the function of making law and the function of applying it). Institutional roles can encompass a number of different functions and we know that the judicial role includes both making and applying law. Nor does the distinction between institutional roles map directly onto different subject areas or types of issue each would address, or indeed forms of reasoning each might employ. In other words, it does not map onto a distinction between law and social policy, principle and policy, or polycentric and non-polycentric issues; in fact, it cuts across those distinctions. The differences between the branches of government do not reside in this kind of carve-up of appropriate subject matter or method of reasoning for each institution.[30] It resides in the way in which each branch of government deals with all of these issues (principle, policy, polycentric and non-polycentric problems) given the various procedural features of their institutional design, the tasks that are assigned to them and the role each branch plays vis-a-vis the others.[31] Let us see how this applies to understanding the institutional role of the courts.

II. THE ROLE OF THE COURTS: PARTNERS IN A JOINT ENTERPRISE

The first point to note about the role of the courts is that they do not act in their own name. Like all the other branches of government, they act as organs of the political society. For this reason, judges in the UK are called the Queen's judges,

---

[28] Thomas Merrill, 'The Constitutional Principle of Separation of Powers' [1991] *Supreme Court Review* 225.
[29] For the idea that we should distinguish between the branches in terms of institutional roles, see Kyritsis (n 12).
[30] Kyritsis (n 22).
[31] For a further development of this way of understanding the separation of powers, see Kavanagh (n 27).

where the Queen is a symbol for the state as a whole.[32] Therefore, we cannot develop an account of the judicial role in isolation from the other branches. This is because the role of judges is constituted in large part by the way in which they relate to the other branches. In particular, the way in which the courts depend on the legislature is a crucial defining feature of the judicial role.

To work out a role-conception for the courts, we have to step back and look at the set of tasks which any political society will need to perform. All political societies need an effective institution capable of making clear, open, prospective, stable, general rules for the community. They also need an independent and effective institution to resolve disputes about the rules and to settle doubt about the scope and application of a given rule in particular circumstances.[33] In democratic societies, we need a *deliberative and representative* body (a legislative assembly) to make general rules for the community which can be deliberately made and changed. And we need an *independent* body (the courts) to resolve disputes about what those rules require in particular cases.

As Lord Sumption points out, the representative nature of the legislative assembly helps to ensure that the views of the populace are appropriately factored into policy decisions. It also helps the assembly to garner popular support for its chosen policies. Its deliberative nature helps to ensure that it scrutinises legislative proposals in a meaningful way whilst drawing on a wide range of expertise from across the assembly. In the joint enterprise of governing, Parliament takes the lead role in proposing, devising and changing the legal rules which govern our lives. It has 'the general initiative in the project of governing'.[34]

By contrast, the role of the courts is to resolve disputes about what the law requires in individual cases. They must work out what the rules enacted by the legislature require in order to resolve disputes about them. They must be responsive to individual complaints or claims about what those rules require. In common law systems, they have the power to make some rules themselves, developing doctrines gradually and incrementally, resolving potential conflicts between those norms or doctrines in order to resolve the claims which are brought before them. This is a significant law-making power, but it is more limited than the power of the legislature to enact laws on any matter it wishes in any way which seems appropriate to it.

Here we can see that the distinction between the legislature and the courts does not lie in a distinction of function, but in the way they exercise that function. Both institutions make law, but they do so in different ways.[35] In general, judicial law-making tends to be piecemeal, incremental and interstitial, working within the

---

[32] Timothy Endicott, *Administrative Law*, 2nd edn (Oxford, Oxford University Press, 2011) 14–15.
[33] ibid 15; HLA Hart, *The Concept of Law*, 2nd edn (Oxford, Clarendon Press, 1994) ch 5.
[34] Kyritsis (n 12) 312.
[35] For a more detailed account of the difference between legislative and judicial law-making, see Aileen Kavanagh, 'The Elusive Divide between Interpretation and Legislation under the Human Rights Act 1998' (2004) 24 *OJLS* 259, 270–74.

frameworks set by the legislature and the laws enacted by them.[36] Much judicial law-making occurs by way of filling in gaps in the existing legislative framework, resolving legal disputes through the application of general legislative provisions to particular circumstance. They cannot choose which areas of the law they wish to adjudicate—they are constrained by the vagaries of the litigation which comes before them.[37] In general, judges have to reason according to law even they are developing or making new law as part of common law adjudication, and certainly when they are interpreting laws enacted by Parliament.[38] Not so the legislature. Parliament can reform a whole area of the law in a root-and-branch fashion. As John Gardner put it, 'a legislature is entitled to make new legal norms on entirely non-legal grounds, i.e. without having any existing legal norms operative in its reasoning. A legislature is entitled to think about a problem purely on its merits'.[39] The legislature 'takes an idea or a policy and turns it into law'.[40] The courts have to help Parliament to implement that policy by applying that law to particular circumstances.

Having sketched some of the functions that the courts perform, let us now pause to ask: what is the value which underpins the judicial role and the value of their contribution to the joint enterprise of governing? We saw that the legislative assembly has democratic legitimacy on its side. What does the judiciary bring to the joint enterprise of good government? The central value of the courts as an institutional actor is their independence.[41] It is their independence which makes them well-placed to apply the law to individual cases in a fair and impartial manner, and to appear to do so. It is also their independence which enables them to resist the pull of popular opinion in their decision-making function and to resist certain forms of political pressure. Reflecting on the value of independence for the courts reveals the Janus-like nature of the judicial role. On the one hand, judges have a 'receptive role' vis-a-vis the legislature.[42] They have the job of understanding, applying, interpreting and implementing the laws laid down by the legislature. Crucial to this role is the duty on the courts to respect the legislature and give effect to its decisions. As the courts emphasise when articulating the standards which inform their role, 'substantial respect should be paid by the

---

[36] For an account of the piecemeal nature of judicial law-making, see Joseph Raz, *The Authority of Law: Essays on Law and Morality*, 2nd edn (Oxford, Oxford University Press, 2009) 200ff; Sir Philip Sales, 'Judges and Legislature: Values into Law' (2012) 71 *CLJ* 287, 291–92.

[37] These various limitations of the power of the courts to make law led Lord Devlin to describe the judge as a 'crippled lawmaker' in comparison to the less restricted legislative law-making powers of the legislature. Lord Devlin, 'Judges and Lawmakers' (1976) 39 *MLR* 1, 10.

[38] John Gardner, 'Legal Positivism: 5½ Myths' (2001) 47 *American Journal of Jurisprudence* 199, 216–17 (reprinted as ch 2 of John Gardner, *Law as Leap of Faith: Essays on Law in General* (Oxford, Oxford University Press, 2012) 40–41).

[39] ibid 217 or 41.

[40] Lord Devlin (n 37) 4.

[41] Lord Devlin thought that impartiality and the appearance of impartiality were 'the supreme judicial virtues', Lord Devlin (n 37) 4; see also Lord Reid, 'The Judge as Lawmaker', reprinted in (1997) 63 *Arbitration* 180, 181.

[42] Kyritsis (n 12) 315.

courts to the considered decisions of democratic assemblies'.[43] They must act with comity towards the legislature, respecting its role in the constitutional division of labour.

Nonetheless, their independence means that the courts can also perform a meaningful *supervisory role* vis-a-vis the other branches of government. Thus, the government is answerable to the courts for the lawfulness of its acts.[44] This is a more limited form of accountability than the political modes of accountability exercised by Parliament. Parliament can hold the government to account for any matter it wishes, whereas the courts can only hold the government to account for violations of the law. Despite being limited, it is nonetheless important and a significant part of the judicial role. It is a power that judges in Britain have performed since medieval times.[45]

I now want to suggest that the supervisory role of the courts strikes more broadly than their role in holding the executive legally to account. In fact, the courts have a general duty to uphold the law and the legal principles which underpin it and can perform an active role in ensuring that these values are protected both when developing the common law and when interpreting statutes. Again, the independence of the courts from the other branches of government (as well as from various popular pressures) makes them well-placed to carry out this role.

It is worth bearing in mind that the receptive role of the courts vis-a-vis the legislature should not be equated with an entirely passive role. We have long ago rejected as a fairy tale the idea of the judge as the mere 'bouche de la loi', mechanically declaring or discovering what the law requires without any role for the judicial evaluation or creativity.[46] We know that judges are more than mere technicians. Not only do they develop the common law, we also know that statutory interpretation is not reducible to a purely passive or applicative task. As Lord Sumption points out, the courts sometimes assume an active interpretive role over the course of time, as they gradually adapt legislative measures to fit changing social needs (an updating construction).[47] In this way, the courts give effect to legislation in new circumstances, thus helping the legislature to implement the law over time.[48] Similarly, judges actively participate in implementing the law by integrating disparate legislative measures into the broader backcloth of fundamental legal principles and doctrines. They knit together ongoing legislation with background principle in a way which produces a coherent whole. By reducing or eliminating potential conflict between different aspects of the law, they help to

---

[43] *Sheldrake v DPP* [2004] UKHL 43 [23].

[44] *R v Inland Revenue Commissioners ex p National Federation of Self-Employed and Small Businesses* [1982] AC 617, 618.

[45] Endicott (n 32).

[46] The classic statement of this 'fairy tale' is Lord Reid (n 41).

[47] John Bell and George Engle, *Cross: Statutory Interpretation*, 3rd edn (London, Butterworths, 1995) ch 7.

[48] Kyritsis (n 12) 316.

ensure coherence in the law, whilst also helping to uphold core legal values which form the stable framework of the law.[49]

The active nature of this integrative work is vividly illustrated by the way in which judges rely on presumptions when interpreting statutes.[50] These include a presumption against unclear changes in the law, a presumption in favour of a strict construction of penal statutes, a presumption against interference with property rights and a presumption of interpretations of revenue statutes favourable to the taxpayer. These presumptions can sometimes be rebutted by clear statutory language to the contrary, but if the language of the statute is general or ambiguous, judges will interpret them in line with these presumptions. One presumption which is well-known amongst public lawyers is 'the principle of legality'. This is 'the familiar and well-established principle' that:

> [G]eneral words ... should not be read as authorising the doing of acts which adversely affect the basic principles on which the law of the United Kingdom is based in the absence of clear words authorising such acts.[51]

What values do those basic principles protect? There is no authoritative list of such values, but they include the rule of law,[52] due process, the value of individual liberty[53] and fundamental rights.[54] Thus, it is now 'a familiar principle of statutory interpretation'[55] that: 'The courts will ... decline to hold that Parliament interfered with fundamental rights unless it has made its intentions crystal clear.'[56] As Lord Hoffmann observed in his canonical exposition of the principle in *Simms*: 'In the absence of express language or necessary implication to the contrary, the courts therefore presume that even the most general words were intended to be subject to the basic rights of the individual.'[57]

---

[49] Joseph Raz, *Ethics in the Public Domain: Essays in the Morality of Law and Politics*, revised edn (Oxford, Clarendon Press, 1995) 376. Lord Reid (n 41) 183; Sales (n 36) 292; see also Lord Sedley, 'Autonomy and the Rule of Law' in Richard Rawlings (ed), *Law, Society and Economy: Centenary Essays for the London School of Economics and Political Science 1895–1995* (Oxford, Clarendon Press, 1997) 313.

[50] See generally Bell and Engle (n 47) ch 7.

[51] *Jackson and others v Attorney General* [2006] 1 AC 262 [28] (Lord Bingham, quoting Sir Sydney Kentridge QC); *R v Secretary of State for the Home Department ex p Pierson* [1998] AC 539, 575 (Lord Browne-Wilkinson); see further Sir Philip Sales, 'A Comparison of the Principle of Legality and Section 3 of the Human Rights Act 1998' (2009) 125 *LQR* 598.

[52] *Pierson* (n 51) 591 (Lord Steyn); Mark Elliott, *The Constitutional Foundations of Judicial Review* (London, Bloomsbury, 2001) 123; Timothy Endicott, 'Constitutional Logic' (2003) 53 *University of Toronto Law Journal* 201, 208.

[53] Bell and Engle (n 47) 175; Endicott (n 32) 270–71; *R v Hallstrom ex p W (No 2)* [1986] QB 1090, 1104.

[54] This includes basic rights at common law as well as Convention rights; see *R (Anufrijeva) v Secretary of State for the Home Department* [2003] UKHL 36 [27]; *Axa General Insurance Ltd v The Lord Advocate* [2011] UKSC 46 [150].

[55] *Axa* (n 54) [151].

[56] *Jackson* (n 51) [159]; *Bank Mellat v Her Majesty's Treasury (No 1)* [2013] UKSC 38 at [55].

[57] *R v Secretary of State for the Home Department ex p Simms* [2000] 2 AC 115, 131; see also TRS Allan, 'Legislative Supremacy and Legislative Intention: Interpretation, Meaning and Authority' (2004) 63 *CLJ* 685.

For some commentators, these presumptions are principles which judges use to infer parliamentary intent. For others, they are not related to parliamentary intent—they are grounded in fundamental, common law principles that the courts have a constitutional duty to uphold, unless Parliament expresses an intention to the contrary in unequivocal terms.[58] Either way, judicial reliance on these presumptions exemplifies how the courts are partners in the collaborative enterprise of making law, where each branch of government makes a distinct institutional contribution to the overarching task of the state to govern well.

To be sure, even on this collaborative conception of the separation of powers, judges do not and should not have the job of enacting legislation, initiating large-scale policy changes or setting out new frameworks for whole areas of the law. They have neither the institutional competence nor the legitimacy to do so. They are, if you like, the junior partner in the joint enterprise. But they are not a mere personal assistant, carrying out mundane, mechanical tasks at the behest of a demanding boss, constantly at their beck and call. The courts perform their own distinct tasks in a joint endeavour, drawing on their particular kind of expertise and legitimacy which the legislature and executive must also respect. The courts have 'a will of [their] own'[59]—a valuable perspective they bring to the joint enterprise of good government.

Thus, in the course of carrying out their task of interpreting and applying that law to the circumstances of individual cases in a way which respects the decisions and constitutional role of the legislature, they can (and must) strive to ensure that certain fundamental principles which protect the liberty of the individual are upheld. Judges are well-placed to make *this* contribution to the collaborative enterprise, because by virtue of their composition and decision-making processes, the courts are well-placed to adjudicate claims where the individual has a particular salience. Another valuable contribution they can make is to ensure that ongoing legislation is integrated into the stable framework of fundamental legal doctrine. It used to be said that judges were conservative in their politics. I do not know whether that is still the case, but it is certainly true that the courts are a conservative institutional body, designed in part to ensure a broad measure of stability, certainty and coherence in the law, even if the political winds are changing rapidly.[60]

The operation of these presumptions also highlights the Janus-faced aspect of the judicial role.[61] On the one hand, their role vis-a-vis the legislature is receptive—they have the task of applying the law enacted by Parliament, respecting 'the settled will of a democratic assembly'.[62] On the other hand, they have an active role in developing the law, sometimes updating it to meet new circumstances and

---

[58] Endicott (n 52) 209.
[59] Alexander Hamilton, James Madison and John Jay, *The Federalist* (1788) no 51 (Madison).
[60] Raz (n 49) 54.
[61] Joesph Raz, 'On the Authority and Interpretation of Constitutions: Some Preliminaries' in Larry Alexander (ed), *Constitutionalism: Philosophical Foundations* (Cambridge, Cambridge University Press, 1998) 181.
[62] *R v Lichniak* [2002] UKHL 47 (Lord Bingham).

interpreting it in the light of fundamental principles. So, the courts must be loyal to legislation which emerges from a democratic legislature, thus giving effect to the will of Parliament and implementing the law it wished to enact. But they also have an important role to ensure that certain constitutional values are protected and upheld in that legislation. We need 'principled as well as faithful adjudication'[63] from the courts.

This Janus-like characterisation of the judicial role is exemplified in many of the tasks that judges have to undertake. When making decisions on the basis of the common law, judges have to weigh the values of certainty, stability and legal continuity against the values of equity and justice in the individual case.[64] They are entitled to develop and change the law in order to do justice in the individual case, but only when they can establish that the interests of the individual are important enough and can be protected without undermining the certainty and stability of the law in unacceptable ways or to an unacceptable extent.

Similarly, when interpreting statutes, the primary task of the courts is to give effect to legislative intent, but in doing so, they also have the possibility in certain circumstances of interpreting the statutes in light of new circumstances, of rectifying apparent absurdity in statutory meaning and of interpreting legislation in light of underlying common law doctrine. In both contexts, judges face a choice between conservation and innovation. They can preserve an existing line of common law authority or they can depart from it, changing it, adapting it and ameliorating it if the circumstances are right. When interpreting statutes, they are also faced with a similar choice. Considerations of continuity, stability and authority of law are naturally very important in legal interpretation, but judges also have a role in striving to ensure a just decision for the parties before them. The application of general rules in statutes should be mediated by equity to ensure that no injustice results from their application. This means that judges do not always need to 'down tools whenever they meet a defect in the law'.[65] They have various doctrines and tools at their disposal to rectify the problem, in order to implement law and make it work. The propriety of using such tools requires careful consideration. They should not be used if the courts are unsure whether they will do any good. Ongoing maintenance, repair and conservation of the law is part of the role of the courts—a role which they must exercise responsibly and with care, being mindful of the institutional limitations under which they labour.[66]

In doing so, the challenge for the courts is to work out the correct balance between legal certainty, stability and continuity on the one hand, and the values

---

[63] Raz (n 49) 375.
[64] Kavanagh (n 35) 267ff.
[65] Lord Devlin (n 37) 4.
[66] Of course, such maintenance and repair is the function of much legislated law as well; see Raz (n 36) 200. The point is simply that legislated law can do much else besides, including root-and-branch radical reform. The courts are less well-suited to performing those larger tasks.

of equity and justice on the other.[67] Sometimes the damage to legal certainty, stability and continuity would be so great (and the consequences of the decision so uncertain) that the correct and most responsible judicial decision is to stick with the legal status quo, hoping that Parliament will intervene to change the law using the broader legislative techniques of law-making combined with the political techniques of generating popular support for that change. Sometimes the courts can reconcile both sides of the equation, doing justice for the individual whilst preserving to some extent the values of continuity and stability. On occasion, the injustice to the individual may be so egregious and the value at issue so fundamental within the legal system that this may outweigh potential detriment to legal certainty and stability in the law. So, if someone is arbitrarily detained without trial, then the courts have a supervisory role over the executive to correct this abuse of power. They also have an active role in statutory interpretation to strive to ensure protection for personal liberty where it is possible and responsible to do so.

III. POLITICAL QUESTIONS AND INSTITUTIONAL DESIGN

In 'The Limits of Law', Lord Sumption outlines the institutional strengths of the legislature and the various institutional values it instantiates. It has democratic legitimacy. It is accountable to the people. It can assess the degree of popular support for a measure and can strive to increase such support if it so wishes. These are good reasons to give the legislature a lead role in the project of governing. But as with all issues of institutional design, it is a matter of balancing the pros and cons.[68] Lord Sumption does not mention the downsides to these otherwise valuable attributes or the potential risks of democratic decision-making. We need not succumb to a disdainful attitude towards political life to realise that some of the virtues Lord Sumption outlines carry with them some potential vices. It is true that the legislature (and elected politicians generally) are responsive to popular views and can give those views a role in the policy agenda. But this responsiveness to popular views carries with it some potential risks. These are the risks of pandering to populist (but misguided) views, especially close to a general election and succumbing to short-term interest at the expense of long-term values. Their focus on the big-picture policy issues may lead them to overlook some implications for individuals. Moreover, simply because the legislators have access to wide sources of information and have some ability to assess the potential impacts of the government's policy initiatives, this should not lead us to be naïve about legislative

---

[67] Lord Irvine had something similar in mind, I think, when he said that the challenge of the courts is 'to work out where the correct balances lies between these competing imperatives of activism and restraint': Lord Irvine, 'Activism and Restraint: Human Rights and the Interpretative Process' (1999) 10 *King's Law Journal* 177, 180.

[68] Neil Komesar presses this point home in *Imperfect Alternatives: Choosing Institutions in Law, Economics, and Public Policy* (Chicago, University of Chicago Press, 1994).

foresight. Especially in relation to large-scale law reform, legislative prescience is limited. Whatever institutional strengths legislatures possess, they are necessarily 'partial virtues'.[69] It is only by seeing the pros and cons of each institution that we can make any advance with the large questions of institutional design posed by Lord Sumption.

Naturally, this applies with equal force to the courts. Given their composition, expertise in the law and decision-making processes, the courts are good at resolving disputes about the application of legal norms to particular circumstances, including the resolution of potential conflicts between such norms. They are also good at evaluating how a statute impacts on the individual and resolving disputes where the individual has particular salience. And their independence enables them to play a meaningful supervisory role vis-a-vis the executive and to curb some forms of legislative excess, harnessing legislation to legal doctrine. But precisely this strength is also a weakness. Judges base their decisions on a limited range of information. They are less well-equipped than the government or the legislature to assess the wider consequences for society as a whole. So the question naturally arises: in cases where courts can see that a case before them has 'multiple consequences' and 'wide implications' including resource-implications for government, should the courts declare those issues non-justiciable? Should they say that these are polycentric matters of social policy in which they have no role to play? If democratic assemblies are better than the courts on matters of 'social policy' and are better able to see the big policy picture and its impact on society as a whole, should the courts step out of the fray altogether?

I think that whilst a finding of non-justiciability may be the correct conclusion in some cases, it is inappropriate as a general judicial response to 'polycentric problems' or 'questions of social policy'. Rather than speaking in broad terms about whether issues of social policy are a matter for the legislature *or* the courts, I think it more helpful to reflect on the appropriate contribution each or both institutions should make in resolving and regulating such issues on behalf of the political community.

Immigration, national security, social housing, education, access to health services, prisoner voting, conditions in prisons—these are all issues of social policy. It is undoubtedly true that the legislature (and the executive) should play the lead role in deciding on the national immigration policy, how to respond to terrorist threats, how to distribute scarce resources in providing for health, education and health, as well as how to run prisons in a fair and just manner. But the courts also have an important role to play in relation to these issues. They are well-placed to evaluate the impact of these laws on individuals. They have a role to play in correcting potential abuses in power when the executive gives effect to its statutory powers in a way which either runs contrary to the statute or fundamental legal

---

[69] K Whittington, 'In Defence of Legislatures' (2000) 28 *Political Theory* 690, 693.

principle. The courts must also interpret primary legislation in light of the well-known presumptions outlined above, including the principle of legality.

So there is a division of labour in the roles played by the courts and the legislature, which is not captured by an all-or-nothing distinction between law and politics, or principle and policy. The difference resides in the different way each institution approaches issues which combine principle and policy—ways which are marked out by each institution's sense of the proper scope and limits of their constitutional role. As Lord Bingham put it in *R v Ministry of Defence ex p Smith*:[70]

> It is not the constitutional role of the court to regulate the conditions of service in the armed forces of the Crown, nor has it the expertise to do so. But it has the constitutional role and duty of ensuring that the rights of citizens are not abused by the unlawful exercise of executive power. While the court must properly defer to the expertise of responsible decision-makers, it must not shrink from its fundamental duty to 'do right to all manner of people'.[71]

Similarly, in the national security context, the courts have emphasised that they are:

> [V]ery much aware of the heavy burden, resting on the elected government and not the judiciary, to protect the security of this country and all who live here. All courts are acutely conscious that the government alone is able to evaluate and decide what counter-terrorism steps are needed and what steps will suffice.[72]

This does not mean that the courts have absolutely no role to play in those areas. On the contrary, Parliament has charged the courts with a responsibility of its own, namely to scrutinise such legislation for compliance with individual rights.[73] This responsibility is complementary to—rather than in conflict with—Parliament's own tasks. It means that the courts and Parliament have a shared responsibility to deal with national security, but they discharge that responsibility in different ways, in accordance with different institutional roles.[74]

Issues of social policy (like national security or immigration or the state of our prisons) comprise a number of different aspects, some of which may be non-justiciable and some of which may not. The courts must differentiate between those different aspects when assessing whether it is institutionally appropriate for them to intervene.[75] Some issues involved in a legislative scheme may 'depend on a political judgment which the court is ill-qualified to assess', whereas others

---

[70] *R v Ministry of Defence ex p Smith* [1996] QB 517.
[71] ibid 556.
[72] *A v Secretary of State for the Home Department* [2004] UKHL 56 (*Belmarsh* case) [79] (Lord Nicholls).
[73] ibid.
[74] Murray Hunt, 'Introduction' in Murray Hunt, Hayley Hooper and Paul Yowell (eds), *Parliament and Human Rights* (Oxford, Hart Publishing, 2015) 8ff.
[75] See, eg, *R (Baiai) v Secretary of State for the Home Department (Joint Council for the Welfare of Immigrants Intervening)* [2009] 1 AC 287 [25].

'may not turn on considerations of broad social policy but on an accurate analysis of the scheme and the law'.[76]

Though the courts sometimes use the distinction between issues of social policy (which are for the legislature) and issues of law (which are for them) as a useful shorthand, there are also lots of dicta where they distinguish carefully between the kinds of task they are well-equipped to perform and those which they are not. Thus, the distinction we discussed earlier between legislative and judicial lawmaking is often invoked. A classic example is provided by *Bellinger v Bellinger*,[77] which concerned the question whether section 11 of the Matrimonial Causes Act 1973 violated a transsexual female's right to marry under the Convention. Whilst the court found that the claimant's rights were clearly violated by the Act, it refused to interpret section 11 compatibly with the Convention using the interpretive tools of section 3 of the Human Rights Act 1998. Acknowledging the piecemeal and incremental nature of the judicial role, Lord Nicholls explained why it would be inappropriate for the courts, sitting in its judicial capacity, to accede to Mrs Bellinger's claim:

> The recognition of gender assignment for the purposes of marriage is part of a wider problem which should be considered as a whole and not dealt with in a piecemeal fashion. There should be a clear, coherent policy. The decision regarding recognition of gender reassignment for the purpose of marriage cannot sensibly be made in isolation from a decision on a like problem in other areas where a distinction is drawn between people on the basis of gender.[78]

Lord Nicholls pointed out that the issue raised wider questions about the nature and status of marriage in our society. Therefore, it 'ought to be considered as part of an overall review of the most appropriate way to deal with the difficulties confronting transsexual people'.[79] Changing the interpretation of the Matrimonial Causes Act would:

> [R]epresent a major change in the law, having far reaching ramifications. It raises issues whose solution calls for extensive enquiry and the widest public consultation and discussion. Questions of social policy and administrative feasibility arise at every point, and their interaction has to be evaluated and balanced. The issues are altogether ill-suited for determination by courts and court procedures. They are pre-eminently a matter for Parliament, the more especially when the government, in unequivocal terms, has already announced its intention to introduce comprehensive primary legislation on this difficult and sensitive subject.

A similar understanding of the appropriate division of labour was outlined in the recent *Nicklinson* case, which concerned the question whether the prohibition on assisted suicide in section 2 of the Suicide Act 1961 violated Articles 8 and 14 of the Convention.[80] The Supreme Court held that it did not. This was a classic example

---

[76] ibid [25].
[77] *Bellinger v Bellinger* [2003] UKHL 21.
[78] ibid [45].
[79] ibid [48].
[80] *R (on the Application of Nicklinson and another)* [2014] UKSC 38.

of a case where the courts had to choose between conserving the legal status quo on the one hand and developing the law on the other. The Supreme Court chose the former option. However, it did not declare the issue to be non-justiciable. As Lord Neuberger observed, 'the mere fact that there are moral issues involved plainly does not mean that the courts have to keep out'.[81] The courts should not abdicate their scrutinising role, whilst nonetheless being mindful of the need to exercise caution, circumspection and restraint in some contexts.[82]

Despite disagreeing on many points, their Lordships were at one in insisting that Parliament's decision to maintain a legal prohibition on assisted suicide was entitled to great respect for a number of reasons. The question whether the provisions of section 2 should be modified raised 'a difficult, controversial and sensitive issue, with moral and religious dimensions.'[83] If an incompatibility existed, it was not easy for the courts to identify, still less to cure. Such far-reaching reform, requiring an assessment of the relative merits of various types of scheme, would be best performed by Parliament rather than the courts. Lord Mance pointed out that legislative law-making was a better way of regulating this issue than relying on the more piecemeal tools available to the courts because 'the courts could not themselves fashion any scheme which would define circumstances in which or safeguards subject to which assisted suicide might be appropriate'.[84] And Lord Sumption observed that 'the question what procedures might be available for mitigating the indirect consequences of legalising assisted suicide, what risks such procedures would entail, and whether those risks are acceptable'[85] are more appropriate for legislative decision-making. Many of their Lordships gave weight to the fact that the issue had been 'considered on a number of occasions in Parliament' and was due to be considered again shortly.[86] That Parliament had debated the issue was not determinative of the Convention-compatibility or preclusive of the court's role, but Parliament's considered decision was entitled to respect.[87] This seems like an appropriate judicial response to the challenges faced by this case. The court exercised a constitutionally appropriate measure of respect for the role of the legislature, but it did not declare the issue to be non-justiciable.

IV. CONCLUSION

In public law adjudication over the last generation, there has a marked shift away from holding that entire areas of public policy are inherently non-justiciable

---

[81] ibid [98].
[82] See further A Kavanagh, 'Judicial Restraint in the Pursuit of Justice' (2010) 60 *University of Toronto Law Journal* 23.
[83] ibid [98]–[164].
[84] ibid [188].
[85] ibid [234].
[86] ibid [115].
[87] See [191] (Lord Mance).

towards a more flexible judicial approach which accepts that they are amenable to adjudication, whilst exercising an appropriate degree of judicial restraint in response to particular features of the case.[88] Social policy is no longer a no-go area for the courts. Nonetheless, judges stress that 'substantial respect should be paid by the courts to the considered decisions of democratic assemblies'.[89] In working out how much weight to give the decision arrived at by the legislature, the courts take into account whether the issue concerns one of the 'broad social policy' whose implications they may be less able to evaluate; the complexity and sensitivity of the issue and whether it is subject of deep societal controversy. Also relevant is whether Parliament has debated and scrutinised the issue.[90] Such factors may increase the respect that judges will accord to the legislature's decision, but they are not determinative. They have to be balanced against other concerns, such as whether the impact of the legislation on the individual is disproportionately burdensome or clearly unjust, or whether the courts are well-placed to provide a suitable remedy.[91] Even if the courts conclude that they are less well-placed to remedy a problem, if Parliament consistently refuses to grasp the nettle, this may give the courts reason to intervene.[92] It is not the ideal solution. But if no other state organ is willing to reform the law and an injustice might otherwise result, it may fall to the courts to intervene.[93]

In his lecture, Lord Sumption concludes that 'politics is quite simply a better way of resolving questions of social policy than judge-made law'.[94] To evaluate the truth of that claim, we would need to know what kind of question is under consideration and what kind of decision is required, together with information about potential consequences of deciding one way or the other. I would resist the suggestion that we are dealing with an either/or situation here. In my view, both the courts and the legislature have a proper role to play in addressing questions of social policy and rights. Law-making is a collaborative enterprise where different aspects of the law are made by different institutions at different times. It is important that each institution contributes the right elements at the right time in a way which is respectful of the contributions of the others. They have to work together. In this enterprise, the legislature plays the lead role and the courts have

---

[88] See Aileen Kavanagh, 'Constitutionalism, Counterterrorism and the Courts: Changes in the British Constitutional Landscape' (2011) 9 *International Journal of Constitutional Law* 172.

[89] *Sheldrake* (n 43) 469.

[90] For a detailed consideration of this issue, see Aileen Kavanagh, 'Proportionality and Parliamentary Debates: Exploring Some Forbidden Territory' (2014) 34 *OJLS* 443.

[91] For an analysis along similar lines, see Murray Hunt, 'Sovereignty's Blight: Why Contemporary Public Law Needs the Concept of "Due Deference"' in Nicholas Bamforth and Peter Leyland (eds), *Public Law in a Multi-layered Constitution* (Oxford, Hart Publishing, 2003).

[92] *Nicklinson* (n 80) [233] (Lord Sumption).

[93] As Lord Neuberger observed in *Nicklinson*, 'despite pleas from judges, Parliament has not sought to resolve these questions through statute, but has been content to leave them to be worked out by the courts'. ibid [98].

[94] Lord Sumption (n 1) 12.

a supporting role, assisting the legislature in the implementation of its laws whilst being prepared to stand up for certain values and principles in the appropriate case.

It is important not to overstate the role of the courts. Judges should not be prima donnas who wish to fashion an ideal society according to their own blueprint. Lord Sumption's lecture is a salutary reminder that they have neither the competence nor the legitimacy to perform such a pioneering role. But it is important not to understate it either. The courts provide a valuable forum in which individuals can bring claims and grievances about the application of the law to their circumstances. Given their independence and their legal expertise, the courts can hear and adjudicate individual claims, resolving the difficult legal issues which arise in the context of an individual case. They have a role to play in upholding the rule of law—and enforcing it against the other branches—even when complex and controversial issues of social policy are at stake.

8

Three Wrong Turns in Lord Sumption's Conception of Law and Democracy

JEFF KING

IN THIS SHORT chapter, I object to three rather central claims in Lord Sumption's speech 'The Limits of Law'[1]: about the legitimacy of judicial interpretation in public law; about his conception of democracy and the role of judicial review therein; and about the utility of the concept of polycentricity as a guide to justiciability.

I. LAW, POLITICS AND JUDICIAL LAW-MAKING

Lord Sumption's task in this speech, when read in conjunction with his FA Mann lecture 'Judicial and Political Decision-Making: The Uncertain Boundary',[2] is to assert that there is a workable border between legal and political decisions, and that judges applying British and European public law frequently transgress it. He illustrates the claim in the English law of judicial review by reference to cases that he claims were wrongly decided, namely *Ex p Witham* and, as indicated in the FA Mann lecture, *Ex p World Development Movement* and *Ex p Joint Council on the Welfare of Immigrants*.[3] I think that Lord Sumption's position on *Witham* and *Joint Council on the Welfare of Immigrants* is incompatible with his claim in the FA Mann lecture that he supports the *Simms* principle of legality, which is that Parliament must use clear language when it exercises its undoubted power to infringe human rights. *Ex p Witham* was about restricting access to justice by statutory instrument, without explicit parliamentary authority. *Ex p Joint Council on the Welfare of Immigrants* was about barring public authorities from offering

---

[1] Lord Sumption, 'The Limits of Law', 27th Sultan Azlan Shah Lecture, Kuala Lumpur, 20 November 2013, available at: http://supremecourt.uk/news/speeches.html.
[2] Lord Sumption, 'Judicial and Political Decision-Making: The Uncertain Boundary' (2011) 16 *Judicial Review* 301.
[3] *R v Lord Chancellor ex p Witham* [1997] 2 All ER 779 (CA); *R v Secretary of State for Social Security ex p Joint Council for the Welfare of Immigrants* [1997] 1 WLR 275 (CA); *R v Secretary of State Foreign and Commonwealth Affairs ex p World Development Movement* [1995] 1 WLR 386 (QB).

142 *Jeff King*

financial support to late-claiming asylum seekers, making them destitute and unable to work legally, again without explicit parliamentary authorisation. I am not sure whether Lord Sumption is aware that in the case of *Ex p Limbuela*, a substantially similar policy scheme embodied in legislation was found by all UK judges who considered the question (including a unanimous Appellate Committee of the House of Lords) to be incompatible in spirit with Article 3 of the European Convention on Human Rights.[4] Perhaps they too were unaware of the distinction between politics and law.

The *World Development Movement* case is in my view often misrepresented not only by Lord Sumption but also previously by Lord Irvine.[5] Both of these accounts claim that the High Court was principally concerned with assessing whether the Pergau Dam in Malaysia was economically efficient. But that was not the key issue in the case. Rather, it was whether a manifestly uneconomic project was a project 'for the purposes of promoting the development or maintaining the economy of any foreign country' within the meaning of section 1 of the Overseas Development and Co-operation Act. It was common ground in the case that the project was uneconomic, because the Minister's own Permanent Secretary (Tim Lankester) had advised him so and there was no evidence rebutting this view, and there was also evidence that the decision was taken to further wider British diplomatic and of course economic interests.[6] This case essentially concerned a minister using funds earmarked by the statute for certain statutorily defined purposes to support projects that were not for those purposes. The fact that Parliament voted separate funds for the project after the case not only does not prove Lord Sumption's point, but rather it vindicates the outcome of the judgment. If the government wanted to give Malaysia some £316 million for reasons pertaining to British interests, it can ask (tell) the Commons to vote that supply separately. The judgment left the £316 million in the development budget, where it belonged.

---

[4] *R v Secretary of State for the Home Department ex p Limbuela* [2005] UKHL 66.
[5] D Irvine, *Human Rights, Constitutional Law and the Development of the English Legal System* (Oxford, Hart Publishing, 2003) at 164–65: '[After explaining the statute, he continues] The court held that, properly understood, this meant "sound development", and concluded that the decision to make the grant was unlawful because, in the view of the court, the grant was economically unsound. By reading an additional requirement into the statute in this way, the court took away from the executive a considerable degree of autonomy. It is this type of judicial activism which begins to blur the boundary between appeal and review, thereby undermining the constitutional foundations on which the courts' supervisory jurisdiction rests.'
[6] Rose LJ: 'Whatever the Secretary of State's intention or purpose may have been, it is, as it seems to me, a matter for the courts and not for the Secretary of State to determine whether, on the evidence before the court, the particular conduct was, or was not, within the statutory purpose … A political purpose can taint a decision with impropriety.' Sir Tim Lankester's minute [ie, the Permanent Secretary] stated: 'The project was an abuse of the aid programme in the terms that this is an uneconomic project. [This was not contradicted.] Accordingly, where, as here, the contemplated development is, on the evidence, so economically unsound that there is no economic argument in favour of the case, it is not, in my judgment, possible to draw any material distinction between questions of propriety and regularity on the one hand, and questions of economy and efficiency of public expenditure on the other.' On the link between the aid and arms sales, see Foreign Affairs Committee, *Public Expenditure: The Pergau Hydro-Electric Project, Malaysia, The Aid and Trade Provision and Related Matters*, 13 July 1994, HC 271-1 (1994–95) at [88].

Let me turn to 'living tree' interpretation, which is the major target in Lord Sumption's speech.[7] The charge in his speech is that the Convention was originally intended as a charter against despotism and totalitarianism, *and* this implies a degree of minimalism to which present judges must adhere. This seems a perhaps incompletely stated version of originalism and, in particular, of the 'original meaning' version associated with Justice Antonin Scalia of the US Supreme Court.[8] I respectfully disagree on the helpfulness of this idea for interpreting the European Convention, both because it is an unsound approach to interpretation and because the evolutive approach has been democratically ratified on a number of occasions.

On the substance of the originalist argument, I should be clear that I agree with Lord Sumption that the original intentions and scheme of a convention's drafters should always be important and given weight. That much is merely purposive statutory interpretation. But 'original meaning' originalism holds that we must interpret the words in the legal instrument as those words were widely understood at the time the instrument was adopted. In the debate between Ronald Dworkin and Antonin Scalia on the merits of originalism, Dworkin's most convincing argument is that there is no strong evidence that the drafters of the US Constitution intended to enact their own particular understandings of what the text meant.[9] They intended to lay down general principles, not their own expectations of how those principles would be understood and applied. I want to argue here that this is exactly what legislators and drafters ought to do with certain vague statutory language and the types of norms found in international conventions (if perhaps not bilateral treaties).

When law-makers enact abstract language, even in a criminal law, they intend to give legislative force to normative standards and they thereby empower *both* the executive and the judiciary with interpretive authority. They intentionally employ vague language in order to preserve the flexibility of a legislative scheme. If this at first sounds strange, then the contrary proposition is upon consideration much stranger. When the authors of the Napoleonic Code created a sweeping set of civil rights and obligations for the private sphere, is it remotely reasonable to think that concepts like person, private, offer, delict, and good faith are to be understood as they were in nineteenth-century France? And when we enacted a general obligation in Britain not to dismiss employees unfairly, are we to read the term as a general normative standard, subject to evolving understandings, or as the words 'unfair dismissal' were understood when the Industrial Relations Act of 1971 was

---

[7] Lord Sumption (n 1) 7ff. Lord Sumption uses the phrase 'living instrument'. On this point, see Martin Loughlin's contribution in ch 3 of this volume.

[8] A Scalia and A Gutmann (eds), *A Matter of Interpretation: Federal Courts and the Law* (Princeton, Princeton University Press, 1997). For an excellent defence of living tree interpretation from non-Dworkinian starting points, see A Kavanagh, 'The Idea of a Living Constitution' (2003) 16 *Canadian Journal of Law and Jurisprudence* 55.

[9] ibid 119ff.

adopted (or do we rather go with the understandings in the consolidating amendments of 1974, 1978 and 1996)? It seems there is little doubt that the advantage of purposive, updating interpretations is so clear that we would need some special interpretive statement in a legal instrument saying otherwise.

Similarly with constitutions and international conventions, drafters realise that most such documents are meant to have a longevity unlike any other legal instrument.[10] Cass Sunstein calls these incompletely theorised agreements,[11] but, also, any public lawyer knows that the so-called 'dead hand of the past' problem is perhaps the largest single issue grappled with in constitutional theory. Purposive and living tree or evolutive interpretation, like purposive statutory interpretation, were very often meant to accommodate the changing nature of the state and societal mores. Constitutions do not just empower claimants, but they disable defendant public authorities, and evolutive interpretation can thus also protect public authorities. An originalist understanding of the US Constitution would devastate the regulatory capacity of the US federal government,[12] and it nearly did destroy Obamacare,[13] and may have done enormous damage to its regulation of election financing.[14] It is no accident that originalists in the US strike down far more legislation than their liberal colleagues,[15] under the absurd theory that they are being more democratic and less activist when they do so. Let me offer a hypothetical example closer to home. Suppose a public employee is dismissed on account of using racist language and racially offensive reasoning in emails at work. He complains that his free expression is abridged under Article 10 ECHR, and the issue in litigation is whether the dismissal is justified under Article 10(2) as necessary for the 'protection of ... public morals' or the 'rights of others'. If we read Article 10(2) as originalists would have it, we could not suppose that public morals would condemn racist speech or reasoning, because it was pervasive at the time across the political spectrum. But there is no doubt, one would hope, that both public morals and the rights of others now, properly understood, would justify legislation abridging expression rights in this type of context.

The more mundane reason why Lord Sumption's assault on living tree interpretation is unpersuasive is that the Strasbourg Court's approach has been ratified democratically on several occasions. Unlike Lord Sumption, I am not an historian

---

[10] There may be a different approach to traditional bilateral treaties than for conventions. Public international law recognises evolutive interpretation at times, but not nearly as the dominant mode of interpretation: see J Crawford, *Brownlie's Principles of Public International Law*, 8th edn (Oxford, Oxford University Press, 2012) 379–80. *cf* R Bernhardt, 'Evolutive Treaty Interpretation, Especially of the European Convention on Human Rights' (1999) 42 *German Yearbook of International Law* 11.

[11] C Sunstein, 'Incompletely Theorised Agreements' (1995) 102 *Harvard Law Review* 1733; see also his *Legal Reasoning and Political Conflict* (New York, Oxford University Press, 1996).

[12] Just such an argument is made in RA Barnett, 'The Original Meaning of the Commerce Clause' (2001) 8 *University of Chicago Law Review* 101, also supporting findings by Justice Clarence Thomas on the same issue.

[13] *NFIB v Sebelius* 567 US __ (2012); *King v Burwell* 576 US __ (2015).

[14] *Citizens United v FEC* 558 US 310 (2010).

[15] A Liptack, 'How Activist is the Supreme Court?' *New York Times* (13 October 2013) SR4.

and do not want to express a strong view on the intentions of the states that adopted the original Convention. But it seems that the text of the Convention was always capable of regulating domestic policy as it has done, and this is indeed also the understanding of Ed Bates, who has written the most authoritative exploration of the subject.[16] Provisions regarding the right to marry, translation services for the criminally accused, the detailed nature of Articles 5 and 6 and the restrictive nature of Article 14, together with the right of individual petition to the Commission, all suggest that it was known that the Convention would certainly address domestic policy. Above all, the detailed limitation provisions, and the emergency powers provision in Article 15, would hardly make sense if the Convention were regarded as a reference point during times of democratic collapse only.

What clearly was radically different at the outset was the role of the Strasbourg institutions in protecting the Convention's scheme. They were weak and inaccessible at the outset, and their interpretive assertiveness, admittedly, was not foreseen or welcome at first, nor can it be said that this role was part of the scheme that the drafters intended to set up.[17] But that is beside the point, because the Court's interpretive jurisdiction has been accepted by separate accession of states party, at a time when Sir Humphrey Waldock was advocating the vision of the Convention as a European Bill of Rights.[18]

Evolutive interpretation was announced by the Court in 1978 in the *Tyrer v UK* case,[19] and the UK has affirmatively renewed its commitment to the Court's jurisdiction three additional times since its acceptance of the Court's jurisdiction in 1966.[20] Most remarkably, the Human Rights Act 1998 was adopted in the same year as Protocol 11 to the Convention, which abolished the European Commission on Human Rights and made the Court the central interpretive organ. I can quote, as well, from the White Paper *Rights Brought Home*, which the Labour government laid before Parliament in 1997:

> 2.5   The Convention is often described as a 'living instrument' because it is interpreted by the European Court in the light of present day conditions and therefore reflects changing social attitudes and the changes in the circumstances of society. In future our judges will be able to contribute to this dynamic and evolving interpretation of the Convention.[21]

---

[16] E Bates, *The Evolution of the European Convention on Human Rights: From its Inception to the Creation of a Permanent Court of Human Rights* (Oxford, Oxford University Press, 2010). Bates also confirms that the Convention, as Lord Sumption maintains, was initially understood as a 'pact against totalitarianism'o though he explains how that conception evolved politically as well as juridically. See generally ch 4.

[17] ibid 89ff.

[18] ibid 366ff.

[19] *Tyrer v UK* [1978] ECHR 2. For another defence of evolutive interpretation at the Strasbourg Court in particular, see G Letsas, 'The ECHR as a Living Instrument: its Meaning and Legitimacy' in G Ulfstein, A Follesdal and B Peters (eds), *Constituting Europe: The European Court of Human Rights in a National, European and Global Context* (Cambridge, Cambridge University Press, 2013).

[20] Ed Bates, 'What was the Point of the ECHR?', http://ukhumanrightsblog.com/2011/03/21/what-was-the-point-of-the-european-convention-on-human-rights-dr-ed-bates.

[21] *Rights Brought Home: The Human Rights Bill* (CM 3782) (1997).

This exact feature of Strasbourg jurisprudence was also debated in Parliament at the time of the Human Rights Bill.[22] The issue was live and the choice was clear. So the assault on the legitimacy of evolutive interpretation is an assault on that very democratic choice.

II. THE CONCEPT OF DEMOCRACY[23]

So far as I can tell, there is no clear conception of democracy to be found in this speech, though there are a few comments indicating what it might consist in. The most direct claim in the speech is that: 'Democracy is a constitutional mechanism for arriving at decisions for which there is a popular mandate.' But neither Hitler, nor Mao, nor even Vladimir Putin can be regarded as democratic leaders, despite having had popular mandates. And Napoleon loved plebiscites too. The procedurally minimalist conception of democracy as formal voting equality, that it is, to quote Joseph Schumpeter, 'that institutional arrangement for arriving at political decisions in which individuals acquire the power to decide by means of a competitive struggle for people's vote'[24] has long been distinguished as wholly unconvincing.[25] And of course Lord Sumption's statement is incompatible with his own claim on the very same page—which I agree with—that we should not confuse popular sovereignty with democracy.

It is absolutely right that, in a democracy, the output of legislative decision-making must be defended as democratic. Democracy is more than tallying voting inputs.[26] The best defences of legislation against judicial review have focused on the claim that legislative decision-making is a better way of respecting the value

---

[22] See, eg, HL Deb 3 November 1997, vol 582, cols 1227–312 at col 1266 (Lord McCluskey).

[23] On this point, see Martin Loughlin in ch 3 of this volume.

[24] J Schumpeter, *Capitalism, Socialism and Democracy* (London, Routledge 1976 [1943]) 241.

[25] Lord Sumption confirmed in the seminar discussion that in his view this Schumpeter's statement that I reproduced here is precisely the right definition of democracy. Schumpeter's conception more generally is known as the 'elitist theory' of democracy. The theory advocates a role for governing elites that rejects any ongoing role for the views, preferences and wishes of the people as a guide to how elites should govern. As Gerry Mackie explains, Schumpeter was a 'reactionary monarchist' who 'did not welcome socialism, but even less did he welcome popular democracy.' G Mackie, 'Schumpeter's Leadership Democracy' (2009) 37 *Political Theory* 128, 128. Furthermore, Schumpeter disclaimed any need for an egalitarian conception of the franchise. See RA Dahl, *Democracy and its Critics* (New Haven, Yale University Press, 1989) 121–22 (showing that Schumpeter's conception led to absurdities such as that the exclusion of black Americans from voting in the American south, or the rule of the Bolshevik party in the Soviet Union, were not in principle undemocratic because we must simply accept each community's own definition of its demos). For these and other reasons, Amy Gutman refers to it only in passing in her discussion of democracy as 'one of the least inclusive, least inspiring conceptions of democracy that have gained currency in contemporary political theory.' A Gutman, 'Democracy' in RE Goodin, P Pettit and T Pogge (eds), *A Companion to Contemporary Political Philosophy* 2nd edn (Cambridge, Blackwell Press, 2007).

[26] R Dworkin, 'Introduction: The Moral Reading and the Majoritarian Premise' in *Freedom's Law: The Moral Reading of the American Institution* (Cambridge, MA, Harvard University Press, 1996).

of political equality.[27] And in my view the best theories of democracy tend to have the goal of securing political equality as their ultimate normative aim and thus this is the standard they must be judged by.[28] Democracy is about securing a mode of decision-making in which we strive to achieve equal potential influence on political decisions taken for the community. Formal voting equality is a logical starting point for giving effect to that view, but it is not the end point.

Lord Sumption's comments about the role of compromise and liberalism's rejection of it provide more clues to his understanding of democracy. I agree with the basic idea that political compromise is an important and legitimate aspect of politics, and a feature that has been marginalised in modern liberalism, especially, one might add, under Ronald Dworkin's notion of integrity as a distinct political virtue.[29] But why is compromise a good thing? The apparent answer to this question in Lord Sumption's analysis is inclusion. It goes against winner-takes-all politics and towards consensus decision-making where possible. But inclusion is not always good. The hyper-proportionality of party representation in the Weimar-era German Reichstag is widely seen as a key reason for its ineffectiveness and subsequent fall. Inclusion is *ordinarily* good for a further reason that we have already seen: it tends to respect the value of political equality and tries to give other groups a slice of the pie, some representation in the overall governing scheme. In corporatist political and economic systems[30] and some Christian doctrine,[31] compromise is seen as good because it facilitates social peace and thus the common good. But obviously in politics and corporatist systems of all types, one only compromises with those who have some power. Powerful groups normally compromise when

---

[27] J Waldron, *Law and Disagreement* (Oxford, Clarendon Press, 1999); J Waldron, 'The Core of the Case against Judicial Review' (2006) 115 *Yale Law Journal* 1347. For a more wide-ranging and challenging critique, see R Bellamy, *Political Constitutionalism: A Republican Defence of the Constitutionality of Democracy* (Cambridge, Cambridge University Press, 2007).

[28] See RA Dahl, *On Democracy* (New Haven, Yale University Press, 1998) chs 5 and 6 for a readable introduction; and RA Dahl, *Democracy and its Critics* (New Haven, Yale University Press, 1989) ch 6; CR Beitz, *On Political Equality: An Essay in Democratic Theory* (Princeton, Princeton University Press, 1990); T Christiano, *The Constitution of Equality: Democratic Authority and its Limits* (Oxford, Oxford University Press, 2008); A Gutman and D Thompson, *Democracy and Disagreement* (Cambridge, MA, Belknap Press, 1996) 26 ('Democracy … is a conception of government that accords equal respect to the moral claims of each citizen').

[29] R Dworkin, *Law's Empire* (Cambridge, MA, Belknap Press, 1986) chs 6–7. There is a debate to be had about whether the theories of Rawls and Dworkin could quite easily make space for compromise. This debate and discussion more generally is not new: JR Pennock and JW Chapman, *Nomos XXI: Compromise in Ethics, Law, and Politics* (New York, New York University Press, 1979); D Braybrooke, 'The Possibilities of Compromise' (1982) 93 *Ethics* 139–50 (reviewing the Pennock and Chapman volume); R Bellamy, *Liberalism and Pluralism: Towards a Politics of Compromise* (London, Routledge, 2002); A Margalit, *On Compromise and Rotten Compromises* (Princeton, Princeton University Press, 2009).

[30] See, eg, A Lipjhart, *Patterns of Democracy: Government Form and Performance in Thirty-Six Countries* (New Haven, Yale University Press, 1999); K Armingeon, 'The Effects of Negotiation Democracy: A Comparative Analysis' (2002) 41 *European Journal of Political Research* 81.

[31] The influence of Catholic thought in particular had important links to political and social corporatism: see H Wilensky, 'Leftism, Catholicism, and Democratic Corporatism' in P Flora and AJ Heidenheimer (eds), *The Development of Welfare States in Europe and America* (New Brunswick, NJ, Transaction Books, 1981).

they feel they have to. And if the compromises run too deep, they become a type of power-sharing arrangement with clientelist features that are downright regressive. Greece provides one example, and Colombia yet another. So if compromise is not always good, but is often good because it promotes equality, then we must ask whether we can design institutions that can correct for the process of political compromise when we can reasonably predict that political compromise can offend and not protect equality. Only a fool would be oblivious to the influence on professional politics of concentrated media, access by wealthy elites, and straightforward majoritarian bias and misinformation. And as a footnote, we should also be clear that the British political system in fact exemplifies a winner-takes-all system rather than a compromise democracy.[32]

In constructing democratic systems that respect the value of political equality, nations often depart from the norm of formal voting equality in a number of ways. The most widespread departure is representative rather than direct democracy. Direct democracy is no longer in fact impossible, and the call for referenda and ballot initiatives on all manner of issues is a major development in contemporary politics, as is the rise of protest parties, some of which offer software designed for real-time polling on minute political issues.[33] This is direct democracy 1.0, showing in real political theatres as we speak. We have all sorts of good quintessentially democratic reasons for stemming this tide and defending representative democracy.

Another frequent departure is bicameralism with weighted representation of federal sub-units in the second chamber. The US model is radically inegalitarian and thus probably undemocratic,[34] but there are many others that are more defensible in terms of political equality. A related example would be consociational systems with minoritarian veto players, such as in Northern Ireland, Switzerland, the Netherlands, Belgium and many other countries.[35] The point of consociational democracy is to preserve stability, but also to facilitate inclusion of groups at risk of harm in winner-takes-all politics, like in Britain and America. A step further still is legislative quotas for race and gender, which are used in well over fifty countries around the world.[36]

---

[32] A Lijphart, *Democracy in Plural Societies*, (New Haven, Yale University Press, 1977) ch 2; A Lijphart, *Patterns of Democracy: Government Form and Performance in Thirty-Six Countries* (New Haven, Yale University Press, 1999). For critique, see B Barry, 'Political Accommodation and Consociational Democracy' (1975) 5 *British Journal of Political Science* 477; DL Horowitz, *Ethnic Groups in Conflict* (Berkeley, University of California Press, 1985) 568–76.

[33] Especially Germany's 'Piraten Partei'aand its use of 'Liquid Feedback' software, something I criticise as incompatible with the practice of *good compromise* in J King, 'Down with Pirates' *UK Constitutional Law Blog* (20 October 2012), available at: http://ukconstitutionallaw.org.

[34] RA Dahl, *How Democratic is the American Constitution?*, 2nd edn (New Haven, Yale University Press, 2003) 43–54 (also confirming American exceptionalism on this issue).

[35] A Lijphart, *Patterns of Democracy: Government Forms and Performance in Thirty-Six Countries* (New Haven, Yale University Press, 2012) especially ch 3.

[36] ML Krook, 'Quota Laws for Women in Politics: Implications for Feminist Practice' (2008) 15 *Social Politics* 345; D Ruedin, 'Ethnic Group Representation in Cross-national Comparison' (2009) 15 *Journal of Legislative Studies* 335.

Yet another departure is found in the appointment of executive officials and even judges. In this country, the Conservative Party introduced the election of police and crime commissioners, which went ahead with an average voter turnout of 15.1 per cent.[37] And in the United States, state judges campaign on conviction rates. Is it undemocratic to regard that as pure folly? On the popular mandate theory offered by Lord Sumption, these officials would be yet more legitimate than those appointed by the executive and who are not accountable periodically to the people. But in a true democracy, we want efficient and non-corrupt crime prevention by career professionals rather than careerist politicians. The same is true of central bank independence, appointments to major agencies and so on.

Now we defend each of these institutions, or some of them, not as some infringement of democracy, but as arrangements that secure the value of political equality and thus democracy itself (or they may secure other ends, such as common welfare, stability etc). Judicial review of legislation on human rights grounds is best understood in precisely the same way. It is one possible mode of institutional design to protect political equality and basic rights in a system where formal voting equality creates a predictable problem. It might work poorly in some countries, like in the US. But in this country,[38] of the 21 statutes to date found incompatible with the European Convention by UK courts and not overturned on appeal, the overwhelming majority of cases concerned groups that are marginalised in the political process: homosexuals, transgender people, mental health patients, foreign terror suspects and, yes, prisoners—and, contrary to Lord Sumption's claim, there are good reasons to think prisoners are a politically marginalised group. The remainder concerned groups that were not politically marginalised, but not influential either: lorry drivers, care workers and children of deceased fathers conceived by fertility treatment. Moreover, about one-third of these cases involved legislation where the legislature had never even debated the rights-issue at stake in the case. There was no deal on the matter. On the whole, the record of the Human Rights Act suggests it has contributed to egalitarian outcomes and, at any rate, the remedies have been remarkably timid and required only minor legislative tweaking in almost all cases. That record may change and it may do more to harm than to help political equality. But for the moment, the legislative review under the Human Rights Act appears to have promoted rather than impeded the value of equality that inspires any convincing conception of democracy.

---

[37] Electoral Commission, *Police and Crime Commissioner Elections in England and Wales: Report on the Administration of the Elections held on 15 November 2012* (London, HMSO, March 2013) 3.

[38] I examine the experience with s 4 declarations and the responses of Parliament in detail in J King, 'The Role of Parliament Following Section 4 Declarations of Incompatibility' in H Hooper, M Hunt and P Yowell (eds), *Parliaments and Human Rights* (Oxford, Hart Publishing, 2015), and see 179 for an illustration of judgments relating to marginalized groups.

III. THE PLACE OF POLYCENTRICITY

Although Lord Sumption borrows his own title from Lon Fuller's famous essay 'The Forms and Limits of Adjudication', the idea of polycentricity makes only a late appearance in his speech. Essentially, the idea is that polycentric issues should not be adjudicated. Polycentric issues are those that comprise vast web of interlocking interests, such that changes to any interest are communicated through the web to other relationships of interest, ad infinitum.[39] Decisions concerning how to regulate an industry, or fund a school system, for instance, are polycentric because the policies adopted will affect a multitude of interacting parties who must adjust in myriad ways to the demands imposed upon them. Fuller thought these issues ill-suited to adjudication because the complexity led to judges making guesses, consulting non-represented parties and so on. His key point was that the distinguishing feature of adjudication as a mode of decision-making is that it gives to the party affected by the decision a right to participate in the adjudication. Polycentric issues affected many dispersed parties who cannot even be identified, let alone heard in court.

This idea continues to have huge purchase in English public law, even though it has died a slow death in the US. It died there because everyone knew that common law adjudication and American constitutional law were rife with polycentric issues. In the common law, we allow our judges to fashion the rules in cases that decide whether pure economic loss is recoverable; whether private parties should be able to recover compound rather than simple interest from public authorities; the scope of public policy in commercial contracting; the nature and grounds of judicial review; and of course supervision of the taxation system, one subject I explored in some detail in an article.[40] Fuller never adequately answered the challenges posed by these types of counter-examples.[41]

In my book *Judging Social Rights*, I tried to rescue Fuller's idea from dismissal by clarifying how we could admit its relevance on the one hand and non-decisiveness on the other.[42] There are factors that attenuate the weight a judge ought to give to the polycentric character of an issue presented to litigation. One of these factors is the mandate the legal framework gives to judges, and it is important for the present discussion. If the legal regime tells the judge to adjudicate a question of proportionality, then it is not for the judge to refuse to do this, as Lord Justice Laws proposed doing in the case concerning David Miranda and Glenn Greenwald,[43] and as Lord Sumption has remarkably argued in this very speech.

---

[39] L Fuller, 'The Forms and Limits of Adjudication' (1978–79) 92 *Harvard Law Review* 353. The paper was a draft published posthumously. As explained on the editor's opening note on the paper, the first draft was written in 1957 and was revised in 1959 and 1961. For my own discussions, which elaborate on the points made here, see J King, 'The Pervasiveness of Polycentricity' [2008] *Public Law* 101; and J King, *Judging Social Rights* (Cambridge, Cambridge University Press, 2012) ch 7.

[40] King, 'The Pervasiveness of Polycentricity' (n 39) 111–23.

[41] On this question, see Paul Craig in ch 10 of this volume.

[42] King, *Judging Social Rights* (n 39) ch 7.

[43] *R (Miranda) v Secretary of State for the Home Department* [2014] EWHC 255 (Admin); [2014] 1 WLR 3140 (Queen's Bench Division) at [40].

I should at this point remind some of the more left-leaning advocates of the idea of polycentricity that Lon Fuller borrowed the concept from Michael Polanyi's book *The Logic of Liberty*.[44] Polanyi was concerned not with adjudication, but with government control of the economy, and his book was a tract against central planning. Friedrich Hayek and Polanyi largely agreed with one another on the libertarian implications of the idea.[45] The idea of polycentricity advocated limiting regulation of the economy for the same reasons Fuller advocated limiting adjudication of those issues—the epistemic challenge for the decision-maker.

The riposte to this line of libertarian reasoning is that even if market regulation involves executive attempts to regulate extreme complexity, the alternative of self-coordination is harmful enough to justify certain trade-offs. The same is true of adjudication. We let our judges make up the private law because they are good at it (so the argument runs) and it suits the market and private persons. In the EU, for instance, Member States wanted the Court of Justice for the European Union to adjudicate issues that are highly polycentric simply because, I assume, these remedies were seen as necessary for a viable common market. National legislatures often do the same with consumer protection legislation, employment protection, judicial review of tax authorities and much else. The UK has recently adopted a general anti-abuse rule empowering Her Majesty's Revenue and Customs to counteract 'abusive' tax arrangements, following on from years of debate on the merits of a general anti-avoidance rule.[46] No doubt such a rule will raise polycentric issues for adjudication, but it was a good idea because the status quo ante was far more costly.

Parliament chose to give the UK courts a mandate under the Human Rights Act to adjudicate polycentric issues. I would respectfully argue that it is not for Lord Sumption to second-guess that choice, least of all under a theory that it is best for judges not to tell parliamentarians what to do. Parliament decided this was a step towards greater accountability and greater political equality, and that it was consonant with the values to which modern democratic orders aspire. The problem they recognised was that there was a deficit in a legal order in which nationals and foreigners alike could not raise human rights claims in our own courts. The belief that giving a domestic avenue for raising Convention claims could provide a remedy and enhance the accountability of executive and legislative authority has not been shown to be wrong. And nothing in the idea of polycentricity shows it to be wrong.

---

[44] M Polanyi, *The Logic of Liberty: Reflections and Rejoinders* (New York, Routledge & Kegan Paul, 1951) especially 170ff.

[45] King, 'The Pervasiveness of Polycentricity' (n 39) 104–05; FA Hayek, *The Constitution of Liberty* (London, Routledge Classics, 2006) 140–41.

[46] Part 5 of and schedule 43 to the Finance Act 2013. For context on the new institutions, see J Freedman, 'Creating New UK institutions for Tax Governance and Policy Making: Progress or Confusion?' [2013] *British Tax Review* 373. For further consideration of the anti-abuse rule, see J Freedman, 'Defining Taxpayer Responsibility: In Support of a General Anti-avoidance Principle' [2004] *British Tax Review* 332.

9

The Human Rights Act and 'Coordinate Construction': Towards a 'Parliament Square' Axis for Human Rights?

CAROL HARLOW

I. FUNCTIONAL SEPARATION OF POWERS AND THE HUMAN RIGHTS ACT

A CURIOUS FEATURE of the debate about law and democracy in the context of the Human Rights Act (HRA) is the extent to which it has been dominated by a certain idea of separation of powers. Lord Sumption has traced this to a judicial source: Lord Diplock's description of a 'balanced constitution' in which Parliament possesses 'the sole prerogative of legislating' and ministers are doubly accountable—on the one hand to Parliament 'for their policies and for the efficiency with which they carried them out' and on the other to 'the courts for the lawfulness of their acts'.[1] Many years later, Lord Hoffmann based a similar analysis overtly on separation of powers, distinguishing 'questions of law' from questions of 'judgment and policy'.[2] Courts and executive in these depictions exercise different functions and are functionally separate. Lord Sumption, on the other hand, dismisses this type of functional analysis as 'neat' and 'elegant', but 'perfectly useless, because it begs all the difficult questions ... The Diplock test will yield a different answer depending on how you define the issue'.[3] Functional analysis is reductive—perhaps deliberately so. Its effect is to transmute complex polycentric questions into a simple legal question and thus to re-allocate them to the judiciary without further discussion of justiciability. This is in fact precisely the way in which human rights campaigners present their case for human rights adjudication as primarily a judicial function.

---

[1] *R v Inland Revenue Commissioners ex p National Federation of Self-Employed and Small Businesses* [1982] AC 617, 619. But see similarly Sir Stephen Sedley, 'The Sound of Silence: Constitutional Law without a Constitution' (1994) 110 *LQR* 270.
[2] *Home Secretary v Rehman* [2003] 1 AC 153 [50].
[3] Lord Sumption, 'The Limits of Law', 27th Sultan Azlan Shah Lecture, Kuala Lumpur, 20 November 2013, 1.

But a striking characteristic of the Westminster model of governance is the absence of any clear dividing lines between the classical triad of governmental institutions. Indeed, until the passage of the Constitutional Reform Act in 2005, the House of Lords served the dual function of second chamber of the legislature and highest court in the land, and its judges were Law Lords, with rights to sit and vote in the House when acting in its legislative capacity. Although their legislative interventions were rare and governed by convention, Law Lords did participate in debates during the passage of the Human Rights Bill. Arguably then, it was the Constitutional Reform Act that effected the dramatic change in the constitutional order generally attributed to the HRA, infusing the constitution with a soupçon of separation of powers that runs against the grain of the doctrine of parliamentary sovereignty, which is the keystone of our constitution.

For Ewing, the HRA marks a break with constitutional tradition, involving an unprecedented transfer of political power from the executive and legislature to the judiciary and fundamental restructuring of our 'political constitution'.[4] Yet the doctrine of parliamentary sovereignty possesses 'surprising vigour, deep roots and unshakeable strength' and 'behind all the hyperbole about the emergence of legal constitutionalism, we find a strong sense of deference by the courts to the political branches'.[5] Lord Hoffmann too believes in the enduring strength of the sovereignty doctrine. The HRA does not alter the fundamental principle of parliamentary sovereignty, and 'people expect' human rights issues to be decided by Parliament 'as they have been in the past' and not by the Law Lords assuming the role of 'Platonic guardian'.[6] For Lord Bingham, speaking eloquently in favour of the Bill in the House of Lords, the HRA would change nothing. The judges would not be empowered—and did not wish to have the power—to 'overrule, set aside, disapply, or—if one wants to be even more dramatic—strike down Acts of Parliament'; following incorporation, 'nothing will be decided by judges which is not already decided by judges'.[7] Lord Hoffmann's view is more nuanced. The function of a judicial declaration of incompatibility is to draw a difficulty to the attention of Parliament. 'The sovereign Parliament' must then 'squarely confront what it is doing and accept the political cost'; it must then decide whether or not to remove the incompatibility.[8] Declarations of incompatibility are, in Conor Gearty's words, 'courteous requests for a conversation, not pronouncements of truth from on high' and 'all that the non-judicial branches of the state are required to do [is] think twice, not blindly obey'.[9] This is a cooperative model of institutional dialogue in which responsibility for a human rights regime is shared and judges and legislators

---

[4] K Ewing, 'The Human Rights Act and Parliamentary Democracy' (1999) 62 *MLR* 79.
[5] K Ewing and J Tham, 'The Continuing Futility of the Human Rights Act' [2008] *PL* 668, 670, 692.
[6] Lord Hoffmann, 'Human Rights and the House of Lords' (1999) 62 *MLR* 159, 160–61.
[7] HL Deb 3 November 1997, vol 582, col 1246. Lords Scarman and Ackner also participated in the debate. See also *Rights Brought Home: The Human Rights Bill*, Cm 3782 (1997) [211]–[213].
[8] *R v Home Secretary ex p Simms* [1999] UKHL 33.
[9] C Gearty, *Can Human Rights Survive?* (Cambridge, Cambridge University Press, 2006) 96.

are (to put this differently again) partners 'engaged in a common enterprise'.[10] This is, I shall argue, the model on which the HRA is premised.

By 'bringing rights home', Lord Irvine (then Lord Chancellor) proclaimed in presenting his Bill to the House of Lords, our courts would develop human rights throughout society and 'a culture of awareness of human rights would develop'. Responsibility for developing the culture of rights would be shared. The logic of the Bill was to 'maximise the protection of human rights without trespassing on parliamentary sovereignty'. The role of Parliament would be enhanced in that 'there would have to be close scrutiny of the human rights implications of all legislation before it goes forward' and this would be doubly underpinned: first, by the duty in section 19 of the Act for ministers to make a 'statement of compatibility' before the second reading of every bill in each House; and, second, by the section 10 power for ministers, following a declaration of incompatibility, to take remedial action by ministerial regulation.[11] Finally, the Lord Chancellor declared his confidence that the 'incorporation of the European convention into our domestic law will deliver a modern reconciliation of the inevitable tension between the democratic right of the majority to exercise political power and the democratic need of individuals and minorities to have their human rights secured'.[12] Courts and legislators must, in other words, work together to develop a human rights culture and construct a human rights framework consonant with the Westminster model of governance.[13]

Janet Hiebert has questioned the tendency to allocate responsibility for human rights exclusively to the judiciary, insisting that Parliament must also engage in a process of rights review. She argues too that separation of functions is dysfunctional:

> Political actors can benefit from the exposure to the judgement of judges who have more liberty from the electoral, public and political pressures that may constrain political decision making and whose rulings may provide important insights into why legislation represents an inappropriate restriction on a protected right. This is particularly significant for parliamentary systems where a majority government may not otherwise face serious constraints on legislative decisions.[14]

Judges too, Lord Sumption argues, must bear in mind that the parliamentary process may be:

> [A] better way of resolving issues involving controversial and complex questions of fact arising out of moral and social dilemmas. The legislature has access to a fuller range of

---

[10] Lord Woolf of Barnes, 'Droit Public—English Style' [1995] *PL* 57, 69.

[11] All the citations are from HL Deb 3 November 1997, vol 582, cols 1227–34.

[12] ibid. Every declaration of incompatibility—save one—has been implemented by the government of the day.

[13] See similarly H Fenwick, 'Prisoners' Voting Rights, Subsidiarity, and Protocols 15 and 16: Re-creating Dialogue with the Strasbourg Court?' UK Constitutional Law Blog (26th November 2013), available at: ukconstitutionallaw.org/2013/11/27/helen-fenwick-prisoners-voting-rights-subsidiarity-and-protocols-15-and-16-re-creating-dialogue-with-the-strasbourg-court.

[14] J Hiebert, 'Interpreting a Bill of Rights: The Importance of Legislative Rights Review' (2005) 35 *British Journal of Political Science* 235, 240.

expert judgment and experience than forensic litigation can possibly provide. It is better able to take account of the interests of groups not represented or not sufficiently represented before the court in resolving what is surely a classic 'polycentric problem'.[15]

Judges cannot afford—and are not required—to be 'insensitive to questions of democratic accountability'.

Mutual recognition is part of a process that Alec Stone Sweet calls 'coordinate construction'. This may in time lead courts habituated to deciding constitutional and human rights issues to engage in a form of 'sustained and intimate judicial-political interaction' in which they 'tell legislators how they ought to have written the law in the first place'. This in turn may promote a reaction in which legislators engage in 'the re-elaboration of a censured text in conformity with constitutional jurisprudence to secure promulgation'.[16] Danny Nicol has suggested that something similar may be beginning to happen in the context of the HRA. Rights-orientated interpretation, which tends towards generalities, has 'instilled a general sense of judicial interpretative liberty, giving courts a degree of legislative freedom'. They have, in other words, begun to 'act legislatively' and, 'although it would be open to a sovereign Parliament to alter or flesh out the Convention rights, Parliament has yet to sanction such a practice on any grand scale'.[17] But rather than a process of coordinate construction, Nicol depicts a formalist straitjacket in which law develops as a 'cordon within which politics is allowed to take place'.[18] Power is, in other words, draining away from Parliament towards the courts.

In the remainder of this chapter, I shall examine these ideas through the medium of four cases in which the relationship between Parliament and the courts was engaged and where human rights were problematic and often contentious. I shall argue that a dialogue model of human rights adjudication is a necessary antidote to the growing climate of rivalry, distrust and dissonance in which increasingly we find ourselves. I shall look for evidence of enhanced horizontal dialogue between national courts and the Westminster Parliament, but also at instances of parliamentary engagement with the Strasbourg Court and Council of Europe institutions. I shall consider the possible development of a web of multi-party horizontal, vertical and multi-level relationships, and I shall argue for a 'Parliament Square axis' in which courts and Parliament work together through a polycentric human rights dialogue to achieve a reasoned outcome.

---

[15] *R (Nicklinson and others) v Ministry of Justice and the DPP* [2014] UKSC 38 [28] and [231].
[16] A Stone Sweet, 'Constitutional Politics in France and Germany' in M Shapiro and A Stone Sweet, *On Law, Politics and Judicialization* (Oxford, Oxford University Press, 2002) 184, 189.
[17] D Nicol, 'Law and Politics after the Human Rights Act' [2006] *PL* 722, 729.
[18] ibid.

II. STUDIES IN CONFLICT RESOLUTION

A. Political Advertising, Careful Preparation

Of my four case studies, that which comes closest to the paradigm of 'coordinate construction' intended by the drafters of the HRA is the political advertising affair. Its largely coordinated and constructive outcome was doubtless facilitated by the facts that it began in Strasbourg with a case that did not involve the UK directly and that the challenged British legislation was initiated by a Labour government in a favourable climate shortly after the passage of the HRA when everyone was anxious to play by the rules. In *Verein gegen Tierfabriken* (*VgT*),[19] a panel of the European Court of Human Rights (ECtHR) had unanimously decided that a Swiss law prohibiting all political advertising on the state-owned television service violated Article 10 of the European Convention on Human Rights (ECHR) because it was too inclusive a ban to be necessary in a democratic society. Political advertising was not prohibited altogether and might be compatible with Article 10 ECHR (freedom of speech) in certain situations, but the reasons for a ban must be both 'relevant' and 'sufficient' in respect of the particular case. In *VgT*, which involved an innocuous advertisement from a group campaigning against cruelty to animals, the Swiss authorities failed to satisfy the Court in a 'relevant and sufficient' manner why the grounds advanced generally in support of the prohibition of political advertising served to justify the interference in the particular circumstances of the case.[20]

The main concern of the UK government in its Communications Bill was the establishment of communications networks and of Ofcom, a new regulator of communications services in the interest of consumers. Political advertising was not at the forefront of their minds and the draft Bill turned to the subject only in clause 314, which did not receive much attention during passage of the Bill. The clause (which became sections 319 and 321(2) of the Communications Act 2003) contained a ban on political advertising drafted widely enough to cover all 'objects of a political nature' or 'political ends' as defined in the Act. This policy could be traced back to the introduction of independent television in 1954 and it reproduced a similar prohibition under the Broadcasting Act 1990 premised on the recommendations of the 1998 Neill Committee on political party funding.[21] There had been a three-month public consultation on the 2002 Bill; it had been considered by two parliamentary joint committees and was supported by the

---

[19] *Verein gegen Tierfabriken v Switzerland* (2001) 34 EHRR 159.
[20] ibid [74] and [75].
[21] 5th Report of the Committee on Standards in Public Life, *The Funding of Political Parties in the United Kingdom*, Cm 4057-I (1998), ch 13. The Committee discussed the implications of the earlier ECtHR decision in *Groppera Radio v Switzerland*, Series A 173 (28 March 1990), but recommended maintaining the ban on political advertising (Recommendation 94).

Independent Television Authority[22] and the Electoral Commission.[23] Yet the government was well aware of the problem posed by *VgT* and the Secretary of State for Culture introducing the Bill made the following section 19 statement:

> I am unable (but only because of clause 314) to make a statement that, in my view, the provisions of the Communications Bill are compatible with the Convention rights. However, the Government nevertheless wishes the House to proceed with the Bill.

The Joint Committee set up to consider the Bill expressed support for the principles underlying the proposed ban in a cursory paragraph, while at the same time urging the government to give careful consideration to methods of carrying forward the ban in ways not susceptible to challenge for incompatibility with Convention rights.[24] As might be expected, the Joint Committee on Human Rights (JCHR) paid particular attention to the question of possible incompatibility with *VgT*, recommending that although it would be a formidable challenge to put in statutory form 'a more circumscribed ban applied more discriminatingly', the government 'should seek restrictions short of an outright ban which could be shown to advance one of the legitimate aims in Article 10(2), and to be a proportionate and non-discriminatory way of pursuing that aim'.[25] In addition, the JCHR wrote asking the Minister to explain why it would be impossible to introduce 'transparent and proportionate' controls on political advertising that would secure a fair balance between competing rights and interests.[26] The Minister responded with a memorandum explaining that the government had looked at ways to include 'workable and Convention-compatible restrictions' in the Bill, but had concluded that the schemes would be unworkable and would not only 'fall significantly short of the present outright ban' but would also allow a substantial degree of political advertising to be broadcast;[27] in other words, the Bill's legitimate objective would not be achieved. Somewhat grudgingly, the JCHR conceded that the course of action taken by the government did not evince a lack of respect for human rights and was 'legitimate in the circumstances',[28] and the Bill passed into law with the political exceptions.

Some five years later, the ban was challenged in court by Animal Defenders International, a campaigning group seeking to broadcast an advertisement about cruelty to primates. The Divisional Court refused a declaration of incompatibility and the case leapfrogged to the Lords.[29] Lord Bingham's speech was significant.

---

[22] Letter of 10 October 2002 from Sir Robin Biggam.
[23] Electoral Commission, *Party Political Broadcasting: Report and Recommendations* (January 2003).
[24] Joint Committee on the Draft Communications Bill, *Draft Communications Bill*, HC 876-1 (2002–03) [301] and Recommendation 100.
[25] JCHR, *Nineteenth Report of Session 2001–2002*, HC 1102 (2001–02) [64] and [57]–[63].
[26] See JCHR, *First Report of Session 2002–2003*, HC 191 (2002–03) [16].
[27] ibid, Appendix 6.
[28] JCHR, *Fourth Report of Session 2002–2003*, HC 397 (2002–03) [41].
[29] *R (Animal Defenders International) v Secretary of State for Culture, Media and Sport* ([2006] EWHC 3069 (Admin); *R (Animal Defenders International) v Secretary of State for Culture, Media and Sport* [2008] UKHL 15. Lord Bingham spoke for Lords Carswell and Neuberger and the decision was unanimous.

After referring in some detail to the parliamentary stages of the Communications Bill, he summarised the government's position as being that it believed and had been advised that the proposed statutory ban on political advertising was compatible with Article 10 ECHR, but because of the ECtHR decision in *VgT*, it could not be sure of this. He went on to look at the *VgT* decision, weighing it against a later ECtHR ruling involving the banning of a religious advertisement under virtually similar Irish legislation[30] and concluding that there was no clear consensus on the broadcasting either of religious advertisements or of political advertising. It followed that the national margin of appreciation should be wider in such cases and 'it may be that each state is best fitted to judge the checks and balances necessary to safeguard, consistently with article 10, the integrity of its own democracy'.[31] In the instant case, the judgment of Parliament should be accorded great weight:

> First, it is reasonable to expect that our democratically-elected politicians will be peculiarly sensitive to the measures necessary to safeguard the integrity of our democracy. It cannot be supposed that others, including judges, will be more so. Secondly, Parliament has resolved, uniquely since the 1998 [Human Rights] Act came into force in October 2000, that the prohibition of political advertising on television and radio may possibly, although improbably, infringe article 10 but has nonetheless resolved to proceed under section 19(1)(b) of the Act. It has done so, while properly recognising the interpretative supremacy of the European Court, because of the importance which it attaches to maintenance of this prohibition. The judgment of Parliament on such an issue should not be lightly overridden.[32]

Thus, the groundwork had been fully prepared by a government professing itself anxious to be compliant, a Parliament that had apparently taken its scrutiny obligations seriously, and courts that had both considered the parliamentary proceedings carefully and, perhaps more importantly, set out the course of events in some detail. Consequently, when, five years later, the ECtHR finally adopted its judgment, the national position was solid, sound and set out in a way that was easy for the ECtHR to follow with a clear message of support for government policy in Lord Bingham's speech. The importance of this is clear from the following passage in the majority judgment, which described the legislative ban as 'the culmination of an exceptional examination by parliamentary bodies of the cultural, political and legal aspects of the prohibition as part of the broader regulatory system governing broadcasted public interest expression in the United Kingdom and all bodies found the prohibition to have been a necessary interference with Article 10 rights':

> It was this particular competence of Parliament and the extensive pre-legislative consultation on the Convention compatibility of the prohibition which explained the degree of deference shown by the domestic courts to Parliament's decision to adopt

---

[30] *Murphy v Ireland* (2003) 38 EHRR 212.
[31] *Animal Defenders* [2008] UKHL 15 [35].
[32] *Animal Defenders*, ibid [33].

the prohibition ... The proportionality of the prohibition was, nonetheless, debated in some detail before the High Court and the House of Lords. Both courts analysed the relevant Convention case-law and principles, addressed the relevance of the above-cited *VgT* judgment and carefully applied that jurisprudence to the prohibition. Each judge at both levels endorsed the objective of the prohibition as well as the rationale of the legislative choices which defined its particular scope and each concluded that it was a necessary and proportionate interference with the applicant's rights under Article 10 of the Convention.

The Court, for its part, attaches considerable weight to these exacting and pertinent reviews, by both parliamentary and judicial bodies, of the complex regulatory regime governing political broadcasting in the United Kingdom and to their view that the general measure was necessary to prevent the distortion of crucial public interest debates and, thereby, the undermining of the democratic process.[33]

Even so, the government victory was marginal. The ECtHR decided by only nine votes to eight that the legislation—supported by Judge Bratza, the national judge—was not disproportionate and that there had been no violation of Article 10. A strong dissenting judgment carried the following warning:

The fact that a general measure was enacted in a fair and careful manner by Parliament does not alter the duty incumbent upon the Court to apply the established standards that serve for the protection of fundamental human rights. Nor does the fact that a particular topic is debated (possibly repeatedly) by the legislature necessarily mean that the conclusion reached by that legislature is Convention compliant; and nor does such (repeated) debate alter the margin of appreciation accorded to the State. Of course, a thorough parliamentary debate may help the Court to understand the pressing social need for the interference in a given society. In the spirit of subsidiarity, such explanation is a matter for honest consideration. In the present judgment, however, excessive importance has been attributed to the process generating the general measure, which has resulted in the overruling, at least in substance, of *VgT*, *a judgment which inspired a number of member States to repeal their general ban—a change that was effected without major difficulties*.[34]

Underlying these conflicting judgments are two very different models of human rights adjudication. The majority shows respect for the 'particular competence of Parliament' and takes note of the cultural background against which the prohibition has been adopted and the 'exacting and pertinent reviews, by both parliamentary and judicial bodies', which are envisaged as cooperating as partners. The minority judgment adopts a diametrically opposed model in which the human rights court has legislative responsibility for the construction of human rights law and national legislatures merely transpose judicial rulings into national legislation. At the same time, *Animal Defenders* provides an exemplary model of 'coordinate construction' and the dialogic approach. It also underlines a point made

---

[33] *Animal Defenders International v UK* (2013) 57 EHRR 21 [114]–[116].
[34] ibid, Joint Dissenting Opinion of Judges Ziemele, Sajó, Kalaydjieva, Vučinić and De Gaetano [9] (emphasis added).

by Lord Bingham concerning the significant contribution of British judges to the development of human rights law. In the debate on the Bill, he had argued that the HRA would give the Strasbourg Court the benefit of a considered judgment by a British judge, with the consequence that 'some of our more idiosyncratic national procedures and practices may be better understood'.[35] This is an important point to bear in mind.

B. Prisoners' Voting Rights: Disobedience or Dialogue?

In *Hirst v UK*,[36] the Grand Chamber of the ECtHR ruled that section 3 of the Representation of the People Act 1983 imposed a 'blanket ban' on voting by convicted prisoners. This was disproportionate and a violation of Article 3, Protocol 1 of the ECHR (A3, P1), which provides that:

> The High Contracting Parties undertake to hold free elections at reasonable intervals by secret ballot, under conditions which will ensure the free expression of the opinion of the people in the choice of the legislature

The margin of appreciation accorded to states under the ECHR was wide but not all-embracing and the automatic disenfranchisement of all convicted prisoners in prison fell outside any acceptable margin of appreciation, 'however wide that margin might be'.[37] The Court demanded legislation within six months.

For human rights lawyers in particular, this is simply a case of disobedience. As the JCHR put it in one of its three reports on the matter, the current 'blanket ban' on the enfranchisement of prisoners was 'incompatible with the UK's obligations under the European Convention and must be dealt with'. The issues were 'not legally complex' and:

> [T]he continued failure to remove the blanket ban, enfranchising at least part of the prison population, is clearly unlawful. It is also a matter for regret that the Government should seek views on retaining the current blanket ban, thereby raising expectations that this could be achieved, when in fact, this is the one option explicitly ruled out by the European Court.[38]

That the issue was controversial and that 'the Government would be taking a generally unpopular course if it were to enfranchise even a small proportion of the prison population' was swept aside by the JCHR as irrelevant. It was not open to the government to question the merits of the ECtHR. A year later, the JCHR was lamenting the fact that 'the case appears destined to join a list of long standing

---

[35] HL Deb 3 November 1997, vol 582, col 1245.
[36] *Hirst v UK (No 2)* (2006) 42 EHRR 41. For a full account of the affair, see I White, *Prisoners' Voting Rights*, House of Commons Research Centre, SN/PC/01764 (updated to 2014).
[37] *Hirst* (n 36) [83].
[38] JCHR, *Monitoring the Government's Response to Court Judgments Finding Breaches of Human Rights*, HC 728 (2006–07) [77]–[78].

breaches of individual rights that the current Government, and its predecessors, have been unable or unwilling to address effectively within a reasonable time frame'.[39]

From this standpoint, the prisoners' voting rights affair seems to epitomise the dualistic character of the law/democracy debate. Thus, Thorbjørn Jagland, Secretary-General to the Council of Europe, giving evidence to a parliamentary bill committee, described himself as 'a rule of law man, so I have to respect the fact that the Court has the final word'. The explicit refusal to implement was a 'first'; no country had ever refused to execute an ECtHR judgment and if the UK—seen as the leading nation regarding human rights and rule of law in Europe and worldwide—were to do so, it might be 'the beginning of the weakening of the Convention system and probably after a while there may also be dissolution of the whole system'.[40] From the opposite end of the spectrum, Chris Grayling, the Justice Secretary, described the issue as one 'of totemic importance in a debate about who governs Britain',[41] while Eurosceptic MP, Philip Hollobone, called it in a parliamentary debate 'a golden opportunity' for the Coalition government 'to put Britain first' and consider 'pulling out of the Convention'.[42]

Yet Thorbjørn Jagland's evidence also provides support for a dialogic interpretation of the *Hirst* saga. Although there had not been a case of overt disobedience, he admitted, states had come to the Committee of Ministers and said: 'We have problems. We cannot do it now. You have to give us more time.'[43] Moreover, in response to questions from Lorely Burt MP, who asked 'You are saying that perhaps they should have talked to us then? We should have been able to have that dialogue?', Mr Jagland replied: 'If Protocol 16 had been in place, then one had this opportunity to have an exchange, but there are other possibilities to have a dialogue, which are not so based on formal articles.'[44] The new Protocol 16, which was not then in force, provides for dialogue in the form of advisory opinions between the highest national court and the ECtHR.[45] In a dialogic framework, stages in the *Hirst* saga can just be read as moves in a multi-level dialogue in which the participants change position and inch forward towards compromise.

In *Hirst*, for example, the majority took Parliament on directly, remarking that there was no evidence that it had, since 1968, 'ever sought to weigh the competing interests or to assess the proportionality of a blanket ban on the right of a convicted prisoner to vote'.[46] Unusually, the House of Commons struck back with

---

[39] JCHR, *Monitoring the Government's Response to Human Rights Judgments: Annual Report 2008*, HC 1078 (2007–08) [62].

[40] Evidence to the Joint Committee on the Draft Voting Eligibility (Prisoners) Bill, HC 924 (2013–14) 224.

[41] ibid 185.

[42] HC Deb 11 January 2011, vol 521, cols 5 and 6WH.

[43] HC 924 at 184–85.

[44] ibid 190.

[45] But see K Dzehtsiarou and N O'Meara, 'Advisory Jurisdiction and the ECtHR: A Magic Bullet for Dialogue and Docket-Control?' (2014) 34 *Legal Studies* 444.

[46] *Hirst* (n 36) [79]. There was a 12:5 majority.

a Westminster Hall debate calling for a 'proper parliamentary debate on the issue, so that colleagues can debate the pros and cons and be given the opportunity to vote to maintain the status quo'.[47] A cross-party, backbench motion followed, which asserted that 'legislative decisions of this nature should be a matter for democratically-elected lawmakers' and supported 'the current situation in which no prisoner is able to vote except those imprisoned for contempt, default or on remand'. At the end of a lengthy debate, the motion passed by 234 votes to 22.[48]

The ECtHR had asked for legislation within six months and the Labour government made gestures at compliance with a two-stage consultation on policy options, but the judgment remained unimplemented at the time of the General Election in 2010. Left to clear up the mess, the Coalition announced legislation that would provide for offenders sentenced to a custodial sentence of less than four years to vote in Westminster and European Parliament elections, unless the judge stated this to be inappropriate in sentencing.[49] In the same year, the ECtHR, treating *Greens and MT* as a 'pilot case', extended the six-month deadline by six months, while warning that the UK government was exposing itself to 'stockpiled' compensation claims.[50] Finally, in 2012, the Ministry of Justice submitted to a committee of both Houses a draft bill containing three options: a ban on prisoners sentenced to four or more years; a ban on prisoners sentenced to six months or more; or a restatement of the existing ban. The Bill Committee recommended that prisoners serving sentences of 12 months or less should have the vote,[51] but no legislation has been timetabled.

Alongside, the government had intervened in the *Scoppola* case[52] to ask the ECtHR to reconsider *Hirst*. Although it firmly declined to depart from precedent, the Court did soften *Hirst* by expanding the margin of national discretion. Caught between the ECtHR and Parliament, the Supreme Court manoeuvred skilfully in *Chester*, the first case to reach it. It held itself bound to follow the law as repeatedly confirmed by Strasbourg, yet declined to grant a declaration of invalidity on the ground that one had already been made.[53] Perhaps thankfully, Lord Mance declared that it was 'now for Parliament as the democratically elected legislature to complete its consideration of the position'[54] and the issue was neatly side-stepped when a claim to vote in the Scottish Referendum was dismissed by a majority on the ground that Article 3, Protocol 1 did not extend outside parliamentary elections.[55]

---

[47] HC Deb 11 January 2011, vol 521, cols 5 and 6WH (Philip Hollobone MP).
[48] HC Deb 10 February 2011, vol 523, col 584.
[49] HC Deb 20 December 2010, vol 520, col 151WS (Mark Harper MP).
[50] *Greens and MT v UK* (2010) ECHR 1826 [97].
[51] Joint Committee on the Draft Voting Eligibility (Prisoners) Bill, HC 924 (2013–14).
[52] *Scoppola v Italy (No 3)* (2013) 56 EHRR 19.
[53] *R (Chester) v Secretary of State for Justice* [2013] UKSC 63. A declaration of invalidity had been granted by the Scottish Election Appeal Court in *Smith v Scott* (2007) SC 345.
[54] *Chester* (n 53) [42].
[55] *Moohan v Lord Advocate* [2014] SC 67. Lords Kerr and Wilson dissented.

A differently constituted Supreme Court was gently changing its position and a wider case law was starting to reclaim the authority of British courts in human rights adjudication.[56] A spirited extra-judicial discourse was developing. Lady Hale addressed the question of supremacy directly[57] and we find Lord Kerr arguing in a lecture that if the Court had ever seen itself as subservient to Strasbourg, we should 'stop it at once', 'kick the habit', 'stiffen our sinews and stride forward confidently'.[58] Lord Irvine—who had introduced the Human Rights Bill—exhorted the Supreme Court 'to re-assess all its previous statements about the stance it should adopt in relation to the jurisprudence of the ECHR in order to ensure that the Supreme Court develops the jurisdiction under the HRA that Parliament intended'. The Court should 'decide the cases before it for itself' and, in case of disagreement, should bear in mind that 'the resolution of the resultant conflict must take effect at State, not judicial level'.[59] Finally, Lord Sumption added to his extra-judicial defence of political decision-making[60] judicial warnings that parliamentary process may be 'a better way of resolving issues involving controversial and complex questions of fact arising out of moral and social dilemmas'[61] and that 'there remain areas which although not immune from scrutiny require a qualified respect for the constitutional functions of decision-makers who are democratically accountable'.[62] There should be no assumption that a court of review is entitled in human rights cases to substitute its own decision for that of the constitutional decision-maker: 'However intense or exacting the standard of review in cases where Convention rights are engaged, it stops short of transferring the effective decision-making power to the courts.'[63]

The Queen's Speech for 2014 contained no mention of legislation, but the government negotiated a further period of delay with the Committee of Ministers. The ECtHR has further eased the pressure by ruling that the finding of a violation of Article 3, Protocol 1 is in itself 'just satisfaction' for non-pecuniary damage sustained by applicants.[64] Fragmentary, disconnected, incoherent and incomplete, the exchanges are nonetheless part of a dialogue.

---

[56] The stages by which the Supreme Court has been led 'substantially to modify the *Ullah* principle' are provided in a timeline by Lord Wilson in *Moohan* (ibid) [104].

[57] Baroness Hale of Richmond, 'Argentoratum Locutum: Is Strasbourg or the Supreme Court Supreme?' (2012) 12 *Human Rights Law Review* 65.

[58] Lord Kerr, 'The UK Supreme Court: The Modest Underworker of Strasbourg?' Clifford Chance Lecture (25 January 2012). See text at nn 67 and 68 below.

[59] Lord Irvine of Lairg, 'A British Interpretation of convention Rights' (December 2012), www.ucl.ac.uk/laws/judicial-institute/files/British_Interpretation_of_Convention_Rights_-_Irvine.pdf.

[60] Lord Sumption (n 3).

[61] *R (Nicklinson and others)* (n 15).

[62] *R (Lord Carlile of Berriew) v Home Secretary* [2014] UKSC 60 [28].

[63] ibid [31].

[64] *Firth and others v UK* [2014] ECHR 874 (12 August 2014).

C. The Immigration Bill 2013: Structuring Judicial Discretion

Efforts by the Coalition government to strengthen and re-shape the Home Secretary's power to deport convicted criminals of foreign nationality afford a more advanced example of coordinate construction, involving a prolonged process of judicial-political interactions. Powers to deport are now statutory; the Immigration Act 1971 provided that a person who is not a British citizen is liable to deportation if 'the Secretary of State deems his deportation to be conducive to the public good', a term that is not defined, and the UK Borders Act 2007 provides more specifically that the Secretary of State must make a deportation order in respect of a 'foreign criminal'. The question whether a deportation is in the public interest was, until very recently, a matter of ministerial discretion. How the discretion would be exercised was set out in Immigration Rules, defined by the Immigration Appeals Act 1969 as 'rules made by the Secretary of State ... which have been published and laid before Parliament'; when laid, the Rules can be disapproved by a Resolution of either House. The precise legal status of the Rules is uncertain and has given the courts a good deal of trouble; however, they are generally agreed to be something more than 'practice' or policy guidance, but less than regulation. A rule acquires the force of law if it is used as a ground for appeal to an immigration tribunal.[65]

The position changed radically after the HRA came into force, triggering growing recourse to Article 8 ECHR (which mandates respect for family life and limits the grounds on which the state can interfere with the right) to prevent deportation of non-national convicted criminals on grounds of intrusion into their family life. By 2010, this practice was having a considerable impact; indeed, it was claimed that such cases accounted for up to 50 per cent of immigration appeals.[66] The problem was exacerbated by the effect of the so-called 'mirror principle', which tied the UK courts tightly to the Strasbourg jurisprudence.[67] The upshot was the introduction of a two-stage test in Article 8 cases, whereby the ministerial view of the public interest would be evaluated with reference to the Strasbourg jurisprudence and the proportionality doctrine that this enjoined UK courts to apply.[68] Put crudely, the domestic view of the public interest in maintaining control over immigration could not, in the light of the mirror principle, prevail over a Strasbourg-dictated view of the ambit of Article 8 family rights. Moreover, in *Huang*,[69] where the

---

[65] In *Secretary of State for the Home Department v Pankina* [2010] EWCA Civ 719, Sedley LJ provides a comprehensive analysis of the legal position. And see also *Odelola v Home Secretary* [2009] UKHL 25 [6] (Lord Hope).

[66] In *MF (Nigeria) v Secretary of State for the Home Department* [2013] EWCA Civ 1192, it was stated that of 602 appeals allowed by the immigration tribunals in 2013, 324 involved convicted criminals who succeeded under art 8. According to a freedom of information request submitted by Dominic Raab MP, the number ranges from 200 to 400 annually and they constitute around 89 per cent of all successful human rights challenges to deportation orders (HC Deb 30 January 2014, vol 574, col 1062).

[67] See *R (Ullah) v Special Adjudicator* [2004] UKHL 26.

[68] *R (Razgar) v Secretary of State for the Home Department* [2004] UKHL 27

[69] *Huang v Secretary of State for the Home Department* [2007] UKHL 11.

government argued that the Immigration Rules had 'the imprimatur of democratic approval as they were made by the responsible minister and laid before Parliament', the House of Lords disagreed; the Rules were not 'the product of active debate in Parliament, where non-nationals seeking leave to enter or remain are not in any event represented'.[70]

Immigration is a high visibility political issue in the UK that can shape the outcome of general elections. It was therefore not altogether surprising that some time after *Huang*, the Home Secretary, Theresa May, announced changes to the Immigration Rules 'to ensure that the misinterpretation of Article Eight of the ECHR—the right to a family life—no longer prevents the deportation of people who shouldn't be here'.[71] The UK Borders Agency, which had just completed a prolonged and thorough consultation on family migration, also announced its intention to 'get the balance between individual rights and the public interest right' by framing rules that would produce 'a decision which is in accordance with our rules and which is also compatible with Article 8 of the ECHR'.[72] A statement from the Home Office announcing changes to the Rules was less conciliatory:

> The Courts have accepted [the] invitation to determine proportionality on a case-by-case basis. They do not defer to the Government's or Parliament's view of where the balance should be struck, as they do not know what that view is. They do not defer to the individual decision-maker's decision on what is proportionate because the Rules fail to establish where the Government considers the balance to be struck ... However, proportionality decisions taken on an individual basis outside the Rules lack transparency and consistency. They do not allow Parliament a role in determining how the balance should be struck. Where legislation in other areas of law gives less discretion to the decision-maker, this has led the Courts to focus more on the policy in the legislation and less on a review of individual decisions.[73]

According to the Explanatory Memorandum, the draft Rules laid before Parliament would:

> [S]et proportionate requirements that reflect the Government's and Parliament's view of how individuals' Article 8 rights should be qualified in the public interest to safeguard the economic well-being of the UK by controlling immigration and to protect the public against foreign criminals. This will mean that failure to meet the requirements of the rules will normally mean failure to establish an Article 8 claim to enter or remain in the UK, and no grant of leave on that basis. Outside exceptional cases, *it will be proportionate under Article 8 for an applicant who fails to meet the requirement of the rules to be removed from the United Kingdom.*[74]

---

[70] ibid [17] and [18].
[71] Speech given at the Conservative Party Conference (4 October 2011).
[72] UK Borders Agency, *Family Migration—A Consultation* (July 2011) [8.18].
[73] Statement by the Home Office: Immigration Rules on Family and Private Life (HC 194) Grounds of Compatibility with Article 8 of the European Convention on Human Rights [13] and [17].
[74] Emphasis added. See Rules 398 and 399 of the Immigration Rules as amended in 2012, HC 395 (2011–12). See also s 65 of and sch 4 to the Immigration and Asylum Act 1999.

It was not to be. It fell to the courts to consider whether the new Rules created a 'complete code' as the government argued, rolling up the Article 8 proportionality test into a single determination governed by the Rules. Both the Upper Tribunal and the Court of Appeal thought otherwise. The primary decision-makers were as much bound by section 6 of the HRA as the judges and the new rules 'maintain[ed] the obligation on primary decision-makers to act "in compliance with" all the provisions of the Convention'.[75] The time had come to try legislation.

The Bill that became the Immigration Act 2014 gave the force of primary legislation to the Rules. It struck directly at Article 8 adjudication in deportation cases by 'requiring a court or tribunal, when determining whether a decision is in breach of Article 8 ECHR, to have regard to the public interest considerations *as set out in the Act*'.[76] The House of Lords Constitution Committee drew the attention of the House to this attempt to 'guide' courts and tribunals in their determination of Article 8, claiming it as 'a significant innovation'.[77] The JCHR's concern was greater. Although the Bill did not 'go so far as to determine individual applications in advance or to oust the courts' jurisdiction', the Committee was:

> [U]neasy about any statutory provision which purports to tell courts and tribunals that 'little weight' should be given to a particular consideration in any judicial balancing exercise, as is proposed by the Bill in relation to Article 8 claims in immigration cases. That appears to us to be a significant legislative trespass into the judicial function.[78]

The Committee recommended that the Bill be amended, but this was not conceded.

As enacted into law, the Act provides that, in considering the public interest question, a court or tribunal *must* have regard in all cases to the public interest considerations listed in the statute.[79] In the case of foreign criminals, deportation is presumed to be in the public interest subject to limited exceptions, which allow a claim to 'a genuine and subsisting relationship' with a qualifying partner or child *only* where the effect of the criminal's deportation on the partner or child would be unduly harsh. The Act also attempts to structure the proportionality test by providing that 'little weight should be given' to private life or to relationships established at a time when a person is in the UK unlawfully.

Can we interpret this as dialogue? It is more like a classic assertion of parliamentary sovereignty and the tenor of some of the parliamentary speeches hinted at a changing climate of opinion. Speakers targeted both the Strasbourg Court for

---

[75] *MF (Nigeria) v Secretary of State for the Home Department* [2013] EWCA Civ 1192 [46]; *MF (Article 8—New Rules) Nigeria* [2012] UKUT 00393 (IAC); *Izuazu (Article 8—New Rules) Nigeria* [2013] UKUT 45 (IAC).

[76] Explanatory notes to s 15 of the Immigration Act 2014 (emphasis added).

[77] House of Lords Constitution Committee, *Immigration Bill*, HL 148 (2013–14) [9]–[18]. Clause 14 became s 19 of the Immigration Act 2014.

[78] JCHR, *Legislative Scrutiny: Immigration Bill*, HL 102 HC 935 (2013–14) Recommendation 9. See similarly Constitution Committee, HL 148 [9]–[18].

[79] Section 19 of the Immigration Act 2014 inserts a new s 117 into pt 5 of the Nationality, Immigration and Asylum Act 2002.

168 *Carol Harlow*

'steadily eroding' UK powers of deportation and also the UK courts, describing them as responsible for tightening the Strasbourg fetters, which was 'rightly or wrongly' a consequence of the HRA. Parliament, one speaker threatened, must 'make it clear which, ultimately, is the supreme court for British law [and] the final word should stay in this country'.[80] And whether this attempt to engage in 'the re-elaboration of a censured text' will be successful or simply extend the dialogue remains an open question. In debate, Dominic Raab predicted that nothing would change. The proposed legislation required that courts, in considering the public interest question, 'must (in particular) have regard to' listed factors, leaving them wide discretion. This, in accordance with sections 3 and 4 of the Human Rights Act, would have to be exercised to comply with existing human rights case law'.[81] The *Huang* principle would, in other words, prevail.

D. The Jobseeker Affair: Decentring the Domestic Constitution

The jobseeker affair is certainly not a case of coordinate construction; indeed, whether it can be classified as dialogue or simply as an old-fashioned attempt by government to 'strike back' at an unwelcome judicial decision with inconvenient financial consequences is largely a matter of opinion. The affair originated with a package of welfare reforms designed to confine welfare benefits to those genuinely seeking work. As an element in the package, claimants were required in certain circumstances to undertake specified 'work-related activity' with a view to gaining work experience. Statute provided that participants could be required 'to undertake work, or work-related activity, during any prescribed period with a view to improving their prospects of obtaining employment', subject to the proviso that the Regulations must contain provisions for notifying participants of the requirements. Any claimant refusing unreasonably to join such a scheme as directed could be sanctioned by loss of the full amount of his or her allowances.[82] The provisions were to be completed by regulations, which became the Jobseeker's Allowance (Employment, Skills and Enterprise Scheme) Regulations 2011.[83] Unfortunately, these regulations were strikingly badly drafted.

In the House of Lords, the Select Committee on the Merits of Statutory Instruments drew the attention of the House to the inadequacy of the Explanatory Memorandum and the information supporting it, which would render parliamentary scrutiny difficult. It also expressed concern that the Regulations 'interpret the

---

[80] HC Deb, 30 January 2014, vol 574, col 1092 (Julian Brazier MP).
[81] HC Deb 30 January 2014, vol 584, cols 1064–65.
[82] Section 1(2) of the Welfare Reform Act 2009, amending ss 17A and 17B of the Jobseekers Act 1995.
[83] The Jobseeker's Allowance (Employment, Skills and Enterprise Scheme) Regulations 2011, SI 2011/917 (the 2011 Regulations).

Act very broadly so that future changes to the Scheme could be made administratively without any reference to Parliament'.[84] In short, neither the text of the Regulations nor the relationship of the Regulations to their parent Act had been adequately thought through or clarified. It was left to the Social Security Advisory Committee to question the merits of the proposals: the mandatory nature of the work experience and the 'sanctions-based conditionality approach' likely to produce hardship.[85]

Therefore, for many reasons, the proposals were controversial and liable to give rise to test cases, and the Regulations were soon challenged on the grounds that they were insufficiently specific, that the general notice provided for was inadequate and that, in the case of one of the claimants, no notification had been given. In the Divisional Court, Foskett J thought the procedural irregularities insufficient to warrant a declaration, but the Court of Appeal thought differently, ruling that the Regulations did not contain an appropriate description of the Employment, Skills and Enterprise Scheme and that the notices sent to claimants did not comply with the requirements of the 2011 Regulations.[86] A passage from the judgment of Stanley Burnton LJ contains a further warning about drafting for purposes of parliamentary scrutiny:

> Description of a scheme in regulations is important from the point of view of Parliamentary oversight of the work of the administration. It is also important in enabling those who are required to participate in a scheme, or at least those advising them, to ascertain whether the requirement has been made in accordance with Parliamentary authority.[87]

The government immediately counter-attacked, resorting to a formula tried and tested in social security cases: retrospective legislation designed to thwart a further appellate judgment.[88] The 2011 Regulations were revoked and replaced by new prospective Regulations, which came into effect on the date of the Court of Appeal judgment;[89] the Jobseekers (Back to Work Schemes) Bill introduced shortly afterwards retrospectively validated all notices served under the 2011 Regulations informing claimants of requirements as to participation and about the consequences of failing to meet requirements. The intention was spelled out unashamedly in the explanatory notes to the Bill; it was necessary to preserve the position under legislation relating to the government's 'Work Programme', which

---

[84] Select Committee on the Merits of Statutory Instruments, *Jobseeker's Allowance (Employment, Skills and Enterprise Scheme) Regulations 2011 (SI 2011/917)*, HL 137 (2011–12) [10], [11].

[85] SSAC, *Report on Jobseeker's Allowance (Employment, Skills and Enterprise Scheme) Regulations 2011*, Cm 8058 (2011) [32], [33].

[86] Respectively *R (Reilly) v Work and Pensions Secretary* [2012] EWHC 2292 (Admin); *R (Reilly) v Work and Pensions Secretary* [2013] EWCA Civ 66.

[87] ibid [2013] EWCA Civ [76].

[88] See T Prosser, *Test Cases for the Poor* (London, CPAG, 1983); *R v Greater Birmingham Appeal Tribunal ex p Simper* [1974] QB 543; *R v Barnsley SBAT ex p Atkinson* [1977] 1 WLR 917.

[89] The Jobseeker's Allowance (Schemes for Assisting Persons to Obtain Employment) Regulations 2013, SI 2013/276.

170 *Carol Harlow*

had been the subject of an adverse Court of Appeal judgment. The effect would be, first, that the government would incur a liability of up to an estimated £130 million in repaying claimants who had been sanctioned under these programmes and, second, inability to impose sanctions in cases that had been stockpiled.[90] The Bill would provide that no decision to sanction a claimant for failures to comply with the 2011 Regulations would be challengeable on the grounds that they were invalid or the notices given under them inadequate. This would blunt the impact both of the Court of Appeal judgment and of the further appeal that the government was making to the Supreme Court if it were to lose it. Self-righteously, the Minister added that the purpose was to ensure that jobseekers previously sanctioned (or to be sanctioned) for non-compliance under the Regulations would not 'receive an unfair advantage over compliant claimants'.[91] The only way to insure against sanction repayments in stockpiled cases was 'to press ahead with emergency legislation'.[92]

Although this plan was lawful and replicated a traditional practice, it raised two questions of constitutional importance. First, was retrospective legislation proper in these circumstances? Second, was resort to emergency or 'fast-track' legislation in order? The main concern of the House of Lords Constitution Committee was with the fast-track procedure, which diminished the opportunity for proper parliamentary consideration and debate.[93] But it also thought the Bill to be suspect on the ground of retrospectivity. It engaged:

> [T]he cardinal rule of law principle that individuals may be punished or penalised only for contravening what was at the time a valid legal requirement. According to the doctrine of the sovereignty of Parliament, retrospective legislation is lawful. Nonetheless, from a constitutional point of view it should wherever possible be avoided, since the law should so far as possible be clear, accessible and predictable.[94]

The Committee therefore drew the Bill to the attention of the House, suggesting that it should consider in particular whether retrospectively confirming penalties on individuals who, according to judicial decision, had not transgressed any lawful rule was constitutionally appropriate in terms of the rule of law.[95]

Unusually, the Supreme Court proceeded to hear the *Reilly* case, although the proceedings were now hypothetical. The explanation given was that even if it was 'rather unattractive for the executive to be taking up court time and public money to establish that a regulation is valid when it has already taken up Parliamentary time to enact legislation which retrospectively validates the regulation', the issue

---

[90] Explanatory notes to the Jobseekers (Back to Work Schemes) Bill [Bill 149].
[91] ibid [10].
[92] ibid [13]–[14].
[93] See Constitution Committee, *Fast-Track Legislation: Constitutional Implications and Safeguards*, HL 116-I (2008–09) [16]
[94] Constitution Committee, *Jobseekers (Back to Work Schemes) Bill*, HL 155 (2013) [22].
[95] ibid [12], [14], [15].

could be of some significance to the drafting of regulations generally.[96] Upholding the Court of Appeal on all points, the Supreme Court invoked the common law to enunciate a rights-based general principle of fairness with respect to notice.[97] It is important to note that the argumentation at this stage was based on domestic law, framed in terms of the rule of law, the doctrine of parliamentary sovereignty and common law principles of judicial review. The only Convention argument before the courts involved a claim that the Scheme amounted to a form of forced labour in contravention of Article 4(2) ECHR, which was easily dismissed by the Supreme Court.[98]

In *Reilly (No 2)*,[99] however, the claimants stood directly on Convention rights, invoking Article 6(1) ECHR to argue that the Jobseekers (Back to Work Schemes) Act undercut the right to a 'fair and public hearing' by an independent and impartial tribunal by arbitrarily determining ongoing judicial proceedings in favour of the government. Although the Convention did not directly rule out retrospective legislation, Article 6(1) cast doubt on its propriety when used to affect the outcome of judicial determination of disputes where the state itself was a party; such an intervention by the executive was permissible only on 'compelling grounds of the public interest'. This argument transformed a domestic squabble into a triangular dispute and incidentally put in issue some complex and confusing ECtHR jurisprudence.[100]

In the High Court, Lang J issued a declaration that the 2013 Act was incompatible with the principle of the rule of law and the notion of a fair trial protected by Article 6(1) ECHR, though not with the right to property protected by Article 1, Protocol 1. Two elements in her reasoning are particularly worrying. First, in her analysis, Lang J overtly invoked separation of powers doctrine while at the same time equating the ECtHR jurisprudence with the 'fundamental principles of the UK's unwritten constitution'.[101] Reflecting the advice of the Constitution Committee, she declared that 'Parliament's undoubted power to legislate to overrule the effect of court judgments generally ought not to take the form of retrospective legislation designed to favour the Executive in ongoing litigation in the courts brought against it by one of its citizens, unless there are compelling reasons to do so'.[102] The judge fails signally to take into account the government's resource-allocation functions, instead drawing an imaginary bright-line between the government acting in the public interest and supposedly in its own interests

---

[96] *R (Reilly and Wilson) v Secretary of State for Work and Pensions* [2013] UKSC 68 [40]–[41].
[97] ibid [65].
[98] See the judgment of Lord Neuberger and Lord Toulson, citing *Van Der Mussele v Belgium* (1983) 6 EHRR 163; *X v The Netherlands* (1976) 7 DR 161; *Talmon v The Netherlands* [1997] EHRLR 448.
[99] *Reilly (No 2) and Hewstone v Secretary of State for Work and Pensions* [2014] EWHC 2182.
[100] *Zielinkski v France* (2001) 31 EHRR 19; *Stran Greek Refineries v Greece* (1995) 19 EHRR 293; *Scordino v Italy (No 1)* (2007) 45 EHRR 7; *National and Provincial Building Society v UK* (1998) 25 EHRR 127.
[101] *Reilly and Hewstone* (n 99) [81].
[102] ibid [82].

as litigant. Thus, she falls directly into the trap that Lord Sumption warns against: transmuting a complex polycentric question into a simplistic legal question re-allocating the decision to the judge with no adequate discussion of justiciability.

Equally noteworthy is the extent to which Lang J crossed traditional boundaries in assessing the 'public interest' argument. Foskett J had quoted the report of the Committee on the Merits of Statutory Instruments, but had resolutely observed the traditional deferential approach to parliamentary material and proceedings.[103] Lang J, roundly rejecting counsel's protest that parliamentary proceedings were a matter for Parliament and not the court,[104] raked through the parliamentary proceedings with a nit-comb, finding a number of 'misconceptions' and 'inaccuracies'.[105] Parliament, she said, had failed to grapple with the Article 6(1) issues, probably because the Secretary of State had made an 'unsatisfactory' section 19 statement to the effect that the Bill was compatible with the ECHR.[106] This statement neither set out the relevant test to be applied by Parliament nor explained to Parliament that it was being asked to justify a departure from the legal norm, which would only be lawful if made for compelling reasons in the public interest. Instead, the statement had led Parliament to believe erroneously that the legislation was designed to 'close a loophole' in order to give effect to the original intention of Parliament.[107]

This 'anxious scrutiny' flies in the face of Lord Sumption's warning that judges cannot afford and are not required by ECtHR jurisprudence to be 'insensitive to questions of democratic accountability', substituting confrontation for partnership.

III. TOWARDS A PARLIAMENT SQUARE AXIS?

I have argued in this chapter for a collaborative approach to human rights issues in which the institutions with the main responsibility for resolving controversies pay due respect to each other's opinions. I have further argued for respect to be shown to variance and diversity; in human rights matters, a 'one size fits all' approach is unnecessary and divisive. The public interest is not monolithic and the judicial corset must not be laced too tightly. Sufficient space must be left for political solutions that, as Lord Sumption reminds us, involve 'a method of mediating compromises in which we can all participate, albeit indirectly, and which we are therefore more likely to recognise as legitimate'.[108]

---

[103] *R (Reilly) v Work and Pensions Secretary* [2012] EWHC 2292 (Admin) [44]–[48].
[104] ibid, James Eadie QC [96].
[105] *Reilly and Hewstone* (n 99) [92]–[98].
[106] ibid [111].
[107] ibid [113] and [114].
[108] Lord Sumption (n 3) 13.

The collaborative model of coordinate construction is shown at its best in the debate over political broadcasting, where the different views of the issue were duly considered and a successful compromise position reached. At the domestic level, the affair illustrates to perfection the elaboration of a text in conformity with human rights jurisprudence that is the hallmark of coordinate construction. But the dialogue was not purely horizontal. In pushing for a solution, the British judiciary 'reached out to Strasbourg' by 'cogently stating their reasoning with a view to influencing the approach which the Strasbourg Court ultimately adopts'.[109] Thus, the affair can be read as the start of a 'Westminster Square axis', whereby the courts and Parliament come together to jointly defend a position of national cultural importance.

Whether the same can be said of the prisoners' voting affair is, as indicated earlier, questionable. The debate is not yet over and it may be that what successive British governments have really been saying is—to quote Thorbjørn Jagland— 'We have problems. We cannot do it now. You have to give us more time'.[110] But following the election of a Conservative government that advocates the repeal of the HRA, compliance now seems unlikely. In parallel, the judicial institutions have been inching towards a potential solution. However, the affair does highlight the dangers of a situation in which a supranational court operates (as the ECtHR does) in a virtual political void, creating a grave accountability deficit while leaving insufficient space for a political solution. Perhaps courts should engage in their own process of coordinate construction?

It is perfectly possible, of course, to read the changes to immigration legislation as a prime example of coordinate construction. There is sustained judicial–political interaction in which judges repeatedly tell the legislators how the law ought to be interpreted, meeting a response in kind from executive and legislature. But although the majority of speakers in the parliamentary debate clearly wished to remain within the parameters of the European Convention, there is an adversarial note in some of the contributions, as when Dominic Raab MP spoke of 'judicial expansion of the right to family life', calling it 'common ground that the Strasbourg Court has steadily eroded United Kingdom deportation powers over the past few decades', but blaming the domestic courts for imposing 'the tightest fetters ... as a result— rightly or wrongly—of the Human Rights Act'.[111] The Bill might therefore be read as a first step in the direction of more complete ways of amending or circumscribing human rights by 'pulling out of the Convention altogether',[112] or, as expressed as a manifesto commitment by the Conservative

---

[109] Lord Irvine of Lairg (n 59).
[110] Above n 40.
[111] HC Deb 30 January 2014, vol 574, col 1063.
[112] ibid.

Party in the 2015 election,[113] by introducing a new British Bill of Rights and Responsibilities to ensure that 'Parliament is the ultimate source of legal authority, and that the Supreme Court is indeed supreme in the interpretation of the law'. Although there is nothing innately unethical in giving the last word to a representative legislature, the power surely carries with it a moral duty to listen, learn and consider. Deference is, in other words, a two-way process, in which both sides must steer between obsequiousness and authoritarianism. It cannot be said that the current debate avoids these vices.

Are we then really stuck with a model of government in which the legislature and the judiciary are doomed to travel forever down separate tracks, veering occasionally into open collision? The undoubtedly provocative use of parliamentary procedure to wipe out inconvenient judicial decisions—called by Lord Pannick in debate 'an abuse of power that brings no credit whatever on this Government'[114]—and the retaliatory judgment of Lang J with its intrusive examination of parliamentary proceedings suggests that we may be. I maintain, however, that a collaborative model is both preferable and within reach. There are many forms of dialogue, both formal and informal, which allow judges to talk vertically to judges and horizontally to legislators. Governments talk to each other horizontally in councils and committees, and also talk diagonally in interventions made to supranational courts. Many bridges are already in place to assist in balancing the debate, such as the JCHR with its two-way legislative and judicial focus or the growing practice of parliamentary committees to call on external evidence from expert witnesses; others may be forthcoming. Dialogue affords the best hope of preserving the distinctive British culture of rights and reinforcing the democratic element of the parliamentary sovereignty doctrine while allowing at the same time for progress. Parliament and the courts must be prepared to engage constructively in a process of coordinate construction; equally, they must face up to the need for tough, multi-level dialogue with Strasbourg. A 'Parliament Square axis for human rights' is needed.

---

[113] Available at https://www.conservatives.com/manifesto.aspx at 58. See also *Protecting Human Rights in the United Kingdom, the Conservatives' Proposals for Changing Britain's Human Rights Laws* (October 2014), available at: https://www.conservatives.com/~/media/files/downloadable%20Files/human_rights.pdf.

[114] HL Deb 21 March 2013, vol 755, col 739.

10

Limits of Law: Reflections from Private and Public Law

PAUL CRAIG

I. INTRODUCTION

THERE ARE A number of enduring themes relating to substantive judicial review, including its intensity, the legal form through which this should be expressed, the extent to which the courts should show deference, respect or appropriate weight to the views of the initial decision-maker, and the capacity of courts to undertake the kind of assessment required of them, given that they may be required to balance considerations that are to some degree incommensurable. These issues are distinct, albeit related. Lurking beneath the surface are more general inquiries concerning the limits of law,[1] connoting in this respect views about what kinds of issues are suited to adjudication and the extent to which adjudication on rights-based claims is qualitatively different from other types of adjudication. These are important questions and they should not be ducked.

It is, however, noteworthy that much of the soul-searching undertaken in this regard by public lawyers is framed pretty exclusively within a public law frame. We, the public law fraternity, pose the preceding questions focusing on the standard fare of constitutional and administrative law. This may be because we have made a considered judgment that the issues that arise in public law are so distinctive as to render any comparison with private law otiose. It may be for more prosaic and contingent reasons, viz that increased specialisation within academia has meant that scholars simply do not know enough about private law to test their assumptions about the limits of law as determined from a public law perspective. My guess is that in empirical terms, the latter rationale is more significant than the former.

Whatsoever the answer to the empirical inquiry, it is surely axiomatic that the conclusion we reach on the preceding issues as judged from a public law perspective must be consistent with any judgment that we might make about private law. To be clear, this does not preclude the conclusion that public and private law are

---

[1] See, eg, Lord Sumption, 'The Limits of Law', 27th Sultan Azlan Shah Lecture, Kuala Lumpur, 20 November 2013, available at: https://www.supremecourt.uk/news/speeches.html.

distinct with respect to the salient issues. It does preclude the reaching of a conclusion about such issues as they arise within a public law perspective, without testing it from a private law standpoint. The reason is obvious. If the principal rationales for disquiet concerning public law adjudication relate to matters such as the balancing of incommensurables or the making of complex normative assessments that are felt to be beyond the judicial role, then we must surely test whether such problems are also to be found in the private law context. If they are, this prompts a series of second-order inquiries. We might condemn private law adjudication to the extent that such considerations prevail therein. We might revise our previous view about public law. We might distinguish the two in accordance with some convincing normative criterion.

II. PRIVATE LAW: NORMATIVE JUDGMENT AND BALANCING

We could conduct this inquiry with reference to numerous areas of private law, and there is no a priori reason why the answer would be the same. Exigencies of space require that choices be made. The focus here will be on the law of torts. There will be analysis of negligence, given its centrality as the principal innominate fault-based tort, and economic torts, which exemplify the judicial approach to an area where the criterion of liability is intent-based and where the jurisprudence is still predicated on a series of nominate torts. It is important to emphasise that the following inquiry concerns both the making of complex normative assessments and the balancing of values that are felt to be incommensurable to some degree.

There is very considerable normative contestation as to the background object or purpose that is to be served by tort law. It plays out most dramatically in the debates between those who conceive of tort as being concerned with economic efficiency and those who adopt a corrective justice perspective. This is just the tip of the iceberg, because there is considerable contestation as to what corrective justice means,[2] which can in turn lead to very different concrete implications for particular doctrines within tort law. There is, moreover, contestation as to whether negligence should be regarded as entailing moral responsibility, so as to trigger ideas of corrective justice at all.[3] The nature of the interests that should be protected through the law of torts, whether the standard of liability should be conceived in terms of fault, intent or strict liability, and the more particular meaning accorded to these standards are all fiercely debated in the academic literature. The normative complexity and contestability raised by these issues matches

---

[2] See, eg, E Weinrib, *The Idea of Private Law* (Oxford, Oxford University Press, 2012); J Gardner, 'The Purity and Priority of Private Law' (1996) 46 *University of Toronto Law Journal* 459; J Gardner, 'What is Tort Law for? Part 1. The Place of Corrective Justice' (2011) 30 *Law and Philosophy* 1; R Stevens, *Torts and Rights* (Oxford, Oxford University Press, 2007); J Oberdiek (ed), *Philosophical Foundations of the Law of Torts* (Oxford, Oxford University Press, 2014).

[3] See, eg, H Hurd, 'The Innocence of Negligence', http://ssrn.com/abstract=2612084.

anything that is found in public law, and what is salient for the present purposes is that the courts make the relevant determinations through the development of tort doctrine and that we accept with equanimity that this is a legitimate part of the judicial role.

The prevalence of complex normative judgment and balancing of incommensurables is further apparent when we move from theory to concrete case law. They are present throughout tort law. The test for negligence as judicially interpreted requires courts to balance a range of incommensurable considerations in deciding whether a duty of care exists.[4] Historically there were doubts raised as to the necessity of duty as a separate juridical concept, with Winfield characterising it as the result of an historical accident[5] and Buckland describing it as the fifth wheel on the coach.[6] These doubts were predicated on the assumption that the criterion for duty was cast simply in terms of reasonable foresight, the argument being that this led to duplication of inquiry, given that the same issue would be considered in more detail in order to determine whether there had been a breach of the duty on the facts of the case. We do not require proof of an antecedent duty in other torts. We simply state that a failure to comply with the legal rules that pertain to nuisance, assault, economic torts and the like is an actionable wrong. The role of duty within negligence has, however, been defended more recently by scholars exploring the philosophical foundations of tort law.[7]

It is nonetheless the case that duty is the medium through which policy considerations are taken cognisance of by the courts in order to decide whether liability should be imposed, even assuming that the defendant has been careless and caused the loss. Current orthodoxy is for a three-stage test to decide whether a duty of care exists: reasonable foresight, a relationship of proximity between claimant and defendant, and whether it would be fair, just and reasonable to impose a duty of care.[8] Duty of care thus conceived has been used as the vehicle through which the courts have denied liability in relation to types of loss, types of defendant and types of act.[9] The considerations that inform the determination whether it is fair, just and reasonable to impose a duty of care will often vary and require balancing

---

[4] J Fleming, 'Remoteness and Duty: The Control Devices in Liability for Negligence' (1953) 31 *Canadian Bar Review* 471; F Lawson, 'Duty of Care: A Comparative Study' (1947) 22 *Tulane Law Review* 111; S Deakin, A Johnston and B Markesinis, *Markesinis and Deakin's Tort Law*, 7th edn (Oxford, Oxford University Press, 2013) 102; B Markesinis and S Deakin, 'The Random Element of their Lordships' Infallible Judgment: An Economic and Comparative Analysis of the Tort of Negligence from *Anns* to *Murphy*' (1992) 55 *MLR* 619.

[5] P Winfield, 'Duty in Tortious Negligence' (1932) 32 *Columbia Law Review* 41, 66.

[6] W Buckland, 'The Duty to take Care' (1935) 51 *LQR* 637.

[7] See, eg, J Goldberg and B Zipursky, 'Tort Law and Responsibility' and S Perry, 'Torts, Rights and Risk' in Oberdiek (n 2).

[8] *Caparo Industries plc v Dickman* [1990] 2 AC 605; *Governors of the Peabody Donation Fund v Sir Lindsay Parkinson and Co Ltd* [1985] AC 210, 241, 245; *Investors in Industry Commercial Properties Ltd v South Bedfordshire District Council* [1986] QB 1034; *Murphy v Brentwood District Council* [1991] 1 AC 398.

[9] *Markesinis and Deakin's Tort Law* (n 4) 102–04.

inter se.[10] This determination may also turn on complex normative judgments as to what justifies the imposition of liability, as exemplified by the distinctions drawn between acts and omissions, personal/property damage and pure economic loss, and bodily harm as compared to psychiatric harm.

It is also readily apparent that balancing is required in order to decide whether there has been a breach of the duty of care. This was given voice most famously by Learned Hand and become known eponymously as the Learned Hand formula:

> The degree of care demanded of a person by an occasion is the resultant of three factors: the likelihood that his conduct will injure others, taken with the seriousness of the injury if it happens, and balanced against the interest that he must sacrifice to avoid the risk. All these are practically not susceptible of any quantitative estimate, and the second two are not so, even theoretically. For this reason a solution always involves some preference, or choice between incommensurables, and it is thought most likely to accord with commonly accepted standards, real or fancied.[11]

For advocates of law and economics, this was a quintessential example of the common law fashioning a rule to enhance economic efficiency, since an accident is deemed to be legally negligent only if the cost of avoiding it is less than the losses incurred by the injured party, discounted by the chance that the injury will actually occur.[12] However, it is important not to forget the language used by Learned Hand J, since this is a corrective to any idea that it is a simple economic calculus reducible to precise monetary amounts. It is more debatable how far English courts take cognisance of the costs of precautions when adjudicating on breach,[13] but it is in any event generally accepted that there can be considerable practical and normative difficulties in ascertaining what constitutes an unreasonable risk for the purposes of negligence liability.[14]

The discussion thus far has highlighted two instances of balancing within the law of negligence: at the level of duty and breach, respectively. This area of the law also exhibits contestable normative judgments over and above any issues of balance per se. Limits of space preclude extensive treatment, so the point can be exemplified by focusing on two examples, both of which are central to negligence liability.

The premise of negligence liability is that to justify the shifting of loss from claimant to defendant, the former must show fault caused by the latter. This has significant distributive consequences, since it means that the risk of non-fault accidents lies with the claimant rather than the defendant, even where the defendant caused the loss. The normative premise is that the defendant was not at fault

---

[10] See, eg, *X (Minors) v Bedfordshire CC* [1995] 2 AC 633; *MacFarlane v Tayside Health Board* [2000] AC 59.
[11] *Conway v O'Brien* 111 F 2d 611, 612 (1940).
[12] R Posner, 'A Theory of Negligence' (1972) 1 *Journal of Legal Studies* 29.
[13] See, eg, *Bolton v Stone* [1951] AC 850; *Latimer v AEC Ltd* [1953] AC 634; *Wagon Mound (No 2)* [1967] 1 AC 617; *Smith v Littlewoods Ltd* [1987] AC 241; *Tomlinson v Congleton* [2004] 1 AC 46.
[14] *Markesinis and Deakin's Tort Law* (n 4) 209–14.

and thus should not be required to pay the defendant. The obvious rejoinder is that neither was the claimant, yet he or she is required to shoulder the loss even where it is unequivocally clear that this was caused by the defendant. This does not, however, in general suffice to establish liability, given that negligence is the dominant tortious cause of action. The legal status quo has been defended on the ground that it comports with corrective justice,[15] but this argument is controversial in various respects.[16] The argument is not that negligence liability is therefore 'wrong', but rather that it embodies contestable normative assumptions, and it was the courts that chose to adopt this standard of liability. Matters were not always so. There were prominent areas where liability was indeed based on cause,[17] such that a plausible interpretation of *Rylands v Fletcher*[18] was that it was drawing together particular instances of strict liability, analogising/expanding from them and enunciating a general principle of liability,[19] thus presaging the reasoning of Lord Atkin in negligence over half a century later.[20]

The judicial choice to foster negligence as the general principle of liability was manifest directly and indirectly. It was directly apparent in the judicial willingness to regard new categories of relationship as subject to the negligence standard, and in the courts' rejection of reasons to deny such liability, as exemplified most famously by *Donoghue* itself, where the House of Lords denied that the existence of a contract precluded negligence liability for cases of physical injury. The indirect preference for negligence liability was less obvious, but very real nonetheless.

This was evident in the judicial limitation or emasculation of the *Rylands* principle.[21] It was not simply that the courts imposed increasingly difficult conditions for the existence of such liability or that they expanded the range of available defences. It was the very reasoning that drove these judicial decisions. It was clear from the seminal rulings that strict liability was regarded as something alien and unnatural, to be confined to the narrowest possible circumstances. This was the message from the House of Lords in *Rickards*, where non-natural user was defined

---

[15] Weinrib (n 2) ch 6.
[16] Compare Hurd (n 3).
[17] D Ibbetson, *A Historical Introduction to the Law of Obligations* (Oxford, Oxford University Press, 1999) ch 4. David Ibbetson provides a balanced assessment of the cause of action for trespass to the plaintiff in person, goods, or land, concluding that this was prima facie strict, albeit not absolute, given that the defendant could plead that the behaviour was justified on grounds of, for example, self-defence. He cautions against too great a contrast between strict and fault liability, noting that issues concerning the ascription of responsibility could arise in either method of analysis. However, he also cautions against the elision of the medieval idea of fault and modern conceptions of negligence. The modern idea that there is no negligence where the Learned Hand calculus indicates that the costs of taking precautions outweigh the seriousness of harm discounted by the risk that it might occur would have been foreign to medieval thought.
[18] *Rylands v Fletcher* (1865) 3 H & C 774; (1866) LR 1 Ex 265; (1868) LR 3 HL 330; A Simpson, 'Legal Liability for Bursting Reservoirs: the Historical Context of *Rylands v Fletcher*' (1984) 13 *Journal of Law and Society* 209.
[19] F Newark, 'Non-natural User and *Rylands v Fletcher*' (1961) 24 *MLR* 557.
[20] *Donoghue v Stevenson* [1932] AC 562
[21] R Bagshaw, '*Rylands* Confined' (2004) 120 *LQR* 388.

as 'some special use bringing with it increased danger to others, and must not merely be the ordinary use of the land or such a use as is proper for the general benefit of the community'.[22] The message was clear: strict liability was reserved for socially unusual or abnormal activities, not ordinary uses of land that might be beneficial. While the utility of the idea of 'general benefit to the community' has been doubted,[23] no judgment did more than *Rickards* to block the development of *Rylands* as a modern principle of strict liability that could be applicable precisely where the activity was normal and yet entailed an inevitable number of accidents where it was difficult to prove fault, such as the running of utilities.[24] The idea that the burden of such losses should be spread among those who take the benefit of the activity rather than being left to lie on the person fortuitously injured is an attractive one, but was precluded by the courts' jurisprudence.

The possibility of using *Rylands* in such instances was further limited by questionable decisions concerning the impact of statutory authority on such liability.[25] The same message was evident in the House of Lords' decision in *Read*.[26] The simple ratio of the case is that liability pursuant to *Rylands* is only applicable where there is some escape from a place where the defendant has occupation or control. The reason for this conclusion is apparent from the judgments: an unwillingness to recognise any distinct rule for dangerous activities and a desire to prevent the tort encroaching on what was felt to be the natural domain of negligence liability.[27] None of the foregoing was pre-ordained, nor was it value free. It was the result of contestable normative judgments, as revealed forcefully by Markesinis and Deakin:

> Not for the first time, an English seed was borrowed by America, combined with indigenous elements and brought to full bloom under the doctrine of liability for extra hazardous activities. On the other hand, in its country of origin the idea had a mixed reception almost from the very beginning … after a moderately welcoming start, given to it by some Victorian judges, the rule was progressively emasculated of all its potential as it struck at the heart of another Victorian favourite: fault. For the Victorian era became (progressively) moralistic and thus any legal rule that encouraged tort to depart from this favoured shibboleth was suspicious, to say the least. In fact it was both suspicious and dangerous in so far as it also challenged the hypocrisy of the age. This is because the fault rule … served this hypocrisy as well, since it protected nascent industries at a time of weak, if not non-existent, insurance practices. For by this time the fault rule had acquired a double aspect: not only did it mean that if you were at fault you must pay; it was also (less convincingly) understood to require that if you are not at fault, you need not pay.[28]

---

[22] *Rickards v Lothian* [1913] AC 263, 280.
[23] *Transco v Stockport MBC* [2004] 2 AC 1.
[24] See, eg, ibid; *British Celanese v A. H. Hunt* [1969] 1 WLR 959.
[25] See, eg, *Smeaton v Ilford Corp* [1954] Ch 450; P Craig, *Administrative Law*, 7th edn (London, Sweet & Maxwell, 2012) 939–41.
[26] *Read v J Lyons and Co Ltd* [1947] AC 156.
[27] J Fleming, *The Law of Torts*, 9th edn (Sydney, Law Book Co, 1998) 383.
[28] *Markesinis and Deakin's Tort Law* (n 4) 518.

The second example of the kind of contestable normative issue that arises within negligence concerns the test for remoteness. The House of Lords settled the matter in *Wagon Mound (No 1)*, stating authoritatively that the test was to be cast in terms of foreseeability, castigating the alternative causal criterion as illogical and unjust.[29] This was in accordance with some academic opinion, which regarded foreseeability as more consistent, simpler and fairer than its causal rival. Thus, Weinrib[30] contends that corrective justice demands the link between culpability and compensation forged in *Wagon Mound (No 1)*, but the reasoning is contestable.

Herbert Hart and Tony Honoré revealed the questionable assumptions underlying this conclusion.[31] They questioned the need for consistency, noting that there is no a priori reason why the same criterion should be used to determine liability, and the extent to which a person should be held liable for the consequences of his action. The fact that a person who has committed an intentional harm may be liable for consequences over and beyond those he intended attests to this. They questioned the argument based on simplicity, which assumes that simplicity is achieved by making culpability and compensation subject to the same test, viz that of foreseeability. The flaw in the argument is the assumption that foreseeability means the same thing in the two instances, which it does not. When used in relation to the determination of culpability it is captured by the elements that constitute the Learned Hand formula, which Hart and Honoré term practical foresight. When used in relation to remoteness and compensation, it bears a different meaning, otherwise it would only be possible to recover for harm if the risk of that specific harm occurring was the reason for calling the defendant's act negligent. The argument concerning fairness, to the effect that it is unfair to burden the defendant with large losses beyond what could have been contemplated, is not at all self-evident. Thus, as Hart and Honoré pithily noted, 'if the liability is out of all proportion to the defendant's fault it can be no less out of proportion to the plaintiff's innocence'.[32] Moreover, the apparent unfairness takes on a different light when it is revealed that the defendant may engage in, for example, negligent driving on many occasions, such that the 'justice of holding me liable, should the harm on that one occasion turn out to be extraordinarily grave, must be judged in the light of the hundred occasions on which, without deserving such luck, I have incurred no liability'.[33]

The *Wagon Mound (No 1)* nonetheless settled the matter in favour of foreseeability, and the rest as they say is history. However, this does not alter the fact that courts routinely make choices in private law based on considerations of justice and

---

[29] *Overseas Tankship (UK) Ltd v Morts Dock & Engineering Co Ltd Respondents (the Wagon Mound)* [1961] AC 388, 424.
[30] Weinrib (n 2) ch 6.
[31] HLA Hart and T Honoré, *Causation in the Law*, 2nd edn (Oxford, Clarendon Press, 1985) 259–75.
[32] ibid 267–68.
[33] ibid 268.

fairness, which are contestable on normative grounds, notwithstanding the fact that the new status quo is embodied in a rule that has been strengthened by the effluxion of time. Indeed, the very fact that the choice is embodied in a rule that is not readily revisited is of more general interest, as will be seen below.

The discussion thus far has focused on negligence liability, but it would be wrong to conclude that issues of incommensurability, let alone difficult normative choice, are confined to this tort. On the contrary, they are present throughout this body of the law. There are numerous instances of incommensurability that are embedded on the face of the 'legal rule'. Consider in this respect the fair/honest comment rule in defamation cases, whereby the common law courts have decided that free speech is sufficiently important that there can be a defence for defamation even where the critic is extreme or unbalanced, provided only that he or she is not malicious.[34] The rule is based on a balance between the value of free speech manifest in the very great freedom accorded to the critic and the interest of the individual whose life may be destroyed by the captious and excessive critique. Consider the rule in nuisance, such that a person who 'comes to' a nuisance will not be able to complain of smell, noise or the like, but can still claim if there is some physical incursion into the property that constitutes an unreasonable use of land by the neighbour. The rule encapsulates a balance between the interests of the property owner and those of the public interest, the rationale being that industrialisation should not be impeded by private complaint of noise, smoke and the like within the relevant area.[35]

Let us now turn to the other principal area adumbrated above. Liability for economic torts is intent-based and a range of competing values have shaped the entire architecture, not merely a particular rule therein. The courts determine the extent to which tort law should impose limits on free competition. It is axiomatic that such competition can impose economic loss on other parties, and this may indeed be the intent or inevitable outcome of a person's action, as exemplified by classic price competition. The legitimacy of such competition is a foundational value in this area.[36] It is, however, qualified by values that serve to define what the judiciary believes to be the limits to that competition. The precise contours of these competing values, their scope and underlying justification are contestable, more especially given that the judicial criteria have often been enumerated in trade disputes between employer and employee. This is readily apparent from the three areas commonly regarded as constituting the economic torts: inducement to breach of contract, interference with trade by unlawful means and conspiracy. There are tensions as to the foundational assumptions as between these areas and within each of them.

---

[34] *Merivale v Carson* (1888) 20 QBD 275, 281; *Slim v Daily Telegraph Ltd* [1968] 2 QB 157, 170; *Reynolds v Times Newspapers* [2001] 2 AC 127, 193; Markesinis and Deakin's Tort Law (n 4) 664–9.
[35] *Sturges v Bridgman* (1879) 11 Ch D 852, 865; Markesinis and Deakin's Tort Law (n 4) 428–29.
[36] *Mogul Steamship Co Ltd v McGregor, Gow & Co Ltd* (1889) LR 23 QBD 598; [1892] AC 25; *Allen v Flood* [1898] AC 1.

The tension between these areas is whether the courts will decide what should be the limits of free competition and make judgments as to the legitimacy thereof. The general assumption in the case law concerning interference with trade by unlawful means is that this is not the correct province for the judiciary, with the consequence that the boundary of legitimate competition is defined by proof of independent illegality. This obviates the courts from making free-standing judgments in this respect, but at the cost of making liability turn on parasitic concepts of illegality, the presence or absence of which may be fortuitous and therefore of questionable relevance for this purpose.[37] Moreover, this approach is in tension with that concerning inducement to breach of contract, where liability is not based on the existence of some independent illegality, such as breach of statutory duty, commitment of a crime, or of another independent tort. The fundamental assumption underlying inducement to breach of contract is that the value of free competition is bounded by the value of the claimant's contractual right to the services of the person induced to break his or her contract by the defendant.[38] There is no a priori reason why this should be so. The court might have decided that the claimant should be left to pursue any contractual claim against the person breaking his or her contract, without any independent recourse in tort against the person who offered the inducement. This might well be regarded as the optimal solution in terms of efficient breach viewed from a law and economics perspective. The choice to regard the contract as generating rights actionable against third parties in tort was not therefore pre-ordained, but was simply reflective of what the judiciary regarded as a legitimate limit on free competition. In true compromise style, the two limbs of the law relating to conspiracy reflect respectively the two preceding approaches: the one predicated on the existence of unlawful means and the other not.

There are, moreover, tensions within each of the three areas. The subsequent case law on inducement to breach of contract revealed contestation within the judiciary as to how far they were willing to press this competing value that embodied a limit on free competition. There was classic incremental case law development whereby the courts expanded the cause of action to include indirect interference with the contract[39] and hindering of the contract,[40] followed by judicial retrenchment disapproving these developments.[41] Analogous tensions are apparent in the case law on interference with trade by unlawful means. It was suggested with good reason, in the light of the expanded case law on inducement to breach of contract, combined with the reasoning in the case law on intimidation,[42] that UK

---

[37] JD Heydon, *Economic Torts*, 2nd edn (London, Sweet & Maxwell, 1978).
[38] *Lumley v Gye* (1853) 2 E & B 216.
[39] *DC Thomson Ltd v Deakin* [1994] EMLR 44.
[40] *Torquay Hotel Co Ltd v Cousins* [1969] Ch 106; *Merkur Island Shipping Corp v Laughton* [1983] 2 AC 570.
[41] *OBG Ltd v Allan* [2008] AC 1.
[42] *Rookes v Barnard* [1964] AC 1129, 1168–69.

law should develop from a series of nominate economic torts to an innominate tort cast in terms of interference with trade by means of action that the defendant was not at liberty to commit.[43] The time seemed ripe for an Atkin-type judgment in this area. It never happened and the courts once again pulled back in this area, through a more constrained definition of what constitutes unlawful means and increased focus on intent to inflict economic damage.[44] While it is therefore unsurprising that the value of free competition should be bounded by the need to pursue competitive aims lawfully, the case law throws into sharp relief the real choices that have to be made as to what constitutes unlawful means for these purposes, both in terms of the nature of the illegality that should qualify in this regard and its causal connection to the harm suffered.

III. PUBLIC LAW: NORMATIVE JUDGMENT AND BALANCING

Normative judgment and balancing are prevalent within public law. They are present in relation to controls framed in terms of purpose/relevancy and reasonableness/proportionality.

Controls over the way in which discretion is exercised commonly operate at two levels.[45] The initial inquiry is as to whether the public body used the discretion for a proper purpose and based on relevant considerations, followed by analysis cast in terms of reasonableness/proportionality.[46] Controls framed in terms of purpose and relevancy are central to the very idea of judicial review. If a legal system has any legal controls over the exercise of public power, then these must include constraints designed to ensure that it is used for the purpose for which it was intended. It would logically be possible to stop there and make this the only form of control over discretionary power. The fact that almost every legal system uses a further method of control is readily explicable. Legal constraints framed in terms of purpose/relevancy are relatively blunt tools, and the courts substitute judgment on these matters, treating them as a matter of statutory interpretation, interpreting the legislation and deciding whether the purpose can be lawfully pursued or whether a consideration can be lawfully taken into account. Legal constraints framed in terms of reasonableness/proportionality allow the court to review in circumstances where it is not self-evident that the purpose was wholly improper or the consideration was wholly irrelevant, enabling the court to

---

[43] T Weir, 'Chaos or Cosmos: *Rookes, Stratford* and the Economic Torts' [1964] *CLJ* 225.
[44] *OBG Ltd v Allan* [2008] AC 1.
[45] Lord Woolf, J Jowell and A Le Sueur, *De Smith's Judicial Review*, 6th edn (London, Sweet & Maxwell, 2007) chs 5, 11; Craig (n 25) chs 19, 21; J Auburn, J Moffett and A Sharland, *Judicial Review, Principles and Procedures* (Oxford, Oxford University Press 2013) chs 14, 17.
[46] *Associated Picture Houses Ltd v Wednesbury Corp* [1948] 1 KB 223, 228–31, 233–34; *Council of Civil Service Unions v Minister for the Civil Service* [1985] AC 374, 410; *R v Lord Saville of Newdigate ex p A* [1999] 4 All ER 860, [32]–[33].

weigh such matters and to do so in accordance with a less exacting standard than substitution of judgment.

Judicial statements[47] that relevancy and reasonableness in its substantive sense can shade into each other commonly capture the situation where the courts are unsure whether to treat a consideration as wholly irrelevant, and hence take it into account and weigh it when undertaking reasonableness review. This may in part be for interpretive reasons, viz that it is unclear from the statutory remit whether the consideration should be deemed wholly irrelevant. It may also be for more conceptual reasons, in the sense that the courts will have to decide on the level of abstraction or specificity with which they pose the inquiry. The broader or more abstract the inquiry at the level of purpose/relevancy, the more likely that the challenged action will satisfy those precepts, the corollary being that the case will be decided through reasonableness/proportionality. By way of contrast, the narrower the initial inquiry at the level of purpose/relevancy, the more likely that the case will be resolved at that level, the corollary being that less remains to be done through reasonableness review. Thus, in the *Wednesbury* case,[48] the hypothetical of the teacher being dismissed for the colour of her hair was tested for conformity with reasonableness review, the assumption being that dismissal on such grounds satisfied the tests of purpose/relevancy. This could only be so if the issue was posed in relatively broad terms, viz that 'physical characteristics could be relevant in hiring or dismissing a teacher'. If, however, the issue was framed in more specific terms, viz that 'the natural colour of a person's hair could never be a relevant consideration in hiring or firing a teacher', then the case would have been resolved without recourse to reasonableness review.

It is, moreover, clear that value judgments and balance pervade both levels of inquiry. The pure theory underlying review for purpose/relevancy is that the courts are simply demarcating the four corners of the relevant statutory power. This may be so in some straightforward cases, but in many it will not. The decision as to allowable purpose, and the determination of relevant considerations, will frequently require judicial assessment of values and application of background principles, as is readily apparent from consideration of any of the leading decisions.[49]

The fact that value judgments and balance are prominent in reasonableness/proportionality is acknowledged, but it is nonetheless worth dwelling for a moment on the variability of such review in cases of rights even prior to the Human Rights Act 1998 (HRA), since it raises more general issues concerning the

---

[47] *Wednesbury* (n 46) 228–31.
[48] *Wednesbury* (n 46).
[49] See, eg, *Roberts v Hopwood* [1925] AC 579; *Council of Civil Service Unions v Minister for the Civil Service* [1985] AC 374; *Secretary of State for Education and Science v Tameside Metropolitan Borough Council* [1977] AC 1014; *Hazell v Hammersmith and Fulham London Borough Council* [1992] 2 AC 1; *Bromley London Borough Council v Greater London Council* [1983] 1 AC 768; *R (Corner House Research) v Director of the Serious Fraud Office* [2009] 1 AC 756.

bounds of judicial legitimacy. The existence of rights increased the intensity of reasonableness review,[50] legislation was interpreted with a strong presumption that it was not intended to interfere with rights,[51] and the courts held that Convention rights were embedded in the common law.[52] These developments were regarded as controversial by some political constitutionalists.[53] They were court-sceptic and opposed to expansion of judicial review—some were also rights-sceptics—and they regarded balancing in such cases as problematic. The judicial decision to recognise rights in the preceding ways was not value-free, but the reality is that there is no neutrality to be had. Thus, the political constitutionalists' objections grounded in either court-scepticism and/or rights-scepticism are every bit as value-laden as the opposing views.

If the courts apply reasonableness review to control discretionary power, there is good reason for varying its intensity depending on the affected interest. It makes no sense in normative terms to assume that a relatively trivial interest is of the same import as an interest that is objectively more significant; indeed, the very statement is a contradiction in terms. It was therefore perfectly defensible for the courts to vary the intensity of such review. This requires the evaluation of the importance of the interest, and whether it should be recognised as a right, in the manner explicated by, for example, MacCormick and Raz.[54] The proposition that statute will be read so as not to interfere with rights unless Parliament made clear its intent to do so is a defensible one. It is normatively sound both because of the importance of the interest that has been denominated as a right and for the reasons powerfully expressed by Lord Hoffmann in *Simms*, viz that Parliament should be mindful of such incursions and should accept the political cost of doing so by making its intent explicit.[55] The development signalled in *Derbyshire*[56] that Convention rights were to be regarded as embedded in the common law was potentially the most far-reaching. While much development in administrative law was remedy-driven, the courts nonetheless had explicit regard for some rights, such as the right to vote, and most notably property rights. Rights-talk was not therefore absent from our legal heritage, but became obscured by the Diceyan formulation of negative residual liberties. There was, however, always a tension in this characterisation. It carried a descriptive connotation, that the scope of, for example, your freedom of speech was the result of the aggregate

---

[50] *R v Secretary of State for the Home Department ex p Brind* [1991] 1 AC 696; *R v Ministry of Defence ex p Smith* [1996] QB 517.
[51] *R v Secretary of State for the Home Department ex p Simms & O'Brien* [2000] 2 AC 115; *R v Lord Chancellor ex p Witham* [1998] QB 575.
[52] *Derbyshire County Council v Times Newspapers Ltd* [1993] AC 534.
[53] A Tomkins, *Our Republican Constitution* (Oxford, Hart Publishing, 2005) 18–25; JAG Griffith, 'The Brave New World of Sir John Laws' (2000) 63 *MLR* 159.
[54] DN MacCormick, 'Rights in Legislation' in P Hacker and J Raz (eds), *Law, Morality and Society, Essays in Honour of HLA Hart* (Oxford, Clarendon Press, 1977) ch 11; J Raz, *The Morality of Freedom* (Oxford, Clarendon Press, 1986).
[55] *Simms* (n 51).
[56] *Derbyshire County Council* (n 52).

limits placed thereon by statute or common law. Nonetheless, it also embodied the normative recognition that the relevant interests were indeed liberties. The real importance of the change to talking openly of rights was that it signified both that duties could flow from the rights and that any limitations of the rights would not simply be acknowledged, but would be rigorously scrutinised.

IV. NORMATIVE JUDGMENT AND BALANCING: REFLECTIONS

A. Polycentricity, Private Law and Social Policy

An oft-voiced element in the discourse concerning the limits of what the courts should and should not do is the stricture concerning the courts to be wary about adjudicating on social policy, more particularly given the fact that judicial decisions given in one context may well resonate more broadly where the problem is polycentric in nature. Such concerns have been raised by Lord Sumption.[57] The extent to which polycentricity should be regarded as problematic in this regard has properly been questioned by Jeff King, who revealed its pervasiveness and the judicial techniques that could be used to deal with it short of judicial abstention.[58] It is interesting that those who express concern about polycentricity normally do so from within the frame of public law. It is public law broadly conceived that is felt to be problematic in this respect.

This does not, however, withstand examination. Reflect for a moment on the foregoing analysis of private law. It has profound social implications in two senses: it embodies social policy choice and has far-reaching consequences for such choices made by the legislature. It would be reductionist to claim that all instances of private law adjudication embody social policy choice, but it would be equally blinkered to deny the link. Tort law sets the boundaries for private responsibility in relations between individuals that are primarily non-consensual. It expresses a social policy choice that is not in any sense pre-ordained as to when a person should bear the costs of loss caused to another, and the social dimension to that choice is not resolved by being cast in terms of corrective justice, given the contestation that surrounds its meaning and application. The courts make the value judgments, and they modify them and amend them over time. The choice thus made then has far-reaching implications for social policy in the second sense. It will determine the respective areas in which losses are borne by a private party and those where they are borne by the state in terms of social welfare payments and the like, as is evident from the seminal literature on accidents, compensation and the law.[59] If there are

---

[57] Lord Sumption (n 1) 15–16.
[58] J King, 'The Pervasiveness of Polycentricity' [2008] *PL* 1; J King, 'The Justiciability of Resource Allocation' (2007) 70 *MLR* 19.
[59] P Atiyah, *Accidents, Compensation and the Law* (London, Weidenfeld & Nicolson, 1970); P Cane, *Atiyah's Accidents, Compensation and the Law*, 8th edn (Cambridge, Cambridge University Press, 2013).

concerns as to the limits of law flowing from polycentricity in a public law context, then they are more than matched by the realisation that defining the boundaries of private responsibility has far-reaching implications for the general social welfare budget. Indeed, the systemic nature of this impact casts many polycentric problems posed in public law into the shadow.

B. Normative Choice, Balancing, Private and Public Law

There is a temptation to think that issues of normative choice and balancing are more common and complex in public as opposed to private law, thus fuelling conclusions that we should conceive of the limits of adjudication differentially in this regard. There is a kindred temptation to think that the ways of dealing with such issues are somehow more tractable in the realm of private as opposed to public law, thereby lending further support to the same conclusion. Both temptations should be resisted.

There is no sound foundation for claims that issues of normative choice and balancing are more common and complex in public as opposed to private law. There is an interesting inquiry as to the relationship between normative choice and balance, more especially balance of incommensurables. Space constraints preclude detailed analysis.[60] Suffice it to say for the present that the former does not necessarily entail the latter, but may often do so. It is thus perfectly possible for the normative choice to be between two or more different foundational precepts that will shape a rule or body of legal doctrine. It is equally possible for the normative choice to express the result, explicitly or implicitly, of a range of incommensurable values. There is, moreover, no a priori reason why a normative choice that does not involve the balancing of incommensurables will be less contestable than one that does. It is in any event the case that issues of normative choice pervade just about every rule in private as well as public law and most certainly every rule of any significance. This is precisely what we unpack when we think about the soundness of common law doctrine in any area. Nor is there any reason to conclude a priori that the issues are necessarily more complex, as judged by any dimension that the word might bear, in public law as opposed to private law. We can all think of morally foundational issues that arise in the context of judicial review, which can affect the life or liberty of particular individuals, as well as many cases that do not raise concerns of this nature. We can, however, readily consider issues of analogous importance that arise in areas such as crime and tort, while recognising that they also regulate matters of less significance.

The idea that such issues can be resolved in a more tractable manner in private as opposed to public law should also be resisted. There are doubtless different

---

[60] See more generally, C Sunstein, 'Incommensurability and Valuation in Law' (1993–94) 92 *Michigan Law Review* 779; Symposium on Law and Incommensurability (1998) 146 *University of Pennsylvania Law Review* 1169.

ways in which the courts can address the balancing of incommensurable values, but these differences do not pan out neatly on a private–public law divide, nor is one such technique unequivocally 'better' than another. The choice of techniques includes: the ad hoc balancing of the relevant factors in each case, as exemplified by the duty concept in negligence and by the determination of the particular hearing rights that should be accorded to the claimant; a modified version of this approach whereby the balancing is undertaken with different intensity for different kinds of case, as epitomised by proportionality review; the formulation of a doctrinal rule that embodies the chosen result of the balancing, as in the context of the rules for nuisance, defamation or restitutionary relief for mistake of law; or the division of the specified area so that its component parts reflect the different balances struck, as illustrated by the sub-divisions within economic torts.

These are different juridical techniques that cut across the public–private divide, and they each have different merits and demerits. It might be felt that it is better in terms of legal certainty for the result of the balancing to become part of the rule, which can then be applied evenly thereafter. However, this is dependent on the issue, whatsoever it might be, being amenable to embodiment in a rule-like format, which will not be the case if the number of variables is too broad or too fact-specific. Even where this is not so, there can be other less obvious disadvantages to rule-type formulations. Thus, where the balancing is not readily apparent on the face of the rule, it is common for the rule to take on a canonical nature and for the balancing that underpins it to be forgotten, such that it is not reassessed. This is in effect what happened in relation to the rule concerning restitutionary relief for mistake of law prior to recent judicial reforms and is also what occurred in relation to the remoteness rules in tort since the 1960s.

C. Statute, Private and Public Law

It might be felt that while private law is reflective of normative choice and while it might entail balancing of incommensurables, it is nonetheless distinctive from public law in three respects.

The first is that private law is largely confined to the terrain of adjudication between private parties, while public law is primarily applicable in the context of power exercised pursuant to a statute. Thus, on this view, the exercise of normative choice/balancing of incommensurables is less problematic when it does not impinge directly on legislative choice. This contains a wealth of contestable assumptions, but let it be accepted for the present purposes that most public law entails statutory interpretation, since most public power dealt with by judicial review has a statutory origin. The normative choices and balancing exercises at common law nonetheless impact on legislative choice in two senses. There are many statutes dealing solely and directly with private law relationships, and the general principles of contract, tort, restitution and the like will be read into the statute, unless there is some clear indication therein to the contrary. The results of the common law choices will in addition inform statutes that deal with public law issues. This is readily apparent from the case law on negligence and public bodies, where the precepts of negligence have been used to shape the confines of such liability, whether through the definition of duty[61] or at the level of breach.[62] It is readily apparent yet again in the way that foundational common law assumptions, such as opposition to strict liability, have been used to limit radically the extent to which such statutes will be read as leading to the imposition of such liability.[63]

The second sense in which it might be argued that private and public law are distinct is that the result of the normative choice or balancing is likely to be more controversial in public law. This argument conceals more than it reveals. It is predicated on the contestable empirical assumption that people are likely to be more engaged by such choices made in the public as opposed to the private law context. This claim is a good deal easier to make than to verify. Thus, while the legislature and the general public might have strong views about an issue such as voting rights for prisoners, this was also the case for high-profile issues in private law, such as the Thalidomide, Bhopal and asbestos litigation, more especially given the victims' difficulties in securing adequate redress based on the existing tort doctrine. The reality in any event is that relatively few Strasbourg rulings have raised the domestic legislative ire.

A third ground of distinction might be said to be that the result of normative choice and balancing is easier for the legislature to overturn in private law. This argument is, however, doubly problematic.

The HRA was a choice consciously made by the sovereign legislature, which entailed judicial oversight pursuant to Convention rights made actionable in UK law. If the sovereign legislature wishes expressly to amend or repeal that choice, it can do so. While the legislation remains in force, it continues to reflect the legislative choice initially made in 1998. Some might feel that the legislature should never have made this choice, since in reality it gives the last word to a judicial organ outside the UK, but this is no reason to deny the democratic legitimacy of that choice. Lord Sumption would say that not everything done by a democratically elected Parliament enhances democracy. He is right as a matter of abstract principle. This argument is, however, fraught with danger. It can be wielded too easily by supporters of democratic choice who wish nonetheless to deprecate a particular exercise of that choice of which they disapprove. The bottom line is that there may be all manner of reasons why a Parliament might be willing to accept constraints, even if the temptations to be avoided are not directly analogous to Ulysses and the Sirens. There will be certain decisions that a particular signatory state does not like, but that is the inevitable consequence of collective action in any

---

[61] See, eg, *X (Minors) v Bedfordshire CC* [1995] 2 AC 633; *Stovin v Wise* [1996] AC 923; *Curran v Northern Ireland Co-ownership Housing Association Ltd* [1987] AC 718.

[62] See, eg, *Barrett v Enfield LBC* [2001] 2 AC 550; *Phelps v Hillingdon LBC* [2001] 2 AC 619.

[63] See, eg, *O' Rourke v Camden LBC* [1998] AC 188; *Hammersmith Railway Co v Brand* (1869) LR 4 HL 171; *Manchester Corp v Farnworth* [1930] AC 171; *Allen v Gulf Oil Refining Ltd* [1981] AC 1001; *Dunne v North Western Gas Board* [1964] 2 QB 806; *Smeaton v Ilford Corp* [1954] Ch 450.

context, which entails the surrender of some freedom of action for the benefits of membership. The reality is, as noted above, that relatively few Strasbourg rulings have raised the domestic legislative ire, and many rulings have been in the government's favour.

The argument is also problematic because the HRA embodies a softer form of constitutional review, such that the legislature still has the last word in relation to primary statute. This was the deal struck when the HRA was enacted so as to respect the tradition of parliamentary sovereignty. It is true, as attested to by the academic literature, that Parliament commonly follows the judicial ruling. This does not alter the preceding point concerning the latitude afforded to the legislature. It may accept the judicial ruling because it had not seen the infirmity and is happy to correct it, which is by definition not problematic in terms of legislative choice since Parliament is in agreement with the judicial result. Parliament might alternatively find it difficult to resist the ruling by a UK court made pursuant to a margin of discretion afforded by Convention jurisprudence, even where Convention demands could be met in some other way. The answer to this is that Parliament should be more robust in this regard. There is something decidedly odd about bemoaning the circumscription of legislative choice where the legislature is not willing to avail itself of the power at its disposal. Parliament might yet again feel compelled to accept the judicial outcome because it is dictated by Strasbourg case law. This is clearly the most constraining in terms of legislative power, but this takes us full circle back to the point made in the previous paragraph, viz that this is the result of the legislative choice embodied in the HRA.

D. Statute, Courts and Respect

The centrality of normative choice and balancing of incommensurables to both private and public law does not mean that the courts should ride roughshod over legislative choice, nor does it mean that they should fail to accord respect to it. My own views in this respect are considered elsewhere,[64] but two more general points should be borne in mind.

We have always taken cognisance of democratic status within the fabric of judicial review. It is built on assumptions concerning the relationship between the legal and political branch of government, as exemplified by the generally accepted proscription on judicial substitution of judgment for that of the administration in relation to the merits of discretionary power. The extent to which primary decision-makers have democratic credentials varies very considerably. The strongest case for such respect is in relation to primary legislation, which embodies the result of legislative choice expressly made after due consideration, although there may, by way of contrast, be rights-based issues that the legislature was unaware

[64] P Craig, *UK, EU and Global Administrative Law: Foundations and Challenges* (Cambridge, Cambridge University Press, 2015) ch 2.

of, more especially in long, complex legislation. The initial determination may be made by bodies such as local authorities, agencies, prison governors, school governors, health boards and bodies to whom power has been contracted out. The extent of their democratic credentials varies considerably. There is clearly a distinction between the existence of democratic legitimacy that inheres by virtue of the vote and the authority given by a democratically elected body to an agency or institution that is not itself democratically elected.

The second consideration should be regarded as a counterpoint to the first. The HRA is not the source of the problem in the manner that some conceive it to be. It is not just that its amendment or repeal might trigger judicial recourse to the common law jurisprudence that pre-dated it; it is more fundamentally because the very recognition of such rights at common law, justified for the reasons set out above, necessarily requires inquiry as to the scope of the right and possible justifications for limitations thereof, thereby raising the same issues that currently require resolution. The only way to avoid such a conclusion is either through some form of rights-scepticism whereby the very denomination of certain interests as rights is felt to be misconceived or through some fairly extreme form of court-scepticism, which would connote not merely the need for respect calibrated according, inter alia, to the nature of the primary decision-maker, but something more akin to judicial abstention. Nor should it be thought that the difficulties of such review at common law or pursuant to the HRA will be obviated or overcome if reasonableness/proportionality control were to be radically limited or even cast aside. The courts would engage in analogous value judgments in the context of purpose/relevancy, and for those concerned about the limits of legitimate judicial intervention, the position would be worse insofar as the courts substitute judgment on these heads of review.

V. CONCLUSION

It is right and proper for there to be informed debate as to the limits of law; indeed, it is vital that such issues should not be ducked or treated dismissively. By a similar token, it is equally important that we test our conclusions as to what those limits should be in a particular legal area against explicit or implicit assumptions that frame our thinking about the legitimate limits of law in other areas. This chapter has sought to contribute to this discourse. Insofar as we are concerned about the limits of law, then this must apply equally to contestable normative judgments that the courts routinely make, as well as to the balancing of incommensurables. Insofar as we are concerned about the limits of law viewed from both dimensions, then our considered conclusions from a public law perspective must cohere with those that inform our thoughts about private law. The assumption that there is some stark dichotomy in this respect as between public and private law does not withstand close analysis.

11
The Limits of Lord Sumption: Limited Legal Constitutionalism and the Political Form of the ECHR

RICHARD BELLAMY

LORD SUMPTION TELLS us that the title of his Sultan Azlan Shah Law lecture, 'The Limits of Law', draws inspiration from Lon Fuller's posthumously published essay on the 'The Forms and Limits of Adjudication'.[1] To a degree, the same can be said with regard to its content. Fuller regarded legal arbitration as pertaining to issues of social order that involve claims of right and guilt for which reasoned arguments can be presented by the litigants and that are not overly 'polycentric' in character—that is, that do not encompass numerous mutually intersecting and largely incompatible and incommensurable claims. Fuller contended that claims within a 'polycentric' context tend to be unsuited to arbitration by the courts because a reasoned appraisal of all the potential issues of right and guilt involved cannot be offered. The resolution of any one case risks being arbitrary in terms of the knock-on effects it has for all the related cases. Such situations are better resolved either by managerial direction, involving a degree of intuition and experience, as is employed by a baseball coach when assigning team positions, or reciprocal bargaining and trade-offs, as is common in contracting and trading, including the bargaining and log-rolling typical of law-making by legislatures.[2]

Lord Sumption goes further than Fuller in regarding most rights claims as having these 'polycentric' features, with their resolution being most appropriately made either by the decisions of elected executives or via the process of compromise between democratic representatives characteristic of parliamentary legislation.[3] Unlike Fuller, though, Lord Sumption considers that adjudication should be largely limited to rights claims that are clearly established in legislation.

---

[1] Lord Sumption, 'The Limits of Law', 27th Sultan Azlan Shah Lecture, Kuala Lumpur, 20 November 2013, 1; L Fuller, 'The Forms and Limits of Adjudication' (1978) 92(2) *Harvard Law Review* 353.
[2] Fuller (n 1) 394–404.
[3] Sumption (n 1) 15.

The partial exception are what he calls 'truly fundamental rights' of the kind found within the text of the European Convention on Human Rights (ECHR), for which he believes a broad consensus already exists, at least within democracies. Even in this case, though, such rights should be regarded as being essentially legislated for by the precise terms of the Convention and the original intentions of the democratically elected politicians who framed it on behalf of their respective peoples.[4] The prime target of his lecture are those judges, chief among them the members of the European Court of Human Rights (ECtHR), who regard the Convention as a 'living instrument' and rights as abstract adjudicative principles to be applied to cases where no settled law exists or to the reinterpretation or even overturning of existing law.[5] In his view, such judicial reasoning proves illegitimate in a democratic society, breaching the limits of what the law allows or is capable of accomplishing.

Lord Sumption's argument can be characterised as a form of 'Limited Legal Constitutionalism'.[6] He seeks to limit constitutional protections to the narrow defence of a minimal set of rights that are enshrined in law and defined and understood in a restricted and non-expansive way, confining the courts to the strict interpretation of the letter and intended meaning of the law, and leaving broader issues of principle concerning how the legal and social order should be configured to the democratically elected representatives of the people. In his view, therefore, the content of constitutional law and the role of its judicial interpreters should both be limited. However, these limits reside in the law itself—judges must simply stick to the law and the limitations it imposes upon them. The error of those ECtHR judges who adopt the 'living instrument' view is a legal one of overstepping their limited and legally permissible jurisdiction and misinterpreting the law in unwarranted, expansive ways that stray into a sphere that ought to be left to democratic politics.[7] The result is to create a 'democratic deficit' that substitutes the arbitrary will of an individual judge for the democratically negotiated will of the people.[8] Nevertheless, he says nothing at all about whether and, if so, how democratic politics might constrain this supposed abuse of judicial power. Democracy appears likewise limited to its own legislative sphere. It has neither a constitutive nor a constitutional role other than the passing of legislation that, to the extent that it does not infringe 'truly fundamental' rights, ought to be faithfully administered by the courts.

This chapter compares Lord Sumption's approach to the apparently analogous views of political constitutionalists. Political constitutionalists express superficially similar concerns to those of Lord Sumption about the democratic legitimacy

---

[4] ibid 8–9.
[5] ibid 7.
[6] On the legal/political constitutionalism distinction, see R Bellamy, *Political Constitutionalism*, (Cambridge, Cambridge University Press, 2007) 2–7.
[7] Sumption (n 1) 6, 8, 11.
[8] ibid 9–10.

of judicial review and likewise advocate the merits of the democratic legislative process for defining the contours of rights within a political community.[9] However, whereas his arguments are institutionally and to some degree politically conservative, this is less so with regard to political constitutionalism. By and large, political constitutionalism has been proposed by those on the left of the political spectrum as much concerned by the judiciary's failure to uphold rights as by their propensity to discover new rights. From the political constitutionalist perspective, Lord Sumption's limited legal constitutionalism is as contentious and as open to abuse as the more extensive versions he criticises, such as those he associates with Ronald Dworkin, John Rawls and the 'living instrument' doctrine of the ECtHR.[10]

Political constitutionalism does not place courts outside politics, but advocates their operating as part of the political system so as to promote the determination and upholding of rights in ways consistent with the constitutional ideal of legal and political equality. Legal and political adjudication are not separated, but are treated as complementary parts of a process designed to ensure that all individuals are treated with equal concern and respect. Bills of rights need not be seen as the exclusive preserve of the courts, but rather as legislative mechanisms that legislatures establish to improve their deliberations and ensure they reason in principled ways when enacting legislation. Likewise, the courts need not be seen as independent of and in some sense above democratic politics, but as democratically constituted and controlled so as to empower those who may not have found a voice within the democratic process to gain a hearing. Political constitutionalism achieves this goal through 'weak review', whereby the courts highlight inconsistencies in legislation, potential unfairness in the legal or political process, or disproportionate impacts on particular individuals or groups that get revealed by particular cases and to which legislatures may have failed to give due consideration.[11] In contrast to 'strong review', 'weak review' does not disapply the law, but rather invites legislatures to reconsider it in the light of particular circumstances of which they may have been previously unaware.[12] On this account, judges may be independent, but the judicial system is democratically dependent not in being limited to following democratically enacted legislation, which may be either insufficient or open to different interpretations with regard to particular cases, but in its institutional composition and working, so that it supports rather than undermines political equality. Thus conceived, these judicial mechanisms

---

[9] The originator of the term and to some degree this approach was JGA Griffith, 'The Political Constitution' (1979) 42 *Modern Law Review* 1. For a survey of subsequent literature, see M Goldoni and C McCorkindale (eds), 'Special Issue on "Political Constitutions"' (2013) 14(12) *German Law Journal*.

[10] Sumption (n 1) 12.

[11] As I have argued elsewhere, the UK Human Rights Act can be more or less assimilated into this characterisation of the political constitutionalist position. See R Bellamy, 'Political Constitutionalism and the Human Rights Act' (2011) 9 *International Journal of Constitutional Law* 86.

[12] For the strong/weak judicial review distinction, see J Waldron, 'The Core Case against Judicial Review' (2006) 115 *Yale Law Journal* 1346, 1354–55.

support a view of the constitutional ideal as inherently linked to the democratic process rather than as a judicial limit on democracy.

The first section outlines the limitations of Lord Sumption's limited legal constitutionalist approach, while the second section traces the political constitutionalist alternative with its focus on promoting political equality through a statutory bill of rights, parliamentary rights review and 'weak review'. The third section then addresses the issue of whether an international legal system, such as the ECHR, could conceivably operate in the manner of a political constitution, in which an international court remains democratically dependent on the domestic legislatures of the contracting states. An argument is given as to why such a system might be necessary and how it could function. The fourth section then details how in certain key respects the ECHR corresponds to such a model. As a result, Lord Sumption's purportedly democratic criticisms of the ECHR are revealed as misconceived, reflecting the limitations of his limited legal constitutionalist approach.

I. THE LIMITATIONS OF LORD SUMPTION'S LIMITED LEGAL CONSTITUTIONALISM

Lord Sumption associates three legal limits as appropriate for rights-based judicial review within a democratic society. First, conventions or constitutions should only entrench the 'limited number of rights that the consensus of our societies recognizes as truly fundamental'—those that protect 'politically vulnerable minorities from oppression'. Anything beyond the realm of this limited set 'enters that of legitimate political debate where issues ought to be resolved politically'.[13] Second, the courts should be limited to the letter of any conventions, constitutions or laws that they have a role in applying, sticking to the plain language and intended purpose of the text.[14] As a result, they can only legitimately strike down legislation that infringes those 'truly fundamental' rights that are associated with what he regards as 'real oppression'. Third, rights can only be extended beyond these 'truly fundamental' and widely agreed protections against oppression through legislation, which must be faithfully followed by the courts. When courts go beyond these limits and seek 'to extrapolate or extend by analogy the scope of a written instrument so as to enlarge its subject matter', they exercise an illegitimate degree of discretion that not only subverts the rule of law by rendering the law 'subjective, unpredictable and unclear' but also 'gives rise … to a significant democratic deficit'.[15]

Lord Sumption puts forward these limits as a way of reining in the power of judges while still preserving respect for 'truly fundamental rights', leaving

---

[13] Sumption (n 1) 10.
[14] ibid 8.
[15] ibid 8–9.

discussion of other rights to the democratic process. Yet, these legal limits are in many respects at odds with his observations concerning the tendency and ability of judges to interpret the law in novel ways, the controversial character of rights, and the difference between popular sovereignty and democracy. At best, his arguments amount to a somewhat conservative exhortation to judges to abide by a supposed consensus agreed in 1950; at worst, they say nothing about how the democratic process might be enhanced and improved so that both legislators and courts take rights and democracy seriously, and engage in an ongoing dialogue as to what they mean for citizens in the here and now.

Lord Sumption's limits belong to a specifically legal form of constitutionalism in the sense of placing trust 'in the power of words engrossed on parchment to keep a government [and, he believes, judges too] in order'.[16] Yet, as Madison pointedly remarked, 'parchment barriers', be they in the form of international conventions, constitutions or written laws, are a 'greatly overrated' device.[17] The danger is that faith in the force of something being written down turns into a fetishism of the text and the nature of interpretation that stymies discussion of the substantive issue at hand. Of course, in some ways that is Lord Sumption's intention—he wants to move the substantive discussion of rights elsewhere into the ordinary political process. Yet, as he acknowledges in his critique of the 'living instrument' doctrine, experience suggests that judges are adept at extending the scope of rights under the guise of textual analysis. There is little he can do by appealing to the 'plain' or 'intended' meaning of words to prevent such exercises. Indeed, the plain or intended meaning of terms often offers little guidance as to how an abstractly formulated right should be applied to particular or novel circumstances. All that such textual fetishism does is to distort the direct normative discussion of issues by turning them into debates about the correct interpretation of the meaning of terms.

Lord Sumption also adopts the dominant legal constitutionalist paradigm in conceiving of conventions as 'a legal limitation on government' in that he does not doubt that judges could justifiably constrain governments and laws that infringed 'truly fundamental' rights.[18] He objects to what he regards as the tendency of the ECtHR and judges more generally to read these rights in a 'maximalist' way, which effectively introduces what he regards as new obligations on governments that may have knock-on effects for other programmes they wish to fund— that, to cite his example, spending on legal aid, say, might get increased by judicial dictat as a result of a given case and thereby, as an unintended consequence in a world of limited budgets, reduce spending on hospitals and schools.[19] But his

---

[16] Walton H Hamilton, 'Constitutionalism' in Edwin Seligman and Alvin Johnson (eds), *Encyclopedia of the Social Sciences*, volume 4 (London and New York, Macmillan, 1931) 255.

[17] Alexander Hamilton, John Jay and James Madison, *The Federalist* (George W Carey and James McLellan (eds) (Indianapolis, Liberty Fund, 2001)) # 48.

[18] Sumption (n 1) 10.

[19] ibid 4–6.

limited approach risks the opposite danger of judicial minimalism of the kind typical of the so-called good old days of judicial passivity. Such minimalism can manifest itself in inaction, where the judiciary ought to have acted, such as their acquiescence in the progressive disempowering of labour unions to foster collective bargaining on the part of workers on the grounds that weakening the power to strike or organise upholds rather than diminishes freedom of association and freedom of speech.[20] It can also encourage the view that government should be limited—that, for example, health warnings on cigarettes interfere with free speech or wage agreements conflict with freedom of contract.

All of which is to say that 'truly fundamental' rights are themselves controversial and that a minimalist reading may be as contentious as a maximalist reading. Lord Sumption tries to get around this issue by asserting that these rights are subject to a 'consensus' and possess democratic legitimacy through having been duly enacted in a convention by our elected representatives. But though there may be a consensus on some abstract formulation of these rights, such as the ECHR provides, there is no such consensus on what they mean in relation to a given case, even among the judiciary—hence the tendency of multi-member courts, such as the ECtHR, to decide most cases by majority vote. Sumption suggests that the courts should defer to the last politically determined view on how such rights should be decided. Yet legislation can be vague and open-ended—often deliberately so, either because such vagueness was a way of securing a compromise or because the legislators appreciated that they cannot anticipate each and every case, not least because new issues may arise. Again, Lord Sumption's narrow conception of constitutionalism as a legal limit on discretion by governments or courts blinds him to the limitations and biases of this view. Even if a convention could be sufficiently detailed as to provide clear guidance to judges in relation to how they should decide future cases, why should it be regarded as more democratic for those subject to it to be bound by the somewhat dated perspectives of its long-dead framers as opposed to the views of recently appointed judges?

Lord Sumption notes that the mere fact that a law or convention has received democratic endorsement or has been enacted by democratically authorised representatives does not in and of itself render that law or convention democratic, especially if it entails taking decision-making out of the democratic arena by handing it over to unelected officials such as judges. As he rightly notes, an authoritarian regime does not become any more democratic simply by virtue of having been established via a democratic process.[21] However, not only is this a somewhat imprecise characterisation of the operation of the ECtHR and most constitutional courts, as I shall detail below, but also his own argument appears vulnerable to a similar

---

[20] For a detailed account of how limited legal judicial review of the kind Lord Sumption advocates supported the curtailment of rights during the 1980s, see KD Ewing and CA Gearty, *Freedom under Thatcher: Civil Liberties in Modern Britain* (Oxford, Oxford University Press, 1990).
[21] Sumption (n 1) 11.

critique. After all, just because a convention was democratically enacted at time x does not mean it can be regarded as still enjoying the democratic endorsement of a quite different people at time z—they have no more authorised or consented to it than they have to the unchanged views and regime of a benevolent dictator elected into power by their parents and grandparents, who pledged to uphold 'truly fundamental rights' as understood in 1951. Lord Sumption might object that whereas the dictator cannot be easily removed by subsequent democratic decisions, legislation can be amended and conventions renegotiated. However, these are also hard to change, especially the last, and the need to do so may not be clear until a case arises that reveals a problem. Of course, he seems to think these issues do not arise so far as 'truly fundamental rights' are concerned, where he believes the past can continue to dictate to the present on the basis of an assumed ongoing consensus. Yet, as we saw, this assumption proves questionable. Over time, citizens have come to view the scope of application of such rights and the sources of oppression both more broadly and, in some cases, even more narrowly than in the 1950s. A better awareness of the nature of discrimination on the grounds of gender, race and religion has greatly changed how many people understand, say, freedom of speech, compared to the dominant understandings of 70 years ago.

Lord Sumption's argument appears to suggest that all the regulators established by democratic governments, from independent central banks to bodies such as Ofcom, must be regarded as illegitimate because they take collective decisions that ought to be made by democratically elected representatives. After all, the logic for outsourcing certain decisions to these bodies is very similar to the rationale behind courts: namely, that such bodies can be more effective, equitable and efficient than elected bodies might be because they can be staffed by experts and be more impartial and have fewer transaction costs than a democratic decision process involving complex bargaining among different self-regarding interests. Yet, it would be wrong to regard such bodies as entirely free from democratic influence. They are usually under the indirect democratic control of citizens and their representatives. Elected politicians or bodies established by them and acting according to democratically enacted criteria generally select their membership, lay down their competences and set their targets, control their funding and implement (or not) their decisions. They are also actively scrutinised by the media and responsive to long-term trends in public opinion. Likewise, though courts are often characterised as 'independent', in reality they are typically democratically dependent to a large degree in precisely these sorts of ways. Indeed, that democratic dependence accounts for many of the characteristics typically regarded as desirable qualities for courts and the judiciary to possess in a democratic society. For example, we expect courts to be democratic in treating all as equally subject to the law and that justice be equally open to all, for related reasons it is also increasingly seen as important that judges should not be a class apart, but should belong sufficiently to the same social world as those affected by their judgments so that they can appreciate their reasoning and situation. These qualities are not achieved simply by virtue of the law being democratically made and judges following it. It reflects the ways judicial institutions are set up, their recruitment policies, and their being a part of rather than outside the political and social system.

Sumption fails to see or explore such issues because of the limited legalistic paradigm that he adopts whereby the law either constrains governments, in the case of fundamental rights, or judges, in the case of everything else. On his account, constitutionalism is about legal limitation, with the role of the courts separated from that of legislatures. As a result, though he advocates that all but 'truly fundamental' rights be subjected to debate and compromise within a legislature, he does not conceive these debates as taking a constitutional form. Rather, he sees rights as emerging from the standard bargaining over social policies, whereby politicians seek to accommodate a sufficiently wide spectrum of interests and opinions to have enough support among the electorate, or their elected members, to obtain a majority.[22] He does not regard 'non fundamental' rights as especially weighty interests or principles that ought to shape the ways in which legislatures deliberate about those policies. He believes political bargaining should simply aim at giving enough people an interest in a policy for it to pass. Its purpose is not to enhance the degree to which that policy promotes the commonly avowable interests of the public to an equal degree. The latter goal involves upholding every citizen's right to equal concern and respect in the consideration of their interests. The former goal, at least in the form advocated by Lord Sumption, merely requires that their limited fundamental rights are not breached and each can bargain on the same terms as everyone else. Yet, on his limited account of the democratic process, it will be enough for a winning coalition of supporters to feel that the policy offers an improvement over the available alternatives, especially that of no policy. But the policy may increase rather than diminish inequalities in the relative power and wellbeing both of the different groups supporting the measure and even more so of those who oppose it, or at best leave them as they are. It suffices that enough feel their preferences are satisfied more than they would be by not compromising, not that the degree of satisfaction each achieves be equitable or fair. Consequently, this trimming of rights from the political process and its reduction to the simple trading of interests risks promoting shallow, purely pragmatic legislative compromises, in which the powerful only concede as much to the relatively powerless as is necessary for them to prevail.[23] It produces a limited account of the constitutional role of the democratic process in all senses—it is limited to a minimal degree by the courts and possesses only limited constitutional qualities.

Lord Sumption may regard this characterisation of his position as unfair given that he says relatively little on the topic. Yet, if he is to counterpose democracy to courts, he needs to offer arguments for why we should regard the legislation

---

[22] ibid 12–13.
[23] I contrast trimming and trading as strategies of compromise with negotiation as part of a democratic form of political constitution in my *Liberalism and Pluralism: Towards a Politics of Compromise*, (London, Routledge, 1997) chs 4, 5, 7.

of the former as having superior constitutional qualities to the judgments of the latter. That he fails to do because he restricts the constitutional to such a limited set and reading of fundamental rights. As a result, the role expected of democracy gets similarly diminished. The aim of legislative bargaining and compromise is not justice on his account, but 'social cohesion', achieved through giving enough people enough of what they want to secure support for the *status quo*—however oppressive or unjust it might be. By contrast, though political constitutionalists share both his worries about judicial discretion and his praise of the merits of legislation, they do so from quite a different perspective. They seek less the mutual limitation of legislatures and courts to their distinct spheres, or of reconciling majorities and minorities through mutually beneficial trade-offs, and more the empowerment of citizens to live as equals. It is to this alternative account of the relative roles of courts and legislatures that we now turn.

II. POLITICAL CONSTITUTIONALISM AND THE DEMOCRATIC DEPENDENCE OF COURTS

Political constitutionalism focuses not on restraint and limitation, but on empowering and enabling. It sees a constitution as a way of structuring deliberation about the nature of law and rights that ensures it is public and treats all involved with equal respect and concern. It does so by seeking to provide processes that ensure political equality so that justice is not only done, but is also seen to be done. As such, it involves focusing more on counteracting the ways in which powerful minorities, such as the possessors of wealth and other forms of social and economic power, can capture the political and judicial process to dominate the majority, as on guarding against the possibility of a tyrannous majority. This latter limitation too often prevents the ordinary citizens who are generally subjected to power from having a voice. So the role of a political constitution is primarily a positive rather than a negative one—that of ensuring that people possess an active and equal influence and control over legislation, so that it addresses their commonly avowable interests rather than simply their being equally subject to it as its passive addressees.[24]

The point of a political constitution, therefore, is to create a public mechanism within which citizens can address each other as equals, thereby showing each other equal respect, about those collective policies needed to treat each other as equals by equally advancing their interests, thereby showing each other equal concern. Since we are all partial to our own views in this regard—as much because of our limited knowledge and experience as self-interest—the best way of overcoming

---

[24] I have elaborated this argument at length in Bellamy (n 6) and my 'Public Law as Democracy' in Cormac Mac Hamhleigh, Claudio Michelon and Neil Walker (eds), *After Public Law* (Oxford, Oxford University Press, 2013) ch 7, 130–50.

our partiality is through being forced to publicly engage and debate with others on as equal basis as possible.[25] On this account, therefore, democracy becomes the means for realising the constitutional ideal rather than the object of constitutional constraint. Political equality within a democratic process provides what, following Hannah Arendt,[26] can be called the 'right to have rights'—that is, the right to be regarded with equal respect and concern.

Does that mean that the courts must be even more subject to democratic control than Sumption suggests? Yes and no. On the one hand, the democratic operation of the courts ceases simply to be a matter of fidelity to democratically made law—a somewhat impractical goal in any case, as I noted above. Rather, democratic control applies more to the institutionalisation of the judicial system—the way in which it is resourced, recruited and structured and the ethos of those involved. For example, it will be important to show that the law serves the people rather than lawyers and does not unjustifiably favour certain groups within the community at the expense of others; that access to justice is not biased or inequitable; and that the judiciary and lawyers do not form a class apart, out of touch with the circumstances and values of the broader society, and that their recruitment is open and meets equal opportunities criteria. Judges may need to be independent of political influence when deciding individual cases, but the system as a whole should be one that operates by public criteria that reinforce political and legal equality through being itself under the indirect influence and control of citizens.

On the other hand, a judicial system that is so structured can play its part in ensuring that the legislative and administrative acts of democratic governments treat citizens with equal concern and respect. As I observed earlier, legislation can never be so framed as to consider each and every possibility. Moreover, even if democratic legislatures fare better than courts in providing a mechanism for the public deliberation of the laws framing our shared social world, no system of representation can ensure that all interests gain an equal hearing or get heard at all. The advantage of the courts lies in their awareness of how measures designed to serve the general good may impact on particular individuals.

What might be the forms and limits of rights-based judicial review within a political constitution? With regard to its form, bills of rights need not be outside of politics—they can be normal pieces of democratic legislation which a legislature enacts to highlight that certain interests deserve especial consideration, establishing special procedures to vet laws and executive acts for compliance. Meanwhile, independent judges operating within a democratically dependent court can be authorised by such legislation to further improve public deliberation by obliging governments and legislatures occasionally to reconsider their decisions in the light

---

[25] T Christiano, *The Constitution of Equality: Democratic Authority and its Limits* (Oxford, Oxford University Press, 2008) 88–96.
[26] H Arendt, *The Origins of Totalitarianism* (Orlando, Harcourt Brace, 1958) 296.

of individual cases that may suggest they overlooked the impact of their policies on certain under-represented individuals. However, such judicial review may be limited to 'weak review', whereby the legislature may choose after due reconsideration to leave a given law or decision unchanged if it holds that rights are best respected by so doing. Note that the emphasis here is on the potentially disempowered rather than the powerful. Almost all the cases referred to by Lord Sumption relate to those minorities who might get an inadequate hearing in legislatures—in cases such as prisoners or asylum seekers through having no vote at all—as opposed to powerful minorities, whose influence might be regarded as likely to be unduly enhanced by their ability to gain access to and shape or employ an often expensive legal process.[27] A political constitutionalist questions the venue shopping of the latter, but upholds the right of contestation of the former.

Arguably, the UK Human Rights Act 1998, which is both a normal piece of parliamentary legislation and gives Parliament the last word, operates in precisely this manner so as to improve rather than undermine the political constitution.[28] It does so by obliging the legislature to explicitly review the degree to which legislation complies with those rights it has itself deemed to be crucial, and by allowing its decisions to be contested, but not laid to one side by the courts. As such, it provides a democratic form of deliberation about rights that can be enhanced by a democratically limited possibility for judicial review for those who may feel overlooked by the legislative process.

Parts of Lord Sumption's lecture could be read as suggesting that he would be happy with such a domestic mechanism, but that he fears that where they exist, then bodies such as the ECHR and the ECtHR are at best redundant and at worst illegitimate precisely because they are not under the ongoing democratic influence and control of the people's elected representatives. Certainly, many who hold seemingly similar views to his have regarded the chief flaw of the current UK Human Rights Act as being what they regard as an obligation under section 2(1) to follow the jurisprudence of the ECtHR, leading them to call for its replacement by a so-called British Bill of Rights.[29] In what follows, I wish to contest both these assertions and argue that such international conventions and courts are neither redundant nor necessarily democratically illegitimate. I shall start by outlining why democratic states might be moved to create such bodies and how they can be so organised as to be democratically dependent in the manner specified above.

---

[27] For examples, see D Nicol, 'Business Rights as Human Rights' in T Campbell, KD Ewing and A Tomkins (eds), *The Legal Protection of Rights: Sceptical Essays* (Oxford, Oxford University Press, 2011).

[28] I have argued for this view in detail in Bellamy (n 11). See also Bellamy (n 24).

[29] See 'Home Secretary Theresa May Wants Human Rights Act Axed', BBC Report, 2 October 2011, www.bbc.co.uk/news/uk-politics-15140742; and 'Protecting Human Rights in the UK: The Conservatives' Proposals for Changing Britain's Human Rights Laws', 3 October 2014, https://www.conservatives.com/~/media/files/downloadable%20Files/human_rights.pdf. In fact, 'take into account' has never been interpreted by British courts as slavishly following, and they have been prepared to disregard ECtHR rulings they regard as unclear or inappropriate in the British context, eg, *Kay v Lambeth London Borough Council* [2006] UKHL 28, 44 and *Brown v Stott* [2003] 1 AC 733.

I shall then turn to the ECHR and shall argue that it conforms more or less to this democratic model, thereby forming a part of the political constitution.[30]

III. THE DEMOCRATIC CONSTITUTION OF INTERNATIONAL COURTS

The previous section indicated that a democratically legitimate system of international human rights protection will need to be limited to weak review and subject to ongoing democratic political control through the ordinary legislative process. Such control must apply to the content of any International Human Rights Convention (IHRC), the running of the legal system charged with its interpretation, and to the competences and—in the ultimate instance—to the decisions of the relevant International Human Rights Court (IHRCt). The challenge addressed in this section is to see whether that is possible without assuming the merging of the various contracting states into a regional or global *demos* and democratic system that might exercise that control.

This argument might seem to require that any IHRC and IHRCt be under the exclusive democratic control of the Member State parties subject to it. If so, that would be an impossible standard for any international body to meet. It suggests that the only democratically legitimate international order would be a world of separate and independent democratic states. However, this picture of autarkic democratic states is unrealistic given the current reality of international interdependence, a condition on which a great deal of our economic wellbeing depends. In these circumstances, decisions in one state can have important consequences for those in another state, undermining exclusive democratic control. Herein lies the reason for creating international regimes, such as an IHRC, in the first place, because they offer a response to this situation. In certain respects, they do involve a weakening of exclusive democratic control. But in other respects, as I shall show, these regimes can be conceived in ways that seek to bolster such domestic democratic control and to render it as feasible as possible in an interconnected world.

Three issues might motivate democratic states to establish IHRCs and IHRCts. All three stem from a commitment to upholding the 'right to have rights' of different peoples to live under democratic regimes that guarantee their citizens the status of political equals, who are entitled to equal concern and respect. First, states may support such mechanisms as ways of promoting democratisation. The move to judicialisation generally occurs when hegemonic elites fear their political opponents may overturn their policies.[31] The governments of new democracies can

---

[30] These two sections draw on my 'The Democratic Legitimacy of International Human Rights Conventions: Political Constitutionalism and the ECHR' (2014) 25(4) *European Journal of International Law* 1019.

[31] R Hirschl, *Towards Juristocracy: The Origins and Consequences of the New Constitutionalism* (Cambridge, MA, Harvard University Press, 2004).

rationally see such international commitments as helping to lock in the domestic status quo against their non-democratic opponents. Mature democracies may doubt the utility or legitimacy of such arrangements for themselves, but still may regard them as helpful for less established democracies. Support for this function can be regarded as a corollary of the political constitutionalist belief that rights are best protected through democracy and because of the threat that non-democratic or unstable democratic regimes may pose to democracies.[32]

Second, even if all states are democratic, democratic states have an incentive to ensure that their ability to operate in a democratic manner is not undermined by the decisions of other states, democratic or otherwise. Therefore, they have reason to create institutions to guarantee that democracies treat each other with equal concern and respect.[33] Examples include trade negotiations, particularly concerning the exploitation of another country's natural resources, and the promotion of global public goods, such as combating climate change and protecting the environment more generally. These arguments also extend to establishing mechanisms to ensure trans- and multinational corporations and organisations respect democratic standards and decision-making.

These two issues can also be related to protecting the stateless and those seeking entry to democratic states. On the one hand, such persons lack access to the democratic process and, since democratic states are committed to spreading democracy, the reasoning underlying the first issue also extends to them. On the other hand, democratic states might fear that unless the burden of admitting them is shared equitably, the democratic quality of certain states could suffer, thereby invoking the second issue. As a result, states have an interest in securing common, democracy-friendly policies in this area.

Third, and finally, even mature democracies can acknowledge that no democratic process is perfect. So long as the imperfections of any judicial process can also be corrected by a democratic mechanism, providing a contestatory channel at the international level may allow lessons to be learned from other democracies and certain unfounded parochial biases and prejudices to be challenged.

These three issues can be linked to three criteria for the governance of the international mechanisms that might be established to address them so as to ensure that these in their turn remain consistent with political constitutionalist assumptions.[34]

First, these courts and the international arrangements of which they form a part must promote and be compatible with the possibility for all individuals to

---

[32] A Moravcsik, 'The Origins of Human Rights Regimes: Democratic Delegation in Postwar Europe' (2000) 54 *International Organisation* 217, 243–46.

[33] P Pettit, 'Legitimate International Institutions: A Neo-Republican Perspective' in S Besson and J Tasioulas (eds), *The Philosophy of International Law* (Oxford, Oxford University Press, 2010) 139, 152–53.

[34] ibid 153–58; T Christiano, 'Democratic Legitimacy and International Institutions' in Besson and Tasioulas (eds) (n 33) 119, 122–24, 126–29.

live in legitimate states that possess democratic systems where collective decisions are made in ways that show them equal respect and concern through being under their shared and equal control. Second, these international mechanisms should be under the equal control of such states. If the legitimacy of democratic states stems from them offering reasonably effective mechanisms for the identification and equal advancement of the interests of their citizens, then the legitimacy of international systems stems from them doing likewise through being in their turn under the shared and equal control of the signatory states. Third, membership of such international systems should be voluntary. Not all states will have an equal stake in collective arrangements on a given issue and many will not have equal bargaining power. Voluntary arrangements allow states to tailor their international commitments to the interests of their populations and ideally to negotiate the terms of their adherence accordingly.

The basic institutional model of the international order stemming from these issues and criteria is that of a voluntary and fair association among democratic states. Such an association offers a 'two level' political constitution,[35] whereby a political constitution at the international level renders an IHRC and IHRCts subject to the democratic authorisation and accountability of the representatives of the contracting democratic states, who are in their turn democratically authorised and accountable to those they represent through a political constitution at the domestic level. A number of recommendations follow from this account as to the competences and scope of judicial review by IHRCts, on the one hand, and the democratic organisation of IHRC systems, on the other. I shall take each in order below.

With regard to competences and scope, four remarks are in order. First, as Thomas Christiano has noted,[36] this model grounds certain international *jus cogens* norms concerning the performance of agreements duly made and against slavery, genocide and aggressive war, since these norms are prerequisites of, or internal to, such an arrangement and the importance it places on the value of consent. Therefore, there can be no problem with IHRCts seeking to uphold such norms unconditionally.

Second, a prime focus of such conventions should be the interactions between states and those who either lack democratic representation or operate outside adequate democratic control, such as refugees and multinational corporations respectively.

Third, if IHRCts are to respect the integrity of the democratic process, particularly in their judgments on domestic legislation and policies, they must be restricted to weak review. Moreover, contestation ought to be limited to cases where domestic political and judicial avenues have been exhausted and only involve those rights that might be considered basic to each citizen within a given

---

[35] R Putnam, 'Diplomacy and Domestic Politics: The Logic of Two-Level Games' (1988) 42 *International Organization* 427.
[36] Christiano (n 25) 123.

polity being able to publicly advance their interests on equal terms to others, though controversy exists as to whether these involve only core civil and political rights or certain minimum social and economic rights too.[37] Allowance also has to be made for the variety of ways in which different legal systems may choose to specify a given right and the numerous circumstances that may lead legislatures to limit the scope of one right in order to secure other rights.

Fourth, given that courts may be as mistaken as legislators, the possibility for a democratic override of an IHRCt judgment must also exist, with such decisions resting with a consensus among the representatives of the democratic governments, who should be ultimately charged with monitoring state compliance with the court's rulings. A number of benefits stem from this arrangement. For a start, from the perspective of the democratic state challenging the judgment, this would be a decision of peers.[38] The governments of other democratic states would appreciate the need to attune rights to domestic situations and the adverse reaction that an IHRCt decision perceived as insensitive to such considerations and in error might arouse. Yet, that need not mean they would tolerate almost any objection to a ruling that proved inconvenient for the government concerned—quite the contrary. For they would also be fully alive to the dangers of allowing states to renege on their solidaristic obligations and of undermining the court's authority through frivolous or self-serving challenges—particularly with regard to democratising states.

The issue of democratic organisation enters here, with three points being pertinent. First, this model is compatible with granting IHRCts a degree of independence from the states that bring them into being so long as the participating states have the right of exit and can determine the competences of these courts. In other words, the functionaries of the IHRC, such as the judges, may act independently, but the system itself must be democratically dependent on the contracting states.

Second, the democratic legitimacy of such dependence rests on the agents of the states involved adequately reflecting the views and concerns of the populations they represent. Consequently, signatories to an IHRC should be limited to states that are at least credibly democratising. The evidence suggests that non-democratic states do not respect the decisions of such bodies in any case—their formal adherence merely serves to give a spurious legitimacy to such regimes.[39] Meanwhile, given the discretion that executives of even democratic states have been accustomed to enjoy in foreign affairs, it is important to ensure that the state officials involved remain accountable for their decisions to the legislature and ultimately the electorate.

Finally, if the system as a whole is to offer equal consideration to the interests of the democratic peoples that it serves, then the signatory states ought to

---

[37] ibid 273–74.

[38] F Scharpf, 'Legitimacy in the Multilevel European Polity' (2009) 1 *European Political Science Review* 173, 199–200.

[39] B Simmons, *Mobilizing for Human Rights* (Cambridge, Cambridge University Press, 2009).

exercise equal control over the IHRC. For example, all states should have an equal vote in decisions regarding changes to the Convention, the selection of judges and instructions as to their working methods, the implementation of the court's judgments, the budget and so on.

Do these arrangements meet the standard objections as to their democratic legitimacy? As I have noted, a prime objection is that such arrangements must be under the exclusive democratic control of each of the contracting states. That is met at a baseline level by insisting that entry into these arrangements is voluntary and includes a right of exit. Moreover, their purpose and operation is structured around respect for democratic self-government. As we saw, this goal lies behind both the three issues motivating the establishment of this system and the three criteria guiding its competences and organisation. In particular, its governance structure does not involve a simple transfer of authority from a domestic to an international actor; rather, it places domestic actors, who remain democratically accountable to citizens or their representatives, in control on an equal and democratic basis. This structure provides a mechanism for democratic control without assuming either a global *demos* or democracy. Instead, the arrangement is one of a democratic international association of democracies and their *demoi*. This sort of 'two level' arrangement has been characterised as *demoi*cratic. There is not so much a transfer of competences as the creation of a jointly controlled mechanism to tackle those common problems that domestic institutions lack the competence to deal with alone. Finally, as a result of this arrangement, the most important objection, of undue judicial discretion, is met through rendering the IHRCt systemically dependent on the collective democratic decisions of the contracting states with regard to their competences and, in the last instance, judgments. Judges may be independent, but only with respect to weak review.

Clearly, many problems stand in the way of realising this system and in practice institutional arrangements may not necessarily always meet the criteria or answer all the relevant issues. In particular, there is the problem of asymmetric bargaining between richer and more powerful states and poorer and weaker states, though coalitions among the latter can to some degree counteract the influence of the former.[40] As with all domestic democratic systems, the international *demoi*cratic system is work in progress, with various groups employing the existing processes to further, and occasionally to hinder, its development. This section has aimed simply at formulating its normative and institutional underpinnings.

IV. THE POLITICAL CONSTITUTION OF THE ECHR

A measure of the plausibility of this approach can nevertheless be gauged by the significant degree to which the ECHR can be assimilated to it. All signatories must

---

[40] Christiano (n 34) 125–26; Pettit (n 33) 158–60.

meet certain minimal democratic standards. The Court and the Convention are overseen by the Council of Europe, the governance structure of which consists of the Committee of Ministers, comprising the Foreign Ministers or their permanent representatives of all 47 Member States, along with the Parliamentary Assembly of the Council of Europe (PACE). The Committee decides the Council's budget, negotiates the treaties and conventions governing its competences, and monitors the implementation of Court decisions. PACE, which includes 2–18 members, depending on population size, from the national parliaments of each of the signatory states, selects the judges—one from each Member State—and the Secretary General of the Council from lists supplied by the Committee of Ministers. As a result, there is a degree of legislative oversight of executive action in this area, with PACE also receiving regular reports from and making recommendations to the Committee of Ministers. The danger of overlooking domestic or transnational minorities is also lessened through the involvement of a Congress of Local and Regional Authorities of the Council of Europe, composed of elected members from these bodies within the Member States, charged with exploring the enhancement of local democracy and, in an advisory role, the International Non-governmental Organisations (INGOs) Conference of the Council of Europe.

Meanwhile, the Court applies a margin of appreciation in making its judgments, especially where no common standard exists across the Council of Europe and it may be necessary to balance rights and other interests,[41] thereby taking account of the diverse ways in which a right may be specified within different legal systems. Moreover, the Court has generally applied a wider margin when the case involves a choice that has been publically debated by a democratic legislature and where opinions reasonably differ, and narrowed it where a legislature has enacted or re-enacted a measure without due consideration.[42] Its judgments also only apply to the given jurisdiction and do not necessarily serve as precedents for rulings in similar cases in another state, thereby minimising the 'one size fits all' problem. The recent Brighton declaration has proposed formally incorporating both the margin of appreciation and the principle of subsidiarity into the Preamble of the Convention,[43] thereby underlining that the primary duty for the implementation of Convention rights rests with domestic legal and especially political organs. Indeed, it proposes that all parliaments should adopt the enhanced pre-legislative scrutiny procedures currently found in the UK and Nordic countries. In fact, the record suggests that the ECtHR already operates at the margins so far as mature

---

[41] See *Rasmussen v Denmark* (1984) 7 EHRR 371 [40]–[41] for the lack of a common approach and *Dickenson v UK* (2008) 46 EHRR 41, GC [77]–[79] for the issue of balance.

[42] *Hatton v UK* (2003) 37 EHRR 28, GC [97]; *Draon v France* (2006) 42 EHRR 40, GC [106]–[108] and—for the converse argument—*Hirst v UK (No 2)* (2006) 42 EHRR 41; *Sukhovetsky v Ukraine (2007)* 44 EHRR 57 [65]–[67]; and the analysis in A Legg, *The Margin of Appreciation in International Human Rights Law* (Oxford, Oxford University Press, 2012) especially ch 4.

[43] High Level Conference on the future of the ECtHR Brighton Declaration, 19/20 April 2012, http://hub.coe.int/en/20120419-brighton-declaration.

democracies are concerned. For example, since 1966, 97 per cent of the cases brought against the UK have been deemed inadmissible, while only 271 out of the 443 cases that were heard were held to involve an infraction—61 per cent or an average of 6.15 cases per year, less than two per cent of all cases brought. Five countries—Russia, Ukraine, Romania, Turkey and Italy—currently account for over half the cases brought before the Court, with Russia alone responsible for 27 per cent of them.

These features of the Council of Europe correspond quite closely to the criteria and corresponding recommendations given in the previous section for ensuring that an international association of democracies itself meets democratic criteria. Not only is it under the equal control of the representatives of democratic states, but these representatives are not simply from the executive branch. The involvement of parliamentary representatives and, to a lesser extent, representatives from local government and NGOs as well increases the likelihood that state policies are more democratically representative of domestic interests than is often the case in foreign affairs, including minority interests. As a result, it addresses at least some of the worries behind those insisting such arrangements be under the exclusive democratic control of the parties subject to them, without assuming the need for a global democratic system. The ECHR can be regarded in some ways as having the qualities of an international legislative charter of rights, with reports from the PACE often leading to changes to the convention or procedures by the Council of Ministers. Last but not least, the ECtHR is politically dependent in being chosen and overseen by a representative body of the contracting states, and is constrained to respect to a high degree their domestic rights-enforcing mechanisms. As a result of these two aspects, the force of the standard worries about judicial discretion are also weakened to a considerable extent.

That said, the ECHR system falls down in two key respects. First, notwithstanding the margin of appreciation, strictly speaking the ECtHR does not adopt weak review. Under Article 46 of the Convention, its judgments have binding force on the High Contracting Parties and once the Grand Chamber has given a final ruling, there are no further grounds of appeal. Still, it does not disapply national laws—they remain in force until the relevant domestic legislature changes them and can only offer a remedy in international, not domestic law. To that extent, the ECtHR could be described as applying a 'soft' version of strong review. Yet, the system could be adapted to deliver weak review relatively easily. As I have noted, the Committee of Ministers is responsible for the implementation of these judgments and can sanction a member for failing to comply and even expel them. However, it would be perfectly possible to allow the Committee to become the final court of appeal as proposed above.

Second, hitherto the focus of the ECtHR has been on the issue of domestic compliance with the ECHR. Although the Council of Europe has explored common issues affecting the relations between states, these have been at the margins. That will change with the proposed accession of the EU to the ECHR, which will introduce monitoring of inter-state economic agreements for compliance with human rights. Already, an important difference between the ECtHR and the Court of Justice of the European Union (CJEU) with regard to labour rights suggests ways in which this move might lead to greater equal respect and concern between the states involved for their internal democratic processes.[44] Yet, how far that happens is likely to depend on the degree to which both the Council of Europe and the EU are regarded as being bound by a political rather than a legal constitution.

V. CONCLUSION

Lord Sumption's critique of the ECtHR reflects the limitations of his rather limited legal constitutionalist approach. He offers a limited view of both rights and democracy that does a disservice to both. As we saw in section I, he places undue and unrealistic reliance on the constraints of the law on judges and, to a limited extent, on governments. Despite his appreciation of the legitimating role played by democratic legislatures in deciding questions of rights, he fails to see its constitutional significance as a mechanism for promoting political equality. As a result, he also does not envisage how courts and legislatures might work in tandem to improve the public deliberation of the other in ways that respect the basic right to equal concern and respect. Section II suggested why and how this might be achieved domestically, and section III why and how it might be important to do so internationally, through IHRC and IHRCts. Section IV concluded by suggesting this model could be applied to the ECHR, which to a large extent complies with it. Thus understood, Lord Sumption's criticisms of the ECtHR appear not only misconceived but also misplaced—of limited value beyond providing a spurious legitimacy to those seeking Britain's withdrawal from the ECHR.

---

[44] J Fudge, 'Constitutionalizing Labour Rights in Europe' in Campbell et al (n 27) 244.

12

*A Response**

LORD SUMPTION

I FEEL RATHER embarrassed that my two public lectures about the constitutional implications of judicial decision-making and international human rights should have provoked such an impressive volume of learning. It was certainly not something that I foresaw when I delivered them. I cannot begin to do justice to all of it in in the time available for response. So I hope that you will forgive me if I offer no more than a short *tour d'horizon* of the major themes which have emerged during the day.

Let me start with two introductory points.

The first is that there is no point in comparing my lectures with my judgments on these issues and finding inconsistencies between them. Of course they are inconsistent. As a judge, I am not there to expound my own opinion. My job is to say what I think the law is. By comparison, in a public lecture, I am my own master. I can allow myself the luxury of expressing approval or dismay about the current state of the law. You might wonder whether, in the highest court of the land, which is bound by no precedent even of its own, there is any difference between my own opinion and my exposition of the law. I have to tell you that there is and that it matters. The personal opinions of the judges in the Supreme Court are only one element in the complex process of decision-making, and not necessarily the most important one. Statutes bind judges absolutely, within the limits of interpretative licence. Established principle, reflected in existing case law, may not strictly bind them, but it is of fundamental significance. Even when the Supreme Court changes the law, it ought to do so within the framework of existing principle, unless there are particularly strong reasons for a more radical approach. Moreover, the Supreme Court's decisions are made collectively. Of course, a judge may dissent or he may concur for different reasons. This can be personally satisfying. But it is not much of a service to the public. It can also leave the ratio of the decision unclear, perhaps the worst sin that an appellate court can commit, short of actually getting the answer wrong.

---

* This is not a paper presented at the workshop. It is the lightly edited text of an extempore summing up by Lord Sumption at the end of a day of papers and discussion.

My second introductory point is prompted by Professor Craig's point that the problems which we have been discussing are not peculiar to public law. The same concerns about the legitimacy of normative rules made by judges arise in private law. So too do the concerns which have been expressed about the polycentric character of many of the problems that come before the court, and the interests of those not represented. Professor Craig is absolutely right to point out that the law of tort in particular exhibits all of these problems. The scope and standard of common law duties of care belong to the realm of judge-made law, but they have major economic, social and budgetary implications. However, it is in the realm of public law that the problems associated with the development of the law by judicial decision have been most acute. This is partly because judges have been more cautious when dealing with private law issues. It is partly because decisions on such issues tend to be less controversial politically. It is also partly because significant changes made by judges to the principles of private law are easier to reverse or amend by legislation. As Lord Hoffmann pointed out, judicial decisions about the law of tort or contract have no constitutional status and are rarely treaty-based. But it is also because the development of public law over the last 30 years has been very rapid, at least by the law's normal leisurely standards, and much of it has had an important political dimension. It has therefore been a matter of public debate extending well beyond the limits of the legal community.

The fundamental principle underlying the views of those who applaud the advance of judicial law-making in the realm of public law was expressed by Ronald Dworkin. 'The issue', Dworkin said, 'is what reasons are, in [the court's] hands, good reasons.'[1] This is a succinct and exact statement of the proposition which I reject. I reject it not so much because it is wrong, but because it is irrelevant to the question before us. We are not concerned with the question whether the rules which judges devise are good rules. The real question is whether they have any democratic legitimacy. We are concerned, all of us in the course of this seminar, with the appropriate methods of arriving at legal rules in a democratic constitution. We cannot decide how we should make law by asking which system produces the best law. The reasons for this are, or should be, obvious. The 'good reasons' to which Ronald Dworkin was referring are reasons which may strike him and those who agree with him as good, but others will regard them as very bad. What do we do then? We need a system for moderating and reconciling divergent opinions about what is good law and what is bad. Beyond a point, judges cannot do that. It is the proper function of representative institutions.

This applies as much to the construction of legislative instruments such as Acts of Parliament and the European Convention on Human Rights as it does to any other source of law. Statutes and international conventions incorporated into domestic law are not simply signposts to the direction of travel. They are statements of law. To extrapolate them into areas lying beyond the limits indicated by the text is to usurp the legislative function. In the case of international instruments

---

[1] RM Dworkin, *A Matter of Principle* (Cambridge, MA, Harvard University Press, 1986) 69.

like the Human Rights Convention, it is to discard the right which every sovereign state possesses of deciding for itself on behalf of its own people to what international obligations it is willing to consent. Lord Hoffmann, in his chapter on the interpretation of treaties, has I think put his finger on this point.

For this reason, I do not share Professor Loughlin's implicit disapproval of the 'originalism and textualism' of Robert Bork and Justice Scalia. We can leave Bork out of it. He never got a chance to show what sort of judge he would be. Justice Scalia, if I read him correctly, has two basic instincts. One is 'originalism' properly so-called. The other is respect for democratic accountability. They are not the same thing, but are different stages of the intellectual process. Originalism is a technique of interpretation. Respect for democratic accountability is one of a number of reasons for adopting it. Some kind of originalism, allied to what Professor Loughlin calls textualism, is not just defensible but also indispensable if we are to interpret statutes or treaties in a manner consistent with the judicial function. The text of a law, properly examined with the aid of the known background, is the only source that we have for discerning the legislature's intention. The text of an international treaty like the Human Rights Convention is the only thing that signatory states have actually agreed. If judges go beyond the text and resort to some more general scheme of values, they must necessarily do so either in accordance with own their personal preferences or else in accordance with what they think that the lawgiver would have done if he had addressed other problems which for whatever reason he left alone. In a democracy, both processes ought to be completely unacceptable coming from a judicial body which is not answerable to the people. As Justice Kentridge said in giving the judgment of the South African Constitutional Court in *State v Zuma*: 'If the language used by the lawgiver is ignored in favour of a general resort to 'values' the result is not interpretation but divination.'[2]

I regard these propositions as obvious, but I am well aware that many people, including some in this room, regard them as heretical. Heresy is of course a treacherous word. We use it to express our disagreement with some proposition without feeling the need to engage with it or articulate our reasons. But I think it worth articulating the reasons why so many distinguished thinkers seek to constrain democratic choice in the interests of a wider scheme of values. Misgivings about adhering to ordinary principles of interpretation when applying legislation or treaties dealing with human rights generally stem from one or both of two instincts.

The first is a feeling that the legislature has not done a good enough job or that if it once did a good enough job, it did it too long ago for the results to be of any continuing relevance. Personally, I do not share this view. But if you do reject the legitimacy of legislation on that ground, then it is incumbent on you to justify some alternative method of decision-making which is preferable. The alternative which is generally put forward is judicial decision. Professor Fredman's basic point, if I understand her rightly, is that parliamentary legislation may have no greater legitimacy than judicial legislation. That may be a stronger point in

---

[2] *State v Zuma* 1995 (4) BCLR 401, 412.

the US than it is in this country, given that the political fault-lines there and the conventions of the two houses of Congress make it particularly difficult to enact or repeal controversial legislation even with majority support. But actually I would not accept Professor Fredman's point on either side of the Atlantic. I would not accept it because it is inconsistent with a democratic constitution to transfer decision-making away from a representative body to an unrepresentative one simply because you do not like the decisions of the former or regard them as out of date.

The second factor stems from a misunderstanding of what originalism really is and what it implies. As Lord Hoffmann pointed out in his chapter, the intention of the original legislators may have been that their text should have an ambulatory effect dependent on future conditions which they could not foresee. For my part, I would not agree with Ronald Dworkin and Dr King that the entire constitution of the US was intended to be read in this fashion. But it is clear that parts of it were. The paradigm case, as Professor Fredman has said, is the prohibition of cruel and unusual punishments by the English Bill of Rights and then the Eighth Amendment to the US Constitution. Opinions about what is cruel or unusual change. Even the most determined originalist would not suggest that it all depends on what would have been unusual or would have been regarded as cruel at the end of the eighteenth century. The same is true of the similar provisions of Article 3 of the Human Rights Convention, as the Strasbourg court held in *Tyrer v UK*.[3] But the problem about the concept of the Convention as a 'living instrument', which *Tyrer* introduced, is that it took a perfectly sensible technique of construction and applied it beyond its proper limits. It is important to distinguish, as the Strasbourg case law so often fails to do, between interpreting existing rights in the light of current conditions and recognising new rights on the ground that, although not in the legislation, they would have been if such an instrument had been drafted in the same spirit today. The latter is not interpretation at all. It is simply judicial extrapolation into territory where the legislator, perhaps deliberately, has not ventured.

The most famous and controversial example of judicial legislation masquerading as interpretation is *Roe v Wade*,[4] which has proved to be the touchstone of opinion on this subject in the US. The real issue provoked by *Roe v Wade* is not whether there ought to be a right of abortion, it is whether the creation of such a right is a proper function of the judiciary. I think that most people, certainly in this country, would say that the answer to the first question is that there should be a right of abortion, within carefully regulated limits. That is certainly my own view. But to derive a right of abortion from the due process clause of the Fourteenth Amendment seems to me to be impossible as a matter of construction. The amendment prohibits states from depriving any person of life liberty or property without due process of law. To construct from the reference to deprivation of liberty a right of privacy and to deduce from that a right of abortion seems to me to be extraordinary. This would certainly not have occurred to the

---

[3] *Tyrer v UK* (1978) 2 EHRR 1.
[4] *Roe v Wade* 410 US 113 (1973).

draftsmen of the Fourteenth Amendment. It would not even have occurred to a hypothetical constitutional convention introducing such an amendment in 1973. If our hypothetical convention had resolved to introduce a right of abortion in 1973, it is inconceivable that it would have chosen to do so in the language of the due process clause. The recognition of a right to an abortion is in reality the result of a change of opinion since the amendment about what rights ought to exist. But the question that one is bound to ask is which organ of the state has the constitutional function of transforming changes of opinion on that question into law. In a democracy, it is surely not the judiciary, but the legislature.

Roe v Wade has had three unfortunate consequences of which European observers should take note. One is that abortion has been incorporated into US federal law as a constitutional right. There is no regulatory framework, such as would presumably have qualified any state legislation on the subject. The right is nearly unlimited (it is subject only to minor restrictions not deemed by the Court to be an 'undue burden')[5] provided that the foetus is not viable, a stage which was originally fixed, quite arbitrarily, at seven months. The second is that being a constitutional right, it is incapable of being modified or qualified without a constitutional amendment, ie, in practice not at all. This is also a problem about decisions about the effect of the Human Rights Convention by the European Court of Human Rights, which is even more difficult to amend than the US Constitution because it would require the agreement of all 47 members of the Council of Europe. The third consequence is that the rule has not been accepted as legitimate in the way it would, at least for most people, if it had been enacted by state legislatures with suitable regulatory safeguards. In Europe, where a qualified right of abortion has almost invariably been introduced by legislation, it has been broadly accepted by the consensus of public opinion. I say 'almost invariably', because the position in Ireland and Poland, the two most strongly Catholic countries of the Council of Europe, is currently uncertain. In *A, B and C v Ireland*,[6] the European Court of Human Rights declined to recognise a human right to an abortion, but only because while there was a European consensus that abortion was acceptable, there was no European consensus about when life in the womb could be said to begin. Sooner or later, the Strasbourg Court may well introduce a right of abortion by holding it to be implicit in Article 8.

This is one of many instances of the immeasurable expansion by the ECHR of what Lord Walker once called 'the indefinite Article 8'. It is Strasbourg's case law on this article which has really converted the Convention into a permanent engine of legal change without any kind of democratic endorsement. I agree with Professor Finnis that this was not what the Convention was designed to do. Article 8 was introduced as a protection against a reversion by the signatory states to the practices of the totalitarian tyrannies of the inter-war and wartime periods: the police state, the unauthorised interception of mail, surveillance by

---

[5] *Planned Parenthood v Casey* 505 US 833 (1992).
[6] *A, B and C v Ireland* (2011) 53 EHRR 13.

public authorities, the knock on the door at 5.00 am. The adoption of autonomy as the guiding principle of Article 8 has very serious implications for democratic governance. The individual's area of autonomy, and the degree to which compulsion may limit it, is ultimately the subject matter of all legislation laying down compulsory rules of conduct of general application. The transformation of autonomy into the touchstone of the individual's relations with the state across the whole range of human affairs has potentially transferred any argument about the limits of individual liberty into the judicial arena where there is no democratic input at all. None of the Member States that put their name to the Convention has consented to such a thing, although it may be said of some of the more recent adherents that they should have seen it coming.

Of course, the Strasbourg Court has not in fact intervened across the whole range of human affairs. In view of the almost unlimited breadth of the principle of autonomy, it has been selective. But given the logically unlimited scope of the principle of autonomy, the court's selectiveness, however admirable, has no rational basis and offers no assurance for the future. No one has yet brought a petition to Strasbourg complaining that their Article 8 rights were infringed by the prohibition on consuming dangerous drugs, even in private, and if they did I imagine that, it would fail. But it is difficult to see how that would differ conceptually from a complaint that the petitioner had been denied the opportunity to have a lawful abortion or lawful assistance to kill himself. The real difference between these cases is that there is a substantial consensus in most Western countries that abortion under controlled conditions is acceptable, whereas heroin consumption is not. Assisted suicide is somewhere between the two, an area where the consensus may be changing. I find it difficult to see how in a democracy the function of translating social consensus into law can belong to anyone other than a representative legislature. I find it equally difficult to see how in countries like Poland or Ireland, where the consensus is that abortion is not acceptable, it can be legitimate to impose it as a matter of judicial decision. It may be said that the extremely restrictive abortion laws of Ireland and Poland are illiberal. And so they are. But I think that it is perfectly possible to have an illiberal democracy. I would not like to live in one, but it certainly exists.

This brings me to the point made by Dr King that Hitler and Putin were democratically elected and Napoleon was fond of referendums. I am afraid that I do not think that these particular historical examples carry him any further. There are plainly certain minimum conditions that must be satisfied if a democratic constitution is to work. First, it requires a minimum level of tolerance of differences. Second, it requires proper mechanisms for ensuring that the campaign and the poll itself are fairly conducted. Third, it requires a constitutional mechanism for selecting between competing views about the policy and legislation of the state, or finding some compromise between them. Fourth, it requires a minimum level of participation. The first three of these conditions did not exist in Hitler's Germany or Napoleonic France and do not exist in Putin's Russia. The fourth was probably present in all three cases, but did not mean much without the first three.

My main objection, however, is not so much to the proposition itself as to the conclusion which Dr King draws from it. The fact that democratic institutions were subverted by Napoleon and Hitler and are being subverted by Putin does not mean that we should all feel at liberty to marginalise or ignore them. And we are certainly not at liberty to subvert them without admitting that that is what we are doing, which is where I fear that Dr King's view leads. Joseph Schumpeter defined democracy as an 'institutional arrangement for arriving at political decisions in which individuals acquire the power to decide by means of a competitive struggle for people's votes'. Dr King quotes this and then says that it has long been regarded as wholly unconvincing. Really? By whom has it been regarded as unconvincing? And for what reasons that the rest of us should accept?

I would suggest with respect that we need to get our terminology straight if we are going to understand each other. A democratic society is not necessarily the same as a liberal one, although historically the two have often gone together. We have to have a word to describe an institutional arrangement for arriving at political decisions in which spokesmen for divergent views are able to compete for votes. Democracy is that word. So Joseph Schumpeter's definition, far from being discredited, seems to me to be invincibly correct. If we start using the word 'democracy' to refer not to a mode of decision-making, but to the outcome that one would expect in a liberal society, we are in danger of confusing our concepts and avoiding some real dilemmas.

Those who believe that democratic choices should be constrained in the interests of preserving certain political values usually do so for one of three reasons. First, they may be saying that democracy is illusory because people's true preferences are not their real choices, being conditioned by their circumstances. This was implicit in the views of Jean-Jacques Rousseau. It is explicit in the views of Marx and the ideology of most totalitarian dictatorships. Second, they may be saying that democracy is not enough because it cannot work without some other values, such as tolerance or freedom of speech. Third, they may be taking the view that democracy is not worth much without conferring on individuals much wider rights than those which are strictly necessary for a functioning democracy, and in particular without protecting minorities against oppression by elective majorities.

Personally, I would not subscribe to the Rousseau-Marx view. So I would not accept the first proposition. But up to a point, I would accept the second and third. To have a functioning democracy, we have to have some of the protections which the Human Rights Convention guarantees, notably freedom of thought and speech and freedom of assembly. What is more, we ought to have some rights which are not essential to a functioning democracy, but are nevertheless indispensable to a just society. The original text of the Human Rights Convention is probably as good a codification of this latter class of rights as one could have. What I cannot accept is that in order to call ourselves a democracy, we must have the immense superstructure of supernumerary rights and constitutional micromanagement which the European Court of Human Right has created by a process of extrapolation and analogy from the text of the Convention. Nor do I accept that in order to call ourselves a democracy, we must delegate the process of recognising those rights to judges, whether of an international or a national court.

I should perhaps say more about the third proposition, which is that democracy is not worth having if it is simply a tool of majoritarian oppression, since this is probably the prime argument in favour of the inventive approach of the Strasbourg Court to the recognition of rights. The problem about it is that its proponents rarely pause to ask themselves what majoritarian oppression is. They therefore tend to confuse the protection of minorities with the protection of others who are not minorities, but are simply adversely affected by some particular principle of enacted law. The distinction is not always easy to make, but it exists and it matters.

In what circumstances can a minority properly claim to be oppressed by democratically enacted laws? The extreme case is an individual who is directly condemned by the legislature. This occasionally happened in England up to the end of the eighteenth century by a bill of attainder, which convicted an accused by a parliamentary vote without any other legal process at all. The last attempt to introduce a bill of attainder occurred in 1820, when the House of Lords passed a bill convicting Queen Caroline of various matrimonial offences, which never became law because it did not pass the Commons. I would not regard that as legislation at all. Therefore, I would not regard it as a proper function of the legislature. There is, as David Hume observed more than two centuries ago, a difference between the sovereign's commands and the sovereign's laws. The use of laws to validate otherwise unlawful commands is usually an abuse. It was the disapproval of English practice among the drafters of the US Constitution which led to their prohibition of bills of attainder by Article 1, section 9. Bills of attainder are hardly a significant problem today, but the argument has shifted onto different terrain. The real issue today arises with minority groups who stand for some common interest and claim constitutional protection from democratically enacted laws.

Most people would agree that minorities are entitled to a measure of protection. But what is a minority for this purpose and what protection should it have? In one sense, it may be said that any group whose defining characteristic is its opposition to or defiance of some democratically enacted law is a minority. But that proves far too much. It would entitle the opponents of every controversial law to be protected against any mandatory legal rule to which they took exception. It would not just limit the choices of the majority, but would deprive the whole concept of majority rule of all meaning. I am not going to attempt a comprehensive definition of a relevant minority here. It is a large and difficult subject. But I would very tentatively suggest that the minorities which can legitimately claim protection against laws in a democracy constitute a relatively narrow category. It comprises groups which stand outside the community constituting the majority, by reason of some common defining feature of their collective identity other than the opinion that they happen to hold about the law in question. The common characteristic may be their religion, ethnicity or nationality, or some other characteristic such as their sexual orientation. It is part of the concept of a constitutionally protected minority that it should be identified by reference to some abiding characteristic, which will place them at a permanent disadvantage as against the majority; in other words, a disadvantage which cannot readily be rectified by ordinary political processes. Minorities are not the same as interest groups. Majoritarian oppression is different from discrimination, although they overlap. Groups such as bankers or higher rate taxpayers or people who believe in corporal punishment in schools may be interest groups. But they are not, simply by virtue of belonging to these categories, minorities entitled to protection against democratically enacted laws which adversely affect them.

Dr King has said that the enactment of the Human Rights Act 1998 was a democratic decision made by Parliament. Moreover, he points out that it was made after the extrapolating tendencies of the European Court of Human Rights had become apparent. I agree with this, but I do not think that it resolves the problem that we are discussing. Of course the passing of the Human Rights Act was a democratic decision. What is undemocratic is not the passing of the Act, but its consequences. The developing jurisprudence of Strasbourg has made it the means by which an essentially legislative power has been transferred to an unrepresentative body, namely the judiciary. Parliament could in principle make a democratic decision to abolish general elections or confer its legislative power upon a dictator. The legislature of the French Third Republic did exactly that in 1940 when with only three dissenting voices it conferred absolute power on Marshall Petain before dissolving both itself and the Republic. This was a democratic decision with undemocratic consequences. We should not be deterred by the parliamentary origins of enacted law from examining its results. The objection to handing over legislative power to unrepresentative bodies lies in the loss of control over what follows. This may well be justified as part of a pooling of sovereignty, as in the case of the Act of Union with Scotland in 1707 or the European Communities Act of 1972. But the incorporation of the developing jurisprudence of the European Court of Human Rights into English law is not in any sense part of a pooling of sovereignty. I can illustrate some of these points by reference to two recent decisions of the Supreme Court about the ambit of the Human Rights Convention.

The first concerns prisoners' votes. The background to this issue is well known and I need not repeat it now. The question whether convicted prisoners should or should not have votes is in itself an issue of very limited significance. There are respectable arguments for giving prisoners the vote, notably that it may encourage in them a sense of engagement and social responsibility. There are respectable arguments against it. Their disenfranchisement reflects their temporary exclusion from the public and collective processes of our society in the same way as their loss of liberty does. But the real issue is not whether section 3 of the Representation of the People Act is good or bad law, but how as a national community we should set about making or adopting law. Although the contrary has been suggested, it seems plain that section 3 of the Act is not an example of majoritarian tyranny. Convicted prisoners are not by any reasonable definition a relevant minority. They are at best an interest group, and probably not even that. The law discriminates against them only in the sense that it singles out those convicted of sufficiently serious crimes as a category that should be in prison and defines the character and incidents of their incarceration. Their disenfranchisement is no more oppressive than any other disagreeable incident of imprisonment for criminal activity. It is an optional choice for any democratic society whether to have such a rule or not. The Strasbourg Court's judgments on the point (which are not all consistent) are law, but they read more like contributions, and not particularly well-informed contributions, to an essentially political debate.

The second decision which I should mention is the Supreme Court's recent decision about assisted dying, which contains the fullest judicial discussion to date of the proper limits of judge-made law.[7] The case actually decided very little, but the nine published judgments have the advantage and disadvantage of offering a wide range of analyses to choose from. The outcome was that the claimants failed in their attempt to obtain a declaration that section 2 of the Suicide Act 1961, which preserved the offence of aiding, abetting, counselling and procuring the suicide of another, was incompatible with the Convention. Two of the nine justices who sat thought that the section was incompatible with the Convention because it invaded the right of an autonomous patient to end his or her life when and how he or she chose. Four of the nine thought that it was a question for Parliament. This was because the Strasbourg Court had already declared that the question was within the margin of appreciation of the UK. The four considered that a major moral issue with important social implications on which our society was profoundly divided could be legitimately resolved only by the representative organ of our constitution. The only basis on which judges could decide it was simply to declare their personal opinions to be law. The other three justices thought that in principle the question was for the courts to decide because, by enacting the Human Rights Act, Parliament had left to the courts the question whether a statutory rule was incompatible with the Convention. They decided against the appellants because there was no evidence to show what alternative statutory regimes might be available to allow assisted dying short of a complete free-for-all.

What are we to make of all this in the context of today's discussions? Section 2 of the Suicide Act 1961 is democratically enacted law. So far, successive attempts to persuade Parliament to change it have failed. The same is true of the corresponding laws against assisted suicide which are in force in 36 of the 42 countries of the Council of Europe whose legal position has been ascertained. In the UK, judges have only become involved in this question because of the Human Rights Act. I can understand why many people feel that the law is immoral or unjust. I can also understand why those who feel strongly about this are ready to petition the European Court of Human Rights as part of a political campaign to have the law changed. But, looking at the issue on a broader basis, can the prohibition of assisted suicide really be categorised as the kind of law which a democracy should not be allowed have? For my part, I have yet to hear of a single convincing reason

---

[7] *R (Nicklinson) v Ministry of Justice* [2014] UKSC 38.

why criminalising the conduct of those who assist others to kill themselves should not be one of the options open to a mature democracy. Up to a point, law may be a good instrument for resolving issues between the state and its citizens. But many of the issues that are resolved by reference to international human rights law are not in reality issues between the state and its citizens at all. They are issues between different groups of citizens, which ought in principle to be resolved by institutions that are representative of all of them. There are no truly legal standards by which to judge a question like assisted suicide. Resort to the courts in cases like this can never be anything but politics by other means.

I confess that I do not have a simple answer to these problems and, if I did, I doubt whether I would want to voice it in the current political environment. But I should say that I do not accept what Professor Loughlin suggests is implicit in my two public lectures on this subject. As I said in my FA Mann lecture, I do not think that it is either feasible or desirable to constrain judicial activism by legislation. If it comes to that, then a valuable constitutional convention will have been cast aside. But the task of avoiding that disaster cannot simply be the responsibility of politicians. The change has got to come from within the judiciary. It requires a greater degree of caution on the part of national judges and even, dare I say it, a bit less of the self-confident assumption which comes naturally to lawyers that the only proper solutions to difficult public issues are legal ones. Above all, it requires a greater respect for the political process, not just among judges but among the population at large, whose facile contempt for politics and politicians and progressive withdrawal from political engagement is to my mind a growing threat to our democracy.

It is, however, undeniable that in cases where the Human Rights Convention is engaged, the solution is only partly within the control of national judges. National judges can make use of the substantial body of domestic law protecting human rights, as they have in fact begun to do in recent years. They can distinguish Strasbourg cases. In a case involving fundamental principle, they can ultimately say that they disagree with its interpretation of the Convention or the way it has been applied to particular issues. But there are two things that it is particularly difficult for a national judge to do.

One is to discard a decision of the Strasbourg Court against the UK itself, which the UK has bound itself by Article 46 of the Convention to give effect to. The courts are a constitutional organ of the UK. They have always sought to avoid deciding issues that come before them in a way which puts the UK in breach of its international obligations. For that reason, I very much doubt whether there is a viable halfway house between total engagement with the Convention and total withdrawal. Hardly anyone is proposing the latter solution at the moment. It would have enormous knock-on consequences, not least for our relations with the EU.

The second thing which it is difficult for a national judge to do is to avoid essentially political value judgments when dealing with the question whether a departure from Convention values is justifiable by reference to one of the various public interests which qualify some of its articles: public order, national security, the rights of others or the like. This requires the courts to apply a proportionality test, which is a fundamental feature of the jurisprudence of the Strasbourg Court. Is the departure necessary to meet a pressing social need under one of the various heads which is recognised by the Convention? The question how far, say, personal autonomy or freedom of speech may be constrained in the public interest is an inherently political question. Recently, in *R (Miranda) v Secretary of State for the Home Department*,[8] Lord Justice Laws expressed strong reservations about my formulation of the test of proportionality in *Bank Mellat v HM Treasury (No 2)*.[9] He said that by requiring a court to assess the balance between private rights and public interests, it gave rise to 'real difficulty in distinguishing this from a political question to be decided by the elected arm of government'. Lord Justice Laws was, I fear, shooting the messenger. My formulation was simply a neutral summary of prior House of Lords authority. But he was absolutely right to be concerned. Proportionality is an essentially political concept unless it is coupled with a principled recognition of the special competence of the executive in certain areas such as national security and an acknowledgment of the broader concept of legitimacy which makes many questions suitable for decision only by Parliament or by ministers politically responsible to Parliament.

It would certainly help if the European Court of Human Rights adopted a wider margin of appreciation which reflected the different constitutional traditions of the 47 countries belonging to the Council of Europe. There are signs that the Court may be moving in that direction. But this will be a gradual process and it will not resolve all the constitutional problems which the Convention poses.

However, although I have no quick fix to offer, no patent medicine to sell you, I am wholly unrepentant about criticising the current state of affairs. Its drawbacks have serious constitutional implications, which need to be recognised and discussed, by judges among others. The UK has a long traditional of achieving significant constitutional change by accident. A century and a half ago, the great Victorian observer of our constitution, Walter Bagehot, celebrated this as a benign feature of our constitution, which made it possible for Britain to adapt to radical social change without disruption or revolution. I think that this was probably true of Victorian Britain at a time when an enlightened oligarchy was in the process of ceding control to a representative democracy. But I doubt whether it is true today. We need to know where we are going. That means that if we choose constitutional change, we should do it on purpose and not as a byproduct of decisions, however enlightened, made by diplomats and lawyers.

---

[8] *R (Miranda) v Secretary of State for the Home Department* [2014] 1 WLR 3140 [40].
[9] *Bank Mellat v HM Treasury (No 2)* [2014] AC 700.

Index

A, B and C v Ireland, 61–62, 217
access to justice, 141–42, 202
  social policy, 17–18
  Witham case, 17–19
Al Rawi v Secretary of State for Foreign and Commonwealth Affairs, 30–31
analogy, *see* reasoning by analogy
Animal Defenders International v UK, 158–61
assisted dying, 73, 91–93, 137–38, 222–23
asylum:
  Art 3 ECHR, 103
  case law:
    Chahal v UK, 108
    Cruz Varas v Sweden, 107–08
    Hirsi Jamaa v Italy, 74, 109–10
    Saadi v UK, 108–09
    Soering v UK, 106–07
  intention of signatory states, 110–17
  logic of norms, 103–06
  moral and legal absolute against torture, 104
Austin, 76
autonomy principle, 118, 218, 224

balancing of values, 9
  duty of care, 177–82
  incommensurability, 177–82
    HRA Act 1998, 190–91
    private law, 176–84
      polycentricity, 187–88
      public law compared, 188–89
      statute, 189–91
    public law, 184–87
      private law compared, 188–89
      statute, 189–91
    statute, 189–91
      courts and respect, 191–92
  normative judgment and:
    HRA Act 1998, 190–91
    private law, 176–84
      polycentricity, 187–88
      public law compared, 188–89
      statute, 189–91
    public law, 184–87, 214
      private law compared, 188–89
      statute, 189–91
    statute, 189–91
      courts and respect, 191–92
  presumptions regarding basic rights, 133–34
  private law, 176–77

economic torts:
  breach of contract, 183–84
  free competition, 182–83
negligence:
  duty of care, 177–80
  foreseeability, 181–82
  remoteness, 181
normative judgment and balancing, 176–84
public law, 184–87, 214
Bates, 145
Bellinger v Bellinger, 137
Bickel, 33–34, 36
Blackstone, 15
Bork, 34–35, 41, 215
breach of contract, 182–84
Brown v Board of Education, 53

Canadian Charter, 50, 53–54, 56–58, 60, 84–85, 97
common law, 2, 20–21, 27–28, 132, 189–90, 192
  'artificial reason', 40
  judicial law-making, 6, 15–16, 22, 26, 35, 39, 74–80, 129–30, 133
  judicial role in the ordering of society, 15–16
  polycentricity and, 150
  rights, 11–12
    ECHR and, 185–87
coordinate construction, 172–74
  case studies:
    Immigration Bill 2013, 165–68
    Jobseeker affair, 168–72
    political advertising, 157–61
    prisoners' voting rights, 161–65
  mutual recognition, 156
Council of Europe, 19, 46, 60–62, 71, 87, 156, 162, 209–11, 217, 222, 224
courts:
  see also European Court of Human Rights; international courts; judges
  access to the courts, 17–19, 141–42, 202
  adjudication, 15
  discretionary powers:
    reasonableness, 186
  dispute resolution, 135
  functions, 127–29
  incommensurability:
    courts and respect, 191–92
  independence, 201–04

international courts:
    competences and scope, 206–07
    democratic legitimacy, 208
    democratic organisations, 207–08
    governance of international mechanisms, 205–06
    human rights, 204–05
joint enterprise governing and, 127–34, 139–40
    declarations of incompatibility, 154–55
limited legal constitutionalism:
    political constitutionalism compared:
        democratic dependence of courts, 201–04
        international courts, 204–08
political courts, 31
    constitutional interpretation and, 32–35
    discretionary powers of judges, 32
    features, 32
    presumptions regarding basic rights, 131–33
    balancing with certainty, stability and continuity, 133–34
    role of legislative assembly distinguished, 128–29
    statute and, 191–92

declarations of incompatibility, 154–55
declaratory theory of law, 6, 15–16, 74–76, 78
democracy, 1–4, 10, 22–25, 63–64
    appointment of executive officials, 149
    bicameralism, 148
    concept, 146, 219–21
        legislative decision-making, 146–47
        role of compromise, 147–48
    institutional design, 149
    judicial law-making and, 2–3, 21–22, 24
    judicial review and, 146–49
    originalism and, 36–37
    sovereignty, 22–23
    statute law, 22–23
    textualism and, 36–37
Derbyshire County Council v Times Newspapers Ltd, 186
Diplock, 17
    'balanced constitution', 154
Dudgeon v UK, 60
duty of care, 177
    balancing of values, 177–78
    negligence, 177–82
    three-stage test, 177
Dworkin, 24, 25, 195, 214
    integrity, 147
    original intent, 47, 49
        Canadian Charter, 54
        US Constitution, 52–53
    originalism, 47, 49, 52–54, 143
    polycentricity, 125–26
    principles v policy, 125–26

Easterbrook, 54–56, 57–58
EB v France, 62
economic torts, 176–77, 189
    breach of contract, 183–84
    free competition, 182–83
Edwards v Attorney-General for Canada (Can):
    'living instrument' doctrine, 56–57
European Convention on Human Rights (ECHR), 1, 19–20, 194
    Art 3, 94–102
        compulsory political and non-political asylum, 103–17
        extending interpreted scope, 102–17
    creating norms, 118–19
    logic of norms, 103–06
    defects, 80
        justifying restrictions with freedoms/immunities, 81–82
        strict scrutiny, 81–82
        true absolute rights, 82
        wording of key articles, 80–81
    domestic law compared, 71, 72
        democratic control, 71
        legitimacy, 71
        variety of law and legal systems, 71
    Immigration Bill 2013, 165–68
    Jobseeker affair, 168–72
    judicial law-making and, 19–20
        concerns, 20–21
        democratic deficit and, 21–22
        interpretation and, 56–63
        reasoning by analogy and, 21
    judicial interpretation, 64–65
        'living instrument', 56–63
    'living instrument', 56–63, 194
        original intent of drafters, 50
        margin of appreciation, 61–62, 209–11
        political advertising, 157–61
        political constitutionalism, 208–11
        prisoners' voting rights, 161–65
European Court of Human Rights (ECtHR), 2
see also individual cases
    Art 3 cases, 94–102
        extending interpreted scope, 102–17
    effectiveness, 120
    growing influence, 30–31
    Immigration Bill 2013, 165–68
    Jobseeker affair, 168–72
    'living instrument' case law, 85–90
    original intent of ECHR, 61, 63–62
        margin of appreciation, 61–62, 209–11
    political advertising, 157–61
    prisoners' voting rights, 161–65
    proportionality, 119–20
    stretching of original intention, 48
evolutive interpretation, *see* 'living instrument' doctrine
Ewing, 154

FA Mann lecture 2011, 2, 11, 223
  law-politics boundary, 29–30, 141
  rise of judicial review, 38
fast-tracking legislation, 170
Fitzmaurice, 52, 86–87, 117–18
Forms and Limits of Adjudication, 15, 150, 193
foreseeability, 181–82
free competition, 182–84
Fretté v France, 62
Frodl v Austria, 99, 102
Fuller, 2, 15, 193–94
  Forms and Limits of Adjudication, 15, 150, 193
  judicial law-making, 2
  polycentricity, 26, 122–26, 150–51, 193–94
  separation of powers, 2
Furman v Georgia, 49, 51–52

Gardner, 129
Gearty, 154
Golder v UK, 49, 52, 59
  defining 'living instrument', 86–87, 117–18
Greens and MT v UK, 163

Hale, 87–90, 164
Hamilton, 33–34
Hart, 99, 181
Hiebert, 155
Hirschman, 42
Hirsi Jamaa v Italy, 74, 109, 115
  ECHR *travaux préparatoires* and, 111–13
Hirst v UK (No.2), 2, 22, 94–97, 120, 161–63
  democracy/law debate, 162
  flaws in judgment:
    circular nature of judgment, 98
    definition of 'arbitrary', 98–99
    proportionality and lack of competence and care, 97–98, 101
    social rights and social duties, 98–99, 101
Holmes, 76
Honoré, 181
Huang v Secretary of State for the Home Department, 165–68
Human Rights Act (HRA) 1998, 30–33, 93–94, 145
  coordinate construction, 172–74
    Immigration Bill 2013, 165–68
    Jobseeker affair, 168–72
    mutual recognition, 156
    political advertising, 157–61
    prisoners' voting rights, 161–65
  functional separation of powers, 153–56
  polycentric issues and, 151
  reasonableness/proportionality, 185–86
Hunter v Southam, 58

Immigration Act 2013:
  Art 8 and, 8

coordinate construction:
  Immigration Bill 2013, 165–68
  incompatibility with rule of law, 171
  proportionality test, 167
  public interest argument, 172
incommensurability, 177–82
  balancing of values:
    HRA Act 1998, 190–91
    private law, 176–84
      polycentricity, 187–88
      public law compared, 188–89
      statute, 189–91
    public law, 184–87
      private law compared, 188–89
      statute, 189–91
    statute, 189–91
    courts and respect, 191–92
institutional competence, 7–8
  judges, 39–41, 132
  judicial review and, 39–41
intention:
  see also legal interpretation; originalism; textualism
  Art 3 ECHR, 110–17
  Brown v Board of Education, 53
  Canadian Charter, 50, 53–54
  Furman v Georgia, 49, 51–52
  'living instrument' doctrine compared, 46–47
  Markin v Russia, 52
  original intent of ECHR drafters, 50, 61
    margin of appreciation, 61–62, 209–11
  South African Constitution, 50–51
  stretching of original intention by ECtHR, 48
  travaux préparatoires, 50, 111
    meaning of '*refouler*'/'*refoulement*', 111–13
  understanding parliamentary intention, 49–52
  US Constitution, 49, 51–52
international courts:
  competences and scope, 206–07
  democratic legitimacy, 208
  democratic organisations, 207–08
  governance of international mechanisms, 205–06
  human rights, 204–05
International Human Rights Convention (IHRC), 204–08, 211
International Human Rights Court (IHRCt), 204–08, 211
interpretation, *see* legal interpretation

Jagland, 162, 173
jobseekers allowance, 8
  coordinate construction and, 168–72
Joint Committee on Human Rights (JCHR), 9, 167, 174
  political advertising, 158
  prisoners' voting rights, 161–62

joint enterprise of good government, 127, 138–40
　declarations of incompatibility, 154–55
　value of courts, 129
　　independence, 129–30
　　presumptions regarding basic rights, 131–33
　　　balancing with certainty, stability and continuity, 133–34
　　protection of rule of law, 131
　　supervisory role, 130–31
judges:
　see also courts
　constitutional role, 223–24
　　politics and, 4
　discretion, 18, 20, 32, 40, 163
　　Immigration Act 2013 and, 165–68
　　normative judgment and balancing, 184, 186, 191
　　reasonableness review, 186
　'living instrument' approach and, 56–63
　normative judgment and balancing, 184, 186, 191
　　reasonableness review, 186
　politicisation, 30
　responsibility for human rights, 155–56
　role in the ordering of society:
　　common law, 15–16
　　Lord Sumption's theory, 38
　　　admonition, 41
　　　constitutionality, 38
　　　democracy, 39
　　　institutional competence, 39–41
　　statutory law, 16
　social conditions and expectations:
　　responsibility to keep abreast of, 17
judicial law-making:
　common law and, 6, 15–16, 22, 26, 35, 39, 74–80, 129–30, 133
　declaratory theory of law, 76–79
　democracy and, 2–3
　democratic deficit and, 2–3, 21–22, 39, 48, 52, 64, 196
　ECHR and, 19–20
　　concerns, 20–21
　　democratic deficit and, 21–22
　　reasoning by analogy and, 21
　expanding reach, 3–4
　legal reasoning:
　　reasoning by analogy and, 21
　'living instrument' doctrine, 82–83
　　common law and, 73–80
　rights adjudication, 9–10
　Vienna Convention of 1969 on the Law of Treaties, 20–21
judicial review, 9, 11–12, 27, 36–37, 175–76
　democracy and role of judicial review, 141–42, 146–50

　polycentricity and, 150–51
　growth, 29–33, 38–41, 186
　IHRCts, 206
　law-politics boundary and, 29–30, 141–42
　　declining respect for political process, 30, 123
　limited legal constitutionalism, 196–97
　political constitutionalism, 202–03
　purpose/relevancy, 184–87
　rights-based judicial review
　　limitations, 196–97

King, 187
Kleinwort Benson v Lincoln City Council, 75–76

law-making, *see* judicial law-making
law-politics boundary, 29–30, 121–22
　declining respect for political process, 30, 123
　impact of ECHR, 30
　judicial review and, 29–30, 141–42
legal interpretation, 4–5, 10–11, 45–47, 67–68, 143–44, 216–18
　constitutional interpretation and, 32
　development in UK, 32–33
　interpretative methodologies, 35
　legal positivism, 32, 34–35
　'living instrument', 32
　originalism, 32, 34–35
'living instrument' doctrine, 144–45
　human rights instruments, 68–69
　originalism and, 69–70
originalism, 5, 7, 11, 46–47, 143, 215–16
　advantages of approach, 47–49
　difficulties of approach, 49–54
　legal positivism and, 34–37
　textualism compared, 54–56, 215
　travaux préparatoires, 47
reasoning by analogy compared, 70–71
textualism, 5, 7, 10–11, 35–36
　originalism compared, 54–56, 215
treaties, 21–21, 59, 68
Vienna Convention of 1969 on the Law of Treaties, 20–21, 59, 68
legal positivism, 32, 36, 41–42
legal reasoning, 1, 9–10, 46, 64, 77
legislature, 92–95
　see also separation of powers
　accountability, 134
　legitimacy, 122–24, 134
　primacy of, 9–10
　principle/policy distinction, 125–27
　unjust acts, 119
　working with courts, 127–34
Letsas, 90
limited legal constitutionalism, 194–96
　limitations, 196–201
　political constitutionalism compared, 195–96
　　democratic dependence of courts, 201–04

ECHR, 208–11
  international courts, 204–08
  weak review, 195–96
  'truly fundamental' rights, 195–98
'living instrument' doctrine, 2, 5–6, 31, 56
  see also legal interpretation
asylum (political and non-political):
  Art 3 ECHR case law:
    Chahal v UK, 108
    Cruz Varas v Sweden, 107–08
    Hirsi Jamaa v Italy, 109–10
    Saadi v UK, 108–09
    Soering v UK, 106–07
  intention of signatory states, 110–17
  logic of norms, 103–06
    moral and legal absolute against torture, 104
Canada, 56–59
  constitutional interpretation and, 32
  ECHR, 59–63
    case law, 85–90
  judicial interpretation and, 56–63
    'warranted deployment of specifically judicial authority and technique', 90–93
  judicial law making and, 73–74, 82–83, 143
  original intent compared, 46–47, 143
  origins and meaning, 83–90

margin of appreciation, 6, 94, 100, 224
  application of ECHR, 12, 61–62, 159–60, 209–11
  assisted dying, 222
  prisoners' voting rights, 161–62
Markin v Russia, 52
Mathieu-Mohin v Belgium, 94–97
Missouri v Holland, 84

negligence law, 9, 176, 189–90
  duty of care, 177–80, 189
  foreseeability, 181–82
  remoteness, 181
Nicol, 156
normative judgment and balancing:
  HRA Act 1998, 190–91
  private law, 176–84
    polycentricity, 187–88
    public law compared, 188–89
    statute, 189–91
  public law, 184–87, 214
    private law compared, 188–89
    statute, 189–91
  statute, 189–91
    courts and respect, 191–92

originalism, 5, 7, 11, 46–47, 143, 215–16
  see also intention
  advantages of approach, 47
    absence of constructive alternatives, 48–49

legitimacy, 47–48
  removing judicial discretion, 48
difficulties of approach:
  legitimacy and democratic deficit, 52–54
  understanding parliamentary intention, 49–52
legal positivism and, 34–37
textualism compared, 54–56, 215
travaux préparatoires, 47

Petrovic v Austria, 62
Polanyi, 151
political advertising, 8
  coordinate construction, 157–61
political constitutionalism, 38–41, 201
  courts and, 202
  ECHR and, 203–04
  HRA 1998 and, 203
  institutional competence, 39
  limited legal constitutionalism compared, 195–96
    democratic dependence of courts, 201–04
    ECHR, 208–11
    international courts, 204–08
    weak review, 195–96
  rights-based judicial review, 202–03
political courts, 31
  features, 32
  discretionary powers of judges, 32
  constitutional interpretation and, 32
  development in UK, 32–33
  legal positivism, 32, 34–35
  'living instrument', 32
  originalism, 32, 34–35
polycentricity, 7–8, 9, 26, 124–27
  non-justiciability and, 135, 138–39, 150–51
prisoners' voting rights, 2, 8, 22–23, 221–22
  coordinate construction, 161–65
  see also Hirst v UK (No 2)
private law, 10–11
  balancing of values, 176–77
  economic torts:
    breach of contract, 183–84
    free competition, 182–83
  negligence:
    duty of care, 177–80
    foreseeability, 181–82
    remoteness, 181
  normative judgment and balancing, 176–84
  polycentricity, 187–88
proportionality doctrine, 6–7, 150
  disenfranchisement, 97–98, 99, 162
  ECtHR and, 81–82, 97–98, 101–02, 119–20, 167
  two-stage test, 165–66, 224
  reasonableness/proportionality, 184–85, 192

public law, 10–11, 175–76
  normative judgment and balancing, 184–87, 214
  purpose/relevancy, 184–87
  reasonableness/proportionality, 184–87

R (on the application of Chester) v Secretary of State for Justice, 22–23, 73, 99–100
R (on the application of Nicklinson) v Ministry of Justice, 73, 91–93, 137–38
R (Reilly) v Work and Pensions Secretary (No 1), 169, 170–71
R (Reilly) v Work and Pensions Secretary (No 2), 172
R v Inland Revenue Commissioners ex p National Federation of Self-Employed and Small Businesses, 17
R v Lord Chancellor ex p Witham, 17–19, 26, 31, 122, 141
R v Secretary of State for Foreign and Commonwealth Affairs ex p World Development Movement, 141, 142
R v Secretary of State for Social Security ex p Joint Council for the Welfare of Immigrants, 141–42
R v Secretary of State for the Home Department ex p Limbuela, 142
R v Secretary of State for the Home Department ex p Simms, 131, 186
Raab, 168, 173
Rawls, 24, 99, 195
Re Spectrum Plus Ltd, 15–17
reasoning by analogy, 20–21, 70–72, 82, 84, 196, 219–20
Refugee Convention, *see* UN Geneva Convention relating to the Status of Refugees (Refugee Convention)
Reid, 16, 74–76, 118
remoteness, 181, 189
Rickards v Lothian, 179–80
Roe v Wade (USA), 11, 25, 216–18
Royal College of Nursing of the UK v Department of Health and Social Security, 69–70, 71
rule of law, 2, 13, 21, 31, 98, 117–18, 131, 140, 162, 170–71, 196
Rylands principle, 179–80

S v Makwanyane, 51
SAS v France, 64
Sauvé (No 2), 100, 101, 120
Scalia, 35, 36, 47–48, 58
  democratic accountability, 35, 215
  originalism, 51, 68–69, 143, 215
  stare decisis principle, 36
  textualism, 55–56
Schumpeter, 146, 219
Scoppola v Italy, 22, 74, 96, 99–102, 120, 163
Senior Courts Act 1981, 17

separation of powers, 2, 6, 26, 30, 40–41, 45–46, 101, 126–27, 136, 171
  HRA 1998, 153–56
Simms principle of legality, 141
social conditions and expectations:
  judges' responsibility to keep abreast of, 17
social policy, 135, 136–38
  access to the courts, 17–18
  compromise, 24–25
  judicial law-making, 24–25
    politics compared, 24
  law-politics boundary, 29–30, 121–22
    declining respect for political process, 30, 123
    impact of ECHR, 30
    judicial review and, 29–30, 141–42
  politics v judicial law-making, 24
Sørensen, 86, 89
South African Constitution, 50–51
sovereignty, 23, 33, 167–68
  democracy and, 146, 197
  HRA 1998 and, 154–55, 191
  international treaties and, 47
  rule of law and, 170–71, 174
stare decisis principle, 32, 36, 45–46
statutory law:
  courts and respect for, 191–92
  judicial role in the ordering of society, 16
  private law, 189–91
  public law, 189–91
Stone Sweet:
  mutual recognition, 156
Sumption (Lord), 27–28
  appointment, 28, 41–43
  constitutional review, 33–35
    judicial review, 35–36
    originalism and, 37
  criticism of ECHR, 48–50
  judges role in the ordering of society, 38
    admonition, 41
    constitutionality, 38
    democracy, 39
    institutional competence, 39–41
  law-politics boundary, 29–33
    declining respect for political process, 30
    impact of ECHR, 30
    judicial review and, 29–30
  limited legal constitutionalism, 194–96
    limitations, 196–201
    political constitutionalism:
      democratic dependence of courts, 201–04
      ECHR, 208–11
      international courts, 204–08
  Limits of Law lecture 2013 (Shah Lecture), 31, 36, 73–74, 193
    institutional design, 121, 134
  LSE Lecture 2012, 30–31

political constitutionalism, 38–41
  institutional competence, 39
  response, 213–24
    legal interpretation, 216–18
    normative judgment and balancing, 214

textualism, 5, 7, 10–11, 35–36, 54–56, 215
de Tocqueville, 19
tort law, 9, 124, 187, 214
  normative judgment and balancing, 176–77, 182–84
travaux préparatoires, 47
  limitations to right to vote, 94–95
  original intent of ECHR drafters, 50
  Protocol 1 ECHR, 94–95
  refouler/refoulement, 111
  unreliability, 49
Tyrer v UK, 45–46, 59–60
  defining 'living instrument', 85–86, 145, 216

UN Geneva Convention relating to the Status of Refugees (Refugee Convention), 110–11, 116

universal suffrage, 95–97
USA, 4, 19, 30, 149
  constitutional review, 33–35
  interpretative methodologies, 35
  original intent of constitution:
    Furman v Georgia, 49, 51–52

Verein gegen Tierfabriken v Switzerland, 157–61
Vienna Convention of 1969 on the Law of Treaties, 5, 6, 20–21, 49, 59, 68
  primacy of language of instrument, 72

Wagon Mound (No 1), 181–82
Waldock, 145
Waldron, 55–56, 63
Weinrib, 181
West Midland Baptist Association Inc v Birmingham Corporation, 16, 74–75

X v Austria, 60–61
Young, James and Webster v UK, 53, 88